T0304515

NEW CONTRIBUTIONS TO TRANSPORTATION ANALYSIS IN EUROPE

New Contributions to
Transportation Analysis in Europe

Edited by
MICHEL BEUTHE
Facultes Universitaires Catholiques de Mons, Belgium
and
PETER NIJKAMP
Free University, The Netherlands

Routledge
Taylor & Francis Group

LONDON AND NEW YORK

First published 1999 by Ashgate Publishing

Reissued 2018 by Routledge
2 Park Square, Milton Park, Abingdon, Oxon, OX14 4RN
52 Vanderbilt Avenue, New York, NY 10017

Routledge is an imprint of the Taylor & Francis Group, an informa business

A Library of Congress record exists under LC control number: 550780

ISBN 13: 978-1-138-33859-3 (hbk)
ISBN 13: 978-0-429-44158-5 (ebk)

Contents

Preface

Economic activity patterns have exhibited drastic changes in the last part of the twentieth century. The gradual shift of regional and national economies towards an integrated network society has caused the emergence of spatial-economic interactivity ranging from local to global scales. As a consequence, transport and communication have become main features of the modern economic era in which the information and communication sector plays an important role.

One of the world regions in which the above factors play a prominent role, is Europe. In some ten years time this continent has gone through wild fluctuations which have offered new perspectives for all European cities, regions and countries. It had to cope with broad policy developments such as deregulation and market integration, but it also had to consider geopolitical changes which made Europe almost a unique laboratory experiment for transportation analysts.

In the past decade these dynamic developments have prompted a large variety of transportation research, not only at the local or national level but also at a European level. The various transportation framework programmes financed by the European Commission have meant an important stimulus for further research progress. Part of the scientific advances in transportation research in the European scene has taken place in the framework of the Network on European Communications and Transport Activity Research (NECTAR). This scientific network is organising on a regular basis workshops and conferences all over Europe with the objective of development and dissemination of new knowledge. The present volume is the outgrowth of one of the NECTAR activities, viz. a research conference held in the historical Belgian city of Mons, at the Facultés Universitaires Catholiques de Mons. A selection of new contributions among the various presentations was made afterwards by the editors of this volume. This book offers a sample of recent advances in transportation analysis with a particular view to Europe and European policy developments.

The following persons and institutions are to be thanked for their support of the above research conference: the Belgian "Services des Affaires Scientifiques, Techniques et Culturelles" (SSTC) and "Fonds National de la Recherche Scientifique" (FNRS), Prof. Dr. W.A.G Blonk and the "Direction Générale des Transports des Communautés Européennes" (DG VII), the Minister J-P. Grafé and the "Direction Générale de l'Enseignement Supérieur et de la Recherche Scientifique", the Minister E. di Rupo and the "Institut Belge des Services Postaux et Communications", Mrs A-M. Straus

and the "Direction Générale des Technologies, de la Recherche et de l'Energie de la Région Wallonne", and the "German Research Association" (DFG).
Finally, the editors wish to thank Diana Raulier, Maureen Shepstone and Angèle Janse whose help was indispensable in preparing the Mons conference and in carrying out the editorial tasks of this volume.

Michel Beuthe   Mons/Amsterdam
Peter Nijkamp

1 Widening Horizons for the Transport Sector

MICHEL BEUTHE AND PETER NIJKAMP

Europe has exhibited remarkable geopolitical and spatial dynamics in the past decade. This has had drastic implications for the transport sector at all spatial levels in Europe. These conditions have also prompted the need for a new and challenging analysis of transport questions in Europe.

This book originated on the occasion of a conference on *European Transport and Communication Networks,* which was held jointly with the research association NECTAR at the Facultés Universitaires Catholiques de Mons (FUCAM) in September 1996. It is also the result of ongoing research, as the topic is of utmost importance and continues to attract abundant research efforts in Europe. Indeed, transportation networks for goods and passengers are seen as important factors in the construction of the European Community, because efficient and complete networks permit easier communication between people in different countries, larger industrial integration by improved spatial processes of production and distribution, and better political cohesion. Thus, over the last decade, the member countries and the European Commission have paid considerable attention to improving the transportation networks by sponsoring large research programs in this area and giving financial support and incentives to network improvements. Some of the following papers bear witness of such European research in transportation.

The first part of the book on *Emerging Network Developments in Europe* will discuss the present situation of the various networks as well as many of the issues which arise in their development. The second part will be concerned with some of the problems which are met in their *Governance.* Most of the papers propose not only formal models of analysis but also empirical research and actual case studies; altogether, they present the main issues of transportation in Europe nowadays.

The first chapter, *Actors and Factors in the Integration of Strategic Infrastructure Networks in Europe* by David Banister, Rico Maggi, Peter Nijkamp and Roger Vickerman, is a reflection on the problem of the European networks integration and on the strategies to adopt for their development and integration. In contrast with many studies which focus on the physical characteristics of networks, they emphasise the need to enlarge the scope

1

of analysis to encompass also concerns of finance, organisation and regulation, software and ecological factors. By the same token, they provide an extensive and complete review of the problems of the present networks and a very useful background introduction to the following chapters.

They start by identifying the necessary components of an evaluation process of networks that includes all aspects of the infrastructure. They propose that it should not be carried only at the individual project level but also at the programme and policy levels with methods appropriate to each case. This leads them to extend the scope of evaluation beyond the direct and indirect impacts on transports to implications for employment, local and regional economies, the use of resources and quality of life. Furthermore, they point out the need at each level of analysis to give as much attention as possible to the decision making processes and factors which can determine a successful integration, from the market regulations to the role of the various transport actors and international agencies. Thus, to analyse the networks and their integration, they advocate to enlarge the scope of inquiry to include all the supporting legal, financial and organisational infrastructures, as well as the decision making processes which determine their setting and evolution.

In a second step, they applied this approach to four separate topics of high interest, peripherality and accessibility, trans-Alpine freight transport, competition and complementarity, and the role of actors, all of which have been thoroughly studied in the course of the European Commission's COST 328 research campaign.

The analysis of peripherality is based on four separate case studies, the main results of which are summarised in comprehensive tables. They bring to light the importance of a good understanding of the linkages and competitive relationships between a peripheral country internal networks and the higher level European networks and actors. They also emphasise that additional infrastructure in peripheral countries may induce some negative effects on these countries. These should be carefully assessed before moving forward with new projects.

Transalpine freight transports were also the object of several surveys which were based on very different methodologies, from the micro level of individual actors behaviour and policy network analysis to network mode choice models (neural and GIS) and qualitative flow forecasts. These studies demonstrate the interest in applying different approaches to cover all the issues involved in this complex international problem. Altogether, it appears that the main barrier which hinders an efficient network integration in this area is organisational, with conflicting national, regional, local and mode-specific interests. Environmental concerns are also a factor, but, to a large extent, they are used and abused to serve other interests.

2

The research on competition and complementarity focuses on an assessment of intermodal transport potential, mainly seen from an actor's perspective in a liberalised transport market and analysed from the five point of views of infrastructure, its financing, its management, the regulation and organisation of its use, and environmental concerns. On the basis of a survey of transport experts, it illustrates that the weakest elements in a co-ordinated European multimodal policy are the financial, technical and organisational problems.

Finally, a questionnaire survey of some twenty European countries on the actors' strategy towards integration of networks was also carried out. It indicates that the European States still have a dominant role in determining investment priorities, while the role of financial institutions and private capital is limited. The major transport operators' influence is also limited. However, the shippers, responding to the demands of their customers, are playing an important role in providing door-to-door intermodal services.

The review of all these problems and of the decision processes involved lead the authors to conclude that a correct understanding of the constraints placed on the choices available to policy and decision makers at all levels is the most critical success factor for the European network integration.

In the line of the above concerns, Roger Vickerman offers a penetrating review of a number of problems which are met by analysts of networks development in the context of peripheral countries. In *The Transport Sector, New Economic Geography and Economic Development in Peripheral Regions,* he is particularly concerned with the assessment of important new infrastructures which are designed to promote the development and integration of these regions within the European Union: the traffic they generate, their impacts on the different modes and nodes in the network and on the localisation of economic activities. However, his critical analysis is based on the most recent researches in regional and transport economics, both theoretical and applied, so that his comments go much beyond the specific problems of peripheral countries, but provide insights and warnings on the present state of network modelling.

Two important research strands are reviewed by Vickerman: accessibility measures and the so-called New Economic Geography. First, the development of GIS spatial modelling has led to numerous accessibility analyses of transport networks. However useful they may be, Vickerman points out that they are often characterised by a double problem of concentration with respect to nodes and to modes. Actually, the representation of a region by its central node may hide part of the transport problems of a region. On the other hand, over an extensive network like the trans-European one, the characteristics of the network and economic activity change very much from one region to another. These characteristics lead to different modal choices in different regions, and a region's relative

3

accessibility should not be measured on the basis of the same mode all over the network.

Then, Vickerman explains the recent developments of economic geography which tries to enrich spatial models by factors of imperfect competition. He develops his views by using the basic elements of the two region Krugman model (1991) which takes into account returns to scale, differentiated products, and, naturally transport cost. This model, taken as an important reference, permits an analysis of some industries' regional concentration on the basis of factors internal to the industry rather than merely of external economies. This approach is particularly interesting, because it integrates some industrial modelling into the classical spatial models. However, the transport market itself is left outside of that analysis, as if it were not very important for the outcome or were not affected by some degree of imperfection.

Thus, Vickerman suggests that transport cost should be made endogenous in the models, that they should depend on the product transported and on all the flows on the network, as well as on the capacity of the network. Then, he supports his views by a discussion of the cases of a few European peripheral regions which offer striking examples of the need to examine closely not only the industrial structure but also the functioning of the transport market: the cases of Portugal, Spain, Ireland and of the Nordic countries. Finally, he discusses the impacts of the Channel Tunnel, where the future outcome in terms of market share between the different means and modes for the crossing of the Channel will depend essentially on the solution which will be found in the transport market.

The chapter on *Methods and Models Analysing Transalpine Freight Transport,* by Simona Bolis and Aura Reggiani, presents an extensive review of recent studies on the problem of North-South freight traffic through Switzerland and Austria. This problem of choice of mode and route for heavy flows of freight between Italy and the northern European countries is a most interesting and important one. It raises fundamental questions of transport policy in relation to the external costs imposed on the population of Austria and Switzerland. Should one build new infrastructures and which ones? Which regulations could alleviate these costs and induce some re-routing of the traffic? How to organise intermodal transport to decrease the negative impacts of such a heavy freight flow? As a consequence, quite a few studies have been devoted already to these problems, which prompted Reggiani and Bolis to review and compare their methodology as well as their results. They classified them under three headings: demand, supply and policy analyses.

Some demand analyses try to forecast the future growth of traffic through the Alpine chain. They use a variety of methods and cover different spatial areas according to the available data, which are often incomplete. Some other studies take a more micro-economic approach by trying to understand the

4

choices made by the shippers and measuring the impacts of regulation on their decisions. The supply analyses examine the characteristics of the present network, its capacity and its bottlenecks. They try to assess what kind of new infrastructure would increase the capacity of the network to absorb future freight flows. In some cases, their analysis attempts to take into account the behaviour of the shippers. The studies focusing on policy issues are mainly concerned with the negative impacts of trucking traffic through the Alpine chain.They cover a very large spectrum of policy solutions and political views, from a national or international perspective. The authors also offer a typology of the reviewed studies in relation to a typology of the data they used.

After this extensive review of many studies and reports which are often published in a very restricted way, Reggiani and Bolis warn us about the incomplete character of existing studies, which are unable for many reasons to provide as yet a comprehensive knowledge of this transport problem with all its socio-economic variables.

The next chapter on *The International Impacts of a New Road Taxation Scheme in Switzerland,* by Michel Beuthe, Laurent Demilie and Bart Jourquin is a follow-up and complements the two papers by the same authors reviewed in the preceding chapter. All these studies use a network software, called NODUS, developed by Jourquin (1995) which, on the basis of a digitised geographic network, generates in a systematic and exhaustive way, another virtual network. The latter is made of virtual nodes and links which correspond to every transport operation of the different modes and means: loading, unloading, transiting, transhipping and moving. The automatic generation of all these elements helps to apply the concept of virtual links to very large networks like the European one. Moreover, the full decomposition of every operation in transport chains, and particularly the explicit introduction of transhipping virtual link, allows a convenient analysis of the problems of intermodality. In these two studies, a Monte-Carlo procedure is applied to generate a point-to-point matrix of origins and destinations on the basis of data on the global flows between a number of European regions and countries. Cost functions are associated to each operation which take into account many variables which define transport costs; they tend to approach the concept of generalised cost. The minimisation of the total cost of the transportation task defined by the O-D matrix produces an assignment of the global flows between modes, means and routes over the network. The calibration of the model output with respect to the observed market share is made through an adjustment of the cost functions. The adjusted model can then be used to compare, through simulations, the results obtained from different specifications of the network and of the cost parameters.

Only the problems relating to the present Swiss regulation on truck tonnage were analysed in the two first papers. In this chapter, the results of that regulation on the international freight flows through and around Switzerland by the different modes are compared to the results which could be obtained from various levels of taxation per ton/km and additional tolls at some Alpine passes. The present regulation on the truck tonnage induces an important modal diversion from trucking to rail transport through Switzerland and a re-routing of part of the trucking through the neighbouring countries. In order to maintain approximately the present situation in Switzerland while abandoning this regulation, it appears that the taxes should be set at a very high level indeed, a level which should lead to a difficult negotiation between Switzerland and the other European countries involved.

Beyond this specific problem, this chapter demonstrates the potential of this network model, with its associated software, to analyse transport solutions on a multimodal network.

To some extent the above model could deal with the interaction between transportation and industrial production activity, by the introduction of different O-D matrixes for different products with specific generalised cost of transportation. However, that would not really permit an in-depth analysis of the full logistic chain of production in which transport operations correspond to a few links only. Such an analysis is proposed by Bo Terje Kalsaas who focuses particularly on the *Networks Impacts of Just-in-Time Production*. The basic principles of JIT transport and production are well known, but, here, Kalsaas comments in much details on all its aspects and methods of organisation, and emphasises the constraints it places on transport organisation and the localisation of the assembling plant's suppliers.

This general analysis of the JIT production model with all its implications is then confronted with the results of case studies realised on the organisation of several car assembling factories, Volvo and Saab factories in Sweden, Toyota and Nissan in Japan. These studies show that JIT organisation is the source of important agglomeration forces which induce suppliers to locate close enough to the plant they supply. However, some other forces also exert their influence in an opposite direction and tend to induce some changes in the logistics of production, mainly the international globalisation and standardisation of production and distribution, and the search for lowest cost suppliers wherever they are located, according to their comparative advantages.

The constitution of the European Union with many different countries obviously raises many problems of convergence of institutions, laws and regulations. Among the political objectives of the Union, the goals of integration and cohesion are therefore considered important. In the field of transportation, these goals translate in a search for inter-operability,

6

intermodality and integration of the national transportation networks. The question is then to find appropriate methods to analyse networks and their components in order to reach a better understanding of their functioning and devise adequate policies. The contribution by Francesca Medda, Peter Nijkamp and Piet Rietveld, *Hierarchies of Spatial Network Systems,* consists of a comparison of two different conceptual approaches of network assessment which correspond to entirely different points of view.

They start by linking organisation processes, as seen by systems theory, to the notion of hierarchy, and propose to contrast networks in terms of the characteristics of their hierarchies. According to that approach, they describe the well known accessibility matrix method as a hierarchy of pyramidal structure based on dominant and subordinate relations between nodes. In effect, this method leads to a ranking of the nodes according to their degree of accessibility in the network. In contrast to that method, they propose to analyse networks as a system of nested sub-networks which are interconnected. The hierarchy between the different layers of network is then of a different nature, somewhat like Chinese boxes of different sizes contained inside each other. In order to provide an operational concept to describe a network from this point of view, they propose to define network membership functions which measure the number of sub-networks to which a node belongs. These measures have the advantage of showing which role a particular node plays at the different layers of the network.

The second part of the book deals with some problems which are met in the *Governance of Networks,* a topic which is present in all European discussions about the organisation of the transport network, particularly with respect to the promotion of intermodality. To some extent, a few of the above papers could have been classified as well in this part of the book, so central is the problem of governance for an efficient use of the networks.

In *Assessing Scenarios on European Transport Policies by Means of Multicriteria Analysis,* by Christian Hey, Peter Nijkamp, Sytze A. Rienstra and Dieter Rothenberger, the question is raised how to set concrete operational targets to define a European transport policy with respect to sustainability, social and economic cohesion, and efficiency. Concerning sustainability, the authors start by an examination of the objectives which are proposed in the literature. They distinguish concepts associated with strong sustainability, which give priority to ecological objectives, from those linked to weak sustainability, taking into account the impacts of environmental aims on the economic system. But both concepts in their various versions appear unable to provide clear targets. Hence, it is necessary to choose targets pragmatically on the basis of current policy documents. Likewise, social and economic cohesion is rather easy to define as the socially acceptable difference between regions, but the critical threshold is politically difficult to

7

assess, and may vary according to the characteristics of the regions and the overall objective of development. As a consequence, a Gini-coefficient of a conventional measure of accessibility could be recommended as a practical indicator, the objective being to improve the accessibility of peripheral centres. Again, concepts for efficiency targets can be found in the welfare economic theories, but it is not evident to translate them into a target for a transportation policy. From the idea that transport should facilitate economic development, several efficiency targets can be nevertheless defined.

Thus, six targets are proposed with respect to which qualitative judgements, at least, can be made: a 25 per cent reduction of CO_2 and a 80 per cent reduction of NO_x from the environmental point of view, an increase of a Gini-coefficient of accessibility and a decrease of unemployment in the poorest regions, from a regional point of view, and, for efficiency, the full cost coverage by transport means plus a reduction of the share of transport activities in the economy.

The next step is to define a set of scenarios corresponding to possible developments of the European society based on the opposed concepts of polarisation and co-operation in three directions: towards competition, towards an equitable society or towards a society with environmental concerns. After an estimation of the scores realised with respect to the above six targets, these scenarios are then assessed by means of the regime method of multicriteria analysis. This is done under various hypotheses concerning the weights given to the different objectives. The reader is invited to assess the conclusion reached by the authors that European and societal co-operation and policies aiming at increasing efficiency and environmental objectives should be recommended for defining a transport policy.

Knut S Eriksen also tackles this difficult question of *Sustainability and the Transportation Sector,* but from a more theoretical and macro-economic point of view. Thus his contribution starts with a review of the main general economic approaches and models which can be used to analyse sustainable consumption of resources over time. At one extreme, there is the Golden Green Rule model that gives full priority to future uses of the available resources, and limit consumption to whatever service the untouched stock of resource can provide. At another extreme, is the Hotelling's Rule approach based on a utility function of consumption only, which leads to the progressive exhaustion of the resources over time. Between these two extremes, it is possible to conceive a rather classical model where utility depends on both the stock itself and on its consumption, in which case it is possible to reach an equilibrium level with a positive stock where, henceforth, no consumption of the remaining stock should be possible. Then, there is also the Chichilnisky criterion model where utility is a weighted sum of the present value of utility over time and the utility obtained in the distant

8

future. This is a more general hypothesis, which can lead to results quite similar to those produced by the other models according to the value given to the weight. This is the specification that Eriksen recommends because it is more flexible in its capacity to model the needs of distant future consumption.

After some considerations on the uncertainty which characterises future outcomes, Eriksen describes the main features of a general equilibrium model of the Norwegian economy, named GODMOD, which gives a large place to transportation demand and supply. He uses the model to compute the shadow price tax, on the basis of the Chichilnisky criterion, which would be necessary to obtain a given decrease of CO_2 emission. He measures also the quantitative impacts on the different transport means that would result from such a taxation.

In *New Governance Principles for Sustainable Urban Transport,* Roberto Camagni, Roberta Capello and Peter Nijkamp examine the particular problems of modern cities where modern technologies of transport and communication have allowed the full exploitation of economies of density and scale, but, at the same time, have created considerable negative factors of pollution and congestion. They first analyse the multiple roles played by modern cities as international gateways, nodes in a network, and places with a particular weight in the network. Then, they examine the conditions under which cities could be organised as a network of several centres with specialised functions, the Multicentric Network City, and succeed in solving the contradictions which bear upon them.

They underline the role played in a modern economy by both communication and transport which are sources of many economic opportunities for development, but also of many costs. For dealing with that complex phenomenon, they propose to distinguish on one hand *accessibility* as the potential source of positive interactions between people and, on the other hand, *mobility* which is the actual realisation of interaction but also the source of costs which reduce accessibility. The problem, as they see it, is to decrease the costs of mobility while enhancing or preserving accessibility.

A way to reach a sustainable compromise between these two contradictory objectives in a urban environment would be to implement market-based solutions in the provision of infrastructure as well as in its use. Trying simply to limit the development of transport probably would be ineffective and constitute an impediment to further social and economic development. Modern telecommunications technologies could also contribute to a cost decrease by making transport more efficient and, maybe, as a partial substitute which does not cause additional external costs.

But the problem of defining a policy for sustainable cities is just as complex as the urban system it should organise, and market-based solutions or the recourse to new technologies will not suffice. It is well known that these are cases where market mechanisms fail to provide a solution and, in any case, some norms and targets must be defined before any market mechanism can be implemented. Camagni *et al.* give a thorough discussion of all the facets of these problems; they also provide useful recommendations about effective ways to design and implement appropriate regulations. They rightly insist that these policies and regulations should be conceived while keeping in mind long term objectives.

In the line of this analysis, Robert E. Paaswell provides a discussion of *Regionalism, Planning and Strategic Investment in the Transportation Sector* in the context of the New York City urbanised area. After identifying the problems of increasing dispersion of activities and suburbanisation in this region, of severe congestion and decaying infrastructure, he underlines the absence of long term and global planning for guiding the region's development and building of infrastructure. Not surprisingly, we find the same problems as in Europe, and it is interesting to examine how and why they are (mis)handled on the other side of the Atlantic. Even though Paaswell recognises the need to think in terms of a network of centres with different functions, his main concern in this paper is to examine ways to sustain the sound economic activity of the core of the region as the main engine of regional growth, i.e. Manhattan as an international centre of finance, entertainment, fashion, tourism and media.

He reviews two major regional strategic initiatives which follow that objective, "Access to the Region Core" (ARC), a joint project of three autonomous regional transport agencies, and the third regional plan of the private Regional Plan Associations (RPA). He discusses the general context into which both plans have been introduced, their objectives and their likelihood of success. Both plans focus on the need for a better and integrated network of transport infrastructure for a better development of the core within the overall region. However, Paaswell points out that both plans are really "without a client" despite their merits. To be implemented, if only partially, both plans would require the support of the present institutions, while these institutions, i.e. local government and agencies, are not designed to manage long term planning of the whole region.

In *Success and Failure Factors for Multimodal Transport Policy in Europe,* Kostas Bithas and Peter Nijkamp endeavour to study the potential of road-rail intermodal transport in the context of the rapid development of freight trucking throughout Europe with all its severe environmental impacts. The paper aims to study the current state of the rail-road freight network in Europe and then to trace the properties of a satisfactory network and finally to define the relevant necessary and sufficient conditions for its efficient operations. This implies taking into account the environmental impacts of the road-rail intermodal solution, the technical, managerial and institutional barriers to its satisfactory operation, the technical performance of current practices, the managerial organisation, and the possible synergy between the two modes.

Given that the data necessary to make such an assessment are very incomplete and not comparable from one country to another, Bithas and Nijkamp have based their approach in this study on answers given to a questionnaire addressed to a broadly composed panel of transport experts in Europe. The survey was composed of two parts. The first one asks for an assessment of the gap between the current intermodal transport and the corresponding desired level at the national and international levels, including the terminals' operations. The second part deals with the main transport barriers, i.e. financial, organisational, software, psychological and hardware, which prevent the development of effective multimodal transport.

A rough set analysis was applied to the questionnaire answers, to which was added three meta-variables relative to the population, the surface and the position of each country. Rough set analysis, which is explained in the paper, is a classification technique leading to 'decision rules' which identify the crucial variables explaining the opinions of the consulted experts grouped in classes of 'common' opinion. Its results pinpoint to the importance of the financial and hardware barriers to the development of intermodal transport, both at the national and European levels. The terminals' poor organisation appears also as an important barrier. The authors complement their analysis by using several more classical statistical methods: factor analysis, principal components and regression analyses. These analyses confirm the results obtained by the rough set approach.

On the whole, the statistical analyses of the survey allow Bithas and Nijkamp to conclude that, while the European transport experts attach a high desirability to an efficient and effective intermodal network, they regret the prohibitive financial, technical and organisational problems which bear upon its development.

Another study based on a survey of experts is provided by Mattias Höjer who examines a set of *Options for Transport Telematics*. This study focuses on how telematics could be used to implement urban transport systems, which would facilitate a sustainable development of cities. In this case, however, the experts were asked to give their opinion about a set of possible but not necessarily probable scenarios about a future urban system organisation which could meet some desirable target. The scenarios are based on concepts developed in the literature and tested in a preliminary round by a few experts; they were formulated as descriptions of the function and use of technical systems for passengers transportation.

Four scenarios were developed which do not exclude each other technically, but take different paths towards fulfilling the basis transport mission. They are fully described in the paper. The first one, the Car Pooling scenario, was designed to show how information technology could raise the vehicles load factor. The Dynamic Route Choice scenario aimed at optimising the performance of the urban transport system with the help of dynamic road user fees, while the Extended Public Transport one focuses on improving information and extending public transport services to include taxis and rental cars. Finally, the Dual Mode scenario combines the potential for efficient energy use in rail transport and the advantages of electric private vehicles. In a first questionnaire, the experts were asked to assess the feasibility, the impact and the economy of each scenario. Then, after some rewriting of the questions, they were asked additional questions on the need for subsidies as well as probability and desirability of the proposed systems.

The expert analysis provides interesting information, as well as interrogation, about worthwhile orientations which could be given to urban transport systems. These are thoroughly discussed in the paper. Suffice it to say here that the Extended Public Transport scenario received the best marks, while some features of the other scenarios were nevertheless positively valued despite various problems. This study, like the preceding one, provides an interesting demonstration of the usefulness of survey methods to assess in a preliminary stage the possible benefits and problems of new techniques and systems which are considered for the future.

The chapter on *Behaviour of Western European Scheduled Airlines During the Market Liberalisation Process,* by Milan Janic deals with the evolution of the aviation industry's legal framework in Europe over the last ten years and with its impacts on the industry behaviour. Following the American deregulation leadership of 1978, the European Union successively launched three deregulation packages from 1987 to 1993. They progressively allowed the European airlines to transport passengers and cargo between all Member States and to freely determine airfares; at the same time, they compiled a set of rules aiming at organising a sound competitive market.

These new conditions of competition could only have substantial impact on the aviation industry. Starting from a presentation of the European industry structure with its numerous flag airlines, Janic comments on the aviation industry growth and analyses its evolution through alliances, equity stakes and mergers. He points out that marketing agreements largely outnumber the other types of co-operation based on equity participation, and discusses the reasons which have slowed the progress towards a competitive market: State ownership and pride, trade-unions, persistence of some monopoly situation due to, for example, congested airports, etc.

Then, beyond this industry analysis from the outside, Janic tries to go deeper into the airlines' behaviour by proposing three statistical analyses of their operations on the basis of available European airlines data on passengers transportation. The first one shows the economies they can obtain from a larger volume of activity and from the exploitation of larger planes on longer distances. The second tries to model the growth and financial performance of some airlines, but the scarcity of data permits only to contrast their conditions of operation at the present time. The third approach shows how the European airlines were able to protect by various means their existing market share from 1989 to 1993 and indicates that pricing competition remained weak. All these results point out how difficult is the path followed in Europe to reach a real competitive aviation market.

The last paper on *Modelling Fees for Freight Transport Services in Eastern European Countries* by Wolfgang Koller, investigates the tremendous differences in the prices for comparable services which are observed between the countries of Eastern Europe. More specifically, it analyses these price differences for road groupage transport, i.e. consolidated transport of small shipments, from Vienna as an origin to Eastern European countries by the technique of hedonic pricing.

On the basis of information provided by an important shipping company, Koller had to create a sample of tripobservations, in which the relative importance of each country in the Austrian export trade was respected. The explanatory variables of the hedonic regression were a number of dummy variables for the destination country, the date of observation and the type of product, the trip distance, and the shipment weights. The transport fees were calculated according to the freight tariff of the shipping company. The shipments weights were distributed according to a log-normal distribution which appeared to fit the available data.

Quite a few interesting observations were obtained from this analysis, where all the variables turned out to be significant with rather stable coefficients for distance and weight. A striking one is that a substantially higher price is set for Eastern hubdestinations compared to Western destinations, while a lower price level is levied for the last part of the trip, from the hub to the final destination. On the basis of the hedonic analysis, it is possible to compute price indexes which facilitate the comparisons between countries and raise a number of questions about the reasons of the differences in prices. Koller relates them to different regulations, unbalance of trade between countries, differences in road infrastructure and in organisation.

The previous contributions have demonstrated that transportation science in Europe is alive and well, and has gone through a rapid evolution in the past decade. The political and social conditions in the transition process in Europe have led to the need for social science and policy oriented research in all countries, including those which were until recently operating under different policy regimes. It goes without saying that still many hurdles have to be taken before the state of transportation research in this region will be able to cope effectively with the vast array of complex policy and behavioural challenges in the transport sector.

PART A:
EMERGING NETWORK DEVELOPMENTS IN EUROPE

2 Actors and Factors in the Integration of Strategic Infrastructure Networks in Europe

DAVID BANISTER, RICO MAGGI, PETER NIJKAMP AND ROGER VICKERMAN

2.1 Introduction

The main objective of the research[1] reported in this chapter has been to contribute to a strategic definition of the integration of the Trans-European networks and to stimulate thought on the development of methodologies for the assessment of performances of transport networks and for strategies for their development and/or integration. This very ambitious objective has arisen out of the realisation that strategic infrastructure networks have in the past been looked at as mainly physical networks. Although physical networks are important, in highly advanced economies it is other characteristics which are also important. We started by taking the five dimensions of the pentagon of concerns (Nijkamp and Vleugel, 1995) where finance, organisation and regulation, software and ecological factors are added to the physical hardware of the infrastructure.

The first stage of the research has concentrated on the necessary components of the evaluation process that includes all aspects of the infrastructure. The second main strand of research has been to examine these processes in more detail through specific case studies which focus on particular key elements within the EU. The chapter ends with the presentation of some more general conclusions on three cross-cutting themes which are at the core of integration, namely the links between networks and integration, appropriate methods for evaluation and analysis, and the contextual factors such as globalisation and internationalisation.

---

[1] This paper is based on work carried out by the COST 328 - Integrated Strategic Infrastructure Networks in Europe group over the last 4 years. We are grateful for the input of all members of COST 328 and of the four Working Groups.

17

2.2 The evaluation framework

New perspectives on evaluation are important as individual links all form part of the network. In the past there has been little evaluation carried out at any level above the individual link where an improvement was taking place. We propose that evaluation should be carried out at three separate levels. In addition to the individual project level where the methods and procedures are well known (e.g. Nijkamp and Blaas, 1994), evaluation should be carried out at the programme and the policy level (Table 2.1).

Table 2.1 Evaluation processes

Evaluation Level	Evaluation Methods	Other Components in Evaluation
Project	Financial Appraisal Cost Benefit Analysis	Environmental Assessment Social Impact Analysis Economic Impact Analysis
Programme	Multicriteria Analysis Framework Approaches	Ensuring that the individual costs and benefits of projects conform to wider programme objectives, particularly on regional development and environment.
Policy	Strategic Environmental Complex Assessment Objectives Analysis, including Meta Analysis	Fitting programmes into the national and international policy context, so that broad economic, social and environmental objectives are met

Different methods are required for programme and policy evaluation as it is important to establish how new links fit in with wider programme objectives (e.g. EU cohesion) and how Common Transport Policy objectives on sustainable mobility and the environment can be achieved. This means that analysis should not be restricted to particular sectors, or the functioning of the networks in particular well-defined contexts. Eventually it could be extended to explore the implications for employment, the local and regional economies, the use of resources and the quality of life.

In addition to the multi-sector analysis, individual links should be assessed in terms of their direct and indirect effects on the transport network. For example, the Channel Tunnel is a major new link between the UK and France and has a direct impact on the transport networks of these two countries. It also has effects on the economies of Kent and Nord Pas de Calais. However, the Channel Tunnel has impacts that are much wider, including those on the airlines and ferry companies (competitors), on freight distribution systems (efficiency) and on other countries (Belgium, The Netherlands and Germany). It is necessary to trace all these impacts as part of the evaluation process, so that the individual benefits of projects can be matched to the overall benefits viewed in combination - the super-additivity of projects and their contributions to programmes and policies.

Table 2.2 Decision making processes

Level of Decision	Key Issues	Critical Success Factors
Local - Project	Individual Links, Terminals, Interchanges for Each Mode of Transport	Restrictions, Competition between Modes, Finance and Subsidy, Individuals, Levels of Integration - *adding value to links and nodes*
National - Programme	Logistics and Network Effects, including questions of Intermodality, Interoperability and Interconnectivity, including the crowding out of investment	Regulation, Competition, Finance (public and private), Companies, Integrators, New Actors, Mergers and Alliances - *adding value to the network and communications*
National and EU - Policy	Competitiveness, Cohesiveness and Environment, but also pricing competition, liberalisation and open access policies	Regulations, Competitive Frameworks, Financial Institutions, Governments, International Agencies, Multinational Companies - *adding value to the competitive position of countries and the EU*

In addition to evaluation processes, there are important implications for decision making processes more generally. Throughout this research, there has been a concern over the critical success factors within the European network of transport links and how value can be added to the network. Again, it is proposed that a three level approach be adopted that attempts to identify both the critical success factors and the nature of the added value (Table 2.2). In the past, most attention has been focused on individual links,

19

terminals and interchanges, often only for one mode of transport. At this local project level, it is argued that the critical success factors for added value would include the availability of finance, the commitment of different individuals (actors), and the levels of integration available (e.g. information and data support systems).

At the programme level, the broader issues of logistics and network connectivity become more important in determining the levels of intermodality, interoperability and interconnectivity. Here again, the critical success factors depend on the availability of finance and the linkages between companies. Financing is often perceived as a problem, but worthwhile projects and programmes will be financed if there are clear benefits. Difficulties are more likely to occur in the organisational and regulatory framework within which transport has to operate as competition is limited by some modes not paying their full social costs. Investment in one location or for one mode may also crowd out other initiatives, and this in turn has implications for efficiency. The means to reduce levels of uncertainty and to permit continuity in finance and investment seem to be the two key conditions for success here.

It is at this scale of activity that new actors and integrators have appeared in the market to assist in obtaining the greatest efficiency from a given (or enhanced) network. The importance of the new technology in facilitating this process cannot be underestimated. In addition to the instrumental role played by technology, the restructuring of companies and the globalisation process (through mergers of companies and alliances between companies) has meant that the use of the network has increased over and above the expected levels. The high quality transport infrastructure has facilitated the use of the new technology and the globalisation process. This is the value added.

At the EU and national policy levels, the transport network in Europe has an important role to play in moving towards the objectives of balanced competition, social and spatial cohesion, and environmental objectives. A high quality network is also a crucial element in maintaining and enhancing Europe's position in the world as well as ensuring regional development objectives and social inclusion. It may have a less important role in achieving environmental or sustainability objectives as transport is a major consumer of resources and producer of pollution (Banister, 1998).

The critical success factors here are the clear support of financial institutions, governments, international agencies and multinational companies in ensuring that the competitive position of the EU is maintained and developed. It is in the interest of all parties that the use of and access to the network is efficient and equitable. This requires agreement on priorities, on investment and on the means to pay for the use of that infrastructure. It is here that the decision processes are sometimes inconsistent, and the means to

20

finance investment or to charge for the use of the infrastructure needs to be established.

In the past, a demand led approach has been followed with heavy investment in the network to meet expected growth. This approach has been modified through management based policies (traffic management and more recently demand management), but even here inefficiencies are increasingly occurring as demand continues to grow and congestion is created. New strategies are required that mix both the physical and financial options in combination with the opportunities that spatial development strategies and technology offer. Location policies and the increasing use of telecommunications can reduce the demand for travel so that the use of the network is improved (Banister, 1997; Salomon, 1995).

In summary, it is important to make evaluations of new links, particularly strategic ones, at different levels. It is also important to include *a wider interpretation of links and networks* so that the supporting infrastructure (finance, regulation, competition, organisational factors, communications etc.) are also included. *The dynamics of the processes* are both interesting and informative, as the use of networks has changed radically, as businesses and people react to congestion and new opportunities. Underlying much of these changes are *the decision making processes* used by all interested parties at all levels. Further investigation is merited of the actors and the critical success factors. As a result of these preliminary findings, a more detailed investigation was carried out along four separate dimensions where it was expected that the actors and the critical success factors would be found - these were peripherality and accessibility, Transalpine freight transport, competition and complementarity, and the role of actors.

2.3   The case studies

2.3.1   *Peripherality and accessibility*

Background - The drive towards the completion of Trans-European Networks (TENs) as an instrument in the removal of barriers to a more competitive infrastructure network in Europe, and a promoter of *greater cohesion, has emphasised the role of improving accessibility* with implications for Europe's more peripheral regions. It is, therefore, clear that any attempt to improve the evaluation and policy making process for infrastructure networks in Europe, has to address the problems posed by the less accessible and more peripheral regions. This raises sets of questions, both for the peripheral regions, and for European level decision making.

At the European level, there is clearly a difficult balance to be struck between those improvements which are seen to be necessary for the greater development of competitiveness of the European Union as a whole, and the recognition that these may imply an uneven development of networks (Vickerman, 1998a). It is tempting to believe that this issue can be addressed through the development of a set of indicators which can capture both of these dimensions. The search for a perfect indicator of accessibility is thus a key element of the development of both the evaluation process and the policy making procedure. We return to this point later.

At the national level, the more peripheral countries of the EU also face some difficult issues. The peripheral countries are those which generally enjoy infrastructure that is both less well developed as a total network, and poorer in the quality of service it offers. This can be measured by the density of both the road and rail networks, and such indicators as the proportions of the road network which are motorways, the extent of electrified rail track, or double track railways. It is also found in the development of airport and port networks. With the latter, the level of service is seen to be particularly important, with lower densities of services linking these regions to the core regions of Europe, customers facing less frequent services, less direct services and higher prices (Vickerman, 1997 and 1998b).

The peripheral countries also face problems within their national territories. The distribution of accessibility varies substantially, typically between their major cities, and more distant poorer rural regions. The choice facing these countries is one of an appropriate distribution of resources between the development of the infrastructures at the higher European level, which will tend to increase inequalities within the country, and concentrate on raising the level of accessibility in the poorest regions.

Accessibility Indicators - It became clear that the variety of experiences in peripheral regions made it unworkable to determine a single universally applicable indicator of accessibility, despite the advances which have been made in the definition of accessibility over the last few years (Vickerman, 1995; Spiekermann and Wegener, 1996). Indicators still tend to be either geographically, or mode, specific. The varying geographic circumstances of the European periphery, ranging from the sparsely populated Nordic countries, through the outer peripheral Atlantic Arc, into the Mediterranean, to Greece and the eastern periphery, clearly poses a major problem for any attempt to define a single accessibility indicator. Critically, improvement in accessibility cannot be unequivocally taken as an indicator of improvement in economic performance or welfare. Thus simply improving the absolute accessibility of a peripheral region does not guarantee improved cohesion within the EU, and may in fact reduce cohesion.

A key factor which emerged during this part of the work was the concept of linking accessibility to that of choice. In all dimensions of travel and transport choice structure, peripheral regions face a more restrained offer, and greater constraints than those in the European core. This choice affects the availability of modes, the range of destinations served directly, or with a single interchange, and perhaps most significantly, the range of choice and competition between different operators and carriers. Defining accessibility thus becomes a question both of a range of factors, and the behaviour, particularly the competitive behaviour, of actors.

Case Studies - In order to develop this concept further, a series of four case studies was undertaken by different members of the group on contrasting peripheries.

The Nordic countries demonstrate the problems faced in sparsely populated regions, which also suffer major physical barriers of sea links to the rest of Europe, whilst at the same time being close to a number of the countries in transition in eastern and central Europe.

Ireland represents the particular case of an island nation highly dependent on sea and air links, with the particular concern that it faces a choice between longer sea routes to the European continental mainland, or a sequence of shorter crossings, using the routes through the United Kingdom.

Portugal, like Ireland, is part of the outer periphery of the Atlantic arc, dependent on links across another member state for its connection by land to the European core, but with strong sea trading links outside the European Union.

Spain is an example of a country with substantial variations in regional degrees of peripherality, but strongly affected by the growth of one industry, tourism.

Summary of Findings - These four studies emphasise the variety of accessibility experiences in different parts of the European periphery. Tables 2.3 and 2.4 provide a summary of these findings in terms of the evaluation processes, and decision making processes identified above. Three particular factors stand out from this which are crucial to future development in the periphery. Firstly, there is the balance between links and networks, and the critical position of key hubs. This affects the way in which local and regional networks within peripheral regions relate to the higher level European networks. It requires a clear understanding of appropriate markets and the threats posed, wittingly or unwittingly, by actors in other regions. Such market opportunities and competitive threats are often sector specific and relate to the existence of scale economies and to the scope for the development of backward and forward linkages within the regions.

Table 2.3 Evaluation processes with respect to peripherality and accessibility

Evaluation Level	Evaluation Methods	Other components in Evaluation
Project	*Financial appraisal and CBA* - Financial appraisal limited given traffic flow levels; need for careful analysis of wider economic factors in CBA; reliance on accessibility indicators can be misleading; many regions already have healthy economies which are protected by inaccessibility rather than constrained by it.	*Environmental assessment* - new physical infrastructure may be seriously ecologically damaging in some remote regions; *Social impact analysis* - some remote regions may have fragile social structures where greater integration is damaging; *Economic impact analysis* - difficult problem of evaluating appropriate forward and backward linkages arising from new transport infrastructure.
Programme	*Multi criteria analysis and framework approaches* - needs a view of overall development of economy to ensure consistency with infrastructure programme, need to consider non infrastructure aspects of transport on consistent basis with physical infrastructure.	*Need for clear objectives on regional development and environment* - programmes must avoid being too oriented to international links to the exclusion or detriment of internal distribution impacts
Policy	*Strategic Environmental Assessment and Complex Objectives Analysis, including Meta Analysis* - need to ensure that transport is treated consistently and transport policy is not being asked to shoulder too large a burden of non transport objectives (e.g. employment creation through construction) and that non transport policies have been adequately assessed for their transport impacts (e.g. other spatial development policy, regional policy, rural development policy etc.).	*Programmes in national and international policy context so that broad economic, social and environmental objectives are met* - A better understanding of the role of transport in the development of the economy and society, especially the distribution of the benefits of growth and economic development, better understanding of the link between economic growth as measured by GDP and welfare (including distributional, social and environmental factors).

Table 2.4 Decision making processes with respect to peripherality and accessibility

Level of decision	Key Issues	Critical Success Factors
Local - Project	*Individual links, terminals and interchanges for each mode of transport* - need to determine most appropriate mode for many regions where conditions do not allow for choice, need to decide between complementarity or competition with adjacent regions (e.g. competing airports or developing surface link to airport in neighbouring region), but intermodality may offer an alternative	*Levels of integration (adding value to links and nodes), finance - individuals* - the need to improve choice, concern about the burden of financing new infrastructure on individuals in sparsely populated areas, cost of tolls, fiscal burden, need for evaluation of relative benefits to local area and to external areas from scale economies, forward and backward linkages etc.
National - Programme	*Logistics and Network Effects/Intermodality, interoperability and interconnectivity* - decide between network choice or preferred network development strategies, problems of linking peripheries directly or through core hubs, crucial role of the design and structure of networks ("network architecture")	*Companies, integrators, new actors, mergers and alliances (adding value to network) - public and private finance* - similar concerns as at local level on incidence of toll and fiscal burdens, need for analysis of "appropriate" network by mode for each country, concern about monopoly power of (often foreign owned) new actors and integrators, which act as limit to choice
National and EU - Policy	*Competitiveness, Cohesion and Environment/ Competition, Liberalisation and Open Access* - fundamental conflict of competitiveness thrusts involving the search for scale economies and simplistic cohesion objectives, contradictions in accessibility indicators. Problem that competition and liberalisation require flows large enough to achieve minimum cost operations by all operators, need for new small scale low cost alternatives	*International agencies, multinational companies (adding value to national and EU competitiveness), institution and government finance* - balance between available Structural Fund and EIB finance and fiscal burden/crowding out effects, distributional concern about competitiveness/cohesion balance, need to identify comparative advantage of peripheral regions in external trade of EU e.g. through ports, development of major "transition" corridors, i.e. choice of destination/trading partner

Secondly, there is the relative importance of competition, both between and within modes. This requires a clear view of the way in which networks are to be viewed as competitive or complementary recognising the typically lower level of flows in peripheral regions. However, some peripheral regions in the EU may face substantial transit or corridor traffic to and from external borders of the EU or ports. Within modes the lack of competition between carriers and the relation of domestic to foreign carriers in strategic alliances may pose particular problems for peripheral regions. This includes the need for reliance for key links on hubs which are controlled by others.

Finally, there are the potential problems of the excess burden of new infrastructure on activities within peripheral regions. New infrastructure provided by the private sector or otherwise requiring the payment of tolls may place extra burdens on the local economy. The replacement of, for example, traditional low cost ferry routes by a new bridge or tunnel may reduce travel times and their variability, but at a high cost to local users. Even where direct charges are not made and where external subsidy is available through the Structural or Cohesion Funds or through EIB loans, the local community will have to bear at least a share of the cost, which places a fiscal burden on it and some crowding out on the local economy. Thus the total costs to the local economy are not reduced by the extent which a simple measure of the enhancement of accessibility might imply. In this case neither competitiveness nor cohesion are improved.

For the development of an evaluation methodology the following features are critical.

The pentagon of concerns identifies the variety of issues which are present in all regions, but the lack of choice in certain dimensions creates particular tensions for its use as an evaluation tool in peripheral regions.

A major issue is the role of actors. In peripheral regions these actors often come from outside the region, or are dependent on other actors outside the region. This blurs the neat distinction into local, regional and national decision makers. Projects in peripheral regions which may have significant effects on local communities, such as the construction of bridges in coastal regions or new roads into inaccessible mountain areas, are typically not viable as free-standing projects, but only as part of a network of new developments. The benefits from a single project can only be realised in full if other projects (often in other regions) are undertaken. It must be evaluated together with the socio-economic development which it has to support. This super-additivity effect makes it difficult to ascribe precise costs and benefits.

2.3.2 Trans Alpine Freight Transport (TAFT)

The TAFT context - The structure of production, distribution and transport is going through a rapid transition phase. Globalisation, outsourcing and just in time delivery are trends that lead to an increased demand for freight transport on the one hand, and to a change in the kind and quality of services demanded on the other. At a European level, these trends are reinforced by the political and economic process of integration and the increase in spatial interaction. The consequence is an increasing stress on the transport networks in the form of congestion and bottlenecks.

The policy responses to these problems are inadequate and in many cases national regulations are at the source of the problem, for example the Transalpine freight transport. But TAFT is not an outcome of market processes alone. On the contrary, the ways in which overall flows are split among the modes and the country is to a very large extent the result of policy intervention in different countries. In the case of Switzerland, the overwhelming role of rail freight, and especially combined transport, is produced by the regulation of road transit (28 tonne limit) and subsidies for piggyback transport.

What generally holds for the European networks is even more true for the Transalpine freight transport networks. TAFT is characterised by spatial friction at national borders, incompatibilities between transport modes, capacity problems on roads, lack of competitiveness on rail, and environmental problems.

Objectives, Approaches and Evidence - The TAFT group analysed problems of network integration in the Trans Alpine context by focusing on the functioning of the network rather than on its overall social impacts. This more narrow perspective permitted concentration on network efficiency and deficiencies and thus the identification of the critical actors and success factors.

The functioning on the network has been considered with respect to the five pentagon dimensions namely: infrastructure (hardware), software, market organisation and regulations, environmental and financial aspects (Nijkamp and Vleugel, 1995). Analysing the functioning of the TAFT network with respect to the five dimensions implied the use of a variety of methods and instruments.

Hence, instead of developing a unified evaluation tool for overall impacts and sets of context, specific tools have been applied to evaluate various cases of malfunctioning. More specifically, the group used the following approaches in the different contexts:

27

- Micro level (individual actors behaviour)
- Stated preference analysis of freight forwarders' behaviour
- Policy network analysis
- Aggregate level (network flow models)
- Mode choice and freight distribution models
- Neural network models
- Qualitative flow forecasts

The application of this diversity of methods produced a number of significant results with respect to singular aspects of TAFT. The research illustrates how various influences, including national, rail, environmental and political forces are all preventing progress towards better use of the infrastructure. This in turn results in a focus on big infrastructure projects, which are only limited by increased funding problems.

The general approach outlined in Section 2 concentrates on value-added use by actors of infrastructure which is itself passive. In line with this approach, TAFT has been viewed as flows, for which the modal links are part of the hardware, but other elements are also involved. There are significant differences in the features of flows by the various Transalpine routes, as well as a modal split between rail and road (Maggi, 1992). Switzerland serves predominantly rail freight, while road use is concentrated on the French and Austrian routes. Combined transport has begun to play a role, mainly through Switzerland.

Infrastructure is not yet a bottleneck on the routes concerned. Although there is some road congestion, there is theoretically a substantial capacity reserve, which could be activated under other circumstances, such as reductions in regulatory restrictions. Although financing is clearly a barrier to the realisation of substantial new links, which may be justified for other reasons such as ecological requirements or organisational shortcomings, this is not seen as a basic barrier to optimisation. The ongoing survival of some combined transport links is not a financial problem, but rather an organisational matter, since subsidy is an aspect of regulatory intervention on market functioning.

The conclusion reached is that the most critical barrier to efficient network integration in the Transalpine sector is organisational. Two features of the findings are highlighted here. Firstly, the TAFT market is over-regulated. National, regional, local and mode-specific interests dominate over the interest of serving transport problems in an integrated way. This regulation reduces the capacity of the network through disintegration. Secondly, the national dimension has a negative impact on TAFT network integration. Most suppliers are local monopolies, and a market structure orientated on the

28

national market dimension has developed. This results in small fragmented operators with inefficient use of scale and market access.

The TAFT studies suggest that the European discussion on the separation of track and operations reflects the need of free access because it is the only way to make competition work, even though in economic terms it is doubtful whether such a disintegration returns higher efficiency and profit than an integrated operation. The existing 28 tonne weight restriction in Switzerland and the ban on night goods vehicle driving has been shown to have an impact equivalent to a 20 per cent price difference, but to provide no incentive to greater efficiency, so inducing the known detours through France and Italy. The existing environmental capacity is used less efficiently. Pricing schemes with fixed and variable elements have an incentive to lower other costs and improve competition.

Critical Success Factors (CSFs) - The critical success factors and the relevant actors found in the research can be listed according to the pentagon of concerns. From the results here, improving the functioning of the TAFT network primarily implies improvements in terms of regulation and market organisation.

More specifically, the research pointed out that *Hardware* is not seen as a scarce factor. Moreover, route and tunnel construction only creates potential, but does not itself improve efficiency. Critical actors in this field are national governments which define infrastructure strategies from a national perspective rather than taking a European view of Transalpine infrastructure needs and respective funding options.

Orgware (organisational and regulatory issues) are shown to be critical. After an examination of several alternative approaches, it was concluded that it is critical to improve the competitiveness of both the rail and the combined transport sectors, by intrinsic improvements following the removal of existing barriers. These include addressing the problems of national monopolies, inadequate internal flexibility, lack of market-orientated behaviour, and confusion of aims through the superimposition of national policy goals - these are the critical success factors.

The available instruments are in general terms re-regulation, privatisation, market opening at a European level and free access. The last of these is the most relevant for the promotion of integrated and intermodal transport. Present operators cannot provide competitive services in today's fragmented market. New entrants require freedom from national policy restrictions and from a dependent relationship with existing railways. Clear rules for infrastructure use, market access, property rights for basic service providers, and an international harmonisation of norms would have an enormous impact upon integration of the networks.

The most feasible approach is probably deregulation, removing existing rules without imposing new rules. This would encourage new partnerships and a more incentive-oriented approach. It is in the orgware domain where we find most of the critical actors. These are the national railways, the national combined transport companies, the road transport sectors which all in one way or in another profit from the current over-regulation of the TAFT market and the subsequent disintegration of the TAFT network. In addition, regulatory agencies have a limited knowledge of alternative modern options for re-regulation and also a limited interest to implement them.

Ecoware (Ecological aspects) has a role to play in that it is at present one of the sources of distortion of choice, and that the concept of ecological capacity is thereby introduced - but this is also a part of the organisational environment. The environmental interest groups represent another set of critical actors in so far as they combine, especially in the TAFT context, narrowly defined local interests with more general environmental concerns.

The other two components of the pentagon of concerns are less important. *Software* has a particular role for rail and combined transport, where open harmonised systems are not yet operational, but this is not seen as a leading critical success factor. *Finware* (Finance) is not seen as a primary barrier to raising efficiency. However, this does not mean that there are no major investment proposals in the TAFT region. There are four tunnel proposals (two in Switzerland, one in Austria and one in France), each of which requires substantial investment. The costs will be borne bilaterally by the connected countries, but the benefits will be spread much wider across Europe. The argument here is that if the project is agreed, the financial package will be put together, but the main barriers to implementation are organisational.

Presenting critical actors and factors this way makes it obvious that actors' behaviour cuts across the logic of the pentagon of concerns. But one important finding is that actors play a strategically critical part in the sphere of regulation and market organisation.

Summary - The TAFT market fails to function efficiently due to various policy failures. First, transport policies have been and are still following a national logic. Regulations in the transport sector on a national level together with national planning perspectives of the infrastructure hinder the emergence of an integrated TAFT network. Secondly, policies which have been designed in the interest of national players, such as railways and combined transport companies, are only slowly giving way to an integrated European approach. Thirdly, the newly arisen focus on environmental issues leads to unholy alliances with the already existing interests. This leads to a situation where different stakeholders strongly support a transport policy focusing on national issues. Under these circumstances, the policy options are severely limited.

These results have been achieved through the application of a variety of methods and a synthesis of the evidence found. Aggregate flow models allowed for the quantification of the overall implications of specific strategies (e.g. the 28 tonne limit), whereas micro-economic analysis has given more precision to strategic potentials in terms of price strategies for forwarders. The combination of this evidence has helped to identify critical success factors. Introducing actors analysis has permitted specific weights to be given to these factors in terms of relevant actors in the case of specific bottlenecks.

Finally, the organisation of the arguments according to the pentagon dimensions has given a coherent overview on the findings. Thus, the pentagon perspective has been used as a reference in terms of critical dimensions of the issue and not as an analytical device – which it is not.

The conclusion is that, in contrast to earlier expectations, organisational issues form the key critical success factor for improving the opportunities of network integration on the Transalpine freight route networks. These findings are clearly not only confined to Alpine routes, however their significance in the concentrated, highly political, and highly competitive environment of the Transalpine range is noticeable.

2.3.3 Competition and complementarity

Background - Recent policy developments in the European transport sector suggest a high degree of deregulation, accompanied by and reflected in a trend towards decentralisation and privatisation. The general view is that the market ought to have a more pronounced place in transport decision making. A market system implies by definition more competition in order to increase the efficiency of formerly bureaucratically organised, over-regulated transport systems (e.g. in aviation, railway operation, or inland waterways transport). However, at the same time, a drive towards the market may encounter two major stumbling blocks which would have to be overcome in order to achieve an efficiently operating market system. Firstly, there is the danger that as a result of market competition a transport system will emerge that is fragmented horizontally (particularly between modes), which suffers from lack of network synergy, critical mass and complementarity between different modes which altogether make up a socially desirable transport system. Secondly, there is the danger that a strict adherence to market principles will favour those transport modes which are economically most efficient, but fail to incorporate the social costs accruing from factors such as environmental decay, congestion and fatalities.

The main aim of this case study on Competition and Complementarity in Road, Rail and Waterway (CoCoRoRaWa) transport was to set out the principles for an evaluation methodology in the transport sector, by investigating systematically the usefulness of the pentagon of concerns for policy assessment regarding the competitive-complementary of transport decisions.

An important focal point of this working group was to identify and develop relevant evaluation frameworks and operational assessments methods in order to judge the socio-economic meaning of extensions or adjustments in transport movements in Europe.

This analysis is crucially important as transport mobility has drastically increased in Europe. For example, in the period 1980-1990 freight traffic in Western Europe has risen by approximately 30 per cent. Car ownership has increased by some 40 per cent, and passenger traffic with approximately 35 per cent. The political developments in Central-and Eastern-Europe leading to a widening of the European transport market and the increasingly recognised need to take care of the environmental stress of the transport sector make it necessary to develop an evaluation system that would incorporate mobility changes, modal shift and environmental constraints in the mobile Europe. Thus, a balance has to be found between efficiency, equity and sustainability.

Objectives and Approach - The objectives of the CoCoRoRaWa case study was to develop a systematic, comparative assessment methodology for road-rail-waterways competition and complementarity regarding intermodal transport in Europe, mainly seen from an actors' perspective in a liberalised transport market. A secondary objective was to position the actual passenger and freight development in a contestable European transport market by means of suitable and measurable indicators depicting the strategic demand and supply characteristics of the evolution of this market. From these two basic objectives the study then develops a cross-modal and cross-national comparative analysis for the performance of various modes and their actors.

The CoCoRoRaWa case study has also made an attempt to establish methodological and applied links with the general evaluation approach (Section 2.2). This has been achieved through the focus on multimodal issues in Europe, with specific attention on the identification and operational definition of indicators for the measurement of integrated European network performance. Attention has also been given to the issue of synergy in European networks by paying attention to the efficient operation (added value) of interoperable networks, and to the analysis of the role that different (new) actors play in the European transport market, with a specific view on the strategic role of market-based initiatives in freight transport (including social costs).

Three methods have been used in the CoCoRoRaWa case study. Firstly, policy scenario analysis has been developed, based on exogenous futures, sustainability policies, and infrastructure options.

Secondly, an assessment of bottlenecks in European transport via a strength-weakness analysis and an analysis of critical success factors for multi-modality (based on the pentagon approach) have been undertaken. Finally, a survey-based and actor-oriented methodology has been developed for setting priorities in intermodal freight transport infrastructures in Europe. The pentagon prism introduced above was used as a general framework for setting up the methodology and for undertaking the empirical studies.

Analysis and Results - The methodological and empirical work was undertaken in two different, but complementary approaches. Firstly, using the five critical success factors encapsulated in the pentagon of concerns, a European survey was held among transport experts in order to identify the bottlenecks and the most promising elements of European intermodal transport policy, in particular regarding freight transport by rail and road. It turned out that financing and organisation were by far the weakest elements in a coordinated European multimodal policy. This means that in future multimodal infrastructure network plans such aspects would need prominent attention. Secondly, a European commodity flow study on road-rail competition was carried out by maximising the benefits of network synergy in Europe. Here neural network analysis turned out to be a fruitful analytical tool. In addition, the environmental costs were introduced by assuming various user charge policy scenarios for European freight flows. Clearly, the implementation of such market-based environmental policies will have an impact on the spatial distribution of flows, but does not lead to a dramatic decline in transport flows.

The assessment and evaluation framework outlined above has been applied to the assessment of the efficiency and the state of transport modes in Europe and of the network as a whole. This has been pursued at two levels. First, the technical elements and their operational aspects have been evaluated. Secondly, the operational-managerial characteristics (environmental, economic, service/network) of a "good" or satisfactorily operating freight transport network have been assessed. Such desired trends have been defined for each mode and for the entire system.

At the more disaggregate level, this case study has tried to trace, identify and assess the decisive barriers that prevent a well-functioning operating of the freight road-rail network. These factors have again been traced at two levels, namely the national level and the European level. In addition, a

33

distinction between intermodel transport lines and terminals has been made. The issue of achieving a satisfactory freight transport network has also been examined. For designing the necessary policy the crucial success factors have been carefully studied and their relative importance systematically assessed. For the identification of both current barriers and success factors the pentagon of concerns has again been used (Table 2.5).

The conclusion reached is that the development of a well functioning multi-modal transport framework emerges as a promising solution for several current transport problems and related factors. However, it appears that the existing state of multi-modal networks is lagging far behind the desired level, especially in the case of road-rail cooperation. The survey exercise performed in the framework of the present study showed thus clearly that transport experts in Europe attach a high desirability to the development of an efficient and effective multi-modal network, and this will be beneficial to the transport sector and society as a whole.

Table 2.5 Survey of the results

	Crucial Barriers	Medium Barriers	Low Barriers
Gap between existing and "desired" intermodal transport. National level	financial hardware	organisational	software psychological meta-variables
Gap between existing and "desired" intermodal transport. European level	financial hardware		organisational software psychological
Gap between existing and "desired" intermodal terminals. National level	financial hardware		software psychological
Gap between existing and "desired" intermodal terminals. European level	financial hardware	organisational	software psychological

However, this evolution is burdened by serious obstacles. It seems that there are prohibitive financial, technical, organisational and other problems. In particular, the cooperation level between European countries for the development of a fully interoperable railways system is rather weak at present. Moreover, railways have an important role to play in the development of an effective network. Other technical problems, such as those related to the existence of specific rolling stock emerge as a decisive barrier and should be taken into account.

Financial issues involved in the creation of sufficient rail infrastructure and intermodal terminals seem to be a rather prohibitive obstacle in almost all European countries and relevant institutions.

On the other hand, the importance of proper intermodal terminals is considered as fundamental by most European experts. They indicate that there is a great lack of intermodal terminals which otherwise could facilitate an effective rail-road network. The development of proper terminals is also burdened by serious financial and intra-European cooperation obstacles.

Conclusion - The socio-economic added value of networks in Europe can be assessed by operationalising the pentagon of concerns and by using environmental policy scenarios for European freight flows. In this context, the final recommendations emerging from our case study suggest that the development of a policy for removing the financial and hardware technical barriers is the main priority, since multi-modal freight transport emerges as a promising evolution in economic, social and environmental terms. Such a policy may have a European (international) perspective which takes into account the particular national characteristics in each country. In this framework, the adoption of common technical standards for railways operation and the introduction of new financial schemes emerges as prerequisites. On the other hand, such development requires new legislation and social adjustments concerning the market structure, the management and the ownership of enterprises and infrastructure in the transport sector.

In the light of the capacity of the current European networks for commodity transport in an integrating economy and in the light of the unacceptably high environmental stress of road transport, new logistic systems based on combined transport as a blend of different modalities are necessary. This will increase capacity, reduce congestion and environmental decay, and make the European network economy more efficient. But this outcome requires dedicated policy strategies on both intermodal transport and on trans-shipment terminals. A more liberalised transport market may increase the efficiency of intermodal transport operations and establish the means by which the environmental factors can be included. The critical success factors of such a market may be mapped out by the application of survey methods among experts and stakeholders, while using multicriteria and disaggregate choice analysis. The resulting transport flows may be gauged by using neural network analysis.

2.3.4   The role of actors

One principal conclusion from the analysis contained in the previous three case studies is that the role of the actors is critical. A comprehensive survey was carried out through a questionnaire survey of some twenty European countries on the actors' strategy towards the integration of networks (Houée, 1995,1997). It was designed to include all those currently involved in decisions relating to the use and integration of networks, and to elicit concerns and opportunities about the future.

At the national level the state still has a dominant role in determining investment priorities for the infrastructure, even though powers are being devolved to regions and to autonomous agencies. It is not just in decisions on investment, but the state controls finances (or access to finance), regulations and taxation. This strategic role also affects the level of integration in networks, but here the experience of different countries is very variable with some having clear central direction, whilst others take a more permissive role as integration and other leave it to the market. The role of autonomous agencies is fairly widespread with respect to ports and airports, but less common for railways and roads. The state has a key role here in ownership and the provision of services, although in some countries the use of contracts and tendering procedures are becoming more common as the state gradually withdraws from service provision.

The role of the regions reflects that of the state at a more local level. Rather than investing in the network, the regions' primary concern is the maintenance of the network and in the provision of services on the network. In some countries, the regions have powers to raise capital, but in others they are restricted to seeking state funding. The regions have only a minor role in the integration of networks as their powers and financing opportunities are limited. Perhaps there is a major role that the regions could play in providing information and advice on the optimal use of the networks to passengers and freight hauliers.

The role of financial institutions and private capital in the construction of infrastructure is limited, except where there are government guarantees. Some potential exists for small to medium scale projects where the risks are low and there are good prospects for returns on investments (e.g. bridges and tunnels). The greatest potential for private sector involvement in infrastructure investment is through joint ventures between the public and private sectors (Banister, Gérardin and Viegas, 1998).

The survey has not found an important role for the major transport operators in the integration of networks. The tendency has been towards greater fragmentation as operators seek to increase their market share at the expense of their competitors. This conclusion relates primarily to the lack of horizontal integration, which is particularly apparent at the interfaces between modes. However, there are some promising examples of greater cooperation through such schemes as park and ride, combined transport and better transfer facilities (including interchanges). The role of the trade unions is very variable as their power is considerable in some countries, but it has been substantially reduced in others. Modernisation is supported by the unions provided that jobs are safeguarded and working conditions improved.

The power of environmental lobbies is again variable between the countries surveyed. Their general influence may be limited, but they are still powerful when focused on particular issues (e.g. a new road or new runway capacity). Similarly, the industry lobbies are still influential when economic factors are debated, particularly jobs, but it is the environmental lobbyists that seem to be more effective in their methods and in influencing opinion on the choices to be made in the transport sector.

The role of shippers is substantial in achieving network integration and in providing door-to-door services, and they have been effective in providing intermodal services. This is particularly important in light of the disintegration of other types of operators. This change has been facilitated by the new logistics, the new integrators (e.g. express delivery) and the requirements of the service sector for immediate response, but often at a premium price. In the initial stage this has led to market opportunities for the integrators to establish dominance in a growing market. In the second phase, alliances have been sought to give manufacturers a complete package for supply/distribution/marketing. This may lead to mergers and the development of global integrators or fixers. The unresolved third phase is whether the market for these new actors is sufficiently large or diverse for it to be contestable. The length and complexity of the supply chains means that there may be opportunities for specialist inputs, where complementarity between supply chains exist or where specialist skills are required to avoid bottlenecks. So the global operators may need local specialist inputs to ensure continuity in the supply chain. However, too many inputs may reduce the effectiveness of the whole process, and in turn lead to higher costs and fragmentation. It is here that the logistics platforms have a crucial role to play in ensuring the weakest points in the chain (the interchanges) operate efficiently (Banister, 1996).

Another set of new actors has arisen in the leisure sector, principally through multi-modal tour operators. Services are again becoming more tailored to the individual at a premium price, rather than being offered as a cheap package. Quality seems to be a key objective. Individual companies are also providing their own integrated distribution networks. Making optimal use of their own vehicles, the information highway and the relatively low costs of transport.

Conclusions - In summary, the survey found that the role of the state (and the EU) is crucial in providing the framework and direction for policy, including regulation, finance, investment, integration and operation of the network. The regions have less of an instrumental role, but more responsibilities for the maintenance of the infrastructure and provision of services. The private sector has a limited role in investment, unless in partnership with the state or in particular projects where risks can be shared. It has a much greater role in the provision of services. Operators are more concerned over their own market share, rather than the integration of the network. Recent changes (e.g. deregulation and privatisation) have led to fragmentation of services, particularly between modes, but also within individual modes.

Environmental and industrial actors are powerful, particularly when focused on single issues or on the employment implications of actions. Shippers have an instrumental role in providing effective door-to-door services, particularly where intermodal services are required. This is a major growth area with the use of logistics and the emergence of new integrators. The growth in leisure-based activities again offers new opportunities for integrated service provision to a new market.

More generally, one of the main findings of the survey was the increased flexibility in the use of the network. Patterns of use changed daily as the requirements of travellers and businesses also changed. This has resulted in the emergence of a large number of small scale creative new actors. The market is in a transition phase - moving from one based on more traditional actors in manufacturing and highly structured forms of distribution, together with regulated travel patterns - to one that is flexible and based on the new service and information economy, with flat slim-lined organisational structures and very variable patterns of travel demand. The new operators will be the customers themselves as supply chains and demand patterns become increasingly personalised. Interactions will take place directly with the providers of goods and services (e.g. through the Internet) - the whole system is customer driven.

If these revolutionary changes take place, then the concepts of integration also change as infrastructure networks become more varied and as general networks are replaced by individual ones. Integration has been seen as a collective responsibility to provide the most efficient service for all users. But now it may be an individual responsibility that requires a particular service to a particular user at a particular time to meet a specific set of requirements. The requirements and the use made of the network will change according to internal and external factors in a dynamic way.

The role of the actors in determining the access to the network and the use made of it is reflected in the figure at the end of this report. The dynamics of change have been underestimated and the role of existing and new actors is also in the process of transformation. The traditional views of a small group of influential decision makers are being replaced by an infinitely flexible arrangement where each person, in each location, on each day determines how they use the network. As a consequence of their individual actions, they affect the decisions of others on how they use (or do not use) the network. Actors, individual and collectively, are instrumental in our understanding of how networks are used.

2.4   Conclusions

Inevitably, there are a wide ranging set of conclusions that have arisen. In the previous section (Section 2.3), the individual results from each of the four case studies have been placed within the evaluation framework (Section 2.2). In this section, the overall conclusions are presented where the findings cut across the four case studies.

The net result of these changes and the dynamics of the processes has meant that the use of the European strategic transport network is in a state of rapid adjustment. The value added is not from the physical use of the transport network as this forms a declining part of the total production process, but value comes from flexible production processes, new users of the network, outsourcing and decentralisation, together with fundamental changes in organisation and management processes.

Transport intensity has grown as both tonne-kms. and passenger-kms. are increasing at a greater rate than the growth in the European economy. Because transport costs are low, this is one part of the production and movement processes that can be increased so that the overall levels of efficiency and value added to the product or traveller are also increased, at least in terms of the provider of the service. The wider social costs of the dramatic increase in transport intensity of movement are paid by society as a whole. Three main cross-cutting conclusions are presented.

2.4.1   Networks and integration

Throughout this research, it has been realised that networks are much wider than the physical infrastructure which is conventionally considered within evaluation. The starting point was the pentagon of concerns, but this has been extended to cover evaluation of policies, programmes and projects, and the crucial role that actors have in the construction and use of all forms of networks. Actors have a key role to play in network efficiency and the new range of actors, particularly the integrators, add value to the networks.

Network integration is demand led within a market environment. Although the actors can facilitate integration through regulation, price, location and other complementary policies, it is the user of the network which primarily determines the level of integration. The freight sector best illustrates this conclusion through its reorganisation - value added is in the form of the new flexible production processes with outsourcing and decentralisation, together with new management structures. It seems likely that other sectors (e.g. passenger) will adapt in the same way so that the integrated services will respond to the demand of users for high quality "seamless" travel (e.g. in the leisure sector) - this is the customer driven network.

Full network integration requires a linking of transport networks, together with economic, cultural and other networks. All of these networks interrelate, and it is difficult to apply one form of evaluation. Even if it was possible to develop a unified evaluation tool for network integration, the product is likely to be technocratic and only able to tackle part of the problem. This is a feature of current methods which mainly address a single mode in the context of a single project with only one (or a few) impact(s) (e.g. the physical infrastructure). A multiplicity of approaches and methods can be proposed (Section 2.4.2) and the analysis carried out concentrates on the functioning of networks in particular contexts. The organisational dimension of the pentagon of concerns is crucial in the evaluation of the value added from the European transport network.

One unresolved issue is that a necessary condition for the efficient use of networks is the requirement for high quality data, so that decisions are based on the best possible information. Within competitive markets, this is difficult as data have a high value and as competitive advantage may rely on exclusive access to information. Further research is required to assess the overall EU-wide benefits of decisions being made on full knowledge and the best available data, as compared with individual actions based on partial knowledge and information. It is increasingly important that decisions are based on full knowledge and information, and that the most appropriate technology is used if network efficiency is to be improved. The maximum societal value added could then coincide with the maximum individual value added.

2.4.2   Evaluation and methods

Across and within all four case studies, a multiplicity of evaluation methods have been used. This is in stark contrast to the starting point of the research where it was proposed to develop a single evaluation tool. It was found that a unique evaluation method is neither feasible nor desirable. As all four case studies opted for a comprehensive evaluation of the various aspects of a network (project, programme, policy level, and the pentagon of concerns), a single method could not comprehend the complexity of the evaluation task. Various individual methods are very precise on single aspects and it is not desirable to lose this precision.

Consequently, this multi-method strategy has proven to be essential to our understanding of the key components of evaluation rather than a common logic for ordering the evidence. This has been found along the two dimensions, namely the evaluation/decision level (actors perspective) and the pentagon of concerns (factors perspective). There is no single valued relationship either between evaluation/decision level and type of method, or between the diverse dimensions of the pentagon and the kind of approach used. On the contrary, a methodological conclusion from this research is that at any object level it pays to apply either more than one method or to use non orthodox approaches. In concrete terms, this means that it is necessary to analyse actors' behaviour in a policy context using a policy network approach and a micro-economic approach, or to evaluate aggregate impacts on a project level, as well as behavioural aspects on a programme level.

Obviously, the above implies that the action has taken a political economic view on the evaluation task in the case of networks. Evaluation needs to consider the potential for actors to exploit new opportunities to give them a comparative advantage or to profit by providing services – and this applies in both core and peripheral areas in Europe.

2.4.3   Globalisation and internationalisation

One of the principle factors affecting the development of transport in Europe has been the increasing internationalisation and globalisation of economic activity. This acts as both a cause and effect of changes in transport. As a cause it leads to changing patterns of demand and flow as multinational companies alter their patterns of investment in the global market. Thus the transport system has to change to meet these changing needs, and governments at all levels are conscious of the need to respond in anticipation of new investment to ensure the investment takes place. As a result, these changes in the transport system, which both confirm the centrality of some locations and open up others, present new possibilities to the internationalising firm, and stimulate new clusters of activity.

This internationalisation occurs both within Europe and between Europe and the rest of the world. Within Europe, firms from one country are involved in new investment in another country, but at the same time there are non European firms investing within Europe. In the latter case the investment is seen as evidence of the increasing attractiveness of European locations for production (i.e. increasing competitiveness). In the former case, it not only reflects changes in "competitiveness" between different regions within Europe, it also has effects on the process of convergence or divergence in the economic performance of these regions (i.e. cohesion). In both cases decisions which have a significant impact on the transport network in any region are being taken outside the region most affected, the distribution of power and control is thus crucial to efficient decisions about new investments, how they are financed, their detailed planning and their operation.

The restructuring of industry within Europe is part of a world-wide process of change, involving the introduction of new technology and new patterns of production to existing sectors, and the introduction of new, more customer-oriented services. This is seen in various ways. Traditional manufacturing is concentrated in fewer, larger plants, controlled by fewer multinational enterprises.

Large investments are made depending on a variety of local conditions, of which good transport is only one. These are investments which can be less permanent than in traditional sectors, adding further to the loss of control by actors within a particular region or country. However, such investments may have very specific infrastructure requirements, which become part of the package necessary to attract large investments into a region. Improved local transport, better telecommunications, airport and seaport investment all feature strongly in this, with new competition between regions being created.

Hence it is not sufficient just to identify the balance of critical concerns from the pentagon used as a starting point in this study, nor even a simple division into the scale of the impact and the identification of the responsible level for decision making. Actors and their influence cut across all of these concerns. These influences involve competition between actors for favoured locations and preferential access to improved networks, competition between regions within Europe and between Europe and the rest of the world for new investment.

Policy actions and reactions by government authorities and other agents at all levels, local, regional, national and supranational (e.g. European Union) become as important as the physical environment and the structure of networks which were previously seen as the major barriers. Understanding the constraints placed on the choices available to policy and decision makers at all levels is the most critical success factor. This is the main lesson for the integration of strategic transport networks in Europe.

References

Banister, D. (1996), *The Dynamic Response of the Actors in the Freight Sector*, Paper prepared for the COST 328 Working Group 4 on the Actors' Strategy, December.

Banister, D. (1997), "Reducing the Need to Travel", *Environment and Planning, B* 24(3), 437-449.

Banister, D. (ed.) (1998), *Transport Policy and the Environment*, Spon: London.

Banister, D., Gérardin, B. and Viegas, J. (1998), "Partnerships and Responsibilities in Transport: European and Urban Policy Priorities", in Button, K., Nijkamp, P. and Priemus, H. (eds.) *European Transport Policy*, Edward Elgar: London, 202-223.

Houée, M. (1995), *Relations Entre Opérateurs et Régulateurs, et Intégration des Réseaux*, Paper presented at the COST 328 Colloquium on Integrated Strategic Infrastructure Networks in Europe – Lausanne, 2-3 March 1995.

Houée, M. (1997), *Survey about Actors Concerned with the Integration of Networks*, Paper prepared for the COST 328 from the results of the Actors Strategies Questionnaire, September 1997.

Maggi, R. (1992, "Swiss Transport Policy for Europe? Federalism and the Dominance of Local Issues", *Transportation Research*,26A(2), 193-198.

Nijkamp, P. and Blaas E. (1994), *Impact Assessment and Evaluation in Transportation Planning*, Kluwer: Dordrecht.

Nijkamp P. and Vleugel J. (1995), "Transport infrastructure and EU developments", in Banister, D. Capello, R. and Nijkamp, P. (eds) *European Transport and Communications Networks*, Wiley: London, 3-30.

Nijkamp, P., Vleugel, J.M., Maggi, R. and Masser, I. (1994), *Missing Transport Networks in Europe*, Avebury, Aldershot.

OECD (1997) *Meeting the Needs of Cities: Transportation, Infrastructure, Finance and Urban Development*, OECD Urban Affairs Division, Paris, October.

Salomon, I. (1995), "Telematics, Travel and Environmental Change: What Can Be Expected of Travel Substitution", *Built Environment*,21(4), 214-222.

Spiekermann, K. and Wegener, M. (1996), "Trans-European Networks and Unequal Accessibility in Europe", *EUREG European Journal of Regional Development*, 4(1), 35-42.

Vickerman, R. (1995), "Location, Accessibility and Regional Development: An Appraisal of Trans-European Networks", *Transport Policy*, 2(3), 225-234.

Vickerman, R.W. (1997), *The Transport Sector, New Economic Geography and Economic Development in Peripheral Regions*, Paper presented at the 37th European Congress, European Regional Science Association, Rome, August.

Vickerman, R. (1998a), "Transport Provision and Regional Development in Europe: Towards a Framework for Appraisal", in Banister, D. (ed.), *Transport Policy and the Environment*, Spon: London, 133-162.

Vickerman, R.W. (1998b). "Accessibility, Peripherality and Spatial Development: The Question of Choice", in Reggiani, A. (ed.), *Accessibility, Trade and Location Behaviour*, Avebury: Aldershot.

3 The Transport Sector, New Economic Geography and Economic Development in Peripheral Regions[1]

ROGER VICKERMAN

3.1 Introduction

There is a renewed interest in peripherality in Europe. The completion of a Single Market, pressures towards Economic and Monetary Union and the threat of competition between the southern and eastern peripheries have all raised important policy dimensions. There is increasing questioning of the traditional reliance on the use of infrastructure, especially transport infrastructure, as a policy instrument. The traditional approach to peripherality has been through the use of conventional measures of accessibility and economic potential, broad macro-measures, which make important, but largely implicit, assumptions about economic structure, production and markets.

This chapter aims to bring together two strands from recent work which cast the peripherality problem in a new light. On the one hand there have been advances in the definition of accessibility which take a more disaggregated approach, concentrating on accessibility within regions and to networks. On the other hand models in the "New Economic Geography" tradition concentrate on the interplay between production characteristics, imperfectly competitive markets and transport costs to demonstrate the potential ambiguity of convergent and divergent forces in the economic integration process. To this we aim to add a third strand, which is typically absent from both approaches, a more detailed consideration of the transport sector itself. Accessibility measures concentrate on objective measures of impedance, distance, time and cost, but do not usually allow explicitly for the role of market structure in the transport sector. Similarly, New Economic Geography models rely too heavily on the simple representation of transport costs as an "iceberg" formulation. This makes for a more tractable model, but misses one of the key dimensions which is of particular relevance to peripheral regions.

The chapter will discuss a largely theoretical approach to these issues, but illustrated with some specific examples which look at the impact of new transport infrastructure on changes in traffic flows, location and logistics. There are four main sections dealing with accessibility, new economic geography, transport sector imperfections and some proposals for a revised model. Two further sections deal with some evidence from two applied projects relating to European networks in peripheral regions and the consequences of a major new infrastructure. The principal finding is that peripheral regions suffer constraints on their economic development as much from imperfections in the structure of transport markets as they do from conventional geographic peripherality.

3.2   Accessibility

The key element in recent approaches is one of disaggregation. Traditional measures of accessibility have been concerned with assessing the accessibility of a *region* rather than the accessibility of individual *economic actors*. Despite attempts to give accessibility and potential measures a firm theoretical basis (e.g. Rietveld, 1989), in practice they have been used in a way which aims to express a single measure for a region. This carries two aggregation problems: spatial and sectoral aggregation.

Spatial aggregation arises because of the attempt to provide a single measure for a given geographical area. Thus the traditional accessibility-potential measures following Clark et al (1969) and Keeble et al (1982, 1988) use geographical regions and measure the accessibility by a given mode of transport to a specific node which is representative of that region. The problems arise because of the assumption of both *nodal* and *modal* concentrations.

Nodal concentration implies that all places within a region can be represented by the accessibility of its key centre. That node, typically the main concentration of population in a zone, may be representative of some of the activities of a region, but not all. Use of traditional measures based on nodes tends to produce smooth accessibility surfaces which peak at the most central node of the set chosen.

Modal concentration uses a single mode of transport as representative of the set of transport opportunities available to a region. This is typically chosen as road transport since it is this mode which will tend to dominate most transport of goods, and of people over shorter distances. It may, however, be particularly inappropriate for more peripheral regions which perceive their (lack of) accessibility in terms of air transport and for which the alternative use of short sea shipping over varying distances may be an important element in any journey choice. Moreover, the increasing interest in multi-modal or combined transport makes road distances alone a less relevant measure. Refinements of indices, such as that proposed by Lutter et al (1992) which uses (subjectively chosen) best modes for each origin-destination pair, can provide a basis for a more subtle index which is able to differentiate rather better between different degrees of peripherality. However, they still suffer from the basic spatial aggregation problem.

One solution to this problem has been proposed by Vickerman et al (1999) which uses a 10 km raster basis for calculating accessibility. An application of this model to the European rail network produces an index which is much more sensitive to intra-regional variations in accessibility. This distinguishes not just the usual centre-periphery differences but also urban-rural differences ion both centre and peripheral regions. Not only does this provide a clear picture of a complex pattern of accessibility across the European Union, it identifies how corridors of higher accessibility with good access to networks come about and similarly how various degrees of "shadow" and "desert" areas of *relatively* poor accessibility can co-exist in relative proximity to nodes of good accessibility, but penalised by the need for network inter-connection and/or a change of mode. This model has also been applied to the *changes* in accessibility resulting from the adoption of the proposed European high-speed rail network by the year 2010. Although this does not change in a major way, emphasising the increasing concentration of accessibility in a small number of high accessibility zones, there are some more subtle changes in the *relative* accessibility of individual locations.

Thus the proposed solution to the nodal concentration problem is one of disaggregating regions into small, independently defined, units, such as raster squares, to avoid the implicit logical bias that the point with the best accessibility is defined as the node of the region and its accessibility attributed to the whole region.

The sectoral bias in traditional models is related to the way that aggregate flows along networks are treated as homogeneous. This implies that distance and/or time can be taken as valued at the same rate in all situations, and specifically that the value of time is the same in all situations and for all users of a given type of infrastructure.

3.3   The new economic geography

The accessibility models discussed above assume a simple correspondence between activities and their demands for transport which enables a change in transport provision, which leads to a change in accessibility, to be transformed simply into part of that sector's costs. In this section we explore further the possible complexities of changing that relationship. This has been done most forcefully recently in what has become known as the "new economic geography", but is simply a development of spatial economic models to allow for imperfect competition.

Traditional models of transport demand take a given structure and distribution of industrial production and final demand and proceed to model the implicit demand for transport within this framework. The emphasis is on first identifying a set of flows of goods within the system necessary to sustain the production structure and then allocating this to appropriate modes and routes within networks. In this sense the transport demand model is a derived demand from the demand for goods in a flow matrix. This flow matrix can be derived, for example, from an input-output type model converted to an multi-regional format. The I-O model shows the demands of each sector (including final demand by consumers and exports) from each other sector. If we know about the regional location of particular industries then, assuming given transport costs, the implicit inter-regional flow of goods to satisfy equilibrium between demand and supply in each regional market can be derived. This demonstrates a degree of circularity since it is usually necessary to make assumptions about transport costs in order to estimate transport demand.

On the other side, the location of industries, depends *inter-alia*, on the assumptions made about transport costs, but the output and the choice of production technology for these industries typically is determined independently of transport factors.

This mismatch of theoretical structures leads to some problems in interpreting the effects of changes in transport costs, since there is typically no assumption of any trade-off between the transport cost factors and other factors. Thus improvements in transport lead to extensions to the market areas of existing firms (see Figure 3.1).

Two firms are located at A and B: firm A has unit production costs of OP_A and B of OP_B. Transport costs are at a fixed unit cost per ton-km, identical for both firms, as shown by the lines RT_A and ST_B. The market area boundary between the two firms occurs at C. Suppose transport costs now fall to RT_A' and ST_B', now the market area boundary will move to the right to E and Firm A gains from the reduction. If only A were to benefit from the fall in transport costs then it would benefit by even more. Of course if B could reduce its higher production costs then it could obtain market area from A. The difference in production costs could arise because of greater scale economies, due for example to a greater density of population at A than B.

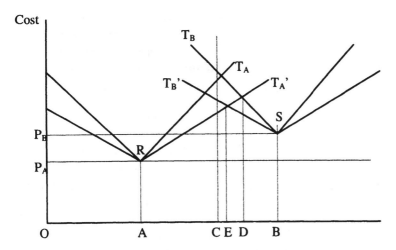

Figure 3.1 Simple spatial economic model

However, this simple model looks only at a single industry. If there is more than one industry at location A then there may be external economies which would also enable the firm to benefit from lower input costs, and also from lower transport costs. Traditional industrial economics models dating back to Marshall (David, 1991) used the idea of localisation economies deriving from factors such as a pooled market for workers and the growth of production of non-tradable specialised inputs. Traditional models of agglomeration have relied on this external economies argument and this leads to a clear benefit to be gained from infrastructure improvements since these can act like a public good. What is needed, however, is a model which allows for the existence of internal economies of scale to generate the agglomeration effect. This is principally required to be able to use a model to explain not just the location of individual firms within industries, but to be able to explain the pattern of agglomeration of industries which leads to a particular economic geography.

The Krugman model (Krugman, 1991a) has been the most influential of the new models of economic geography. The model has its basis in international trade theory and thus provides a common basis from which to explore both international and interregional patterns of economic activity. The model assumes two regions, two factors and two types of production, one displaying constant returns to scale and the other increasing returns, but which can be located in either region. Individuals are assumed to have a utility function of the type developed by Dixit and Stiglitz (1977). This assumes a composite choice process by which individuals choose between broad types of goods and within each of these can choose between

49

differentiated products. This enables easy consideration of monopolistic competition in markets where differentiated products occur. The key point here is that the perceived elasticity of substitution to the individual firm producing the individual product depends both on the overall elasticity of substitution of individuals for goods of that type and the firm's perceived elasticity for its product relative to those of other firms. This perception depends not only on the actual elasticity of substitution but also the firm's perception of its rivals' responses to any change in price or output it makes.

Such a representation lies at the base of modern trade theories which emphasise the significance of intra-industry trade in which regions with similar production structures still find advantages in trading with each other. Welfare gains arise from the increase in choice faced by consumers as well as from scale and other economies achieved by increasing the output of each individual product brand. This could be a significant feature in determining the distribution of induced costs and benefits between regions as a result of a change in the transport costs incurred in moving goods between them.

The key objective of the model is to investigate ways in which industries will concentrate in particular locations as a result of factors internal to the industry, scale economies, product diversity, imperfect competition etc. rather than through the traditional reliance on external economies as a determinant of industrial concentration. This is not the place to repeat the full details of the model (see Krugman, 1991a, for a basic statement), but it is useful to summarise the key findings which will be used in the subsequent discussion.

The model identifies three key parameters, the relative values of which determine the outcome in terms of whether there is a change in the distribution of economic activity between regions resulting in increased or reduced concentration. The three parameters are:

- the share of total expenditure in a region spent on the output of the sector with increasing returns, called here "manufacturing", μ
- the elasticity of substitution within the "manufacturing" sector, σ, which gives a measure of the potential scale economies in the sector since the greater is the elasticity of substitution the lower is the scope for achieving scale economies;
- the level of transport costs, τ, measured as the proportion of the output of a sector in one region delivered to a market in another region and thus not used up in transporting the output, such that low values of τ imply high transport costs and high values of τ imply low transport costs, the "iceberg" principle.

These three parameters determine relative wage rates and the prices of traded goods in each region. Labour is assumed to move towards higher real wages (either because nominal wages are higher and/or price levels lower). This process induces either convergence or divergence of regional wage levels and deconcentration or concentration of the labour force.

The simplest way of developing the regional implications is to consider the conditions under which a new firm will establish in one region or the other. Suppose initially all the "manufacturing" industry is in region 1, which therefore has a larger market, and all the income from "manufacturing" goes to region 1. If the firm wants to set up in region 2 it will have both to pay a higher wage to attract appropriate labour to move to that region and sufficient to compensate that labour for the likely higher price of "manufactures" in that region, which (except for the output of the new plant) will have to be imported. Thus the relative wage must depend on τ and μ. The value of sales transferred will depend on the elasticity of substitution facing a particular firm, σ. Note that the firm in region 2 has a potential monopoly in that region, but a disadvantage (because of transport costs) in selling to region 1 and because of its higher labour costs.

The net outcome of this model depends on the values of all three parameters relative to each other. The key relationships are as follows:

- the larger is μ, the lower will be the relative sales of the new firm in region 2 because workers demand a larger wage premium;
- if transport costs are zero, $\tau = 1$, location becomes irrelevant. If transport costs are large, τ is small, the firm could set up profitably in the new region because it is relatively protected, unless there is a very small elasticity of substitution, σ, implying large scale economies, or a very large home market in region 1, μ, which would be difficult to compete against;
- there is a critical value of τ, at which there will be no incentive to set up in region 2; at values of τ less than this a rise in τ (fall in transport costs) will therefore lead to an increase in concentration, but at values of τ above this critical value, further increases in τ will lead to deconcentration toward the location indifference at $\tau = 1$;
- as σ increases (indicating less significant scale economies), the relative profitability of setting up in region 2 increases. The higher is σ, the higher is the critical value of τ for any given value of μ which will enable profitable operation in region 2. As scale economies increase in importance, σ gets smaller, the possibility of deconcentration is reduced and the trade off between market size, μ, and transport costs, τ, becomes critical - if μ is large then τ must fall (transport costs rise) if concentration is not to occur.

The nature of these results can be shown as a simple numerical example (Krugman and Venables, 1990). This assumes two production locations, one, Belgium, which has relatively high production costs, and the other, Spain, which has lower production costs. If production is concentrated in either of these "regions" scale economies lead to lower costs than if production is distributed between the two. Now consider the role of transport costs, where the higher volumes produced in Belgium allow lower transport costs, total costs equal production costs plus transport costs. This shows that with high transport costs it would be cheaper to divide production between the two locations, with a total cost of 12 against 13 in Belgium and 16 in Spain. As transport costs fall the situation changes. A halving of transport costs would lead to concentration in Belgium, but a reduction in transport costs to zero ($\tau=1$ in the formal model) would again cause concentration of production, but in the other region.

Table 3.1 Numerical example of transport costs and convergence

	Production costs	Shipping costs High	Shipping costs Medium	Low
Produce in Belgium	10	3	1.5	0
Produce in Spain	8	8	4	0
Produce in both	12	0	0	0

Source: Krugman and Venables (1990)

The model outlined above is just one of a range of new economic geography models with many similarities which have been developed (for a full survey see, for example, Fujita and Thisse, 1996). More recent work has concentrated on improving the specification and adding some further features. Martin and Rogers (1995) include a measure of infrastructure in the regions which is allowed to influence productivity and market area. This suggests that internal infrastructure in a region or country is more important than external (inter-regional or international) infrastructure. This shows the importance of distinguishing the transport costs of serving the "domestic" and "foreign trade" markets. Ciccone and Hall (1996) look more carefully at the differences in labour productivity in different locations. Venables (1996) takes up the important question of how vertical linkages between industries affect their optimal location decisions. As well as being able to produce similar types of outcome of the simple Krugman model, with changes in transport costs being able to produce both divergence and convergence results depending on the starting point and the size of the change, this model also shows that similar results can occur without the mobility of labour which characterised the operation of the Krugman model. This is of particular interest since there are clear limits to labour mobility within the EU where this would involve international mobility.

3.4   Transport market imperfections

The main problem area with the new economic geography model and its derivatives is in its treatment of transport. The principal interest of those developing the models has been in imperfections in the markets which use transport with an implicit assumption that transport markets themselves are not so important. To the extent that transport costs are an increasingly small proportion of total costs this may seem reasonable, but on the other hand transport has been identified as a potential major source of economic progress in Europe, delivering both competitiveness and cohesion gains (Vickerman, 1997, 1998b). Furthermore imperfections in the transport sector itself may be the source of important costs which fall disproportionately on different regions (Vickerman 1998a).

The use of the "iceberg" principle is quite reasonable as a starting point and does allow for equal treatment of all impedance effects, but it fails to take into account specific features of the transport sector. Martin and Rogers (1996) have made a first attempt at dealing with infrastructure, but this is within the "iceberg" tradition, although they try and separate internal and external infrastructures. Martin and Rogers make the point that dealing with infrastructure as a "price" interacting between producers and consumers is more satisfactory than the production function approach used by the macro studies in the Aschauer (1989, 1990) tradition. However, the problem is then one of turning any improvement in infrastructure into the appropriate price, which is particularly difficult given the public good characteristics of infrastructure which lies behind the Aschauer approach - the specific point is that it is not market priced.

A further point is that the price charged for any given unit of transport depends critically on the market structure within the transport sector. Increasingly, firms in peripheral regions complain about poor levels of service and high levels of price which are related to the firms being held captive by monopolistic suppliers of transport on sparsely served parts of networks (see Vickerman, 1998a). This suggests that there is a case for a more explicit modelling of the transport sector, the determinants of transport price in the model (even if it is the "iceberg" variable τ). The key point here is that τ is typically taken as constant, or constant for a particular type of good, rather than dependent on the market for transport. Here we are suggesting that in a region which is poorly served, there will be a greater problem in getting access to good quality transport (a lower τ) than in core regions, although it is possible to argue that where there is a large imbalance in trade, backhaul rates may well be very low compared with those in the direction of the greatest flow.

There have been relatively few studies of the incidence of imperfections in competition in international transport, with the exception of passenger air travel. It has been a sector characterised by a high degree of regulation, either through the sort of explicit regulation and bilateral quota systems, which have been used in road haulage, or simply through the consequences of state ownership, which has dominated air transport and railways. The more advanced degree of privatisation and deregulation in the airline industry and the comparative example of deregulation in the US market have been behind the greater interest shown in the airline sector.

For peripheral regions, air travel connections dominate choices for passenger travel and demonstrate clearly some of the problems arising from market structure. Peripheral regions tend to be served by smaller national or regional airlines which have higher costs through lower exploitation of scale and scope economies, but also through their lack of competitive power in gaining slots at core hub airports which puts them at a competitive disadvantage in offering the best flight times relative to airlines based in the core hubs.

Freight transport depends principally on road for most regions. Here again the existence, until recently, of strict quantitative regulation, including the dominance of bilateral quotas for international transport, can have strongly discriminatory impacts on peripheral regions. This may be particularly problematic if there are strong imbalances in the value/bulk ratios of inward and outward flows. The more specialised a region's output, the more likely it is to have specialised transport needs which also make it more vulnerable to monopoly power of transport providers.

The growth of specialist total logistics providers has led to a degree of vertical integration in transport and distribution which has the potential for reducing costs. However, the scope for this may be greater in more diverse and developed core regions where competition between such firms is likely than in the more specialised peripheral regions.

This discussion implies that the behaviour of transport costs is not exogenously given by the nature of the product. It depends on a complex interaction between the structure of product markets and their inputs and the organisation of markets for individual models of transport (and the competition between them). For us to understand the different ways that different regions are affected we need to understand this relationship more fully.

3.5 The basis for a revised model

As indicated above, the major theoretical need is a better specification of the τ variable in the new economic geography model. As it stands τ is not clearly specified. It is a single parameter which appears to be determined by the characteristics of the product and the costs of transport between the two regions which, it is presumed, depends on the distance between the regions and the incidence of other impedances to transport such as borders, tariffs etc. The key point is that it appears to be exogenous to the model.

Our suggestion for revision is that τ is actually endogenous, dependent on the product, but also on the implied flows of the product between the regions, the total flows of all products and the capacity of the transport network(s). This latter point is potentially the critical one since most models have assumed that improvements in transport will automatically lead to lower transport costs and modelled the effects of the assumed improvements. Where there is excess capacity in the provision of transport this need not be the case. In fact there are circumstances in which the provision of additional capacity leads to increase costs on the users of a network. For example, if the additional capacity is funded either by user tolls or by increases in taxation on local communities perceived as benefiting, the rise in firms' total costs could be greater than any perceived reduction in direct transport costs from the improvement. Moreover, if the improvement of one transport mode leads to a shift in usage towards it then the increasingly monopolistic position of that mode could be exploited and lead to a rise in real transport costs.

3.6 Some evidence: peripheral regions

We are not in a position to derive an estimable model from this discussion. The next stage is the development of a simulation model which would enable us to explore the sensitivity of a model to changes in the assumptions about the transport market. Here, however, we just offer an initial view of some evidence on the relevant characteristics of transport markets in peripheral regions, to give some view of network effects, and in the following section on the impact of a single new infrastructure, where some of these impacts can be more precisely identified.

The work on peripheral regions owes much to the valuable case studies prepared as part of the COST328 initiative for the Nordic countries (Pasi and Himanen, 1996; Beilinson, 1997), Ireland (Crowley, 1996), Portugal (Fortunata Dourada, 1996) and Spain (Zaragoza-Ramirez, 1996). This section draws on the preliminary analysis of this evidence in Vickerman (1998a).

Peripheral regions have been adept at adjusting both their structure of production and their trade to suit their locational circumstances. For example, 80 per cent of Portuguese exports and over 90 per cent of imports (by weight) are transported by sea, mainly the import of raw materials (including oil) from, and the re-export of processed materials to, former colonies of Portugal. This is consistent with Portugal's extreme maritime situation. Ireland, however, appeared to specialise less in goods which exploit its location, rather those which can exploit its labour skills and adaptability to international technology. Portugal's economy is thus less integrated in any real sense into the EU economy than that of Ireland and its transport needs are therefore substantially different. In the Nordic countries, the situation is different again with a heavy emphasis placed on the exploitation of natural resources, including forest products, which have very particular transport needs, and for which the main markets are in the core regions of Europe. However, the Nordic countries are less completely "edge" economies than Ireland and Portugal with an important though changing transit traffic role with Russia.

All of these countries experience problems of transit traffic with other states. In the case of Portugal this is reduced in importance by the bias of trade away from land transport to the rest of Europe. However, this lack of heavy flows has presented problems in justifying the upgrading of appropriate routes to and through Spain. In addition there are five different frontier crossings which splits the given volume of traffic into even smaller flows (only one exceeded an average of 3500 vehicles per day in 1985). In the case of Ireland the choice is between short sea versus long sea ferry crossing. All UK transit routes also face a further sea crossing, with again a choice between the longer North Sea routes and the shorter Channel routes. The longest sea routes (e.g. Rosslare-Roscoff) can avoid the UK completely but these are only appropriate for certain destinations. This choice of direct but longer sea routes against shorter sea routes, often a combination of such crossings, is particularly relevant to the situation in the Nordic countries. This is further complicated by some of the shortest and most direct routes involving transit of non-EU states with poor infrastructure such as Estonia and Poland. All of these countries therefore face complex transport cost structures involving several degrees of choice.

The development of air transport has been a major factor in improving the accessibility of peripheral regions. However, there is an unevenness in the impact of this within peripheral regions. In Ireland almost 50 per cent of all passenger movements are concentrated in Dublin and almost 85 per cent in the main three airports. In Spain, Madrid is less dominant with only 20 per cent of total traffic and 17 per cent of international traffic, given the importance of holiday traffic to the Mediterranean coast and islands.

Nevertheless, almost 48 per cent of total traffic is concentrated in the three airports of Madrid, Palma de Mallorca and Barcelona and 66 per cent of international traffic is carried by the five largest airports. In Portugal only three airports carry any significant international traffic, nearly 50 per cent of which is handled by Lisbon. Of the five main Nordic airports (Helsinki, Stockholm, Gothenburg, Oslo and Copenhagen), Copenhagen, the major hub airport for the Nordic countries, handles nearly 40 per cent of the total traffic to other EU destinations (outside the Nordic countries) compared to under 30 per cent of Nordic traffic. Oslo, by comparison, has only 14 per cent of the EU traffic but nearly 22 per cent of the inter-Nordic traffic.

The development of infrastructure in peripheral regions also follows rather different paths. Ireland, for example, has seen a major contraction in its once extensive railway system, with recent investment concentrated on improving suburban transport in Dublin and cross-city connections in Belfast. In contrast the road network has remained dense with responsibility falling to local administrations (County Councils) with an interest in improving local access. Road surface per 1000 inhabitants is well over twice the EU average and second only to that in Luxembourg, five time the Spanish provision and almost four times the Portuguese provision. The development of motorway standard roads has, however, fallen well behind that in other European countries. In Portugal the diversity of possible routes into Spain has led to a multi-route strategy and a deliberate multi-modal strategy. This has led to substantial investment in both road and rail over the four major routes. However, effort has been concentrated on the one route which maximises the investment within Portugal in an attempt to promote internal regional development independently of improved European level accessibility.

In the Nordic countries much of the emphasis has been on a series of major new infrastructures across the seaways dividing Scandinavia from continental Europe: the Great Belt and Øresund crossings currently under construction and the proposed direct link across the Fehmarn Bælt. These will have a major impact on the internal accessibility of Denmark and on the ease of access to southern Sweden and the Oslo region as well as creating a major new metropolitan region out of the Copenhagen and Malmo areas. For comparison it can be noted that around 700,000 passengers a year used air services between Copenhagen and Stockholm in 1994/5 and a further 300,000 between Copenhagen and Gothenburg whilst some 23 million passengers travelled between Denmark and Sweden by ferry. New links between Sweden and Denmark and continental Europe will also have the tendency to accentuate the relative remoteness of Finland which remains accessible only by a relatively long ferry crossing.

Thus a preliminary look at some evidence confirms the diversity of experience in peripheral regions. This diversity of experience does, to some extent, represent deliberate policy choices in the different countries and also reflects the availability of European level funding. Nevertheless it illustrates above all the complexity of the transport cost function to be experienced in these countries.

3.7   Some evidence: New infrastructure

We also introduce some evidence occurring as the result of individual new infrastructure, in this case the Channel Tunnel. The potential influence of the Tunnel is extremely wide and is being felt over a wide area and variety of routes. We have, therefore, to take into account both passenger and freight traffic and diversions from sea (ferry) and air routes. Diversions from sea routes can involve a simple switch of carrier from ferry to Tunnel, or a more complex switch of mode, e.g. from car ferry, to through rail (3.2). Furthermore, the ferry operations need to be split into short sea and long sea routes (Figure 3.3). Diversion from long sea ferry routes to the Tunnel, or from air to the Tunnel carries with it implications for the public authorities for the provision of adequate road and ail access infrastructure. Thus, accurate measurement, not just of traffic on the cross Channel sections of the route, but also on the appropriate routes taken to reach the various ports, is also an essential feature.

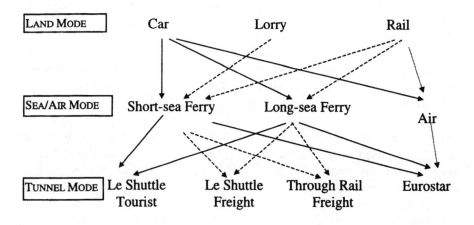

Figure 3.2   Structure of Demand Choices for Cross Channel Traffic

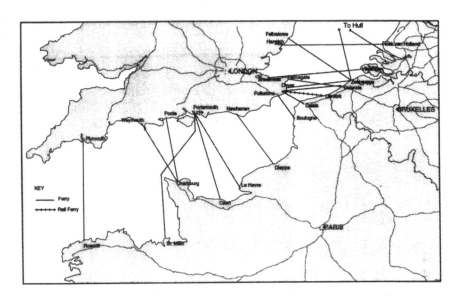

Figure 3.3 Cross-Channel ferry routes

As reference to Figures 3.2 and 3.3 demonstrates, attempting to define the precise boundaries of the appropriate markets for either passenger or freight traffic, does raise issues of great complexity. When attempting to assess the potential market for a new travel opportunity, we have to have some basis for assessing the potential diversion rates. When that new travel opportunity is a completely new mode, the basis for assessing those elasticities does not exist prior to the collection of data, and therefore, how we collect the data can have important implications for the end result. What is clear from simple inspection of 3.3 is that it is not sufficient to identify the appropriate cross channel routes as being the area susceptible to diversion to the Tunnel. We also need to know the initial origin and ultimate destination. Thus, although, for example, the potential diversion rate from one of the long sea crossings such as Portsmouth to St. Malo or Hull to Zeebrugge might be relatively small, some categories of traffic within the markets for those particular ferry routes may be quite substantial. The same point is clearly true of diversion from air traffic. Although a considerable proportion of London/Paris or London/Brussels traffic is not likely to divert to Tunnel use, there will be particular categories of traffic typically conditioned by their central city origins and destinations, and their business nature, which may find the diversion rates are likely to be much higher.

This makes it clear that a project such as the Channel Tunnel is much larger than the simple definition of the tunnel from one end to the other, it involves all of the feeder road and rail networks and their capacities as a critical determinant of the true costs of using this as opposed to any other mode.

The problem of traffic generated by new transport links is a difficult one. The argument is that given lower costs, principally lower time costs, people will make more journeys between any two points. Some of this apparent traffic generation is in fact traffic diverted from other destinations. This is, of course, distinct from diversions from other routes. This is of potential importance in the Channel Tunnel case, but possibly not so much related to the Tunnel itself as to some of the associated infrastructure. Thus, the completion of new motorway links and of high speed rail links has brought certain destinations within easy reach of day return journeys or long weekends. Similarly, freight traffic may change because of opportunities to re-site depots, or to change other aspects of the logistical process. Experience with new high speed rail services in France had certainly suggested that substantial traffic growth could be ascribed to new links in this way, and recent evidence from the Government's Standing Advisory Committee on Trunk Road Assessments (SACTRA, 1994) has confirmed this for new trunk roads in the United Kingdom. In some respects the financial viability of the Tunnel did depend on being able to identify substantial traffic growth, since unlike a number of other new fixed links (e.g. those in Denmark) there were no plans to remove the ferry services from even the most competing short sea routes, and especially given the enormous capacity of the Tunnel system.

The Channel Tunnel finally opened for service progressively during 1994. This means it is still a little soon to get an overall picture of the reliability of initial forecasts. Furthermore, the intensive competition between all of the operators on the cross channel routes does mean that it has been extremely difficult to monitor actual traffic on a regular basis. Some idea of the impact of the Tunnel can, however, be obtained from Figures 3.4, 3.5 and 3.6.

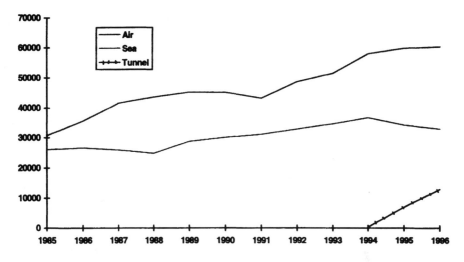

Source: Transport Statistics, Great Britain, HMSO, London

Figure 3.4 Passenger traffic, UK-EC Europe 1985-1996

Figure 3.4 shows how the opening of the tunnel in 1994 led to a reduction in the rate of growth of air travel between the UK and EC Europe and an actual reduction in ferry traffic. Total traffic grew nearly twice as fast in 1994 (+10.4 per cent) as in 1993 (+5.7 per cent) and by a further 6.6 per cent in 1995. The final 1996 figures need careful interpretation due to the disruption in Channel Tunnel services following the fire in November 1996. On the evidence of the first three quarters of 1996 however, ferry traffic continued to decline, though at a lower rate (3.6 per cent compared to 9.3 per cent in the previous year) largely due to a continuing price war. Air traffic growth picked up again in 1996 (+9.1 per cent compared to +3.3 per cent) in total terms, though closer examination of Paris and Brussels routes suggests quite substantial falls in traffic.

Figures 3.5 and 3.6 give some more detailed monthly data for lorry and car traffic (by number of vehicles) through the Port of Dover and on Le Shuttle services. This shows the considerable seasonal variations on a month by month basis, but also the recovery of ferry traffic towards the end of 1996, even without the effects of the tunnel fire which make Eurotunnel carryings non-comparable. Le Shuttle freight services were suspended from November 1996 to June 1997 due to the fire. Since then they have struggled to achieve the levels of traffic experienced during the same period of 1996 whilst ferry traffic has continued to grow. Despite some disruption to car services in early 1997, carryings continued to show some growth, though at lower rates than previously, a situation which continued after the resumption of full services in June 1997. Overall car carryings in 1997 showed only a modest increase on 1996 and Eurotunnel achieved no growth in market share.

The evidence does demonstrate clearly that both a diversion of traffic to the short crossing (ferry or Tunnel) from longer routes and a generation of new traffic as a result of the increased level of service on these routes have been obtained. This does, however, have to be set against the background of intensive price competition during 1995 to 1997, as the Tunnel and the ferry Companies have struggled for market share. Particularly noticeable is the extent to which Eurotunnel captured a larger portion of road freight traffic than it had originally forecast, though this traffic was abruptly halted by the fire in the Tunnel in November 1996. This situation will change with the recently agreed merger of the two main ferry companies on the short-sea Dover-Calais route.

This demonstrates the complexity of the impacts of major international transport projects involving new modes or new links. The evidence is still somewhat sketchy, but it is clear that there has been a substantial impact on the volume and pattern of UK-continental Europe traffic over the past two to three years. Both growth and diversion are taking place and diversion occurs between both modes and routes. Changes in the latter have important implications for connecting infrastructure. For example, it is clear from detailed examination of figures that there has been a continuing diversion from the Belgian Straits (Ostende and Zeebrugge) ferry routes to the French Straits (Calais) largely as a result of the near completion of good road links to Calais, regardless of whether the Tunnel or ferry are used. The road links were largely justified on the basis of the tunnel, but have substantial impacts on ferry traffic patterns. Similarly, problems of access to Dover and the Tunnel due to traffic congestion in and around London have led to a revival of traffic growth (especially freight) through longer distance sea routes, e.g. via Hull.

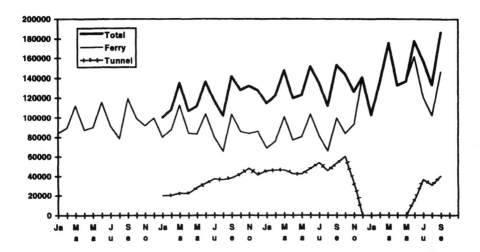

Source: Dover Harbour Board, Eurotunnel
Figure 3.5 Dover ferry and tunnel lorry traffic 1994-97

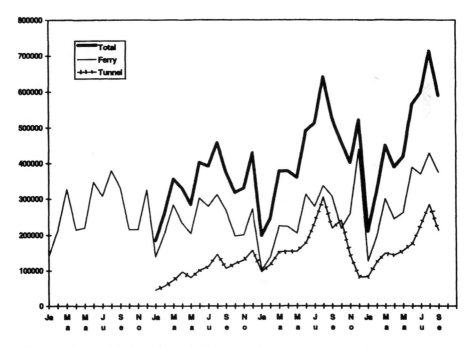

Source: Dover Harbour Board, Eurotunnel
3.6 Dover ferry and tunnel car traffic 1994-95

63

3.8 Conclusions

In this chapter we have identified the way in which specific characteristics of the transport sector can have an important influence on the potential economic performance of regions, especially peripheral regions. This is an extension to the microeconomic model of regional specialisation and convergence of the "new economic geography" in which we have recognised some specific issues in the specification of the transport cost recognising imperfect competition within that sector. As a precursor to the development of a full model we have identified various theoretical issues which need to be taken into account and provided some evidence of the importance of these, both from a general survey of transport in peripheral regions and a case study of the impact of a specific project.

References

Aschauer, D.A. (1989), "Is public expenditure productive?", *Journal of Monetary Economics*, 23, 177-200.

Aschauer, D.A. (1990), "Why is infrastructure important?" in Munnell, A.H. (ed.), *Is there a Shortfall in Public Capital Investment?*, Conference Series, 34, Federal Reserve Bank of Boston.

Beilinson, L. (1997), *Passenger Transport between the Nordic Countries and other EU Countries*, Report to COST328. VTT, Helsinki, Finland.

Calmette, M-F, and Le Pottier, J. (1995) "Localisation des activités: un modèle bisectoriel avec coûts de transport", *Revue économique*, 46, 901-909.

Ciccone, A. and Hall, R.E. (1996), "Productivity and the Density of Economic Activity", *American Economic Review*, 86, 54-70.

Clark, C., Wilson, F. and Bradley, J. (1969), "Industrial Location and Economic Potential in Western Europe", *Regional Studies,* 3, 197-212.

Crowley J. (1996), *Case Study: Ireland,* Report to COST328, University College, Dublin.

David, P. (1991), 'The Marshallian Dynamics of Industrialisation: Chicago', 1850-1890, *Journal of Urban Economics*.

Dixit, A.K. and Stiglitz, J.E. (1977), 'Monopolistic Competition and Optimum Product Diversity', *American Economic Review*, 67, 297-308.

Fortunata Dourada M. (1996), *Acesso de Portugal ao Centro Europa*. Report to COST328. Junta Autonoma de Estrados, Almada, Portugal.

Fujita, M. and Thisse, J-F. (1996), 'Economics of Agglomeration', *Journal of the Japanese and International Economics*, 10, 339-378.

Glaeser, E.L., Kallal, H.D., Scheinkman, J.A. and Shleifer, A. (1992). "Growth in Cities", *Journal of Political Economy,* 100, 1126-1152.

Hanson, G.H. (1996), "Economic Integration, Intra-Industry Trade and Frontier Regions", *European Economic Review*, 40, 941-949.

Keeble, D., Owens, P.L. and Thompson, C. (1982), 'Regional Accessibility and Economic Potential in the European Community', *Regional Studies*, 16, 419-432.

Keeble, D., Offord, J. and Walker, S. (1988), *Peripheral Regions in a Community of Twelve Member States*. Luxembourg: Office for Official Publications of the EC.

Krugman, P. (1991a), Increasing Returns and Economic Geography, *Journal of Political Economy*, 99, 483-499.

Krugman, P. (1991b), *Geography and Trade*, MIT Press: Cambridge, MA.

Krugman, P. and Venables, A.J. (1990), "Integration and the Competitiveness of Peripheral Industry", in Bliss, C. and Braga de Macedo, J. (eds), *Unity with Diversity in the European Economy*, Cambridge U.P and CEPR: Cambridge.

Krugman, P. and Venables, A.J. (1995), "Globalization and the Inequality of Nations", *Quarterly Journal of Economics*, 110, 857-880.

Lutter, H., Pütz, T. and Spangenberg, M. (1992), *Accessibility and Peripherality of Community Regions: the Role of Road, Long-distance Railways and Airport Networks*. Report to DGXVI, Commission of the European Communities. Bundesforschungsanstalt für Landeskunde und Raumordnung: Bonn.

Martin, P. and Rogers, C.A. (1995), "Industrial Location and Public Infrastructure", *Journal of International Economics*, 39, 335-351.

Pasi S, Himanen V (1996), *Transport of Goods Between the Nordic Countries and Central Europe*. Report to COST328. VTT, Helsinki, Finland.

Rietveld, P. (1989), "Employment Effects of Changes in Transportation Model Infrastructure: Methodological Aspects of the Gravity", *Papers of Regional Science Association*, 66, 19-30.

SACTRA (1994), *Trunk Roads and the Generation of Traffic*, Report of the Standing Advisory Committee on Trunk Road Assessment (Chairman: D. Wood), HMSO: London.

Venables, A.J. (1996), "Equilibrium Locations of Vertically Linked Industries", *International Economic Review*, 37, 341-359.

Vickerman, R.W. (1997), *Trans-European Networks: Balancing Mobility, Competitiveness, Cohesion and Sustainability*, paper to Internationale Wissenschaftstage Eisenbahn '97, Technische Universität, Dresden, October.

Vickerman, R.W. (1998a), "Accessibility, Peripherality and Spatial Development: The Question of Choice", in Reggiani, A. (ed.), *Accessibility, Trade and Location Behaviour*, Ashgate: Aldershot, 79-93.

Vickerman, R.W. (1998b), "Transport Provision and Regional Development in Europe", in Banister, D. (ed.), *Transport Policy and the Environment*, E. & F.N. Spon: London.

Vickerman, R.W., Spiekermann, K. and Wegener, M. (1999), "Accessibility and economic development in Europe", *Regional Studies*, 33, 1-15.

Zaragoza-Ramirez A. (1996). *Peripheral Regions and Their Access to Networks. Case Study: Spain,* Report to COST328, Asociacion Espanola de la Carretera: Madrid, Spain.

Note

1. The chapter draws on work undertaken as part of the European Union's COST 328 (Integrated Strategic Infrastructure Networks for Europe) and STEMM (Strategic European Multi-Modal Modelling, Contract ST-96-SC.301) projects.

4 Methods and Models Analysing Transalpine Freight Transport: An Overview

SIMONA BOLIS AND AURA REGGIANI

The present paper aims to offer a specific contribution to the general issue of search of evaluation indicators and assessment methods for complementary and competing trans european networks, by investigating recent studies, analyses and models which have been conducted in the context of the Transalpine freight transport flows.

From a methodological viewpoint, this paper presents a structural organisation of objectives, typologies of studies, methods of analysis, models and typologies of related data.

The report intends to show the correlation between given typologies of data and given typologies of studies which have been applied thus far. The final step of the analysis is oriented towards the identification of a 'structural review' of objectives, typologies of studies, methods of analysis, models and typologies of related data in the Transalpine freight transport network.

4.1   Introduction

Within the last few decades, significant changes in the structure and nature of economic and social relationships have stimulated a sudden growth of the mobility pattern. Freight transport in Europe has become a multi-modal / multi-nodal activity. The emergence of an integrated and open market between the European Free Trade Association (EFTA) and East European countries, in tandem with the development of new infrastructures for international connections, are the forces driving towards market globalisation. In addition, a new definition of strategic behaviour within a global framework, as well as a strong and crucial interaction of transport cycles, will result.

Parallel to the quantitative/qualitative modification in the transport demand, the quantity of transported goods and the quality level of service significantly changed. In order to face this new and increased mobility of demand/supply, and to reach the goal of developmental and economic convergence, the European Union (EU) has proposed the idea of 'transnational' infrastructures and transport networks.

The context of the Transalpine freight transport presents extremely interesting phenomena. For years, the Alps have been represented as a 'barrier' and have played a dramatic role in the EU development. By causing relevant asymmetries between Central, Southern and Eastern Europe in terms of opportunity, growth and implementation of an 'integrated' territorial evolution, the Alpine region has been defined as a 'border region'.

Furthermore, until a few years ago, the Alpine region had not been influenced by the trend of economic cooperation from a European perspective, because strong national pressures have characterised and directed the management of their common area, the Alps. Only recently, with the introduction of new countries in the EU, the creation of the European economic space, and changing economic relations between EU and Eastern countries, have the Alpine regions experienced discord regarding their own regulations (see also Reggiani, 1999).

Nowadays, the problem of the neutral countries in the Alpine arch in relation to north-south traffic directions is coming to the fore together with the problem of transport infrastructure in Eastern Europe (see e.g. Maggi *et al.*, 1993). In this context, many studies have recently been conducted by different operators involved in the so-called 'Alpine problem'.

The understanding of the actual and anticipated scenario of Transalpine transport flows and the analysis concerning the situation of the measure supplied at the Alpine chain seems essential in this context (see, among others, Müller and Maggi, 1998). In particular, further studies are required on the following:

- the 'missing grids' inside the network: these network interruptions are represented both in the material infrastructure shortage and in the transport market organisation;
- the optimal use of the network: the presence of under-utilised infrastructure or infrastructure which could be more efficiently operated with a different organisation and traffic information system.

Clearly, these analyses can also be oriented towards a greater understanding of the hypothetical strategic options for the Transalpine infrastructure performance in order to improve European transport system integration.

In order to fulfil the above goals, the first necessary step is to acquire knowledge of the *state of the art* of the analyses/studies conducted thus far in the framework of the Alpine case. Our examination aims to investigate the most recent studies and models so as to compile a 'structural review' of objectives, typologies of studies, methods of analysis, models, and typologies of related data in the TransAlpine freight transport network.

4.2   Objectives in Transalpine freight transport studies: A review

4.2.1   Introduction

The growing interest in Transalpine transport analysis really began a few years ago when several studies and research projects were undertaken on this topic (the bibliography appended to this essay presents a partial list of them). On the basis of such a list, this work intends to select and investigate the studies — according to the chosen methodology — in order to emphasise the goals of these analyses and their evolution, namely, changes of such goals in space and over time (see Table 4.A.1 in Annex A).

Some studies are based on a comprehensive demand/supply estimation model (see Austrian FM, 1992; EU-Commission, 1990; Istra-Italferr Sis-Tav Spa/B, 1992; SFTDE, 1988; FS-SNCF, 1993; Maggi and Müller, 1995; FS Spa, 1994); others develop a database (see DFTCE-Sigmaplan Sa, 1991; Graf, 1995; Sandonnini, 1991; Istra-Italferr Sis-Tav Spa/A, 1992); and still others use traffic data taken from various studies by developing alternative methodologies or objectives of analysis (see Beuthe *et al.*, 1998; Freudensprung *et al.*, 1994; Rossera, 1994, 1995; I.Re.R., 1992, Nijkamp *et al.*, 1997; Reggiani *et al.*, 1997, 1999). The list also considers studies which examined specific aspects without developing original methodologies or forecasts (see Chatelus and Torricelli, 1994; Gruppo Clas, 1994; Maggi, 1992; Russo, 1995; see again Annex A for the list and the abbreviations used within the text).

It is worthwhile to present the objectives of the studies related to the Transalpine transport network under the following headings:

- Demand analysis
- Supply analysis
- Policy issues.

4.2.2   Demand analysis

The formation of the European Market Union generated an intense concentration of intra-community exchanges crossing the Alpine massif. The objective pursued in many of the examined studies is a correct estimation of the growth rate of the intra-community business relationships. Generally, these studies have been carried out in order to supply a database for feasibility analyses of infrastructural projects, owing to the lack of a homogeneous and complete database (see Austrian FM, 1992; EU-Commission, 1990; FS-SNCF, 1993; Istra-Italferr Sis-Tav Spa/A, 1992; SFTED, 1988).

It should be noted that in many cases, demand analyses are limited to partial areas of the Alps because of an insufficient number of reliable statistical documentation (see Table 4.5 for the geographical area covered by the studies under analysis).

Until now, demand analyses have mainly been studied by minimum-cost/time flows models (see e.g. Fs Spa, 1994; I.Re.R., 1992). Other studies, on the contrary, underline the importance of developing performance functions and answering the question of how users react to certain given conditions on the supply side (see e.g. Rossera, 1995).

The distinctive feature of the Alpine sector concerns the difference between the actual and the potential use (according to the shortest time or to the minimum traffic cost criterion) of transit corridors through France, Switzerland and Austria. Some studies examine the extent to which transport policy measures implemented in Switzerland (and recently in Austria), have caused traffic flows to diverge from their potential minimum distance pattern. For example, the models proposed by Rossera (1994), Beuthe *et al.* (1998) and Demilie *et al.* (1998) strive to understand the impact of restraining the restriction on road haulage on the Swiss side.

It should also be noted that current studies of the Alpine area examine the traffic impact to and from Eastern Europe (see Austrian FM, 1992; Istra-Italferr Sis-Tav Spa/B, 1992).

In Table 4.1 the objectives pursued by the studies have been classified as follows:

- *Evolution of flows*: these studies attempt to forecast the quantitative movements in the analysed area in the short or long-term. They are usually built on economic growth forecasts. The range of variables involved, as well as the coverage and the reliability of databases essentially changes from one study to another.

Indeed, there are studies which point out the impact of new infrastructures upon the demand level (see Austrian FM, 1992, FS-SNCF, 1993; Istra-Italferr Sis Tav Spa/B, 1992; SFTED, 1988).[1] It should be noted that most do not consider all the Alpine transits, but instead narrow the analysis to particular geographical areas (see Austrian FM, 1992; FS-SNCF, 1993; SFTED, 1988).

70

Other studies examine the trend for freight transport demand under the hypotheses of different macro-economic scenarios, such as Graf (1995), which focuses on freight traffic in Switzerland, the I.Re.R. (1992) analysis of the Italian Alpine flows, and the EU-Commission (1990) analysis of road passenger/freight traffic across the Western Alpine regions. A comprehensive overview of forecasts with reference to cross-Alpine traffic is offered by Gruppo Clas (1994).

Table 4.1 Demand analysis objectives concerning the Transalpine freight transport network: a review of major studies

STUDIES	Evolution of Flows		Demand Behaviour	'Deviation' of Flows from:	
	All Transit	Not all Transit		Minimum Cost	Minimum Time
Austrian FM, 1992		x			
Beuthe et al.,1998				x	
EU-Commission, 1990		x			
FS Spa, 1994	x				
FS-SNCF, 1993		x			
Graf, 1995		x			
Gruppo Clas, 1994	x				
I.Re.R., 1992	x				
Maggi and Müller, 1995			x		
Nijkamp et al., 1997	x				
Istra-Italferr Sis-Tav/A, 1992	x				
Istra-Italferr Sis-Tav/B, 1992	x				
Reggiani et al., 1997,1999	x				
Rossera, 1994				x	x
Rossera, 1995			x		
SFTED, 1988		x			

And finally within this context, we mention Nijkamp et al. (1997) and Reggiani et al. (1997, 1999), who conduct forecast analyses — on the basis of policy/environments scenarios — by means of two (methodologically different) modal split models, such as logit and neural network models.

We note that the forecast analyses are primarily accomplished for the years 2000 and 2010/2015; only a few studies offer forecasts beyond these years (see SFTED, 1988). Others offer a range of sensitivity analyses concerning variations in transport cost and time (Nijkamp et al., 1997; Reggiani et al., 1997, 1999).

- *Demand behaviour*: these studies attempt to understand the transport network with special attention given to the qualitative characteristics of the market.

Maggi and Müller (1995) propose a micro-economic approach for analysing "the behaviour of the shipper, which determines the impact of network characteristics on the cohesiveness of networks" (p. 3). Following this approach, Rossera (1995) puts forward a first attempt at modelling the transport Alpine network by taking into account the impact on the demand side, of the related performance levels with particular attention on congestion phenomena.

- *Deviation of flows from minimum cost and/or minimum time direction*: these studies propose methods of understanding how Swiss and Austrian prohibitions have modified the Alpine distribution of flows. The objective of the studies is to reveal the difference between actual and potential use in transit corridors through France, Switzerland and Austria (see Beuthe *et al.*, 1998; Rossera, 1994).

4.2.2.1 Concluding Remarks By analysing the above studies, the following general remarks can be made:

- several studies aim to forecast Transalpine freight transport flows in the short and long-term; however, the related analyses often suffer from the lack of an adequate database;
- the economic principles guiding behaviour on integrated networks are often unclear. The shortage of adequate knowledge of the behaviour of shippers compromises the efficacy and efficiency of any European integration policy. With regard to the central issue of Transalpine transport flows, it seems extremely important to consider the 'transport networks' as a whole, embedding all the synergy effects produced by the 'infrastructure (physical) network';
- mechanisms producing competition between road and rail are often underestimated. Generally, the models used for studying freight traffic crossing the Alpine chain are the classical economic models minimising cost/time flows. However, given the complexity of the Alpine context, a performance view (including punctuality, reliability, shipped, price/tariff, flexible/customised services, flow control, safety, etc.) would certainly offer more insights;
- the hypothetical saturation level concerning the economic sectors and traffic relations is missing;

- the effects of the Market Union for the European community are not developed in terms of labour division and transport market liberalisation. In particular, the impact of the liberalisation process on the flow distribution inside and outside the European countries has not yet been completely analysed.

In summary, a complete knowledge of the typology and territorial diversification of the market, together with the business network — which is able to influence traffic relationships more than the average economic trend — is often missing in the aforementioned studies.

A comprehensive knowledge of technical-functional and economic-productive aspects of the Transalpine system seems necessary in order to move towards European integration. Until now it seems that the studies based on Transalpine demand analysis have not developed such a precise and painstaking research.

4.2.3   Supply Analysis

The studies under analysis particularly focus on the estimation of the network capacity in the short (2000) and long-term (2010/15/20/40). In many cases, one goal is to forecast the capacity of attracting an increasing number of flows along one (or more than one) transit due to new infrastructures (see e.g. Austrian FM, 1992; FS-SNCF, 1993; SFTED, 1988).

The transport policies of Swiss and Austrian Federal Governments push towards rail and combined transports in accordance with an increasing socio-ecological sensitivity. This sensitivity is one reason why studies began to focus on railway performance (only the EU-Commission's study (1990) concentrates on road transport). Several of these studies were commissioned by public institutions in Switzerland and Austria (see Austrian FM, 1992; DFTCE-Sigmaplan Sa, 1991; SFDTE, 1988).

In relation to the changes invoked by these Alpine countries, many studies have attempted to illustrate the actual situation of rail and combined transport through Transalpine links. The particular objective of these studies is to show the bottlenecks in the network that cause an under-utilisation of the existing potential (see FS Spa, 1994; Russo, 1995). The area considered by the examined analyses is limited to one or two nations (i.e. only Italy or Italy and Austria), and they ultimately develop the concept of interoperability.[2] Less attention is given to interconnectivity[3] and intermodality.[4]

A novel interpretation in this context is given by the analysis of Maggi and Müller (1995), which emphasises that the behaviour of the supply side actors can capture cohesive aspects of the TransAlpine network. The specific goal of their research is to understand the relationship among various network characteristics and the quality of transportation services on the supply side sectors.

In Table 4.2 the objectives pursued by the examined studies are classified as follows:

- *Capacity forecasts of the network*: these studies forecast quantitative movements in order to analyse Alpine transits in the short or long-run. Models also involve modal distribution forecasts.

Table 4.2 shows those studies focused on the impact of new infrastructure (forecasts) both in the short and long-term (see Austrian FM, 1992; FS-SNCF, 1993; Istra-Italferr Sis-tav Spa/B, 1992; SFTED, 1988). As was emphasised for the demand side, the majority of these studies do not consider all the Alpine transits.

Other studies analyse the capacity of the network in the short-term. In this case, the forecasts include the technical improvement of the physical network done recently (see DFTCE-Sigmaplan Sa, 1991; EU-Commission, 1990; Sandonnini, 1991), or which should be implemented before the year 2000 (see FS Spa, 1994).

- *Supply behaviour*: these studies investigate the transport network with a special focus on the qualitative characteristics of the market.

Maggi and Müller (1995) propose a micro-economic approach for analysing the behaviour of carriers as well as the cohesiveness of the Transalpine network.

Russo (1995) proposes an analysis of combined transport between Italy and Austria based on the so-called Pentagon Prism of Five Critical Success Factors (see Section 3). The analysis pays specific attention to the political behaviour of operators.

- *Evaluation of bottlenecks in infrastructures/organisation/legislation*: these studies highlight missing links as well as offer suggestions for removing existing bottlenecks.

Such studies (except FS Spa, 1994) try to uncover the causes that generate an under-utilisation of the Alpine network. Freudensprung *et al.* (1994) and Russo (1995) develop the research in light of the Pentagon Prism analysis (see Section 3), and both studies analyse the Italian-Austrian border. Sandonnini (1991) and FS Spa (1994) focus on the Italian Alpine area.

Table 4.2 Supply analysis objectives concerning the Transalpine freight transport network: A review of major studies

STUDIES	Capacity Forecast of the Network				Supply Behaviour	Evaluation of 'Bottlenecks' in:		
	Short Time	Long Time	All Tran.	Not all Tran.		Infrastructure	Organisation	Legislation
Austrian FM, 1992	x	x		x				
EU-Commission, 1990	x			x				
DFTCE-Sigmaplan Sa, 1991	x			x				
Freudensprung et al., 1994						x	x	x
Fs Spa, 1994	x		x			x	x	
FS-SNCF, 1993	x	x		x				
Gruppo Clas, 1994	x	x	x					
Istra-Italferr Sis-Tav Spa /B, 1992	x	x	x					
Maggi and Müller, 1995					x			
Russo, 1995					x	x	x	x
Sandonnini, 1991	x		x			x	x	x

4.2.3.1 Concluding Remarks In summary the following remarks can be made:

No study has yet achieved the objective of a comprehensive knowledge on the effects of competition among all the infrastructures related to the Alpine transits. For example, although the Istra-Italferr Sis-Tav Spa/B (1992) study makes different hypotheses for the year 2010, none of these simultaneously considers all infrastructure projects.

While on the short-run, analyses are available concerning the potential of the network by promoting technical innovations (for the links and the carriage material) and/or by improving the existing organisations, forecasts for the long-term are not available and only evaluations of new infrastructures have been produced.

Very often the objective of the studies is to design the future potential of the railway sector. In this context, it should be noted that the modal distribution procedures which have been used are significantly in favour of rail transport. Consequently, if the purpose of the study is to forecast the competition between rail and road by assigning a high capacity to rail, it is likely that the results will be biased. Furthermore, studies on the assessment of the future railways capacities on the demand side are missing. In other words, given the probable discrepancy between speed of dynamics of infrastructure potential/feasibility and speed of dynamics of actors' behaviour/ reactions, it becomes necessary to develop further insights in this respect.

It is important to underline the dearth of studies investigating overall characteristics of the Transalpine network. Moreover, the operators' knowledge of the structure (such as road, railways and combined transport companies) and the level of interoperability, interconnectivity and intermodality of the network should be the key issues for understanding the competitive force of each transport mode.

4.2.4   Policy Issues

The need to respond to European economic world demand for market liberalisation is the principal driving force of the planning and development of the Alpine system. The Alpine massif can no longer be considered as a border element, but rather as a further opportunity for economic development and policy integration, according to the definition of 'active space'[5] introduced by Geenhuizen and Ratti (1995), and Ratti (1998).

However, until now, the Alpine countries have played a dominant role in the national transport policy by being protective and insensitive to Market Union needs. This is also reflected in several studies (see e.g. DFTCE-Sigmaplan Sa, 1991, Graf, 1995, SFTED, 1988), which take into account national or regional decisions instead of promoting European driving action. Meanwhile, many studies invoke an active policy towards rail and combined transport (see FS Spa, 1994; Istra-Italferr Sis-Tav Spa/A, 1992; Maggi and Müller, 1995; Russo, 1995; SFTED, 1988).

Nowadays, the environmental aspect of transport receives considerable attention from national policy makers. The main guideline is that transport policy must contribute to an effective distribution of the resources of the society as a whole by involving economic, social/environmental and cultural aspects. Swiss and Austrian policies have totally embraced this value. The effects should become clear in the coming years, above all for the *cultural changes* that this approach entails. This issue is reflected in a few studies (see e.g. Freudensprung *et al.*, 1994; FS-SNCF, 1993; Graf, 1995; Russo, 1995).

In Table 4.3 the policy issues underlined and/or promoted by the studies are classified as follows:

A - Transport policies (in a strict sense)

a) policy in favour of liberalisation,
b) policy in favour of protectionism,
c) promotion of active policies (in relation to the behaviour of public institutions),
d) promotion of neutral policies,

e) predominance of private culture and resources,
f) superimposition of private and public culture and resources.

Table 4.3 shows that the majority of studies favour active policies. Several authors give prominence to the need for a systematic approach in the infrastructural field (see e.g. DFTCE-Sigmaplan Sa, 1991; FS Spa, 1994; I.Re.R., 1992; Istra-Italferr Sis-Tav Spa/B, 1992). Other studies emphasise the necessity for active policies aimed towards political harmony and the development of transport modes compatible with ecological concerns (see e.g. Freudensprung *et al.*, 1994; Russo, 1995).

Some studies highlight the transport impacts and costs with respect to the prohibitions and impositions existing in the Alpine system (see **Reggiani** *et al.*,1997; Rossera, 1994).

Much less attention is devoted to the private interests involved in the Transalpine transport network. Only recently have private resources been used in the field of large infrastructural projects, such as the European High-Speed rail system. In particular, the presence of private interests in the Alpine sector may change the criteria used in transport policies both for the financial and the socio-cultural aspects.

B - Socio-environmental policies

Here the studies have been classified as follows:

g) promotion of policies which do not regard the social effects of transport activities,
h) promotion of policies which do explicitly regard the social effects of transport activities,
i) environmental policy.

Current studies are not apparently and significantly oriented towards analysing social effects of transport policies upon the Alpine system. Previous studies aimed at the analysis of the Alpine region have always been fragmentary and incomplete; thus the social effects of transport decisions for the Alpine region as a whole have often been underestimated.

On the other hand, the environmental problem is being scrutinised. There are studies that promote combined transport as a feasible alternative to congestion phenomena (see Istra-Italferr Sis-Tav Spa/B, 1992; Russo, 1995), while others point to the role of politicians in the realm of the Transalpine transport market (see Maggi and Müller, 1995). In some cases, environmental parameters are used for feasibility analyses of new infrastructural projects (see e.g. Freudensprung *et al.*, 1994); in others environmental scenarios are used for forecasting/sensitivity analyses on Alpine transport flows (Nijkamp *et al.*, 1997; Reggiani *et al.*, 1999).

C - Type of legislation

In this context, classification of the studies results as follows:

j) European decisions (studies referring to policies published by EU institutions),
k) National or regional decisions (studies referring to or following policies made official by national or regional institutions).

Not long ago, EU presented several documents concerning the legal framework for the entire traffic sector in order to offer a 'global approach' perspective. Many studies in our analysis refer to the common traffic policy with respect to different areas of the Alps (see e.g. EU-Commission, 1990, for the road transport in the Western Alps; FS Spa, 1994, for the European technical harmonisation from the Italian perspective; Beuthe *et al.,*1998, and Russo, 1995, for combined transport through the Alps).

Other studies develop their analyses on the basis of particular aspects of national or regional legislations. Many of them concern the Swiss policy (see e.g. DFTCE-Sigmaplan Sa, 1991; Graf, 1995; Maggi, 1992; Rossera, 1994; SFTED, 1988).

Table 4.3 Policy issues concerning the Transalpine freight transport network: a review of major studies

STUDIES	A Transport Policies						B Socio-Environmental Policies			C Legislation	
	a	b	c	d	e	f	g	h	i	j	k
Beuthe *et al.*,1998			x				x				x
Chatelus and Torricelli, 1994			x		x		x				x
EU-Commission, 1990	x						x			x	
DFTCE-Sigmaplam Sa, 1991		x	x					x			x
FS Spa, 1994			x				x			x	
FS - SNCF, 1993			x		x				x	x	
Freudensprung *et al.*, 1994		x	x					x			x
Graf, 1995		x	x					x	x		x
I.Re.R, 1992			x		x				x		
Istra-Italferr Sis-Tav Spa/B,1992			x				x	x	x		
Maggi, 1992								x			x
Maggi and Müller, 1995	x		x				x		x	x	
Nijkamp *et al.*, 1997								x	x		
Reggiani *et al.*, 1997,1999								x	x		
Rossera, 1994	x										x
Russo, 1995			x					x	x		
SFTED, 1988		x	x		x						x

4.2.4.1. Concluding Remarks In accordance with the review of the studies dealing with policy issues the following remarks can be made:

The resources within the transport sector must be made as profitable as possible with respect to the 'social cost' for the Alpine countries rather than the 'economic cost' for the operators. These external costs are generated by transport users and imposed upon the non-travelling public. Formally, factors exist when the activities of one group (either consumers or producers) affect the welfare of another group without payment or compensation being made. This assertion is especially true for Alpine countries because of the difficulties related to the ecological vulnerability of the Alps.

In following the previous point, Switzerland and Austria have adopted national policies directed at financing the transport cost associated with a 'green policy'. The problem is how to govern the increase of flows crossing the Alps and, simultaneously, how to favour the socio-economic development of the Alpine population with respect to their culture, their economy and the environment. There is now a strong trend towards piece-meal information and technical approaches, as well as single projects that compete with each other. This delays any resolution of the Alpine problem in an efficient and systematic way (Senn, 1995).

Given the above constraints, the Alpine region offers few options and limited capacity to the transport sector. Active policies directed at full exploitation of the existing potential should support the maintenance of the structural Alpine topology. The need for European thinking is especially evident.

4.3 Critical success factors and cohesiveness indicators in Transalpine freight transport studies

Studies on the Alpine links have highlighted the importance of dealing with the concept of 'missing' networks. This term refers to the absence of strategic components of transport and communications infrastructure which may be either material or immaterial in nature (see Maggi et al.,1993).

The Pentagon Prism of Five Critical Success Factors developed by Nijkamp (1995a, 1995b) systematically identifies the strategic factors responsible for a sub-standard functioning of networks.

The components of the Pentagon Prism — which correspond to critical success factors — are the following:

- HARDWARE, which refers to the tangible material aspects of transport infrastructure. They serve to physically facilitate transport services or flows generated by consumers or firms.
- SOFTWARE, which refers both to computer software used to control sophisticated hardware and to related services such as information systems, computerized booking and reservation systems, communications facilities, route guidance systems, and so on.
- ORGWARE, which comprises all regulatory, administrative, legal, management and coordination activities and structures regarding both the

80

demand and the supply side in the private and the public institutional domain.

- FINWARE, which refers not only to the socio-economic cost-benefit aspects of new investments, but also to the way of financing and maintaining new infrastructures, to fare structures, or to state contracts for guaranteed finances for public transport deficits.
- ECOWARE, which refers to environmental and ecological concerns, including safety and energy questions.

In Table 4.4 below, the studies on Alpine transport have been typified with reference to their correspondence with each critical success factor previously defined in conjunction with the main cohesiveness characteristics: intermodality, interoperability and interconnectivity, as illustrated in Section 4.2.3 and notes 1, 2, 3.

Table 4.4 Cohesiveness characteristics in relation to five critical success factors according to the studies under analysis

Cohesiveness Feature	Hardware	Software	Orgware	Ecoware	Finware
I Intermodality	Russo, 1995 Fs Spa, 1994	Russo, 1995	Russo, 1995	Russo, 1995	
II Interconnectivity	Freudensprung et al., 1994		Rossera, 1995 Maggi and Müller, 1995 Sandonnini, 1991	Rossera, 1994 Freudensprung et al, 1994	Rossera, 1994 Freudensprung et al., 1994
III Interoperability	Beuthe et al., 1998 Gruppo Clas, 1995		Beuthe et al., 1998 Maggi and Müller, 1995	Maggi, 1992	Gruppo Clas, 1995

4.4   Typologies of studies and data

4.4.1   The physical network covered by the studies

In Table 4.5, the geographical areas — in the framework of Alpine transits — covered by the studies have been outlined. In this context it is necessary to address the problem of a shortage of studies investigating the Alpine region as a whole. Studies focus on partial aspects, not only in terms of the 'physical network', but also in relation to the transport network. For example, most studies

81

tend to concentrate on the rail/road mode and neglect the role and potential impact of the air and maritime modes. Furthermore, scant attention is given to transit axes in the Eastern Alps.

The absence of a comprehensive view on the problem of Alpine crossings is partially due to the number of institutions involved — each has different responsibilities and interests — and also because of the result of fragmentary and heterogeneous data.

Table 4.5 Geographical areas covered by the studies

STUDIES	GEOGRAPHICAL AREA OF INTEREST	ALPINE TRANSITS							
		V	M	MB	S	L	G	B	T
Austrian FM, 1992	'Brenner Relevant' traffic				x	x	x	x	x
Beuthe et al., 1998	EU freight flows across Swiss Alps				x	x	x		
Chatelus and Torricelli, 1994	Italy/France/Switzerland traffic		x	x	x	x	x		
EU-Commission, 1990	Western Alps	x	x	x					
DFTCE-Sigmaplan Sa, 1991	'Swiss Relevant' traffic		x	x	x	x	x	x	
FS Spa, 1994	Italian Alps	x	x	x	x	x	x	x	x
FS - SNCF, 1993	Mont Cènis		x						
Freudensprung et al., 1994	Brenner							x	
Graf, 1995	Swiss Alps		x	x	x	x	x	x	
Gruppo Clas, 1994	TAFT								
I.Re.R., 1992	Italian Alps	x	x	x	x	x	x	x	x
Istra-Italferr Sis-Tav Spa/A, 1992	Italian Alps	x	x	x	x	x	x	x	x
Istra-Italferr Sis-Tav Spa/B, 1992	Italian Alps	x	x	x	x	x	x	x	x
Maggi, 1992	Swiss Alps					x	x		
Maggi and Müller, 1995	Swiss Alps				x	x	x		
Rossera, 1994	Swiss Alps		x	x	x	x	x	x	
Rossera, 1995	TAFT								
Russo, 1995	Italian/Austrian Alps							x	x
Sandonnini, 1991	Italian Alps	x	x	x	x	x	x	x	x
SFTED, 1988	Northern Alps		x	x	x	x	x	x	

Legend: Alpine Transits

V= Ventimiglia, M= Mont Cènis/Frèjus, MB= Mont Blanc, S=Simplon, L= Lotschberg, G=Gottard, B=Brenner, T=Tarvisio.

In Table 4.6 the main Transalpine links are shown together with the examined regions. The total number of passages is about 400; the primary mountain passes number about fifteen, but only some of them are served simultaneously by rail and road infrastructure.

Table 4.6 Main Transalpine links

TRANSITS*	MODE	GEOGRAPHICAL LINKS	RELATED NATIONS
Ventimiglia	ro/ra/m	Savona-Nice	I/F
Tende	ro/ra	Cuneo-Nice	I/F
Frèjus/Mont Cènis	ro/ra	Turin-Chambèry (Grenoble)	I/F
Mont Blanc	ro	Aosta-Annecy/Geneva	I/F
Great Saint Bernard	ro	Aosta-Martigny	I/F
Simplon	ro/ra	Domodossola-Brig	I/CH
Lotscheberg	ra	Brig-Thun(Berne)	CH/CH
Gotthard	ro/ra/m	Bellinzona-Altdorf	CH/CH
San Bernardino	ro/m	Bellinzona-Altdorf	CH/CH
Brenner	ro/ra/m	Bolzano-Innsbruck	I/A
Croce (San Candido)	ro/ra	Tolmezzo- Lienz	I/A
Tarvisio	ro/ra/m	Tolmezzo - Villach	I/A
Tauernautobahn	ra/m	Villach-Salzburg	A/A
Phyrn Autobahn	ra/m	Graz-Linz/Salzburg	A/A
Karawanken	ra/m	Ljubljana -Villach/Klagenfurt	SL/A

Legend:

Mode: ra= Rail   ro= Road m = Motorway

Related Nations: F= France I= Italy CH= Switzerland A=Austria SL = Slovenja.

* The principal links are written in bold type.

4.4.2 Typologies of studies

Since the final purpose of this review of studies related to the Alpine case is to identify evaluation indicators and assessment methods for the development of an integrated trans european network,[6] each study can be classified according to the following scenarios/directions:

1. analysis of traffic evolution up to 1992
2. traffic forecasts (short, medium or long-term)
3. impact of new or improved transport alternatives
4. impact of policy measure.

The above issues will be discussed in Section 4.4.4. An overview of the studies considered, classified according to the type of analysis, methodology and data, is illustrated in Table 4.A.1 in Annex 4.A.

4.4.3   Typologies of data

Depending on the type of scenario concerned, different analyses, methods and models have been used. The application of different methods presumes the existence and use of various qualitative data. Therefore, by considering studies about the Alpine sector, the following types of data have been analysed (ordinal and cardinal information) (see again Table 4.A.1 in Annex 4.A):

1. data concerning movements of origin-destination (volume of traffic and transported goods broken down by mode, number of origin-destination broken down by mode, characteristics of the transport users) (see e.g. Austrian FM, 1992, Beuthe *et al.*, 1998, DFTCE-Sigmaplan Sa, 1991; I.Re.R., 1992; Istra-Italferr Sis-Tav Spa A/B, 1992);

2. data concerning the 'critical success factors' for the suppliers (speed, comfort, flexibility, reliability, cost, safety, use of telecommunications technologies, etc.) (see e.g. Freudensprung *et al.*, 1994; Maggi and Müller, 1995; Russo, 1995);

3. data describing the effects on the demand side, of a change in the transport supply or in the socio-economic context (see e.g. DFTCE-Sigmaplan Sa, 1991; FS Spa, 1994; Istra-Italferr Sis-Tav/B, 1992; Maggi, 1992; Rossera, 1994);

4. data referring to transport infrastructure or tangible physical aspects, such as technical equipment, terminals, railways, road networks (see e.g. Chatelus and Torricelli, 1994; Istra-Italferr Sis Tav Spa/B, 1992);

5. data referring to transport information systems, such as computer software, communications facilities, data sets and route guidance systems (see Freudensprung *et al.*, 1994; Russo, 1995);

6. data referring to the private and public institutional framework of the transport system, such as all regulatory, administrative, legal, management and coordination activities; (see Freudensprung *et al.*, 1994; Graf, 1995; Maggi, 1992; Russo, 1995);

7. data referring to the environmental and ecological impacts (see Freudensprung *et al.*, 1994; Graf, 1995; Russo, 1995);

8. data describing the social-economic context, such as population, mobility rate, G.N.P. (Gross National Product), etc. (see Austrian FM, 1992; EU-Commission, 1990; FS-SNCF, 1993; Graf, 1995; Istra-Italferr Sis-Tav Spa/A, 1992).

4.4.4   Relationship between typologies of studies and typologies of data

The choice of the type of data clearly depends on the objectives as well as the chosen method of analysis. Therefore, in order to gain greater insight into the development of studies carried out thus far in the Alpine context, we will examine the most relevant correlation between   types of studies, types of data   and methods (see Table 4.A.1 in Annex A) in the framework of the types of studies underlined in Section 4.2.2.

4.4.4.1   Analysis of traffic evolution up to 1992   The interest in the Alpine network is quite recent. It was motivated by the necessity to create the European Common Market and by the exceptional growth of mobility for passengers and freight. For this reason, this first approach, which began in the late 1980s, showed the necessity for analysing how these important changes were revolutionising market relationships among countries, particularly within the Alps. The major problem was in collecting useful data for the Alpine transit system (see DFTCE-Sigmaplan Sa, 1991; Sandonnini, 1991).

Many of these studies have represented the 'starting point' for further investigation in the field of traffic forecasting or in the impact of new or improved alternatives studies, etc. (see Istra-Italferr Sis-Tav Spa/A, 1992).

Concerning the basic information of these studies, the data used mainly refer to quantitative movements or to socio-economic data.

4.4.4.2 Traffic forecasts These studies do not incorporate changes in the transport system or within the socio-economic context. They do include the evaluation analysis of the bottlenecks in Transalpine freight transport. The concept of missing networks applies to poor performance in terms of convenience, speed, comfort, flexibility, reliability, costs, safety and social costs of European infrastructure (see Maggi et al.,1993). Traffic volumes are the most important data for traffic forecasts, especially at a strong level of aggregation of the demand. In this context, it is possible to identify secondary objectives — as an addendum to the overall objective — both temporal (annual, monthly or traffic peak forecasts) or spatial (prediction of transport evolution in specific corridors or networks) (see Russo,

1995). The detail of the data depends on the sub-objectives listed above as well as the method used. The adopted method is often the aggregate forecast based on trends or extrapolations of transport data (see FS Spa, 1994; I.Re.R., 1992). It should be noted that the studies do not integrate volume of traffic data with an analysis of development in mobility and modal choice.

4.4.4.3 Impact of new or improved transport alternatives This type of study presupposes a geographical approach based on origin-destination flows data. The covered area can vary from a regional corridor to a national or even transnational network. In theory, multi-modal models should be a preferred instrument for this type of study: they generally lead to the construction of an origin - destination matrix broken down into modes and/or typologies of transported goods (see Austrian FM, 1992; EU-Commission, 1990; FS-SNCF, 1993; Graf, 1995; Istra-Italferr Sis-Tav Spa/B, 1992; SFTED, 1988). The problem is the low availability of data (see Beuthe et al., 1998).

Multicriteria models for evaluating different transport system alternatives are often used. Multicriteria analysis aims to identify the most realistic option from a set of discrete alternatives by systematically investigating relevant impacts of each alternative on the basis of a set of evaluation criteria (see Freudensprung *et al.*, 1994). This approach requires different kinds of data concerning characteristics of the movements, of the transport users, and of the transport supplier.

For the special case of the Transalpine network, a political-economic model has been applied (see Maggi, 1992), which considers the importance of local aspects for the national decisions on road transport issues. In this context, transport projects are evaluated according to the spatial distribution of their local impacts in terms of costs and benefits. In this model, data on the aggregate level — formulated in terms of frequencies of the stochastic indirect utility functions — are used; the estimation equation also uses qualitative variables.

4.4.4.4 Impact of policy measure Private and public transport suppliers are directly responsible for many measures which can influence transport flows evolution in the Transalpine area. These measures are generally studied in market analyses. Other important kinds of measures are those provided by national governments or international bodies, such as the European Union. These measures are particularly concerned with taxation, tariffs, subsidies, legislation, regulation, and operating methods or practices. This typology of study generally requires detailed information on user behaviour, users' sensitivity to different factors, and primarily to the critical success factor for the supplier. Forecast of global variations in time and tariffs is generally carried out by multimodal models which, in some cases, include data concerning mobility, but also include cost factors data or indicators of the quality of services (see Rossera, 1994). When the effects of certain measures on demand are not available in econometric terms, it is possible to rely on market analysis technique. This method presupposes that transport operators (qualified or not; it depends on the objectives of the analysis) are asked to assess how they might change their strategic policy or how they might react to certain changes in the structure of the transport market (see Maggi and Müller, 1995).

Studies concerning the impact of policy measures have been carried out by using a cost function approach (see Beuthe *et al.*, 1998; Rossera, 1995).

4.5   General conclusions

By analysing the aforementioned studies, we can confirm that comprehensive knowledge of mechanisms governing the transport system performance is still missing; moreover, the available data show a lack of homogeneity from all points of view. No study thus far has clearly identified the socio-economic variables that characterise the evolution of the Transalpine flows.

In the examined studies, the use of quantitative data prevails, especially for analysis of origin-destination flows. Quantitative and qualitative data are also used with reference to private and institutional frameworks as well as to environmental and ecological aspects. Multi-modal and aggregate forecast analyses are the most frequent methods. The results of the above studies do not conflict, but a systematic viewpoint is still missing.

In the policy issue context, the studies under analysis emphasize two major emerging problems:

1. lack of national policy agreement,
2. lack of optimisation of the transport system in light of both the ecological vulnerability of the Alps and limited infrastructural space.

On the basis of the above observations, it seems necessary to develop contributions oriented towards the analysis of the effects of new/improved transport alternatives, as well as of policy measures in conjunction with studies associated to traffic forecasts.

Acknowledgements

The authors wish to thank the group *Funzione Strategie, Studi e Mercati - Ferrovie dello Stato S.p.A.* (Rome) for their fruitful contribution. In particular, Dott. Pietro Spirito, Ing. Giuseppe Baldassarri and Dott. Maurizio Caruso Frezza are gratefully acknowledged. Furthermore, the authors wish to acknowledge the Italian project MPI 40 per cent and CNR n.97.000264.PF74, as well as the European Action COST 328 'Integrated Strategic Infrastructure Network in Europe'. We would also like to thank Dr. Antonio Nicoletti for his contribution to a previous version of the present paper.

References

Beuthe, M., Demilie, L., and Jourquin, B. (1998), *The International Impacts of a New Road Taxation Scheme in Switzerland*, Paper prepared for the Cost 328 Research Action, Final Seminar, 1998, Bilbao.

Chatelus, G. and Torricelli, G.P. (1994), *Cooperations transalpines et infrastructures de transport*, INRETS and I.R.E: Paris.

Demilie, L., Dupuis, V., Jourquin, B. and Beuthe, M. (1998), "On the Crossing of the Alpine Chain and the Swiss Regulation of Trucking", in A. Reggiani (ed.), *Accessibility, Trade and Location Behaviour*, Ashgate: Aldershot.

DFTCE - Sigmaplan Sa (1991), *Traffico merci attraverso le Alpi 1989*, Sintesi dell'evoluzione dopo l'apertura della galleria stradale del San Gottardo nel 1980, Bern.

Ferrovie dello Stato (1993), *Le direttrici di traffico. Pianificazione e sviluppo dei servizi merci* . L'Offerta merci FS '94-'96, Rome.

Ferrovie dello Stato SPA and Societé Nationale des Chemins de fer Francais (1994), *Nuovelle liaison ferroviarie Lyon-Turin* - Etude du franchissement alpin.

Freudensprung, P., Nijkamp, P. and Simons, R. (1994), *Bottlenecks in Trans Alpine Freight Transport - A Multicriteria Analysis on Future Brenner Corridor Alternatives*, Department of Economics, Free University, Amsterdam.

Frybourg, M. and Nijkamp, P. (1994a), "Integrated Strategic Infrastructure Networks in Europe (ISINE)" - *In Search of Evaluation Indicators and Assessment Methods for Complementary and Competing Trans-European Networks*, Cost Secretariat 328, Brussels.

Frybourg, M. and Nijkamp, P. (1994b), *An Assessment Methodology for Integrated European Transport Network Operations*, COST 328 Paper, Brussels.

Geenhuizeen, M. Van and Ratti, R. (1995), *New Network Use and Technologies in Freight Transport: an "Active Space" Approach*, I.R.E. Report, Bellinzona.

Graf, H.G. (1995), *Prospettive del traffico merci alpino 1993 - 2015*, St.Gallen Zentrum fur Zukunftforschung: St.Gallen.

Gruppo Clas S.r.L. (1994), *Studies on Alpine Crossings: A Survey*, Milan (mimeo).

I.Re.R. (Istituto Regionale di Ricerca della Lombardia) (1992), *Il trasporto di merci e di persone attraverso le Alpi, Situazione e prospettive di evoluzione*, I.Re.R. Report, Milan.

Intraplan and Kessel & Partner (1992), *Verkehrsstudie Brennertunnel commissioned by the Austrian Federal Ministry of Public Works and Transport*, Forschungsarbeiten aus dem Verkehrswesen Band, Wien.

Istra S.p.A. - Italferr - SIS. T.A.V. S.p.A. (1992), *Studio del Traffico*, Rome.

Istra S.p.A. - Italferr - SIS. T.A.V. S.p.A. (1992), *Studio di fattibilita' Sempione e Gottardo*. Studio di prefattibilita' Villa Opicina: Rome (mimeo).

Maggi, R., (1992), "Swiss Transport Policy for Europe? Federalism and the Dominance of Local Issues", *Transport Research*, Vol.26a, No.2, 193 - 198.

Maggi, R., Masser, I. and Nijkamp, P. (1993), "Missing Networks: the Case of European Freight Transport", *European Planning Studies*, Vol.1, No.3, 351-365.

Maggi, R. and Müller, K., (1995), *Trans-Alpine Freight Transport: a Case Study on Cohesiveness*, Position Paper prepared for the COST 328 Seminar 2/3 March 1995 , Lausanne.

Motor-Columbus AG and Electrowatt AG (1988), *Neue Eisenbahn-Alpentransversale. Basisbericht*, commissioned by the Swiss Federal Transport and Energy Department, Zurich.

Müller, K. and Maggi, M. (1998), "Price Effects of Regulation", in A. Reggiani (ed.), *Accessibility, Trade and Location Behaviour*, Ashgate: Aldershot, 219-312.

Nijkamp, P. (1995a), *The Competitive Edge of Rail Freight Transport -* Position Paper prepared for the COST 328 Seminar, 2/3 March 1995, Lausanne.

Nijkamp, P. (1995b), Trans Missing Networks to Interoperable Networks, *Transport Policy*, Vol. 2, No. 3, 159-167.

Nijkamp, P., Reggiani, A. and Bolis, S. (1997), "European Freight Transport and the Environment: Empirical Applications and Scenarios", *Transportation Research D*, Vol.2, No.4, 233-244.

Ratti, R., (1998), "The Active Space: A Regional Scientist's Paradigmatic Answer to the Local-Global Debate", in A. Reggiani (ed.), *Accessibility, Trade and Location Behaviour*, Ashgate: Aldershot, 219-237.

Reggiani, A. (ed.) (1998), *Accessibility, Trade and Location Behaviour*, Ashgate: Aldershot.

Reggiani, A., Nijkamp, P. and Bolis, S. (1997), "The Role of Transalpine Freight Transport in a Common European Market: Analyses and Empirical Applications", *Innovation: The European Journal of Social Sciences*, Vol.10, No. 3, 259-271.

Reggiani, A., Nijkamp, P. and Nobilio, L. (1999), Spatial Modal Patterns in European Freight Transport Networks: Results of Neurocomputing and Logit Models, in A. Reggiani, D. Fabbri (eds.), *The Role of Spatial Economic Networks: New Perspectives*, Ashgate: Aldershot (forthcoming).

Rossera, F. (1994), *Freight Traffic Through the Alps: Peculiarities and Impacts of Abnormal Routing*, Discussion Paper, Istituto di Ricerche Economiche: Bellinzona.

Rossera, F. (1995), *Modelling Transalpine Freight Transport*, Discussion Paper, Istituto di Ricerche Economiche: Bellinzona.

Russo, R. (1995), *Combined Transport Through the Alps: A Comparative Analysis at the Austrian-Italian Border*, Vienna University of Economics and Business Administration, Department of Economic and Social Geography, Vienna.

Sandonnini, P.P. 1991, *Ricerca sulle problematiche dello scambio internazionale delle merci attraverso i valichi alpini*, Unione Italiana delle Camere di Commercio.

Senn, L. 1995, *Il trasporto attraverso le Alpi. Nuove infrastrutture di trasporto nelle Alpi: la necessita' di un approccio globale e sistemico*, UnionTrasporti, Milan.

Setec and Inarco 1990, *Franchissements alpins entre la France et l'Italie*, EU/DG Commission for Transport, Brussels.

Notes

1. Austrian FM, 1992 analyses the effects of the construction of a new Brenner rail tunnel (Fortezza-Innsbruck); FS-SNCF, 1993 analyses the Lyons-Turin high-speed train project; Istra-Italferr Sis-Tav Spa/B, 1992 analyses five alternative scenarios in which different schemes concerning Brenner, Gotthard and Simplon projects are combined; SFTED, 1988 analyses the effects of five mutually-exclusive future infrastructure schemes for the Swiss Alp transits.
2. It basically consists of the possibility for a train to freely circulate throughout the European rail network like a road vehicle would circulate throughout the European road network (Russo, 1995).
3. Interconnectivity refers to horizontal coordination of and access to networks of a different geographical coverage (Frybourg and Nijkamp, 1994a, 1994b; Nijkamp, 1995a, 1995b).
4. Intermodality addresses the issue of a sequential use of different transport modes in the chain of transport (Frybourg and Nijkamp,1994, and Nijkamp,1995a, 1995b).
5. Active space integrates the capacity for a region to manage dynamic internal and external relationships (openness) with the capacity to reach a sustainable development.
6. See also the objectives underlined by Frybourg and Nijkamp (1994a, 1994b) in the framework of EU/COST 328 Action.

Annex 4.A Classification of the studies concerning the transalpine freight transport network

Table 4.A.1 A general overview of studies related to the Transalpine freight transport network

AUTHORS	STUDIES				DATA								METHODS							LINKS/NETWORKS
	A	B	C	D	1	2	3	4	5	6	7	8	a	b	c	d	e	f	g	
Austrian FM., 1992	x				x							x	x	x						Brenner relevant Traffic
Beuthe et al.., 1998			x	x	x				x		x								x	EU Countries' Freight Flows across Swiss Alps
Chatelus and Torricelli, 1994			x				x	x	x							x				Italy/France/Switzerland Traffic
EU Commission, 1990			x		x							x	x							Western Alps from Ventimiglia to Mont Blanc
DFTCE-Sigmaplan Sa, 1991	x						x	x						x						From Mont Cénis/Frejus to Brenner
Fs SpA., 1994			x	x			x	x	x				x							Six Directions/seven Rail Alpine Transits
FS-SNCF, 1993			x						x			x	x	x						Mont Cénis
Freudensprung et al..., 1994			x	x	x		x	x	x	x	x				x					Brenner Corridor
Graf, 1995			x					x	x	x	x	x	x							Swiss Alps
Gruppo Clas., 1994			x		x									x						Whole Alpine Network
I Re.R., 1992	x				x	x	x						x							Matrix O-D /EU Countries and Switzerland
ISTRA-ITALFERR SIS TAV/A., '92	x				x						x			x						Alpine Transit between Italy and Europe
ISTRA-ITALFERR SIS TAV/B., '92			x	x			x	x				x		x						Euro-Trans System 1st Version
Maggi., 1992			x					x			x	x					x			Swiss Alps
Maggi and Müller., 1995		x				x											x			Swiss Alps
Nijkamp et al., 1997	x	x	x		x			x					x	x						Whole Alpine Network
Reggiani et al., 1997	x	x	x		x			x					x	x						Whole Alpine Network
Reggiani et al., 1999	x	x	x		x			x					x	x						Whole Alpine Network
Rossera, 1994			x	x		x	x						x							From Mont Cénis/Frejus to Brenner
Rossera, 1995		x																	x	Whole Alpine Network
Russo, 1995	x				x	x	x	x	x									x		Austrian–Italian Axis
Sandomnini.,1991	x				x								x	x						Italian Alps
SFTED,1988			x		x							x	x							Northern Alps from Mont Cénis to Brenner

STUDIES

A = Analysis of Traffic Evolution up to 1992
B = Traffic Forecasts
C = Impact of New or Improved Transport Alternatives
D = Impact of Policy Measures

DATA

1 Concerning quantitative movements
2 Concerning critical success factors for the suppliers
3 Describing the effects of a change on demand
4 Referring to transport infrastructure
5 Referring to transport information system
6 Referring to private and public institutional framework of the transport system
7 Referring to the environmental and ecological impacts
8 Referring to socio-economic data

METHODS

a Aggregate Forecasts
b Multi-modal Models
c Multicriteria Analyses
d Political-Economic Models
e Market Analyses
f Pentagon Prism Model
g Cost Function Approach

References to Table 4.A.1

The studies examined are listed below in alphabetical order and with the abbreviations used in the text as follows:

1 - Austrian FM, 1992
INTRAPLAN AND KESSEL & PARTNER (1992), Verkehrsstudie Brennertunnel commissioned by the Austrian Federal Ministry of Public Works and Transport, Forschungsarbeiten aus dem Verkehrswesen Band, Wien.

2 - Beuthe et al., 1998
BEUTHE, M., DEMILIE, L., and JOURQUIN, B. (1998), The International Impacts of a New Road Taxation Scheme in Switzerland, Paper prepared for the Cost 328 Research Action - Final Seminar, 5-6 November 1998, Bilbao.

3 - Chatelus and Torricelli, 1994
CHATELUS, G., TORRICELLI, G.P. (1994), Cooperations transalpines et infrastructures de transport, INRETS and I.R.E., Paris.

4 - EU-Commission, 1990
SETEC AND INARCO, (1990), Franchissements alpins entre la France et l'Italie, EU/DG Commission for Transport, Brussels.

5 - DFTCE - Sigmaplan Sa, 1991
DFTCE- SIGMAPLAN Sa (1991), Traffico merci attraverso le Alpi 1989, Sintesi dell'evoluzione dopo l'apertura della galleria stradale del San Gottardo nel 1980, Bern.

6 - FS Spa, 1994
FERROVIE DELLO STATO (1994), Le direttrici di traffico. Pianificazione e sviluppo dei servizi merci . L'Offerta merci FS '94-'96, Rome.

7 - FS - SNCF, 1993
FERROVIE DELLO STATO SPA AND SOCIETE' NATIONALE DES CHEMINS DE FER FRANCAIS (1993), Nuovelle liaison ferroviarie Lyon-Turin - Etude du franchissement alpin.

8 - Freudensprung et al., 1994
FREUDENSPRUNG, P., NIJKAMP, P., SIMONS, R. (1994), Bottlenecks in Transalpine Freight Transport. A Multicriteria Analysis on Future Brenner Corridor Alternatives, Department of Economics, Free University, Amsterdam.

94

9 - Graf, 1995
GRAF, H.G. (1995), Prospettive del traffico merci alpino 1993-2015, St.Gallen Zentrum fur Zukunftforschung, St.Gallen.

10- Gruppo Clas, 1994
GRUPPO CLAS S.r.L. (1994), Studies on Alpine Crossings: A Survey, Milan (mimeo).

11- I.Re.R., 1992
I.Re.R. (Istituto Regionale di Ricerca della Lombardia) (1992), Il trasporto di merci e di persone attraverso le Alpi. Situazione e prospettive di evoluzione, I.Re.R. Report, Milan.

12 - Istra-Italferr Sis-Tav Spa/A, 1992
ISTRA S.p.A. - ITALFERR - SIS. T.A.V. S.p.A. (1992), Studio del traffico, Rome.

13 - Istra-Italferr Sis-Tav Spa/B, 1992
ISTRA S.p.A. - ITALFERR - SIS. T.A.V. S.p.A. (1992), Studio di fattibilita' Sempione e Gottardo - Studio di prefattibilita' Villa Opicina, Rome.

14 - Maggi, 1992
MAGGI, R. (1992), Swiss Transport Policy for Europe? Federalism and the Dominance of Local Issues, *Transport Research*, Vol. 26a, No. 2, 193 - 198.

15 - Maggi and Müller, 1995
MAGGI, R., MÜLLER, K. (1995), Transalpine Freight Transport: a Case Study on Cohesiveness, Position Paper prepared for the COST 328 Seminar, 2-3 March 1995, Lausanne.

16 - Nijkamp et al., 1997
NIJKAMP, P., REGGIANI, A., BOLIS S. (1997), European Freight Transport and the Environment, Empirical Applications and Scenarios, *Transportation Research D*, Vol.2, No. 4, 233-244.

17 - Reggiani et al., 1997
NIJKAMP, P., REGGIANI, A., and BOLIS, S. (1997), The Role of Transalpine Freight Transport in a Common European Market: Analyses and Empirical Applications, *Innovation: The European Journal of Social Sciences*, Vol.10, No.3, pp.259-271.

18 - Reggiani et al., 1998
REGGIANI, A., NIJKAMP, P., NOBILIO L., (1998), Spatial Modal Patterns in European Freight Transport Networks: Results of Neurocomputing and Logit Models, in A. Reggiani, D. Fabbri (eds.), *The Role of Spatial Economic Networks: New Perspectives*, Ashgate, Aldershot (forthcoming).

19 - Rossera, 1994
ROSSERA, F., (1994), Freight Traffic Through the Alps: Peculiarities and Impacts of Abnormal Routing, Istituto di Ricerche Economiche, Bellinzona.

20 - Rossera, 1995
ROSSERA, F., (1995), Modelling Transalpine Freight Transport, Discussion Paper, Istituto di Ricerche Economiche, Bellinzona, (Mimeo).

21 - Russo, 1995
RUSSO, R., (1995), Combined Transport Through the Alps: a Comparative Analysis at the Austrian-Italian Border, Vienna University of Economics and Business Administration, Department of Economic and Social Geography, Vienna.

22 - Sandonnini, 1991
SANDONNINI P.P., (1991), Ricerca sulle problematiche dello scambio internazionale delle merci attraverso i valichi alpini, Unione Italiana delle Camere di Commercio.

23 - SFTDE, 1988
MOTOR-COLUMBUS AND ELECTROWATT, (1988), Neue Eisenbahn-Alpentransversale. Basisbericht commissioned by the Swiss Federal Transport and Energy Department, Zürich.

5 The International Impacts of a New Road Taxation Scheme in Switzerland

MICHEL BEUTHE, LAURENT DEMILIE AND
BART JOURQUIN

5.1 Introduction

Switzerland is an important transit country for freight traffic through Europe, and its population is very much concerned by the pollution and the congestion that road traffic creates over its network. Indeed, the geographic configuration of the country, its circuitous and mountainous network, tend to increase these problems and their impacts on the population, while the natural beauty of the country and its important tourism activity militate in favour of their control. These concerns led the Swiss government to impose some restrictions on trucking over its territory: since the early seventies, transport movements by trucks of more than 28 tons are forbidden in Switzerland, and trucking is not allowed during the night and on Sundays.

That weight limitation was proven to be very effective in reducing the number of trucks transiting through Switzerland, even though it induced to some extent a substitution of more numerous 28 t. in place of 40 t. trucks. First, this restriction increases the cost per ton of road transportation, so that rail transportation becomes relatively more competitive and part of the road traffic is switched to the rail. Second, it induces the choice by truckers of different routes through longer itineraries through France and Austria.

In an earlier paper by the same authors (Demilie, Dupuis, Jourquin and Beuthe, 1998), these effects have been estimated using a multimodal network analysis, which will be used again in this paper. Since these results provide the reference situation for measuring the impacts of alternative restrictive strategies, part of them will be summarised in a following section.

At a later date, Switzerland even decided by referendum that, starting in 2005, all international transit trucks should be banned from Switzerland. However, a compromise solution is presently negotiated between Switzerland and the European Union. First, in 1990, Switzerland committed itself to the development of the Swiss railway infrastructure in order to promote combined transport in place of trucking. It is the "Neue Alpen Transversale" with the boring of new rail tunnels underneath the present tunnels of the St-Gothard and Lötschberg-Simplon links. In 1992, Switzerland also accepted to co-ordinate its road traffic taxation with the European Union's policy of pricing the cost of infrastructure as well as the external cost of transport, and to not discriminate against European Union's truckers for international transport in Switzerland.

The present negotiations aim at implementing concretely these principles. In all likelihood, they will lead to a progressive abolition of the 28 tons restriction and to the introduction of a new tax per ton/km transported. The latter would be defined in principle by the real cost of road transport, infrastructure and external costs included, which is not already paid through other taxes, like, for instance, the excise tax on fuel.

This perspective raises clearly a number of difficult problems and questions concerning the estimation of external costs. It is, nowadays, a very active field of research in various fields of scientific research. The present paper will not deal with these matters, but accept the estimates used by the Swiss Federal government in order to devise a new tax per ton/km which is under scrutiny at the present time. Another important problem is to assess the new tax's impact on road traffic, should the restriction on trucks' size be abandoned. Would such an additional tax limit road traffic through Switzerland to a level similar to the present one? If it is not the case, how much different will it be? And what will be impact on the rail traffic? The answers to these questions are not only important from the point of view of the budget resources the tax will provide or for the management of the railways; they may also affect the political acceptance of the new tax by the Swiss population and its government. These are the questions on which this paper is focused.

The first section of the paper describes the present situation of the network and of the specific road taxation in the Alpine countries. The second section briefly explains the new taxation schemes which are presently under consideration. The third section reviews the applied methodology, which is based on the same multimodal freight transport network model as was used in our earlier paper on this topic (Jourquin and Beuthe, 1996). It gives a short explanation of the transport cost functions, of the database and of the building of the origins-destinations matrix. The fourth section presents the simulations results, the estimated impacts of the new taxes in terms of the different modes' traffic volumes, the choice of routes and the tax revenue. The paper ends up with some short conclusions.

5.2   The present situation in the Alpine Chain

5.2.1   The Infrastructure

The geographic network which is covered by this analysis includes all the Western European countries, from Scandinavia to Spain and Greece, which have some international transport traffic with Italy. This network was digitised on the basis of the list of 'Trunk Lines of International Importance' published by the European Conference of Ministers of Transport (ECMT), updated to the present situation.[1] In principle, this digitised network includes roads, railways, inland waterways as well as short-sea shipping lanes, but, for the present research, only the road and railway networks are used.[2]

Since the Swiss network is at the core of the problem, it is worthwhile to describe the transport corridors which are used for crossing the Alpine chain. Figure 5.1 presents the geographic situation of the main TransAlpine passes which are used by international freight traffic.

On the Western side, i.e. the French-Italian border, the Ventimiglia pass has a single rail line, the Mt-Cenis/Fréjus pass has two tunnels, one for road and the other one for rail, while the Mt-Blanc tunnel is only for road traffic.

The main Swiss tunnels are situated along the central segment: the Gr-St-Bernard tunnel is part the E27 road towards Aoste ; the Lötschberg-Simplon pass provides a road and rail link towards Domolossa, Milan and Novara; the St-Gotthard road and rail tunnel link with Bellinzona and Chiasso; the San Bernardino road tunnel is on the National 13 towards Bellinzona.

The Brenner tunnel for road and rail is also part of the central segment but on the Austrian territory. It is the most important transit point between Germany (and Northern Europe) and Italy.

The Eastern segment between Italy and Austria has six main passes, the most important of which is the Tarvisio rail tunnel.

5.1 enumerates all these passes and indicates the type of traffic they are made for: road, rail, combined road/rail transport accompanied or not.

---

[1]   From information collected from various sources. Among them: DFTCE-Sigmaplan (1991,1995) and CEMAT (1995).

[2]   An example of the use of the full-fledged trans-European network with four modes can be found in Demilie, Jourquin and Beuthe (1996).

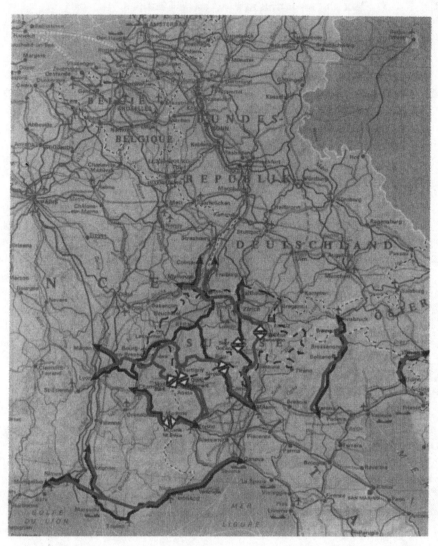

Figure 5.1 Main traffic flows (grey lines = road, black lines = rail)

Table 5.1 Main Alpine passes

	Road	Acc. combined	Unacc. combined	Rail
Western segment of the Alpine arc (French/Italian border)				
Ventimiglia	x		x	x
Mt-Cénis/Fréjus	x		x	x
Mt-Blanc	x			
Central segment of the Alpine arc (Swiss/Italian border)				
Gr-St-Bernard	x			
Simplon	x	(x) 01.01.98	x	x
Gotthard	x	x	x	x
S. Bernardino	x			
Reschen	x			
Brenner	x	x	x	x
Eastern segment of the Alpine arc (Austrian/Italian border)				
Felbertauern	x			
Tauern	x	x	x	x
Schoberpass	x	x	x	x
Semmering	x		x	x
Wechsel	x		x	x
Tarvisio	x			x

5.2.2   Traffic restrictions and road taxation

Some of the European countries have introduced significant road restrictions for heavy trucks. This is particularly the case of Germany, Switzerland and Austria.

In Switzerland, road transport is generally forbidden on Sundays and holidays; they are also forbidden during the night from 10 p.m. to 5 a.m. In Austria, road transport are forbidden from Saturday 3 p.m. to Sunday 10 p.m. as well as during holidays. There is also an interdiction of night transport for trucks which exceed a noise emission level.[3] In Germany, road transport is forbidden on Sundays and holidays.

Various taxes are also imposed on road transport beyond the excise taxes on diesel fuel and taxes on the firms' income. First, there are some tolls that have to be paid on the main international itineraries. These are given in Table 5.2, where they are computed in equivalent cost per vehicle/km.

---

[3] In practice, most of the trucks exceed the noise limit.

Table 5.2 Average toll cost per vehicle/km

Country	Average cost per km (BEF)
France	4.4
Italy	4.1
Spain	6.0
Portugal	4.0
Austria	4.1

Source: Own computation

Second, additional tolls have to be paid at some tunnels or similar points on the network. These are given in Table 5.3.

Table 5.3 Toll per crossing

Name of the crossing	Toll cost per crossing (BEF)
Mont Blanc	3495
Fréjus	3408
Grand Saint Bernard	2716
Brenner	2929
Arlberg	1757
Tauern	757
Felbertauern	2270
Phyrn	2197

Source: Own computation

Four countries have introduced an annual circulation tax on their network. Germany, Benelux and Denmark have fixed it at 29,769 BEF. The annual Swiss circulation tax amounts to 73,431 BEF.

Finally, there is that important Swiss limit on the size of a truck, which already has been mentioned above.

5.3   The Swiss road taxation project

The new Swiss road taxation scheme is entirely in line with the policy promoted by the European Commission that each transport mode should pay its real cost, which includes the infrastructure cost as well as the external costs of pollution, accidents and congestion. In principle, such a policy should lead to a better use of economic resources, and limit the use of road transport, which would become relatively more expensive since its users would pay its full cost.

102

Thus, in order to respect this principle, the Swiss government has based its present proposal on available estimates of total road transport external costs. It has also taken into account the cost of infrastructure which is not covered by the existing tax on fuel, plus the amount of the present circulation tax which would be abolished. Congestion costs are not included because they are directly borne by the users. The marginal cost of congestion, i.e. the congestion imposed by each user on others, is not taken into account. Thus, this taxation will be based on average cost only, and not on marginal cost, as it should be for an optimal allocation of resources. The total cost data are given in Table 5.4.

Table 5.4 Total cost to be recovered by the future tax

	In million of FS
Road external cost	1,001
- Road accident	20
- Noise	260
- Building damages and health	721
Road infrastructure cost not covered by the existent road tax revenue	17
Revenue from the annual circulation taxes	132
Total cost to be recovered by the future tax	1150

Source: Conseil Fédéral Suisse, Message du 11 septembre 1996, p. 10 and 12.

It is acknowledged by the Swiss government that these figures are on the conservative side and that some other methods of computation would likely provide higher figures. Moreover, the damages to agriculture and the negative climatic impacts are not included in that estimate.

Since the nuisances of road transport are roughly proportional to distance, the new tax should also be established on that basis. Two road tax instruments could therefore be considered: an additional excise tax on diesel fuel and a tax per km or per ton/km.

In order to recover the amount of SF 1150 million, it was estimated that an additional tax of between SF1 and 2 per litre should be imposed on diesel. However, despite its administrative convenience, a price increase on diesel fuel would not reach the desired result, since the price of diesel in Switzerland is already higher than in the surrounding countries. A further increase would lead many truckers to fill in their reservoir outside of Switzerland, and the purpose of the tax would be defeated. Actually, an increase on diesel fuel could only be feasible in the framework of a co-ordinated European taxation policy.

Thus, even though the perception of a tax per km or per ton/km is not easy to administrate, this is the solution which has been retained by the Swiss government. This new tax would be imposed over the whole Swiss territory for various practical reasons and also in accordance with a likely proposal of the European Commission concerning the taxation of transport. However, the Swiss government does not exclude introducing a set of specific road tolls at some passes of the Alpine chain, in order to take into account the exceptional cost of some infrastructures. The tolls which are considered at the present time are given in Table 5.5.

Table 5.5 Proposed tolls at Swiss passes

Passage	Toll per vehicle
Saint Gothard	150 SF
San Bernardino	150 SF
Simplon	75 SF
Saint Bernard	40 SF

Source: Conseil Fédéral Suisse, Message du 11 septembre 1996.

On the basis of the ton/kms realised by the Swiss trucks inside and outside Switzerland, it was estimated that a tax of (SF) 2.5 cent. per ton of authorised maximum weight and per kilometre would be needed in order to recoup the required 1105 millions of SF.[4] But, the proposed law admits a minimum of 1.6 cent. as a transitory measure, and a maximum of 3 cent. in order to take into account additional external effects and/or inflation. A third of the tax revenue would be given to the Swiss Cantons for infrastructure maintenance and as a compensation for the external costs. The remaining two thirds would go to the federal government to finance transport infrastructure projects.

A likely scenario of the new tax implementation would be to begin with a level of 1.6 cent. SF in 2001 with a simultaneous easing of the trucks' size restriction to 34 tons. Then, in 2005, a level of 3 cent. would be applied and the trucks of 40 tons allowed on the Swiss territory. In the following analysis of impacts (section 4), these two levels of the tax will be introduced

---

[4] These computations neglect the transport made by foreign trucks in Switzerland. Actually, it is supposed that the transport made by Swiss trucks abroad are equivalent to the transport of foreign trucks in Switzerland. Note also that the computation of the tons transported is based on the authorised tons for each category of trucks. More details on these computations are given in the Message of the Federal Council of 11 September 1996.

successively, and, at the same time, the 28 tons restriction will be raised. The impacts of adding a toll at some Alpine passes will be also examined.

5.4   The network model and its calibration

A thorough analysis of freight transportation on a network, with all its alternative solutions including intermodal transport, requires the separate identification of all the transport operations and their characteristics. In the NODUS network model (Jourquin 1995), which is used in this paper like in our earlier paper on this topic, the modes are naturally distinguished but also the different transportation means used on the same infrastructure. Likewise, the operations of loading, unloading, transhipping and transiting are separated. This separate identification allows the adequate handling of combined transport by creating a fictitious expanded network, or virtual network, made of virtual links corresponding to every operation and linking them in a systematic way in the geographic space.

The difficulty with that methodology is that it leads to the creation of rather large and complex networks. In the present case, there are about 9,500 road and rail links in the digitised trans-European geographic multimodal network, from which something like 180,000 virtual links are generated. But the structured notation used for the geographic nodes and links allows an easy and automatic generation of all the virtual links which are needed (Jourquin and Beuthe, 1996).

With such a set-up it is possible to attach to each type of virtual segment its corresponding cost function. Altogether, the costs included in the modelling have three components: the costs directly related to the vehicles and their crew, the handling cost and the opportunity cost of time. Obviously, for a multimodal transport, the costs of the successive operations of the different modes must be added. But, if we consider a simple unimodal trip by a specific transport unit, the transport cost per ton is assumed to be a linear increasing function of distance, which can be written as:

$$C^{\theta} = (f^{\theta} + l^{\theta} + o^{\theta}) * H^{\theta} + (m^{\theta} + (f^{\theta} + o^{\theta})/v^{\theta}) * s,$$

where θ indicates a particular means/mode choice. H^{θ} is the total time for loading and unloading, and s is the distance. For a particular θ, the first part of the equation is a constant, while the second part is proportional to the distance. The value of all the parameters is given in the appendix with some additional explanations. Their meaning is the following:

- f^{θ} corresponds to the vehicle fixed cost, per ton and per hour of standard use;
- l^{θ} is the additional cost of labour per ton and per hour of handling the goods at the points of origin and destination;
- o^{θ} is the opportunity cost, per ton and per hour, of the capital tied into the goods during the transport;
- m^{θ} is the variable cost of moving one ton over one km;
- v^{θ} is the vehicle's average speed.

For intermodal transport, the transhipment costs are also taken into account. Specific transit costs are also included for the trains' time cost of waiting at the frontiers, and for the road and tunnel tolls imposed on the trucks. Note that the trucks' speed is adjusted somewhat in proportion to the time they are not allowed to run on the different national networks, for instance on Sundays.

Given a matrix of origins and destinations which defines a set of transportation tasks, the total cost of transportation over the virtual network can be minimised by the choice, for each pair of origin and destination, of the cheapest mode, means and route, the alternatives of combined transport included. Thus, summing up all the costs defined above, the following total cost is minimised for each origin/destination:

$$
TC = \sum_{Origin-Destination} \sum_{Mode\,/\,Mean\,/\,Route} \left[\sum_{Unloading} costs + \sum_{Loading} costs + \sum_{Moving} costs + \sum_{Transshipment} costs + \sum_{Simple\,Transit} costs \right]
$$

Naturally, the results of such an exhaustive and detailed analysis can be aggregated in order to compute the modes' market shares; all the itineraries as well as the combinations of modes can also be identified.

It is worth underlining at this point that the cost minimisation is made on the basis of an all-or-nothing procedure for each origin/destination pair, so that all the traffic (of a given commodity) between two nodes is assigned to the same mode/means/route combination. This follows from the specification of the costs per ton which are not increasing functions of the total quantities transported on a particular link. Such an approach supposes normally that there is no capacity constraint. In general, this rather strong hypothesis can be accepted when annual transport flows over a large network are studied. In the present case, we are aware of some capacity constraints at a few passes across the Alpine chain. But, the implementation of an equilibrium model in a large network is a difficult task which will require additional work. In the meantime, the results given by an "all-or-nothing" assignment procedure are worth considering.

The results obtained can be taken as estimates of transport demand for the different modes and means and itineraries under two hypotheses: that the shippers are actually minimising the generalised cost of transport, and that the carriers' tariffs bear a close relationship with the operating transport cost, at least at the margin for 'contestable' transport. Both hypotheses can certainly be debated. But, even if they are accepted as a reasonable approximation, the results of this cost minimisation have to be assessed with caution, and the model must be calibrated before proceeding further. To begin with, despite the number of cost elements included in the functions, the total cost analysed does not fully match the definition of generalised cost that is supposed to be minimised by shippers. Decision factors like reliability, safety, information and other services which are provided by the carriers are not included in the functions, because their cost equivalent for the shippers is not known. Moreover, there may be technical or administrative factors which lead the railways to not choose the shortest (and normally the cheapest) route between some origins and destinations. And, then again, the carriers' cost used in the model is only a proxy for the tariffs paid by the shippers, and which are generally unknown.

For all these reasons, adjustments have been made to the cost functions, in order to obtain a better fit of the initial simulations to the observed market shares, and to take into account in that way the decision factors which cannot be included formally in the modelling of the costs.

5.5   The simulation of the new taxation scheme

The initial simulations used as reference basis are naturally the simulations of the present situation where only 28-ton trucks are allowed in Switzerland. Thus, the calibration of the model made in our earlier paper on the impacts of the suppression of the 28 tons restriction (Demilie, Dupuis, Jourquin and Beuthe, 1998) can be used again. Complete details on the full calibration of the model can be found in this paper. In effect, two distinct basic simulations have been made for the manufactured goods and the non-manufactured goods respectively, in order to take into account the different values of these goods, i.e. 231,000 BEF versus 24,000 BEF, and the corresponding opportunity costs, as well as their specific service requirements. Moreover, since hardly any non-manufactured goods are transported by combined transport, this transport option was not included in the simulation relative to non-manufactured goods.[5]

The database used concerns the flows of goods to/from Italy crossing the Alpine Chain in 1994. Regional origin-destination pairs were available for the following countries: Switzerland (12 regions), Italy (6), France (9), Austria (4) and Germany (11).[6] The other flows were aggregated per country. In order to obtain a point-to-point O-D matrix, centroïds were created in each region as additional nodes of origin and destination. Then, the total flows of goods were assigned by small bundles among these centroïds by random drawing. This 'Monte-Carlo' procedure can be justified by the fact that the centroïds are not evenly distributed over the network, but are more numerous in industrialised areas where the density of the network is greater. To that extent, it is likely that their distribution over the geographic space corresponds to the distribution of the real origins and destinations. A more complete explanation, as well as a test of that procedure, is given in Jourquin and Beuthe (1996).

Table 5.6 gives a comparison of the estimated modal splits of the calibrated model under the constraint of the 28 tons restriction to the observed modal splits.

Table 5.6 Observed and estimated modal splits

		Observed %	Est. 28 t. %
Manufactured goods	Rail	42	44
	Road	68	66
Non- manufactured goods	Rail	32	32
	Road	68	68

Source: Own computation

The first two columns of Table 5.7 give more detailed information on the modal distribution at the different national borders with Italy. Despite some remaining imperfections, which result from the difficulty to model in all details some peculiarities of the network and its functioning, we think that these results suitably fit the observed data, and that they provide a good basis for analysing what would happen if the new taxation scheme was introduced.

---

[5] Practically, the manufactured goods correspond to the NSTR category 9. No category of non-manufactured goods uses combined transport by more than 5 per cent.

[6] These data were provided by the Eidg. Verkehrs- und Energiewirtschaftsdepartement, Dienst für Gesamtverkehrsfragen (Bern).

The results of the two taxation scenarios, at the (SF) 1.6 cent. and 3 cent. levels respectively, are given in the next two columns of Table 5.7. They must be compared to the results of the estimation under the 28 tons constraint which provides the simulation of reference for the other simulations. Naturally, all the simulations have been made under the hypothesis that the tolls and regulations imposed by the neighbouring countries remained unchanged.

Table 5.7 Observed and estimated modal split by border

		Observed		Est. 28 t.		1.6 cent SF		3 cent SF	
		Mi. t.	%	Mi. t.	%	Mi. t.	%	Mi. t.	%
Swiss/Italian border	Rail	14.8	78	14.7	67	2.9	9	11.1	47
	Road	4.1	22	7.1	33	29.7	91	12.7	53
French/Italian border	Rail	8.6	20	8.5	25	7.7	26	8.3	25
	Road	34.4	80	25.6	75	21.7	74	25.1	75
Austrian/Italian border	Rail	9.6	32	10.6	29	9.4	31	10.5	30
	Road	20.4	68	25.4	71	20.5	69	24.1	70
Total	Rail	33.	36	33.8	37	20.0	22	30.0	33
	Road	58.9	64	58.1	63	71.9	78	61.9	67

Source: Own computation

First, it clearly appears that the introduction of a tax of (SF) 1.6 cent. per ton/km, with the simultaneous suppression of the 28 tons limit and of the circulation tax, would change the pattern of traffic dramatically through the Alpine chain. The most important change would occur at the Swiss/Italian border where road traffic would be multiplied fourfold, while rail traffic would decrease in an even greater rate. Hence, the modal split between the modes would be very strongly modified. Globally, traffic through Switzerland would increase from 21.8 to 32.6 million tons. This change of volume through Switzerland would correspond to a decrease of the same amount through Austria and France, but the modal split between these two countries would not be much changed, since both road and rail traffic would decrease. Thus, from the Swiss point of view, the end result of this scheme would be an increase of the total traffic through Switzerland with a strong modal shift towards road transport.

The imposition of a tax of (SF) 3 cent. per ton/km would produce somewhat different results. Then, road traffic at the Swiss/Italian border would also expand, but this expansion would be less dramatic: from 7.1 to

12.7 million ton. Taking into account the larger loading capacity of 40 ton trucks, this would correspond to a 19 per cent increase in the number of truck movements; still a substantial increase. At the same time, rail traffic through Switzerland would decrease from 14.7 to 11.1 million ton. The global traffic increase through that country would be modest: from 21.8 to 23.8 millions of tons. In Austria and France, both rail and road traffic would decrease, but only slightly. Thus, the main result of this particular tax would be a modal shift towards road transport in Switzerland.

Table 5.8 presents the modal splits computed on the basis of the tons/kms transported through the Swiss territory, on one hand, and transported on the networks of the other countries, on the other hand.

Table 5.8
Observed and estimated modal splits in t/km by region (millions)

	28 tons		40 tons		1.6 cent. SF		3 cent. SF	
	Mi. t/km	%	Mi. t/km	%	Mi. t/km	%	Mi. t/km	%
Switzerland								
Rail	3362	67	189	2	658	8	2533	46
Road	1638	33	11347	98	7149	92	2929	54
Total	5001	100	11537	100	7808	100	5462	100
Other countries								
Rail	38451	44	20423	26	29074	35	36937	43
Road	48724	56	59104	74	53811	65	49277	57
Total	87176	100	79528	100	82886	100	86215	100
Total								
Rail	41814	45	20612	23	29733	33	39470	43
Road	50363	55	70452	77	60960	67	52207	57
Total	92176	100	91064	100	90694	100	91676	100

Source : Own computation.

When comparing the modal split at the Swiss/Italian border in terms of tons (table 5.7) and t/km (Table 5.8), it is seen that they are very close to each other in every scenario. This indicates that the average distance of transport by truck and by train in Switzerland is not much affected by the type of scenario.

The comparison of the total tons/kms transported under the different scenarios (last line of Table 5.8) is also interesting. When 40 t. trucks are allowed on the Swiss road network, it is seen that the total decreases from 92,176 to 91,064 millions tons/kms. This is not surprising since the 28 t. weight limit was an incentive to make a detour through France or Austria. Another factor is the rail shipments decrease which are made over somewhat longer distances. Note, however, that the opening of the Swiss network to 40 tons trucks without any compensating toll induces also some truckers to

110

make a detour, this time through Switzerland, in order to avoid the Austrian and French road tolls. This is a practice they will abandon when the 1.6 cent. tax is introduced. This is shown by the further reduction to 90,694 millions tons/kms, when the tax is imposed, despite some increase of the rail shipments. When the tax is set at SF 3 cent. per t/km, Swiss roads become more expensive and rail shipments obtain a larger market share. As a consequence, the total of tons/kms increases to the level of 91,676 million.

Table 5.9 shows clearly that, if the 28 t. limit is abolished, the tax of SF 1.6 cent. per t/km would not be sufficient to dissuade the truckers from using the Swiss roads more intensively. Truck/kms, which include the substitution effect of 40 t. instead of 28 t trucks, would increase by 191 per cent. In the case of a SF 3 cent. tax per t/km, truck/kms would increase by 19 per cent only. This is still a substantial increase, particularly if it is seen in the context of an expanding flow of international transport.

Table 5.9 Variations of veh./kms in Switzerland

	1.6 cent. SF		3 cent. SF	
	Mi. v/km	%	Mi v/km	%
Rail	-5.5	-80	-1.7	-25
Road	282.7	191	28.4	19

Source : Own computation.

Table 5.10 gives an estimation of the tax revenue in the two scenarios. Note that they concern only the traffic between Switzerland and the rest of Occidental European on the one hand, and Italy on the other. The domestic traffic within Switzerland, the traffic from Switzerland to countries other than Italy, or transit traffic not involving Italy, on which the tax would also be imposed on the Swiss territory, are not included in these computations. It is seen that the revenue from the 1.6 cent. tax would be greater than the revenue from the 3 cent. tax., because the higher price effect would be more than compensated by the lower volume effect.

Table 5.10 Estimation of the tax revenue

	1.6 cent. (billions of BF)	3 cent. (billions of BF)
Federal state	4.6	3.5
County	2.3	1.8
Total	6.9	5.3

Source : Own computation

111

As mentioned above, the Swiss government envisages imposing additional road tolls at some Alpine passes in order to take into account the exceptional cost of their infrastructure. The tolls which are considered at the present time were given in Table 5.5. By including them now with the 3 cent. tax, it is possible to compute their joint impact on traffic flows. These are given in the third column of Table 5.11.

Comparing these flows and modal splits with the results of the 3 cent. tax alone, which are given in the second column, it is seen that the tolls mainly have a double effect: a diversion of part of the Swiss traffic to Austria and France, and a very strong change of the Swiss modal split in favour of rail transport, while the Austrian and French modal splits are barely affected by the tolls. This induced modal shift in Switzerland is so strong that it appears also in the comparison with the present situation.

Table 5.11 Observed and estimated modal split by border

		28 tons		3 cent. SF		3 cent. SF + T	
Border ital./		Mi. t.	%	Mi. t.	%	Mi. t.	%
Swiss	Rail	14.7	67	11.1	47	19	96
	Road	7.1	33	12.7	53	0.9	4
French	Rail	8.5	25	8.3	25	8.4	24
	Road	25.6	75	25.1	75	26.5	76
Austrian	Rail	10.6	29	10.5	30	10.4	29
	Road	25.4	71	24.1	70	26.1	71
Total	Rail	33.8	37	30.0	33	37.8	41
	Road	58.1	63	61.9	67	53.4	59

Source : Own computation

It appears then that this joint scheme of taxation would overshoot the target of maintaining approximately the present situation which is a likely objective for the Swiss authorities: the total flows through Switzerland would be reduced by 9 per cent, while most of this traffic would be handled by trains. Obviously, this scheme must be also assessed in the context of the present negotiation with the European Union and the neighbouring countries. Presumably, these taxes and tolls should be seen as much too high by the European Commission: altogether they would amount to more that 400 SF (one way) on some itineraries across Switzerland. It is also likely that the Austrian and French authorities would be reluctant to accept a sizeable diversion of traffic through their territory without any adjustment of their transport policy.

In view of these results, we tried to find out at which level of tolls the traffic flows and modal splits, which are induced presently by the 28 tons limit, could be approximately maintained. A few iterations made with different sets of tolls indicated that only the tolls at the San Bernardino and the St-Gothard needed to be lowered. Indeed, the suggested level of 150 SF for these two tolls is particularly high. We then found out that tolls of about 25 SF at the St-Gothard and 45 SF at the San Bernardino would suffice to maintain the present situation.

5.6   Conclusions

The main conclusion to be drawn from the above results is that the introduction of a tax lower than SF 3 cent. per ton/km, computed on the basis of the maximum authorised vehicle weight, without any restriction on trucks' weight, would lead to such a road traffic increase through Switzerland that it would not be acceptable, in all likelihood, by the Swiss authorities and population.

A tax of 3 cent. per ton/km would not be sufficient to limit road freight traffic to a level similar to the one obtained by the 28 t. limit on a truck's weight. Road traffic, measured in tons or in tons/kms, would increase by 79 per cent, while rail traffic would decrease by 25 per cent. However, larger 40 ton trucks would be substituted by 28 ton trucks, so that the real road traffic measured in trucks/kms would increase (only) by 19 per cent, still a sizeable increase in a context of continuing expansion of international transports.

These changes brought about by the 3 cent. SF tax would result mainly from a modal shift within Switzerland. It does not appear that Austria and France would be much affected by this particular taxation scheme. Hence, these two countries would have no particular reason to change their policy to counter some induced negative effects on their territory.

However, Swiss authorities are also considering the introduction of additional tolls at some Alpine passes. Their joint effect with the 3 cent. tax would clearly overshoot a target of maintaining the present modal split and traffic flows through Switzerland: the total of transports through Swiss territory would decrease by 9 per cent and most of it would be handled by freight trains. In all likelihood, such a result would not be acceptable by the other countries. We then found out that tolls of about 45 SF at the San Bernardino and 25 SF at the St-Gothard, with the other proposed tolls unchanged, would be sufficient to maintain the present modal splits and traffic flows within Switzerland and the other countries.

113

Acknowledgements

This research is part of the E.U. research program COST 328 on Integrated Strategic Infrastructure Networks in Europe. We wish to thank Fabio Rossera (IRE, Lugano), A. Reggiani (U.of Bologna) and R. Maggi (U. of Zürich and Lugano) for helping us with their useful information and comments. Our grateful thanks also to Eidg. Verkehrs- und Energiewirtschaftsdepartement, Dienst für Gesamtverkehrsfragen (Bern) for providing data on international traffic flows. Moreover, we thank M.P. Allain (CNR), A. Bechet (SNCB), S. Bolis (U.of Lugano), M. Caruso Frezza (FS, Italy), M. Clabecq (EUCOTRANS), P. Dooz (TRW), F.Jennes (ITR) J. Langevin (FEBETRA), and W. Zhender (INTERCONTAINER) for their information about costs and transport operations.

Nevertheless, the authors bear sole responsibility for the results presented in this paper. They are grateful to the "Services Fédéraux des Affaires Scientifiques, Techniques et Culturelles" (SSTC) for granting financial support for this research.

References

Beuthe M. and B.Jourquin (1994), *L'influence du tour de rôle sur les coûts de la navigation intérieure*, Revue d'Economie Régionale et Urbaine No. 3, 417-427.

Bolis S., Reggiani A. and Nicoletti A., *Methods and models analysing transalpine freight transport : an overview*, University of Bologna.

CEMAT, (1995), *Europe speaks intermodal*, booklet, Roma.

CFF (1990), *Le printemps du rail*, information booklet of SF, Berne.

Chatelus G. and Torricelli G-P.(1994), *Coopérations transalpines et infrastructures de transport, une étude de cas sur les relations de l'Italie avec la Suisse et la France*, I.N.R.E.T.S. et I.R.E.

Coleman R., (1995), *La "perméabilité" de la chaîne des Alpes charnière entre le nord et le sud de l'Europe*, CEE-Forum dello Sviluppo, Turin.

Comité National Routier., (1995), "Coûts de références", *Les fiches des cahiers de l'observatoire du CNR*, Paris.

Conseil fédéral suisse., (1996), *Message relatif à une loi fédérale concernant la redevance sur le trafic des poids lourds liée aux prestations*.

Crainic T.G., M.Florian, J.Guélat and H.Spiess (1990), *Strategic Planning of Freight Transportation: STAN, An Interactive Graphic System*, Transportation Research Record 1283.

Crainic T.G., M. Florian and D. Larin (1993), *STAN, New Developments*, Centre de Recherche sur les Transports, Université de Montréal, papier de recherche No. 942.

Demilie L., B. Jourquin and M. Beuthe (1996), *A Sensitivity Analysis of Transportation Modes Market Shares on a Multimodal Network, The Case of Dry Bulk Transports between Benelux/Germany and Spain*, Policy Analysis of Networks (ed. by C. Capineri and P. Rietveld) Ashgate: Avebury, 1997, 235-252.

Demilie L., V. Dupuis, B. Jourquin and M. Beuthe (1998), *On the Crossing of the Alpine Chair and the Swiss Regulation of Trucking*, Accessibility, Trade and Locational Behaviour (ed. by A. Reggiani), Ashgate: Avebury, 1998, 303-333.

Deming W.E. (1978), *On a rational relationship for certain costs of handling motor freight over the platform*, Transportation Journal, 17, 5-11.

DFTCE-Sigmaplan (1991), *Transalpiner Güterverkehr, Auswirkungrn des Gotthard-Strassentunnels auf den Güterverkehr, Schlussbericht über die Entwicklung 1980-1989*, Bern.

DFTCE-Sigmaplan (1995), *Alpenqueneder Güterverkehr auf Strasse und Schiene 1994, Alpenbogen Ventimiglia bis Wien*, GVF-Auftrag nr.242, Dienst für Gesamtverkehrsfragen, Bern.

Gathon H-J., (1991), *La performance relative des chemins de fer européens: gestion et autonomie*, Ph.D.thesis, University of Liège.

Guélat J., M.Florian and T.G. Crainic (1990), *A Multimode Multiproduct Network Assignment Model for Strategic Planning of Freight Flows*, Transportation Science, 24, 25-39.

Harker P.T. (1987), *Predicting Intercity Freight Flows*, VNU Science Press, Utrecht, Pays-Bas.

Jourquin B. (1995), *Un outil d'analyse économique des transports de marchandises sur des réseaux multi-modaux et multi-produits: Le réseau virtuel, concepts, méthodes et applications*, Ph.D. Thesis, Facultés Universitaires Catholiques de Mons.

Jourquin B. and M. Beuthe (1996), *Transportation Policy Analysis with a Geographical Information System : The Virtual Network of Freight Transportation in Europe*, Transportation Research C, Vol. 4, No. 6, 359-371.

Ministero dei Transporti e della Navigazione (1995), Conto Nazionale dei Transporti, Roma, Italy.

Russo R. (1995), *Combined transport through the Alps, a comparative analysis at the Austrian-Italian border*, Vienne University of Economics and Business Administration.

Sandonnini P.P. (1991), *Ricerca sulle problematiche dello scambio internazionale delle merci attraverso i valichi alpini*, per conto dell'Unione Regionale delle Camere di Commercio Industria Artigianato e Agricoltura del Veneto.

Schweizer Eisenbahn-Revue (10/1993), *Gotthard and Lötschberg: the finishing line of the third stage draws near*, Bern.

Senn L. (1995), *Il trasporto attraverso le Alpi, Nuove infratrutture di trasporto nelle Alpi: la necessita di un approccio globale e sistemico*, Uniontrasporti, Milan.

U.I.C. (1994), *European Infrastructure Master Plan*, Paris.

Appendix : Values of the parameters[7]

The values are expressed in 1994 BEF: f, l, and o are in BEF per ton and per hour, m in BEF per ton/km.

Table 5.A 1

Parameters	Railway		Truck	
	Combined	Traditional	40 tons	28 tons
f	13	9	63	95
l	-	2.05	60.28	90.42
o (manufactured)	2.64	2.64	2.64	2.64
o (non-manufactured)	0.27	0.27	0.27	0.27
m	0.80 [a]	0.78 [a]	0.75 [b]	1.05 [b]
Average loading (tons)	496.8	488.8	16.6	11.1
% empty	20	17	21	21

a : includes fuel, part of maintenance and various administrative costs.
b : includes fuel, maintenance and repair, and the cost of the tires.

The parameters for the railways are based on the published statistics of the Belgian railway company (S.N.C.B.). As there exists a large number of possible engine-carriage combinations, we have defined a standard traditional and a standard combined train. Note that the Belgian cost data have been adjusted for each national railway company, in order to take account of their varying efficiency. The adjustment coefficients, which are given in the next table, are based on the work of Gathon (1991). Jourquin (1995) gives more details on the computation of the parameters.

---

[7] The road data are from the Comité National Routier, France (1994) and FEBETRA, Belgium. The specific combined railway data are provided by INTERCONTAINER, EUROTRANS and TRW.

Table 5.A 2

Railway company	Productivity index	Relative index to Belgium
SJ	1	0.592
NS	0.762	0.777
SNCF	0.7	0.846
RENFE	0.69	0.858
VR	0.675	0.877
CFF	0.667	0.888
CH	0.666	0.889
BR	0.653	0.907
CFL	0.637	0.929
SNCB	0.592	1
FS	0.583	1.015
CP	0.563	1.052
DB	0.528	1.121
TCDD	0.352	1.682

6 Network Impacts of Just-in-Time Production

BO TERJE KALSAAS

6.1 Introduction

Just-in-time (JIT) production, meaning a system for organising labour processes, is now common around the world. It has its origin in the Japanese automobile industry and in Toyota Motor Corporation in particular (Womack et al. 1990). This paper addresses the mechanisms in JIT-manufacturing related to logistics and location of subcontractors of OEM-parts that provide JIT-supply. The aim is to contribute with causal explanations of these relationships, which are methodologically inspired by Sayer (1992).

The relationship between subcontractors and principal firms is necessary. One cannot exist without the other. They comprise a system of production orders, procedures for logistics, production contracts, quality systems, power relationships, etc. In such a system it is important to identify mechanisms that have the capability to produce spatial impacts that might occur under different societal conditions. The subcontractors and principal firm in the system illustrate a case of quasi integration (Leborgne and Lipietz 1992) where the principal firm is often the dominating agent (Perroux 1955/1979, 1988).

The paper builds on a previous study of Scandinavian and Japanese automotive industries focusing on JIT-production and the impact on transport and location (Kalsaas 1995a, 1995b). The applied case data include Volvo Car and Saab Automobile in Sweden (Figure 6.1), and Nissan and Toyota (TMC) car factories in Japan (Figure 6.2), and subcontractors to these. Data are also gathered from Mitsubishi's headquarters in Tokyo and from carrier companies. Primary data regarding Nissan and Toyota were gathered in 1995, while data from Volvo and Saab were obtained in 1994-95.

Figure 6.1 Volvo and Saab in Sweden

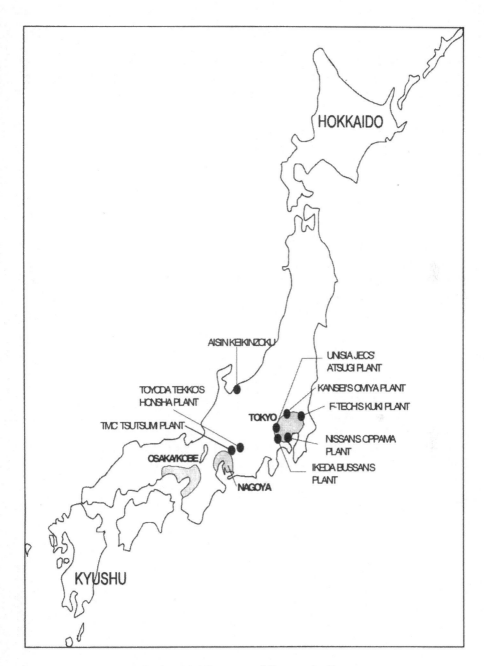

Figure 6.2 Nissan and Toyota in Japan

6.1.1 JIT-production and supply of OEM parts

In the JIT-production paradigm there are two superior operative perspectives, which should be comprised by measures for social organisation, methods and techniques that submit to (op. cit.):

- reduction of all types of waste (reduction of costs), e.g. human effort (working hours), capital to machines and tools, inventory in stock, buffer and process, manufacturing space, etc.; and
- flexible response to changing demand of diversified products (customer orientation).

The principle of fast, continuous and small lot production is derived from these two main operative perspectives while there is also a continual search for best practice, which requires collective involvement by workers, and integration of suppliers to the principal firm's production system. In addition, increased outsourcing of non-core production and services is expected in order to cut costs, reduce risk and improve flexibility. Increased outsourcing is a strategy that enlarges capacity in existing plants without huge new investments. At the same time, in order to cut transaction costs, a tendency is expected where the principal firm puts effort into reducing the number of suppliers followed up by designing vehicles with fewer components (increased sub assembly) and by making more parts interchangeable across models (increased standardised platforms). The same cost-cutting reasons result in a tendency towards organising the supplier base in tiers.

Further splitting up the principles above in subordinate principles, methods and techniques is a matter of necessary detailing. Some attributes that are regarded as core aspects in this respect are listed below in connection with the principle of fast, continuous and small lot production. These are:

- small batch production of diversified products and customer orientation;
- time compression of all linkages and processes in the production chain, response time to end users included;
- minimise stock and buffers;
- increased outsourcing of work;
- increased quasi-integration and integration of suppliers to principal firms' production;
- emphasise total quality control; and
- priority to suppliers that are located in the same area.

Although there are variations, the findings in the Scandinavian cases confirm that there is considerable ongoing restructuring of production in terms of time compression of labour processes, time compression in the links between subcontractors and between final assemblers and subcontractors. The objectives of this are: simplifying material flows, reduction of stock and buffers, small batch production, quality control in production, quality assurance of subcontractors, utilisation of EDI to integrate agents in production chains, increased outsourcing of components, tiering, demand driven production chains and time compression of customers' response time. In these respects, the selected cases are "critical cases" for this study.

The Japanese cases are also expected to follow the model of JIT-production, where logistics play a major role. There are, however, important differences among the cases, and Toyota's Tsutsumi plant is outstanding in respect of controlling the labour process (Kalsaas 1995a, Kalsaas and Takeuchi 1996). The production system found in the investigated cases is also in a process of change. Changes affect location and transport and the JIT-production system. These changes will be discussed at the end of the paper as they do not stem from the JIT-production system, but from other forces of regional change. First, I will try to explain the forces that stem from the production system itself, which is the main purpose of the paper.

JIT-production gives a new role to external transport, that ought to be seen as the conveyor, or pipeline of inventory, which makes it possible to achieve JIT for consignees and manufacturers, or to be so close to this as possible. It can therefore be claimed that transport is a force of production and that JIT-supply is a necessary condition for JIT-production of diversified tangible products. Compressed transport time and supplying OEM (Original Equipment Manufacturing) parts and components in small lots with high frequency make it possible for the principal firm to minimise parts inventories and compress throughput time and make gains in flexibility, customer response and fast capital turnover, and thereby gaining competitive advantages.

Following from this we can argue that the qualities of fast supply (time) and reliability have to be met by the organisation of transport when linking functions together in time and space. Seen in a historical perspective, the transport of OEM material in JIT-production and in other post-Fordist technological paradigms, links together in time and space what was integrated in one firm under Fordism.

6.1.2   Reliability versus geographical separation and time compression

Reliable supply might be described as precise and predictable supply. Reliability might also be thought of as certainty and control of factors that might

123

impose uncertainty and reduce precision in the movement of external goods. This follows the regulation approach by identifying the main contradictions between the reliability of supply on one hand and geographical separation of production and time compression of supply links on the other.

Increasing geographical distance in terms of the time required for moving goods between final assemblers and affiliated subcontractors reduces the reliability of the supply, or material flow, if this is not met with countermeasures. Minimising this distance means that stability of supply is strengthened by close location, for instance as in a vertically integrated plant or in a geographical cluster of networking firms. The same can be said for the links between subcontractors on different tiers in production chains, although perhaps less directly.

What matters for geographical separation in supply chains is time, the time it takes to carry out a consignment; in other words the external transport, and affiliated activities, of the supply lead time in the case of a technical division of labour.

Close location might be thought of as supply from a department within a company (vertical integrated production) while a considerable distance, or remote location, might be thought of as global sourcing. Global sourcing by sea transport is theoretically possible in a JIT-system. However, this is at the cost of flexibility in supply and inventory which is one of the main goals in JIT.

Spatial division of labour is nothing new to capitalist production, even though it is argued that JIT-production works in the direction of further extension of the spatial division of labour. What is specific is the time compression of activities in the relationship between subcontractors and final assemblers and between subcontractors on different tiers. It is thought that this causes a reduction in supply reliability, since there are fewer time buffers present in the actual production chains to balance any disturbances. The contradiction between reliable supply and separation in space is thus growing as a function of increased time compression in production and supply.

A second contradiction is between spatial division of labour and time compression on one hand and reliable supply on the other. This might be overcome or eased by different measures, such as relocation, establishing a deposit and JIT- terminal, improved goods transport concepts (organisation, technology), improved infrastructure for transport (simplifying, removing bottlenecks such as ferries, etc.), improved transport technology (faster and more appropriate means), electronic data interchange (EDI) or other distance-adjusting technologies (Hepworth and Ducatel 1992), such as intelligent transportation systems. Keeping materials in stock and having buffers are also measures to ease matters, though they are not wanted, since zero stock is one of the main objectives of the system.

124

The agents in the outlined concept are the final assembler as the principal firm and layers of suppliers/subcontractors. In addition, there are carriers and forwarders, and authorities on a different level, who deal with regulation and operation of transport infrastructure, land use, allocation of public investments, taxation, planning, etc.

The strength of agglomeration forces and impact of geographical proximity are likely to be weakened over time as the procedures in the relationship become a routine (Burmeister and Colletis-Whal 1997). A counter-force here is the registered increase in the turnover of models (design intensive production) as this will require new procedures, and maybe new relationships have to be established. The Swedish final assemblers are increasing the time compression in this regard to the level of the Japanese cases. They seem to follow the tendency of standardising under-the-skin parts across different models, and new models might not be completely new developments as the practise was before. Changes in logistics etc. are further confirmed when new models are launched.

The importance of establishing a routine between the producing agents and avoiding disturbances of any kind, are also arguments for establishing lasting relationship between the agents. The agents are therefore also likely to strive for "organisational proximity" as well as geographical proximity (Burmeister and Colletis-Whal 1997, Storper and Walker 1989). The strength of these forces will depend on the parts and components in question.

From this basic discussion of reliability of supply, time compression and separation in spatial distance between vendors and customers, the conceptualisation is extended to include different aspects of logistics and external goods movement as illustrated in Figure 6.3.

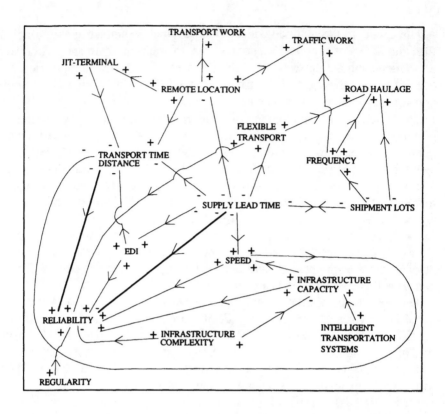

Note: The lines between the text fields in the figure illustrate conceived relationships or links between the actual aspects. The plus or minus signs guiding the relationships indicate expected value of impact. For instance, relatively increased compression of supply lead time (-) is likely to demand faster speed in moving goods (+), which again has a positive impact on the reliability of supply (+). The direction of the arrows in the figure indicates the main direction of influence.

Figure 6.3
Time compression and external movement of OEM material

6.1.3   Transport in JIT-production

The two major contradictions above are highlighted in Figure 6.3 by thicker lines. Reduction of transport time distance (the time it takes to carry out a consignment) in terms of external goods movement is likely to lead to relatively increased reliability in supply links. Compression of supply lead time, or subcontractors' customer response, is expected to decrease the reliability. The pressure towards shorter supply lead time in JIT is thus in itself a cause of instability and a source of distortion in the model.

The emphasis on compressed supply lead time, or subcontractors' customer response, is related to the underlying theory of competitive strategies of firms (Schoenberger 1987). Supply lead time refers to the elapsed time from which call-off is issued to a supplier until the ordered material is received at a defined location (e.g. gate 5, building 2) for unloading. The notion of supply lead time is central to understand the strength of agglomeration forces between subcontractors and principal firms. It represents the available time for goods transport.

When interpreting Figure 6.3, only one link should be considered at a time and the others thought of as fixed, so that the expected relative impact is focused. However, the pressure towards increased compression of the goods movement part of the supply lead time, as in JIT-supply, is considered to be a basic condition for the conceptualisation. The time for production from the supplying agents side is thought of as fixed in the analysis. External goods movement is moreover presupposed to be organised as direct transport, and the scale of the material flows between agents and transport is regarded to be fixed.

The time predictability for delivery associated with reliable supply is of crucial importance in JIT-supply since there is expected to be almost zero stock and only small buffers of parts to balance disturbances. Components are not to be delivered earlier or later. Too early, and thus unexpected, delivery is likely to cause disruptions in the production system. High reliability will therefore be positively related to the stability of the supply system.

The part of the infrastructure that is of interest for transport refers to those assets that make it possible for trucks and other means of transport to move goods from one place to another. Transport telematics and intelligent vehicle highway systems, such as route guidance, vehicle location and traffic monitoring and control, are conceived to be part of the infrastructure. Their presence is expected to increase the infrastructure capacity and thus allow higher speed as well as collision reduction and improved road safety (Levine and Underwood 1995). Contingencies such as road accidents might cause severe disturbances to the material flow if there are blocked roads for instance.

Electronic data interchange (EDI) is conceived in the model to ease the contradiction between reliable supply and spatial division of labour by speeding up the communication process between the agents in production chains, freighting companies and drivers included. EDI is related to intelligent transportation systems such that electronic data interchange between transport means and traffic monitoring technology makes it possible to reduce the transport time distance by selecting the fastest route. The denotation of EDI includes technology for tracking goods, and EDI and intelligent transportation systems might be thought of as distance adjusting technology (Hepworth and Ducatel 1992).

Although it is not shown in Figure 6.3, a specialised logistics service is also conceived to ease the problems that are likely to disturb supply. Logistics services might be so-called "third party logistics" that refer to the outsourcing of extended logistic services. This may include guaranteed reliable delivery, responsibility of the communication between the actual vendors and customers, warehousing, loading and unloading. The market for such advanced logistic services is stimulated by the increased role of transport in production related to JIT and time compressed customer-supplier links. This follows from the uncertainty imposed by JIT that increases the demand for expertise to control material flow and make gains in precision. Third party logistics also represents an extended division of labour.

Remote location for subcontractors in relation to customers becomes increasingly disadvantageous when the supply lead time is compressed, and thus makes agglomeration relatively favourable for the manufacturing agents. This follows from the concept discussed above in relationship to reliable supply. The transport time grows per se for relatively remotely located subcontractors, as indicated in Figure 6.3. While a JIT- terminal and deposit will reduce the transport time distance in relationship to the ordering agent and thus improve reliability, certainty and precision.

The capability of moving OEM materials relatively fast is directly and positively related to the reliability of supply as it makes it possible to balance disturbances and delays by increasing the speed. This is related to both transport means and infrastructure. The capability of the means of transport is not visualised in Figure 6.3.

The growing complexity of the infrastructure for transport also decreases the reliability of the supply system by imposing relative uncertainty and perhaps also reductions in flexibility. Complexity in this sense may be made up of numerous infrastructure elements in the transport route, e.g. ferries, bridges, tunnels, roads, harbours, and not least terminals, which may attract contingencies such as road accidents, bad weather conditions, strikes and lock outs. The complexity aspects of external infrastructure find their parallel in the in-house production sphere, where one of the first steps to improve throughput time is to simplify the material flow by line oriented layout and a reduced number of operations. The throughput time, or total cycle time, in the production of tangible commodities refers to the accumulated time for handling orders, production planning, internal transport, assembly, and shipment of finished goods.

Increased infrastructure complexity is furthermore assumed to reduce the infrastructure capacity, which again is modelled to be positively interrelated with the speed of goods movement and reliability. For example, relatively lower average speeds of transport indicate relatively less reliability or stability.

It is conceived that flexible transport is demanded for increased time compression of supply lead time and quick customer response. Flexible transport refers to the capability of fast response to new material demands, for instance the suppliers' capability to transport components that are to be replaced in assembly on short notice as in the case of emergency orders. Such flexible capability improves the stability of the system by reducing uncertainty, as it is regarded as an element in a "safety-net" for the receiving agent in the supply chain. In this sense it should be obvious that transport and subcontracting substitute for stock and buffers for the final assembler.

Trucks of different types and sizes, according to lot sizes, increase the flexibility in transport in contrast to transport by rail and sea. If an articulated truck exceeds the limits of a road in terms of axle load, a smaller truck or reduced transport loads might be used.

Another aspect of flexibility that might also work in the favour of trucks, is the possibility to achieve more involvement by individual truck drivers compared to that of employees on ships and trains. The theoretical basis for this attribute in the model is to be found in the concept of external and internal flexibility. Following on from this it is possible even in a neo-Taylorism path of development to combine functional flexibility on an individual basis with external flexibility, because of the very individual nature of working as a truck driver (Leborgne and Lipietz 1992, Kalsaas 1995a). This aspect is of course especially evident when truck drivers also own their means of transport, which might be hired out on the spot market or on a long term basis to a carrier company.

The presumably well known impact from JIT-supply and time compressed supply lead time on reduction in shipment lots is further modelled in Figure 6.3. This should also be seen as a necessary feature following from small batch production, which is earlier modelled to be a basic feature of JIT-production. Small batch production in a system of functional division of labour would hardly have made any sense if this was not matched with despatching small lots of material to customers. And as such, it might be argued that the importance of transport is rising and that external movement of OEM material becomes an integrated element of the labour process in production chains based on JIT.

For a fixed volume of production to be despatched over time, smaller shipments lead per se to increased frequency of despatched material. Increased frequency in supply at a fixed volume leads to demand for relatively less capacity in means of transport, and thus increases the advantage of truck haulage over rail and sea.

129

A positive relationship between increased shipment frequency and increased traffic work is also modelled. This is a necessary relationship if other variables are unchanged. However, it might be possible to change the conceived rise in traffic work caused by higher frequency of relatively small lot shipments by some pattern of consolidating external goods movement, for instance collecting parts on a milk-round basis as practised by Volvo and Saab for the bulk of OEM parts. More remote location between vendors and customers leads to both increased traffic work and transport work. Traffic work refers to the utilized trucks multiplied by the length of the haul (truck-kilometre), and transport work refers to the weight of goods carried multiplied by the length of the haul (tonne-kilometres).

The attribute of regularity is finally conceived to be a positive relationship and linked to reliability. Regularity in transport intervenes with the core of JIT as compression of supply lead time, as it is expected to imitate the phase of production as much as possible. Thus sequenced supply follows the sequence in production, delivery 4 times per day comprises the parts and components needed for about one quarter of the day in each shipment, and daily delivery the calculated need for one day of production. Regularity should not be confused with frequency in supply as a daily supply flow might be as regular as a supply flow that is received 8 times per day.

If the infrastructure capacity for road transport is scarce and supply is being disrupted by congested roads, as it is found in some parts of Europe and Japan, this will draw the attention to alternative transport modes such as rail and sea, for instance in order to by-pass problematic areas. Long distance between suppliers and customers also works in favour of alternatives to road haulage, which are strongly interrelated to the cost of transport and the value of material to be moved. For small items of light weight and relatively high added value and maybe of strategic interest, even air transport can be a competitive alternative for reasons of cost, and not least time. The volume of transaction is crucial not only for transport costs, as it exists in fixed costs, but also for frequency in supply as will be demonstrated. In terms of transport costs, growing transaction volumes become increasingly important as the transport distance increases due to the presence of fixed costs (Malmberg 1993). There is a body of literature assessing transport costs for different transport means, and transport by rail might be a competitive alternative for distances exceeding 80-100 km, though flexibility and the transport time involved might be an obstacle (Benson et al. 1994).

JIT-supply and JIT- oriented supply are likely to increase the relative importance of road transport as conceived above, but here it should also be remembered that rail started to lose ground to road transport long before JIT became a notion in Europe. JIT can, however, strengthen this development tendency. See for instance Maskel (1994) who discusses the rise and fall of infrastructures.

The next step is to discriminate between different concepts of JIT-supply that have the capabilities to produce spatial determination of production and differences in transport.

6.2   Different concepts of JIT-supply

6.2.1   Sequential JIT-supply

Sequential supply refers to a supply arrangement where unique components are supplied in sequence and fully synchronised with the final assembly process. The Swedish notion of this phenomenon is applied here. In Japan, Nissan, Toyota, Honda and Mitsubishi denote the identical arrangement as synchronised supply (Kalsaas 1995).

When the components are unique, this refers to the existence of a one-to-one relationship between components and cars. A typical component supplied in sequence from a subcontractor is found to be seats, which are bulky, highly diversified and are used in all car units. Components supplied this way comprise quality assured systems which are ready for assembly.

Two relationships are found to be crucial for deciding the available supply lead time in sequential supply. This is firstly the relative point in time which the final assembler is able to identify which unique car to assemble and then to despatch the sequential call-off to the subcontractors in question. This ordering point is restricted by the time car bodies successfully leave the paint shop (Figure 6.4) and by the size of the actual paint body storage.

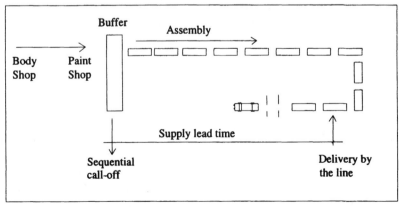

Figure 6.4 Principal layout of a car factory

131

Secondly the length of the throughput time in final assembly constrains the length of available supply lead time. If for instance call-off is despatched 2 hours before a painted body is put into the line and the throughput time in final assembly is 8 hours, the absolute time window available for sequential supply is 6 hours. This time period should comprise order handling, possible sub-assembly and transport and affiliated operations, and there may be a short waiting time by the line.

For specific components, the supply lead time is further restricted by the stage in the assembly process the component is needed (Figure 6.4). Is for instance a component devoted to workstation number 50 or 100? In the first alternative the available supply lead time is obviously more constrained than in the latter. Engines are an example of components that are needed relatively early by the line, while seats, complete wheels and bumpers are needed relatively late in the process.

Furthermore the speed of the assembly line and the number of painted bodies placed on the line per hour compress the throughput time per se, and thus available supply lead time.

6.2.2   Other JIT-supply concepts

The other broader conceptualised category of JIT-supply refers to the supply of parts and components for one day of production, or less, in due time of demand. Compared to warehousing of parts, this JIT-supply concept achieves an inward material flow that is more in accordance with how the production is performed, though less synchronized than sequential JIT.

However, external supply conducted by kanban as in the Toyota case is almost as synchronised. It is found to be supplied with a frequency as high as 16 times per day for some parts. A crucial difference between sequential supply and kanban and MRP controlled flows is that sequential supply operates on a one-to-one basis between parts and unique cars, which is not the case for kanban and MRP.

In its most relaxed pattern this is defined to include the concept of for instance European sourcing where JIT is somewhat diluted in order to accommodate suppliers within an extended trucking radius as in the case of Volvo and Saab.

The material flow from supplier to final assembler in these other supply strategies is confirmed to be less controlled and complex compared to the sequential JIT-supply concept. This follows from the one-to-one relationship between components and unique cars, which is found to be very demanding and expensive to operate.

6.2.3   JIT-supply controlled by MRP and kanban techniques

JIT-supply is found to be controlled by either one of these techniques that are likely to comprise different spatial forces. We start by elaborating the differences between kanban and MRP.

The "pull" principle is a central feature with kanban, and sequential JIT-supply, where subsequent processes are pulling components from previous processes. And as such, the "pull" attribute is a central aspect of the JIT discussion. Kanban is probably also the origin of the JIT notion and has received much of the credit for the success of Japanese production systems (Kalsaas 1995).

Kanban is frequently compared in the literature with the computerised production control system MRP; (see for instance Nørby 1992). MRP originated in the early 1960s in the USA in the golden age of Fordism. The aim was to improve the efficiency of inventory management in manufacturing. The principles digitised in MRP had already been practised in a manual form before World War II (Browne et al. 1988). As time passed, new operational functions were added to the system, such as master production scheduling, production activity control, rough cut capacity planning, capacity requirement planning, and purchasing. The extended MRP was labelled MRP II (manufacturing resource planning), which Browne et al. characterise as an integrated approach to the management of manufacturing resources (op. cit.).[1]

Sugimori et al. (1977) characterise MRP as the general production system, which is used to make production schedules of complete products. The production schedule is projected on components and parts, thereafter schedules are made for those, and instructions are issued to each workstation. Operations further produce parts in accordance with their schedules and instructions by *"employing the method of the preceding process supplying the parts to the following process"* (op. cit., p. 555). Hence the basic procedures in MRP have a "push" character versus "pull" as in kanban. Among the final assemblers studied, TMC is the only case that applies kanban for controlling the bulk of supply. The others utilise MRP, when we do not include supply in sequence and Saab Automobile's kanban supply scheme for a few parts. Kanban literally means card. The JIT-controlled supply system operates in the following way. It is operated with two types of kanban, conveyance card and production card. When a worker at the final assembly plant takes a part from a pallet for the first time he detaches the conveyance card and places it in a nearby box. These cards are collected by the subcontractor during the

---

[1] It is not of significant interest to distinguish between MRP and MRP II in this paper.

next delivery time, and are brought back to the subcontractor's plant where they are attached to each pallet of parts already in stock. At the same time the production card attached to each pallet is removed and becomes an order for the production of more parts by the subcontractor. The pallets with the conveyance card attached are then ready for delivery to the assembly plant at the next scheduled delivery time.

It is widely accepted that kanban is superior to MRP, in terms of reduced need for planning and handling information (Sugimori et al. 1977, Ohno 1982, Sayer 1986). MRP needs workers to update information continually and operates on fixed cycle times (the average time to carry out a specific operation). But in real life, individuals need variable cycle times, e.g., due to skill, social life, health conditions, and disruptions caused by equipment, which in combination with the "push" system is likely to cause pile-ups. On the other hand, the "pull" concept regulates "normal" fluctuations in cycle times at the lowest possible level due to the "pull" principle.

On the basis of a push based system, regularity becomes relatively more central in logistics, cf. the model in Figure 6.3, since the direct pull force is not present and the focus is likely to be imitating the MRP decided production phase, by emphasising the routining of incoming flows to make gains in smooth receiving and internal distribution procedures. It follows from this that the capability of flexible transport becomes relatively more central when "pull" principles are applied for managing supply compared to "push", and thus utilisation of road haulage also becomes more likely, according to the conceived model. In the case of kanban and sequential JIT-supply, parts and components are pulled to the assembly line in accordance with the phase and demand in production. This might be irregular and what is crucial is precision, and thus the capability of a flexible response to achieve this.

Companies employing kanban and MRP, as well as sequential JIT-supply, are, however, all dependent on an overall planning system to handle forecasting and preliminary production plans, which are distributed to suppliers in the chain as frame orders/notifications in order to pull enough materials into the supply chain to close the lead-time gap.

If we extend the analysis of the pull feature to embrace the whole production chain, i.e. also comprising the supply chain and sale, features such as manufacturing to order and JIT-supply (frequently small lot supply) become crucial. These may be combined with a modernized MRP technique for the day-to-day control of production. The pull feature in this approach is the same as a demand oriented production chain, where the pull signal is given by the customer when he confirms his order of a uniquely composed product.

6.3 Volvo and Saab increase the number of components supplied in sequence

It was found that Saab and Volvo are expanding the number of components being supplied in sequence, while TMC and Nissan move in the opposite direction by sequencing in-house what was earlier supplied in sequence by subcontractors. Changes in logistics take place in particular when new models are launched, and Volvo and Saab are speeding up their turnover of models to be comparable to that of the Japanese cases. Logistics is even considered when new car models are developed. An effort is made to identify components or systems that can be outsourced to specialists who take the responsibility for sub assembly, and thereby try to reduce the number of components and suppliers the principal firm has to deal with.

It is confirmed that the reduction in sequential supply in Japan is strongly related to the costs linked to this supply scheme, but it should also be seen in relation to Volvo and Saab's more diversified car products and TMC and Nissan's tendency to make reductions in the level of diversification, which is also found to take place in Honda and Mitsubishi in Japan (Kalsaas and Takeuchi 1996).

Table 6.1
Sequential supply and shipment frequency and lots

Component	Delivery frequency	Shipment lots in number of car sets
Volvo Car's Torslanda plant 1)		
Seats	9 times per day	90
Wheels	8 times per day	96
Bumpers (RPAB)	Every 1.5 hours 2)	60
Saab Automobile's Trollhättan plant:		
Seats (Lear Seats)	Every 45 minutes	20
Bumpers (RPC)	Every second hour	60
Wiring harnesses	Every 45 minutes 3)	12
1) Data for carpets and hat shelves are missing 2) Reduced frequency during night due to reduced production at Volvo. 3) Only for Saab 900		

The supply lead time is measured in a few hours in the cases reported in Table 6.1, which indicates supply frequency for Volvo and Saab's sequential supply. Volvo's respondent emphasised the bulky characteristic of components and the number of variants to be most important in the trade off between sequential supply and daily supply. This is again strongly related to available space by the assembly lines. Saab appears to have a more cost-oriented approach to the question, and calculates the flow cost per part for alternative supply strategies in which inventory cost and transport cost are crucial variables.

At present both Nissan and TMC apply sequential JIT only for complete seats and wheels. Earlier, batteries, windows, carpets and door trims, in addition to drive shafts and ceilings were supplied this way to Nissan.

Data regarding the frequency of sequential supply in the Japanese cases is not available, but Ikeda Bussan's daily supply frequency of seats to Nissans' Oppama plant is calculated to 38, which is equal to 27 consignments every hour when we make corrections for idle time.[2] Each consignment includes seats for 14 car units and orders are received on condition of 2 hours supply lead time.

6.3.1   An example of sequential JIT-supply

I will now look in more detail at the example of Raufoss Automotive's (RAA) supply of bumper systems to Volvo Car's Torslanda plant regarding the generation of transport and the relative impact on location. A modern bumper system is constructed of aluminium bumper reinforcements, shock absorbers of expanded polypropylene, and painted bumper covers of plastic. RAA's bumper systems to Volvo are supplied in 250 variants. Variables that make up bumper system variants are front and rear bumper, car models, geographical market (different traffic safety regulations), 4- or 5-door cars (different rear bumpers), and not least colour.

The 11 different colours used by Volvo Car add considerably to the variation spectrum. According to a respondent at Volvo's Torslanda plant, the painted bumpers are what the customers demand and the next Volvo to be launched in the near future will have even more painted bumper details. Volvo's bumper systems are frequently referred to as something more than a bumper, as it makes up an increasing share of the styling of the car.

---

[2] Ikeda Bussan has a plant located next door to Nissan's Oppama plant (10 minutes' drive). The company is a single supplier of seats to Nissan, but Nissan's Oppama plant is supplying 2 of 3 lines from in-house production. The car plant's daily output at the time of interview was 1,600 car units based on a two shift system each with a length of 9 hours plus two hours overtime between the shifts. The factory was thus operated 22 hours per day. When calculating the supply frequency above it is assumed that the production capacity is similar on the three lines.

Bumpers are very bulky. Therefore they are supplied in sequence to Volvo by Raufoss Automotive Plastics. The bulky feature of bumpers affects the transportability, and this was one reason for Raufoss Automotive's establishment of Raufoss Belgium NV (1989) in Ghent, where Volvo has a car factory.

The transportability of bumper systems has further developed in a direction that makes the product more sensitive to transport costs. At present one truck load from Raufoss to Torslanda represents 150 bumper units (75 cars) while the capacity was 840 units (420 cars) for the last Volvo 240 model in 1986-87. The difference measured in the number of articulated trucks is approximately 1 to 6.

Bumper systems are furthermore vulnerable to scratches and being discoloured on the painted surface. They need therefore to be well protected during transport.

The throughput time in final assembly is 8 hours for the two assembly lines at Volvo Car's Torslanda plant, and at present 30 car bodies enter the assembly lines per hour. They have moreover a painted body storage of one hours production, cf. Figure 6.4.

Bumpers are assembled 3.6 and 6 hours after the car is on line for respectively Volvo's 900 series and the newer model 850 at current line speed. Maximum supply lead time for bumpers is thus 4.6 hours for the 900 model and 7 hours for the 850 model, while Volvo Car requires 3 hours' supply lead time from Raufoss Automotive Plastics. The average available time buffers in-house for Volvo is then 1.6 hours for bumpers for the 900 series and 4 hours for the 850 model. In addition to a certain buffer for balancing disturbances, Volvo uses the time buffer prior to assembly to move the bumpers from the receiving area to the designated workstations.

Raufoss Automotive Plastics receives orders for bumpers from Volvo's Torslanda plant every 7 minutes. Each order comprises front and rear bumpers for 5 cars and defines the delivery address in the factory, sequence number, article number, features with the bumpers and chassis number of the related car.

Raufoss Automotive Plastics despatches a truck with 60 bumper sets to Volvo 14 times per day (Table 6.1). In daytime a shipment is despatched every one and half hours. The driving time between Raufoss Automotive Plastics and Volvo Car's Torslanda plant is 10 minutes. Shipment of 60 bumper sets is equal to 1 hour's production at Volvo's two lines with current speed.

The average time available for the transport of bumpers is 2.6 hours for the 900 model and 5 hours for the 850 model. This is calculated on the basis of respectively 4.6 and 7 hours supply lead time. A further prerequisite is 1 hour for internal handling by Volvo prior to final assembly and Raufoss

Automotive Plastics needs 1 hour for internal execution of orders. It should thus be clear that the available time window for goods transport will shrink further if Volvo speeds up its assembly lines.

However, Volvo-respondents say that the distance is not to go beyond 50 km or 1 hour's driving time for control reasons. Saab in comparison requires sequential suppliers to be located within the upper limit of 20-60 minutes driving time from the final assembly plant.

Volvo is always short of components which are supplied in sequence, according to the former logistics manager at Volvo Car's Torslanda plant, who claimed that the close proximity of subcontractors is an extremely important condition as it facilitates quality assured components. Volvo is supplied with seats in sequence from Bengtsfors with a driving time of about 2.5 hours, but this is a continual cause of worry as, for instance, delays caused by a car accident are enough to interrupt the whole supply scheme.

The respondents reasoned that the upper limit in time distance was due to the very close communication between team leaders on the line and the sequencing agent, which is necessary to smooth the flow and compensate for minor and larger disturbances. Tight human relationships are crucial between suppliers and sequential JIT-supply.

The findings thus confirm the conceived model of agglomeration for this supply scheme (Figure 6.3). Emergency transport is for instance utilised for balancing disturbances. On one occasion in the autumn of 1994 Raufoss Automotive moved 4 bumpers by helicopter from Raufoss to Volvo's factory in Torslanda in order to avoid a line stop. The cost of the helicopter flight was NOK 60,000, at that time approximately SEK 70,000. To stop an assembly line for one hour costs Volvo SEK 300,000.

The confirmed new policy of faster turnover of car models in the case of Volvo and Saab is also likely to impose continual disturbances in the production chain, as changes of this kind appear to be an important source of problems in both final assembly and in subcontractors' production. Hence, when production starts to achieve a routine character in the chain, it might be time to make new radical changes.

Disturbances in final assemblers' production are transmitted throughout the actual production chain. A key factor to success in JIT-production appears to be final producing agents in a production chain who are in control of their own labour process, as well as reliable equipment and a well-developed planning system, which minimize supply demand at short notice apart from the routined order system.

Actual confirmed causes of disturbances in production are listed below:

- Set up time of machinery and equipment;
- breakdowns of production machinery and affiliated technology, for instance computer networks;
- breakage of parts in production and transport;
- misreading of stock;
- inferior quality of supplied parts and components;
- delay in delivery;
- arrival of parts and components in large batches;
- irregular delivery;
- disturbance to transport, such as accidents, weather conditions and traffic congestion;
- strikes and social conflicts and lack of commitment.

Several of the listed aspects stem from the spatial division of labour, which is thus a condition for JIT-production and a reason to get possible problems controlled. The space aspect is for instance crucial when it is needed to get a unique component replaced in a hurry due to breakage in final assembly or transport, or by inferior quality delivered by a subcontractor.

6.3.2 The bulk of OEM parts is not supplied in sequence

As seen from the section above, the bulk of OEM parts and components are not supplied in sequence, but belong to the category of other JIT-supply, where the agglomeration forces between subcontractors and principal firms have less strength than in the case of sequential JIT-supply. It is, however, crucial to discriminate between kanban and MRP controlled supply in this respect.

Among the car plant cases, only Toyota's Tsutsumi plant applies kanban for this purpose. An exception though is Saab who for some time have tried out a simple form of kanban for a few parts. The other Swedish and Japanese cases apply MRP for ordering and controlling the supply of OEM-parts.

For these schemes Nissan applies a supply lead time of 3-5 days for delivery schedules in addition to submitted frame orders of 10 days, 30 days and notification of 3 months. In order to compare with Volvo and Saab, the transport time and the time spent to consolidate flows by milk-rounds has to be added in the Swedish cases, since a different purchasing policy is applied (CIF versus EXW[3]). Nissan's supply lead time of 3-5 days should therefore be compared with 4 days for Volvo (1 day response by subcontractor, 1 day collecting and consolidation, 2 days' transport from hub to hub) and 5-8 days

---

[3] Incoterms 1990, published by the International Chamber of Commerce.

for Saab (2 days' response, 6 days available for transport operations and balancing assemblers' production). For Nissan relatively more time is applied in subcontractors' production and for Volvo and Saab relatively more time on transport.

TMC transfers a 30 day frozen production order to subcontractors in addition to forecasts and more detailed frame orders as in the case of Nissan, while the daily supply is pulled by kanban orders.[4] Data for supply lead time in the case of Toyota is not available, but it is measured in hours, according to the study of the subcontractor Toyoda Tekko. This is also verified in the frequency table below (Table 6.2), as it is most unlikely that parts are supplied several times per day over long distances in the context of Toyota's production system. This argument is not, however, valid for bulky parts that demand several full truck loads.

TMC tries to increase the frequency of delivery in order to reduce the level of inventory. On the day of the visit to the Tsutsumi plant the maximum timetable arrival frequency for the same supplier at one of three receiving areas comprising 12 platforms was 11 times per day, minimum 1 and average 5. Sixty-five subcontractors were designated to the receiving area.

Nissan operates with a supply frequency of maximum 8 times per day. The frequency is derived from a calculated standard number of parts in each consignment. Each kanban order contains also a standard number of parts. The principal difference is contained in the applied "push" respectively "pull" feature regarding impact on local forces and transportation.

The bulk of parts for Volvo and Saab are supplied with a daily frequency. Volvo is restructuring towards a fourteen-day-car concept, in which they can handle 2 days' driving time. This is equivalent to the sailing time for the daily sea transport they operate between their two main hubs in Ghent and Torslanda. Two days covers Europe north of the Alps, which thus is their main JIT region. However, the bulk of parts to GM- controlled Saab is supplied daily. They are operating a global purchasing policy. They put much more weight on cost compared to Volvo who compete strongly on customer response, c.f. the fourteen-day-car concept.

---

4 TMC and Nissan dealers provide TMC and Nissan in practice with fixed orders of 30 days, which include so-called speculation cars that are not sold to end users. In comparison Volvo and Saab's dealers are only responsible for cars sold to end users, the Swedish car makers operate with one week order buffers.

Table 6.2 Volvo's requirements for material flows

Quality aspect	Explanation
Reliable flows	Fixed time schedules for loading at the suppliers' site and unloading at Torslanda Car plant
High frequency flows	Daily or every second day from whole Europe. Once per week from the US and Japan. (The basic idea is to force subcontractors to catch up with the cycles of Volvo's production.)
Fast flows	Fast flows it is for instance defined to 0-1 day from Scandinavia,[5] 2 days from Holland, France, Belgium, Germany, Austria, Switzerland and Finland, 3 days from Spain, UK, Italy and Portugal, 5 days from Ireland, 30 days from North America and 32 days from Japan.
Equal flows	Consignments are always to follow the same route independent of mixed loads, size, etc. (Cycles that go and go in contrast to ad hoc solutions)
Price value flows	Decisions in transport are to consider logistics costs, production costs, inventory costs, etc. (Optimum costs for Volvo)

6.3.3   Spatial impacts from MRP and kanban JIT-supply

Let me consider the difference between Nissan and Toyota in this respect who are comparable in terms of output, line speed and supply frequency.

Nissan's subcontractors have 3-5 days for production and transport and affiliated procedures before delivery. This is only a few hours for the Toyota suppliers. This shows that the agglomeration forces are much stronger between subcontractors and the principal firm in the kanban case, as there is less time available for transport.

Furthermore, it follows from the time available that the MRP case opens possibilities for consolidating transport to an extent that is not possible for the kanban case. This is an important feature in sustainable development. In the MRP case, flexibility in production is necessary in order to avoid the pile up of parts arriving as ordered 3-5 days earlier. In the case of Nissan there had to be a major earthquake before this occurred, as was the situation on the day of interview a few days after the Kobe earthquake in January 1995. In the case

---

[5] "0" day transport distance means it is possible to deliver at Volvo's final assembly on the same day as the consignments are collected at subcontractors' site.

141

of Toyota's utilisation of kanban the necessary flexibility is passed over to the subcontractors. Toyota's Tsutsumi plant is nevertheless very flexible in several senses of the word.

As flexibility in supply is a striking feature with time compressed kanban supply, regularity is a relatively stronger feature with MRP controlled supply. The regularity, however, simulates the scheduled phase in production as close as possible, cf. Table 6.2.

The difference between MRP and kanban in this respect, is, however, diminishing when the supply lead time in kanban orders is extended as in the case of the second tier subcontractor, Aisin Keikinzoku. This company supplies bumper reinforcements on a kanban basis with a supply lead time of 3-4 days and 30 days of frame orders and 3 months' notification. Saab has also experience of kanban which is comparable to this phase. The difference is who is conducting the orders, the shop floor workers on the line as in kanban, or a logistics officer (expert) in the management team as in the MRP case.

6.3.4   Volvo's fourteen-day car concept

Volvo's strategy is to achieve world class standards in customer service, and thus be one of the three best car makers in this respect. Customer response time is a main scope for their restructuring process. The present customer response time is 30 days in Sweden and the rest of the EU, while the goal is 14 days at the end of 1995 associated with the fourteen-day-car concept.[6]

The concept requires Volvo to make up daily production plans for the 7th day ahead of present time based on incoming orders from dealers the same day, or maybe one day before. Hence an order buffer of 7 days is required.

The inward logistics can be explained as follows. If the production plan is made up on day N, the delivery schedules ought to be communicated to the suppliers on the morning of day N+1. The suppliers should be ready for delivery at their site on the morning of day N+2 if they are located in Germany or other relatively remote locations. Day N+2 is further designated to gather parts to hubs (in cases of less than one truck load) by carriers in actual milk-rounds (cargo collecting zones). Day N+3 and day N+4 are applied for transporting the material from the hubs in Europe to Volvo Transport's terminal in Gothenburg, in the case of Torslanda plant. These 2 days for transport are equivalent to the transport time by ship from Ghent to

---

[6] The concept might be inspired from the "three-day-car" utopia where the customers receive their unique cars 3 days after signing the order at the dealer. Unique in the utopia means unique in all elements, even the car body (Twenty-first Century Manufacturing Enterprise Strategy 1991).

Arendal in the district of Torslanda. Days N+5 and N+6 are the non-working days Saturday and Sunday in this example.

The parts and components are finally to be brought to the assembly plant before the first shift starts in the morning on day N+7. Volvo has now 7 days for production and shipment of cars to the end users via dealers.

The 7-day production to order cycle is to be repeated daily, production plans are made up on Tuesday for production on Tuesday the following week, etc. The concept is based on production to order for the European market and on European sourcing.

While trying out the outlined system, Volvo intends to operate with an inventory of three days on average. The aim is to shrink the buffer to two days.

A cornerstone in the concept is an order buffer of 7 days, no more no less. This is problematic as cars are not sold in even numbers every day. Hence, the fixed buffer must be matched by flexibility in production to slow down or raise the phase in production. It is especially problematic to raise the phase in production, as the labour process needs to be re-balanced. The need for different lengths of the working day and numerical flexibility in the labour stock is also an issue in this context. For instance it might be necessary to work 10 hours one day and 7 hours another day.

The board of Volvo has decided to go for the fourteen-day car concept, though without solving the need for flexibility. Another alternative to the 14-day lead time is to apply different customer responses as is done today.

In May 1995 there was a 7-day buffer regarding Volvo 850, but the line has surplus capacity, and it is easier to stop the line than to increase the phase or the working day when there were already 3 shifts per day as is the case for Volvo 900. Volvo 900 has at present a delivery time to customers of 8 weeks, which means the order buffer is about 7 weeks.

In the effort to implement the fourteen-day car concept Volvo Cars' Torslanda plant has developed new logistics and demands of Volvo Transport in this regard "to achieve production free of disturbance", as the respondent at Volvo Transport put it. The new requirements consist of five elements that are summarized in Table 6.2.

The table addresses listed the collection of consignments at subcontractors' site. This is not implemented as documented earlier.

Included in the strategy above is the use of Volvo Transport's logistics terminal at which flows are currently deconsolidated and from which the OEM parts and components could be delivered directly to the different destinations in the final assembly plant.

The respondent at Volvo Transport admitted that there are no particular changes in the speed of material flows compared to previous concepts. It still takes the same amount of time to drive a truck from Germany to Sweden.

The change is found foremost in the concept of reliable flows, high frequency flows, and equal flows.

The previous transport pattern was for instance despatching parts from Germany on Thursday and Friday and driving to Sweden during the weekend for unloading, and to reload for Germany on Mondays. Hence parts were received in relatively large batches which created 'shock waves' through the system compared to the current system of daily delivery. There are, however, remaining problems related to the flows from Germany to be delivered on Mondays as already documented.

Table 6.2 indicates delivery every second day in some cases. Although the policy is daily despatching of consignments from all subcontractors, this has to be traded against shipment lots and volume and economy. Due to the framework of the fourteen-day-car concept, all less than daily and longer than 2 day flows have to be compensated.

6.4   Network and locational impacts

All the investigated Norwegian subcontractor cases are located well within 2 days transport time in relationship to Volvo and thus also within Saab's supply region for daily flow. It should be pointed out, however, that direct transport is unacceptable for less than full truck loads, and in cases of emergency, because of excessive transport costs. The goods thus have to be picked up in a milk-round like arrangement and consolidated. This is noted to be particularly problematic in cases of relatively remotely located Rollag due to the road standard in question and the difficulties in consolidating full truck loads during the time available. Difficulties in consolidating truck loads stem from lack of other export industries in Rollag and proximity to the transport route.

Location of subcontractors to areas where there are also other export industries is thus important for this transport scheme and for suppliers of the car industry. The problems connected to Rollag are not present in a location such as Larvik as it is easy to consolidate full truck loads with goods from companies located in proximity of the E18 highway between Larvik and Oslo.

If the volume of output from each subcontractor is large enough to make full truck loads with acceptable frequency to one or several customers in one destination area, the windows of possible locations grow since the need to consolidate truck loads with other shippers is omitted. This is the case for Raufoss Automobile in Raufoss and Hydro Aluminium Fundo in Høyanger. The relative impact from JIT in this regard is that the development towards demanding smaller lots in each shipment combined with increased frequency, makes it necessary to have contracted relatively larger volumes than before to achieve this relative freedom of location.

It is out of the question to supply Saab in Trollhättan and Volvo in Gothenburg in sequence from Norway, except maybe from a small part of southern Østfold county that has comparable distance to Torslanda as Volvo's supplier of seats located in Bengtsfors. To be supplied with seats from Bengtsfors is, however, too far away and a problematic location for Volvo Car in Torslanda. Raufoss Automotive has followed up on these local forces by establishing branch plants and deposits in the proximity of Volvo's car assembly plants in Uddevalla, Ghent and Torslanda. Strategic investments are also confirmed to follow up new tendencies on the market. If Raufoss Automobile had not carried out this investment, there would have been a great risk that an outsider would have done so. Moreover, it is probably risky to only operate a deposit in Torslanda, and not have any significant production beyond the sequential supply and deposit service. This is related to the current relatively complicated and expensive material flow that adds to the cost and makes the company vulnerable to competition. Raufoss Automobile is thus considering expanding the activities in Torslanda to include a factory. The main Workers' Union, which is strongly opposed to the establishment in Uddevalla, is a counter force in this regard. This time they are not directly opposing the new establishment, but they demand that the loss of jobs in Raufoss must be compensated by new local work. The employees in Uddevalla also argue that they can serve Volvo Car in Torslanda.

It should also be mentioned that Volvo Car subsidised Raufoss Automotive with the establishment in Uddevalla. The reason was to save transport costs, as in the EXW purchasing concept it is a responsibility for Volvo to move the components from the first tier supplier to final assembly and have no responsibility for transport further upstream in the production chain.

It is often said that a central JIT feature is that final assemblers give priority to subcontractors who are located in the local area. This was found to be true regarding sequential supply but not in the daily flow supply scheme, where close location in Europe is within 2 days' transport time and where the actual subcontractors' resource base is relatively more important than the location.

If time distance is considered important for several products and supply arrangements, transport costs matter even more for several products that are produced by the investigated subcontractor cases. To operate on the German market for iron castings produced in Larvik seems to be vulnerable in terms of competitiveness due to transport costs. Such geographical limitation is probably also found for capacity subcontracting products such as machined castings and forged iron parts, and even for the specialised production of

145

bumper reinforcements establishing branch plants in continental Europe is being considered.

6.4.1   The new Øresund link

The planned new bridge across Øresund and the discussed bridge across Fehmarn will certainly ease the transportation of parts from suppliers in Germany, though it will not solve the congestion problems in the Hamburg area in north Germany, according to the respondent from Volvo Transport. However, after the withdrawal of former Board Chairman Mr Gyllenhammar, Volvo has no policy on infrastructure projects. Mr Gyllenhammar, for instance, made a proposal that a new highway should be built between Oslo and Paris.

Saab's respondent did not regard the Øresund and Fehmarn bridge of strategic interest to them with regard to the supply of parts and components. The reasoning of Saab's respondent is founded on logistics and driving time regulations for drivers and is thus different from Volvo's point of view. Saab's reasoning is based on the transport arrangement of exchanging drivers and tractors for trailers at ferries between Germany and Sweden. This arrangement is customised to the driving time regulations in Europe. For instance in the case of a bridge, drivers of trucks with Saab goods have to rest for eight hours anyway, as the maximum 9-10 hours daily driving limit usually is reached at arrival in Travermünde or Saßnitz. A similar argument was made by Volvo's respondent who claimed that the new Øresund bridge will not solve the driving time regulations. Currently drivers from the European continent have no driving time left when they reach Kiel or another ferry port in northern Germany.

The respondent from Saab's Forwarding and Shipping Department argued that the cheapest way of moving goods is by sea and the Øresund bridge means little change for Saab. What the responsible forwarder wanted was morning and afternoon departures by ferry from North Germany to Gothenburg with a reduction in sailing time from 16 to 10 hours.

However, there are also benefits from a new Øresund bridge. The transport from Germany is for instance routed by ordinary car ferry service, often Kiel-Gothenburg (14 h) in the case of Volvo's Torslanda plant. When 30-40 articulated trucks from the ferry bound for Volvo arrive simultaneously at the terminal it causes queues, waiting time and stress for the receiving agent. This can be avoided when Sweden is linked to Germany with a bridge via Denmark, as it opens the opportunity to smooth the arrival of these trucks by scheduled arrivals.

146

The present dependency on ferries is moreover an obstacle to a possible increase in the daily supply frequency from the European continent to for instance twice per day. This aspect exemplifies the point that a road infrastructure that does not include ferries offers considerably more flexibility as it is always available and independent of any sailing schedule. The risk of strikes and bad weather conditions are further in disfavour of ferry links.

The relative increased demand in flexible infrastructure in JIT is further exemplified by the findings regarding emergency supply, which repeatedly occur. Emergency supply or express supply is a substitute to delay in delivery when routine transport schemes become too slow. The point is then to get the delayed consignment to the consignee as fast as possible. Hence a possibility to drive continually at any time is an important feature with the infrastructure.

Goods transport by rail, might benefit most from the new Øresund link, which makes it possible for trains to be driven directly without the delay caused by splitting them up in order to fit the limitation enforced by ferries. Modern freight trains might have a length of 700 meters, or more.

6.5 Conclusion

The findings confirm the expected agglomeration forces in the case of sequential JIT in the relationship between subcontractors and assemblers. It is confirmed that the applied time-space concept is fruitful when studying the most time compressed JIT-material flows. However, some time buffer has to be added for handling possible disturbances.

The importance of geographical proximity is weaker in the daily supply schemes as operated by Volvo and Saab, which are designed for European sourcing. The agglomeration forces are stronger for supply organised by the kanban principles compared to that of MRP. However, the differences between these principles diminish sharply when kanban is operated on supply lead times that are comparable to that of MRP. MRP also opens the possibility for larger opportunities for consolidated goods transport compared to kanban, which again can be operated by means of rail and sea transport as in the case of Volvo's daily Gothenburg-Ghent line that is operated in combination with milk-routing.

In Japan, heavy traffic is found to contract JIT-supply regions. Transport costs still matter for JIT-supply in both Japan and Norway, for some parts cost is more important than time. Parts and components have to be individualised regarding logistics and spatial implications.

The location pattern of subcontractors relative to other subcontractors and other industry that demand transport service is confirmed to be a crucial condition for the milk- round concept and consolidating full truck loads within available time spans. This aspect grows in relative importance as shipment lots are being reduced and supply frequency increased.

If the volume of output from each subcontractor in the milk-round concept is large enough to make full truck loads with acceptable frequency to one or several customers in one destination area, the windows of possible locations grow since the need to consolidate truck loads with other shippers is omitted. The relative impact from JIT in this regard is that the development towards demanding smaller lots per shipment in combination with increased frequency, makes it necessary to subcontract relatively larger volumes than before to achieve this relative freedom of location. This is also an example that transport costs still matter, although, relatively less.

The benefits from the new Øresund link appear to be limited for the investigated cases. However, the bridge leads to gains in flexibility for transport, smoothing of production, and possibilities of increasing the supply frequency, but the regulation of driving time for truck drivers appears to be a hindrance.

The strategy of production for end users' order as operated by Volvo and Saab makes it relatively beneficial for companies to establish production where they have their main market. It is found to be almost impossible to produce cars for orders when production and customers are located on different continents as the customer response time is not likely to be competitive. This follows from the extra lead time enforced by sea transport.

The agglomeration forces are thus relatively strong from JIT-production systems in the relationship to subcontractors of OEM-parts and assemblers when we isolate the impact. There are, however, several other forces that might be more important than JIT. The findings in Japan reveal that a growing number of parts are being imported, and Japanese car assemblers seem to evolve towards globalisation. This implies an increased specialization and division of labour among production units within the companies. Regarding supply, imported parts might be supplied just-in-time to the individual plants, but from a warehouse and terminal for import. Moreover the production system for cars in Japan is increasingly being decentralised in order to secure labour supply. Subcontractors have only partly been following their final assemblers when they have expanded assembly to new production sites. It is also found that companies have a strategy of combining JIT-supply for some components with particular attributes and global sourcing for others. This is, however, contradictory in relation to a strategy of producing highly differentiated cars for the end users' order.

References

Benson, D., R. Bugg, G. Whitehead (1994), *Transport and Logistics: Elements of overseas trade*, Woodhead-Faulkner: London.

Burmeister, A., Colletis-Whal, K. (1997), *Proximity in networks: The role of transport infrastructure*, paper presented at the NECTAR Cluster 2 meeting: The role of networks in economic spatial systems: New perspectives, Bertinoro, Italy, 14-15 March 1997, University of Bologna.

Browne, J., J. Harhen, J. Shivnan (1988), *Production Management Systems: A CIM Perspective*, Addison-Wesley Publishing Company.

Hepworth, M, and K. Ducatel (1992): "Transport in the Information Age: Wheels and Wires", Belhaven Press: London.

Kalsaas, B. T. (1995a), *Transport in Industry and Locational Implications: 'Just-in-time' Principles in Manufacturing, Generation of Transport and the Relative Impact on Location. Scandinavian and Japanese Experiences* Dr.ing. Thesis, Department of Town and Regional Planning, Norwegian Institute of Technology, University of Trondheim.

Kalsaas, B. T. (1995b), *Paths of development in the Japanese Automotive industry: How is the relative loss of competitive advantages affecting the practising of just-in-time in Japan?* IGU Commission on the organisation of industrial space, Seoul August 1995. (Forthcoming: *The problems of the pacific Rim area*, Volume 5 of the Avebury series.)

Kalsaas, B. T., Takeuchu A. (1996), *Path of Development in Japanese and Scandinavian Car Industry*, Paper presented to 28th International Geographical Congress, Commission of Industrial Spaces, The Hague, August 5-10, 1996.

Leborgne, D. and A. Lipietz (1992), "Conceptual Fallacies and Open Questions on Post-Fordism", in Storper, M, and A.J. Scott (eds), *Pathways to Industrialization and Regional Development*, Routledge: London.

Levine, J. and S. Underwood (1995), *Stakeholder Preferences in Urban Transportation Evaluation*, Paper presented at the conference of the Association of Collegiate Schools of Planning, Detroit, October 1995.

Malmberg, B. (1993), *Problems of time-space coordination - A key to the understanding of multiplant firms*, University of Uppsala, Department of Geography, Paper No 40.

Maskel, P. (1994), "Infrastrukturens økonomiske rolle", in *Nordisk Samhällsgeografisk Tidsskrift*, No.18.

Nørby, M (1992): "JIT visjoner og erfaringer", *Samfunnslitteratur*, Denmark.

Ohno, T. (1982), "How the Toyota Production System Was Created", *Japan Economic Studies*, Summer, Vol. X, (4), 83-103.

149

Perroux, F. (1955/1979), "Note on the consept of 'Growth Poles'", in D.L.McKee, R.D.Dean and W.H.Leahy (eds), *Regional Economies: Theory and Practice*, New York.

Perroux, F. (1988), "The pole of development's new place in a general theory of economic activity", in Higgins, B. and D.J. Savoie (eds), *Regional Economic Development*, Boston.

Sayer, A. (1986), "New developments in manufacturing: the just-in-time system", *Capital and Class*, Vol. 30, 43-72

Sayer, A. (1992), "Method in Social Science: A Realist Approach", 2nd edition, Routledge: London.

Schoenberger, E. (1987), "Technological and Organizational Change in Automobile Production: Spatial Implications", in *Regional Studies*, 21(3), 199-214.

Storper, M. and Scott A.J. (1989), "The Geographical Foundations and Social Regulation of Flexible Production Complexes", in J.Wolch and M.Dear (eds), *The Power of Geography: How Territory Shapes Social Life*, 21-40, Unwin Hyman: Winchester.

Sugimori, Y., K. Kusonoki, F. Cho, S. Uchikawa (1977*)*, "Toyota Production System and Kanban System Materialization of Just-in-Time and Respect-for-Human System", in *Int. J. Prod.Res.*, 15(6), 553-564.

Womack, J. P., D. T. Jones, D. Roose (1990), *The Machine that changed the World*, New York.

7 Hierarchies of Spatial Network Systems

FRANCESCA MEDDA, PETER NIJKAMP AND
PIET RIETVELD

7.1 Hierarchy in network: concepts

In recent years we have witnessed drastic transformations in the European geo-political and socio-economic map. Such changes not only pertained to the functional relations between regions, but at times also concerned the morphology of the network system in Europe. These structural developments have prompted various research questions on the relationships between spatial structure and spatial processes in a network economy. A rather common concept - often accepted in European policy decisions - is the notion of spatial hierarchy in networks, which implies a multi-layered configuration with major nodes at the top of the hierarchy. In this context, it is an intriguing research question to ask what these hierarchical concepts precisely mean and how they can be investigated in an operational sense. The aim of this paper is to shed some light on this issue. The starting point of our analysis will be the theory of hierarchical systems.

Frequently, natural as well as artificial systems are defined by complex internal structures. For the description of such systems, one often utilises the decomposition of the whole into parts, so as to be in accordance with organisational principles or developmental laws. The *hierarchy* concept is one of the accepted systems structures that can be considered as a device to interpret and represent reality in a systematically ordered way. But how do we define the hierarchy concept?

According to Bunge, "a hierarchy or hierarchical structure is a set equipped with a relation of domination or its converse, subordination" (Bunge, 1969). We can observe that Bunge's definition follows a very common notion of hierarchy where a hierarchy is considered as a structure in which the different parts are linked by predominance relationships. However, by browsing through the scientific literature, we are not convinced that these conditions are the only necessary prerequisites of a hierarchical structure. The concept of hierarchy has received new interpretations ranging from a conventional vertical authority structure to a configuration which Simon has defined as "a set of Chinese boxes of a particular kind" (Simon, 1973). Such a broadening of the meaning of hierarchy does not determine a predominance of one concept over the others, but as Grene observes "perhaps the meanings of 'hierarchy' form a family in Wittgenstein's sense. Perhaps they even form a hierarchy" (Grene, 1969).

When we analyse the operational definition of the concept of hierarchy applied to spatial networks, and in the majority of cases, we observe the use of a *bossy* structure. By *bossy* structure we mean that through multi-indices, as for example accessibility and connectivity indices, we are able to compare and classify the nodes of the network in a hierarchy which is defined in accordance with relations of dominance and dependence among nodes. But with this perspective the spectrum of the different concepts of hierarchy is then reduced to a single and unambiguous interpretation.

Networks are regarded in our paper as a particular organisation of interactive structures among units based on interconnectivity of nodes. The present paper will focus primarily on hierarchy structures in networks by expanding the *bossy* hierarchy concept and considering the possibility of another interpretation of network hierarchy. First, we consider the concept of hierarchy as part of the spatial systems theory. This theoretical point of view is necessary in order to introduce network hierarchy within two broad categories: a hierarchy of points and the nested hierarchy. In the second part of the paper, we propose and analyse an operational definition of hierarchies in network systems by comparing these two categories in a simple network system.

7.2   The organisation process in spatial systems

Systems theory distinguishes between a system that is organised and a system that is becoming organised (Coffey, 1981). A system is considered organised when it possesses a structure that is orderly, whereas a system is becoming organised when each element that composes it develops its own functions in accordance with the potentialities of the element involved. This implies that within the system there is co-ordination and connection among the elements. Such definitions apply to any system, including not only social systems, but also spatial systems.

Such a concept of systems organisation is closely related to the concept of *entropy* (Coffey, 1981). It is possible to define three different interpretations of entropy. The first interpretation is the thermodynamics one which is based upon the two principles of thermodynamics; it considers entropy by referring to the process of irreversible degradation of energy in a closed system. The second entropy interpretation is the statistical thermodynamics approach which investigates how to quantify the different states of the energy distribution. The third entropy interpretation, the communication theory approach, examines entropy in relation to the information contained in a probability distribution. Our central focus is upon spatial process systems, and therefore the classical thermodynamics definition seems more suitable to our study. In fact, in thermodynamic terms, any system without inner constraints is characterised by a continuous change towards a state of equilibrium or perfect homogeneity. In this state, called the "state of disorder", the system assumes the maximum level of entropy and is unable to produce useful work (Georgescu-Roegen, 1971).

It should be noted that the thermodynamics definition addresses a *closed* system, whereas spatial networks are examples of an *open* system. The difficulty that arises in the application of the thermodynamics approach can be solved if we consider the Theory of Open Systems. This approach examines the capacity of the open system to evolve through states of equilibrium, i.e. the system moves from a state of equilibrium to another state of equilibrium, called "steady equilibrium", with a continuous exchange with the environment. This principle of dynamic equilibrium (Prigogine, 1971) is particularly important when defining the principle of *equifinality*. The principle of equifinality assumes that in an open system, if either the initial process or the nature of the process is altered, the final state will also be changed. In other words, the same final state of a system can be achieved by starting from different initial conditions and from different ways.

Let us depict this concept with a simple example (see Figure 7.1). In the figure a surface is considered as the system where its constraints are represented by the friction effect and two balls. The open system is represented by the balls and possible forces which can move the balls on the surface. If we imagine pushing the two balls with different forces, we will observe that from a certain point of equilibrium, the balls reach the same point of equilibrium. Their state of equilibrium is not static because the intervention of external elements will move the balls again. The movements of these two balls can be considered as a continuous process through equilibrium states.

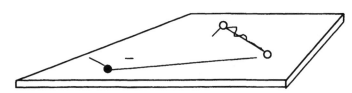

Figure 7.1 An example of the dynamic equilibrium and the principle of equifinality

After having briefly described the organisation concept and its relation to systems theory, we can observe that this concept is often linked to the notion of hierarchies. The logical dependence of these two concepts is shown by the fact that the development of organisation processes can be examined through hierarchies. This does not mean that a system organises itself according to the form of a hierarchically ordered structure as, for example, Bunge's vertical authority structure. We used the concept of hierarchy as a guide to rank, layer and cluster entities, and describe operations of the organisation processes of systems, such as network systems. For our purpose here, the brief examination of different types of *hierarchisation* also applies to transportation and communication networks.

7.3   Hierarchies of network spatial systems

Having considered the concept of hierarchy as a device to map out organisational processes in networks, we will now examine the various interpretations of this analytical tool. We can identify two perspectives from which we can interpret the concept of hierarchy. The first is the distinction between *vertical relations* and *horizontal relations*. By vertical relations we refer to the interactions among subsystems which are not symmetrical and which are uni-directional; while on the other hand, the horizontal relations are the interactions in between top and bottom levels of the system and among subsystems at the same hierarchical level. The second perspective discerns between the interaction *among* subsystems and the interaction *within* subsystems of a hierarchy.

Let us consider a hierarchical structure represented by the Chinese boxes introduced by Simon in 1973 (see Figure 2), where each subsystem interrelates and where each can be identified as a separate entity. In the Chinese boxes each box includes all others through a relationship of subdivision in which each part is distinguishable and has its own properties, but the components always have different properties which depend upon the collective that they form. Grobstein (1973) observes that "in its simplest sense hierarchical order refers to a complex of successively more encompassing sets. In hierarchies a given set must be described not only for itself while in terms both of what is within *it* and what it is *within*".

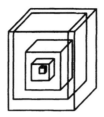

Figure 7.2 Hierarchical order in Chinese boxes

Koestler (1967) described the effect of this stratified boxes hierarchy as the 'Janus' effect, a tribute to the Roman god Janus who has, as a feature, two faces looking in opposite directions which may be interpreted as simultaneously looking inward and outward.

Simon (1973) also identifies another important characteristic of hierarchical structures: the 'Sisyphus' effect. "Two watchmakers assemble fine watches, each watch containing ten thousand parts. Each watchmaker is interrupted frequently to answer the phone. The first has organised his total assembly operation into a sequence of subassemblies; each subassembly is a stable arrangement of 100 elements, and each watch, a stable arrangement of 100 subassemblies. The second watchmaker has developed no such organisation. The average interval between phone interruptions is a time long enough to assemble about 150 elements. An interruption causes any set of elements that does not yet form a stable system to fall apart completely. By the time he has answered about eleven phone calls, the first watchmaker will usually have finished assembling a watch. The second watchmaker will almost never succeed in assembling one" (Simon, 1973). The advantage of modularization which Simon examines implies that complex systems can evolve more rapidly through hierarchical structures organised in a systematic way.

If we consider a set of elements such as A, B, C, and so on, a hierarchical relationship which will connect them may be written as:

$$S = [A, B, C, \ldots N]^R$$

This general definition of a hierarchy structure focuses on the factor R, which identifies the relationship among the different parts of the set. Thus, R establishes the connection of singular elements to the entire structure S, and defines the membership of this element to the hierarchy structure (Grobstein, 1973). The factor R constitutes the major concern in the definition of the hierarchy, since it determines the type of hierarchical structure that we want to adopt. In the previous section 7.2, we have assumed the absence of intrinsic hierarchies in the organisation processes of systems, particularly spatial systems such as networks. Such an assumption is in line with the idea that in order to discern reality, the most fundamental of human intellectual activities is the ordering of experience and the simplification of complexity. For instance, the Babylonian astronomers were the first to classify the stars by ordering them into constellations; the Greeks then divided the homogeneous space into a hierarchy of eight heavenly spheres, each equipped with its clockwork of epicycles (Koestler, 1967). From this viewpoint the factor R, and consequently the hierarchical structure, can be considered as a descriptive organising principle for network structures.

Given this observation, we suggest that the correspondence between the structural and the descriptive levels of the network is the definition of the factor R which allows us to define the hierarchical structure. However, the operational definition of the factor R must take into account the impossibility of an exhaustive description of the structural complexity of the network. For this reason, in the definition of our factor, we assume the uncertainty principle of quantum dynamics (or the Heisenberg principle), which expresses the fundamental indeterminism in any attempt to control all variables defining the state at a given instant in time.

At this point, we can further define the relevant factor R by following the suggestion of Pattee "to study the simplest language-like structure or, if you prefer, descriptive processes, that can create a clear separation of hierarchical levels" (Pattee, 1973). Against this background, the next section will compare two definitions of hierarchy of spatial networks. The first will be based upon the concept of accessibility as the discriminating factor among nodes. The second definition of network hierarchy focuses on the Chinese boxes hierarchy where it is necessary for us to define the interrelationships among the different parts of the networks without establishing a dominant or subordinate relationship among nodes.

7.4 An illustrative network analysis

We will now clarify the notion of network hierarchy on the basis of some illustrations. In order to develop the concept of the 'Chinese boxes' hierarchy, we will examine a simple network and carry out a comparative study of two different approaches which define two different concepts of a spatial system hierarchy.

In the first approach (Section 7.4.1), we will examine the network and its hierarchy through the matrices of *connectivity* and *accessibility*. Such an approach is widely applied in the scientific classification of transport networks. The hierarchies are determined through the analytical concepts of rank and superiority. We notice that leading scholars (Haggett and Chorley, 1969; Taaffe and Gauthier, 1973) have observed the limits of this approach, particularly the difficulty in dealing with network systems with large numbers of nodes and edges. In addition, these measurements are too weak to clearly differentiate among transportation networks. The second approach will be discussed in Section 7.4.2. It focuses upon the analysis of the interrelations among the sets of graphs and sub-graphs of the network.

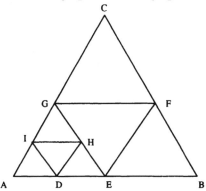

Figure 7.3 Illustrative nested network

We will start here with a simple network structure. The network we choose to examine as an illustrative case has a nested structure; it is characterised according to graph theory by 9 vertices and 15 edges. It is not disconnected and its diameter is equal to 3 (see Figure 7.3). Clearly, one may examine any other network configuration. The mapping in Figure 7.3 is only for illustrative purposes.

7.4.1   Hierarchy of nodes

In our investigation we assume that networks do not have intrinsic hierarchies, but that the definition of the hierarchy structure is a device to describe the network. In this analysis, by means of the connectivity and accessibility matrices (definitions will be given below), we will be able to define a hierarchy of the network according to the accessibility value of the nodes.

In order to define the hierarchy of nodes of the spatial network through the accessibility matrix, we must start with the definition of the connectivity matrix of the graph. The connectivity matrix is a binary matrix, where we assign a value equal to one to the vertices directly connected and a value equal to zero to disconnected vertices. Let us examine our illustrative network of Figure 7.3 and determine its connectivity matrix, ψ, according to the above procedure (see Table 7.1).

Table 7.1 Connectivity matrix

	A	B	C	D	E	F	G	H	I
A	0	0	0	1	0	0	0	0	1
B	0	0	0	0	1	1	0	0	0
C	0	0	0	0	0	1	1	0	0
D	1	0	0	0	1	0	0	1	1
E	0	1	0	1	0	1	0	1	0
F	0	1	1	0	1	0	1	0	0
G	0	0	1	0	0	1	0	1	1
H	0	0	0	1	1	0	1	0	1
I	1	0	0	1	0	0	1	1	0
Tot	2	2	2	4	4	4	4	4	4

The connectivity matrix can be used to yield a simple *measure of centrality*. In a nodal structure the centrality concept is based upon the dominant association (Abler et al., 1972) that is defined by the number of direct linkages of each node of the network. In the connectivity matrix we analyse the degree of centrality through the number of direct routes that join each node. For instance, node D in Figure 7.3 is directly connected to nodes A, I, H, E, and thus it has a centrality value equal to four. However, in our case the degree of connectivity of the network is insufficiently discriminative, because the set of nodes is divided by only two degrees of connectivity; i.e., the degree of connectivity is equal to two for nodes A, B, C, while the degree of connectivity is equal to four for the nodes D, E, F, G, H, I.

A more complex definition of centrality is through the accessibility matrix. The accessibility matrix is the sum of the connectivity matrix and all matrices that enumerate indirect paths between nodes on the network. It is therefore determined by summing the connectivity matrices taken to the powers 1 to n, where n equals the diameter of the network. The diameter of a network is defined as the maximum number of edges in the shortest path between each pair of vertices. In our case study we have calculated that the diameter of our network is three; therefore, we compute the accessibility matrix, χ, as follows:

$$\chi = \psi + \psi^2 + \psi^3;$$

After having determined the accessibility matrix, we then sum the values present in each column of the matrix in order to assign an accessibility value to the network nodes (see Table 7.2). Such a value indicates the number of direct and indirect paths which connect each of the nodes with any other node in (at most) three steps. For instance, the value 6 for the combination A-H in Table 7.2 means that there are four different paths connecting node A with node H in (at most) three steps. The higher the accessibility value, the more accessible is the node by the network routes and consequently, the more central - or predominant - is its position in relation to the surrounding areas and within the network structure.

Table 7.2 Accessibility matrix

	A	B	C	D	E	F	G	H	I
A	4	1	1	8	4	2	4	6	8
B	1	4	3	3	7	7	4	4	3
C	1	3	4	3	4	7	7	4	3
D	8	3	3	10	10	5	7	12	12
E	4	7	4	10	8	10	7	11	7
F	2	7	7	5	10	8	10	6	5
G	4	4	7	7	7	10	8	11	10
H	6	4	4	12	11	6	11	10	12
I	8	3	3	12	7	5	10	12	10
Tot	38	36	36	70	68	60	68	76	70

Now it becomes clear that these accessibility values of the vertices allow us to define the hierarchical structure of the network (see Table 7.3). In our case, the node H has the highest accessibility, whereas the lowest value of accessibility is achieved by nodes B and C. It is interesting to notice that the value of accessibility assumes its highest value for the most 'nested' vertex, i.e. H.

Table 7.3 Hierarchy of nodes

node B	36
node C	36
node A	38
node F	60
node E	68
node G	68
node D	70
node I	70
node H	76

By developing this approach, we have determined the hierarchy through the accessibility matrix. Such a hierarchical arrangement is characterised by a *pyramidal shape,* where the node with the highest value of accessibility is the peak of the pyramid. However, with such a definition of hierarchy, we examine our complex network-reality from a single perspective - the accessibility value - and obtain only a mono-dimensional picture. We may ask, is this attempt satisfactory for our observation and understanding of network systems? Let us now examine another possible approach of *hierarchisation.*

7.4.2   Nested hierarchies

A network represents a connection of points and depicts the interconnection among the different sub-graphs which constitute the graph of the network. According to this definition, a network therefore can be examined as Simon's Chinese boxes, where the nest of subnetworks composes the entire structure of the network. In our earlier discussion of this approach, we recognised not only the necessity to examine the interconnection among the subnetworks - interconnection which depends upon the whole network that the subnetworks form - but also to focus our attention on the single subnetworks which have their distinguishing structures and properties.

In order to establish this hierarchy construction, we need to determine a factor that will identify the rules in accordance to which we will be able to decompose our network. Such an important role in the hierarchy definition is developed by the factor R.

$$S = [A, B, C, \ldots N]^R$$

where : S is the network;
        A, B, C,...N are the subnetworks.

To reiterate our discussion thus far on the factor R, we have observed that such a factor is the analytical device which attempts to organise, simplify and then rank the nodes of networks into hierarchies. The choice of the factor determines the level of detail into which we want to partition the network. It is certainly related to the features of the network being examined, in, for example, its morphology or its functions. Nevertheless, in the selection of the factor R, we need to always keep in mind that we have assumed there to be no hierarchy as a built-in structure in the network, and we can therefore freely decide the number of levels that better describe the network.

Let us consider the triangular figure previously examined (see Figure 7.3). The network depicts a simple structure, all the subnetworks are connected graphs, and in our case the network is a closed graph. We thus decide to break down the network into three hierarchical levels. This will imply that each node of the network not only would belong to a specific hierarchical level more than one time - due to the fact that a node can belong to various subnetworks which compose the partitioned network of the specific hierarchical level - but also that each node can or cannot belong to the three established levels of hierarchy. The membership of the network nodes to these three hierarchical levels will be represented by three *hierarchy membership functions*; $f(n)$ for the first hierarchical subnetwork, $g(n)$ for the second hierarchical subnetwork, $h(n)$ for the third hierarchical subnetwork.

The rules, i.e. the factors R, by which we will subdivide the network, are defined as follows. We observe that the network is constituted by a contour network, the line A-D-E-B-F-C-G-I. We assume that the first hierarchical level is formed by the points that belong to the contour (see Figure 7.4a). In the case of an open graph, we arbitrarily connect the "broken" contour with *dummy* edges. This will not falsify the results of our general procedure, since the approach is focused on the nodes of the network and their interconnectivity rather than the edges of the contour. Each of the vertices along the contour has a value equal to 1 of a membership function *f(n)* (see Table 7.4). This function represents the attachment of the vertices to the contour of the network and therefore indicates how many times the examined node belongs to the different subnetworks. For instance, since node H does not belong to the first hierarchical level, the membership function f(H) is equal to zero. However, when we assign the membership function to the node, we assume that each node must belong to each subnetwork only one time.

The second level of the hierarchy is formed by subnetworks – distinct from the contour – which have all their vertices along the contour of the network (see Figure 7.4b). The membership of the vertices at this level is defined by the function *g(n)* (see Table 7.4). The third level is formed by all the subnetworks which must have at least one vertex which does not belong to the contour of the network (see Figure 7.4c). The function *h(n)* indicates the membership of the vertices to this third hierarchical level (see Table 7.4).

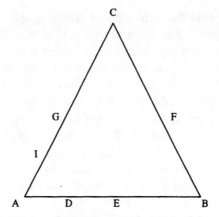

Figure 7.4a First hierarchical level

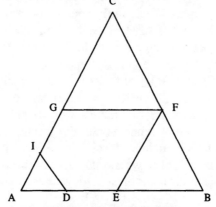

Figure 7.4b Second hierarchical level

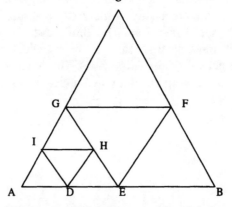

Figure 7.4c Third hierarchical level

If the network presented a more complex structure and the three hierarchical levels were insufficient in describing it, we could add as many levels as is necessary by following the same procedure. For instance, the fourth hierarchical level will be formed by all subnetworks that have at least two nodes which do not belong to the contour of the network; the fifth will have at least three nodes, and so on.

Table 7.4 Network membership functions

n	f(n)	g(n)	h(n)
A	1	4	12
B	1	4	16
C	1	4	16
D	1	8	33
E	1	8	37
F	1	9	32
G	1	8	37
H	0	0	42
I	1	8	33

The values which appear in Table 7.4 represent the number of subnetworks to which the node being examined belongs. For instance, for node A, in the first hierarchical level we have found only one subnetwork where it belongs; in the second hierarchical level, there are four subnetworks which have node A, whereas in the third hierarchical level there are twelve subnetworks that have node A.

Now that we have assigned the values of the three membership functions to all vertices of the network, we can rank these values into three hierarchies (see Table 7.5).

Table 7.5 Hierarchies of the nested network

n	f(n)	n	g(n)	n	h(n)
H	0	H	0	A	12
A	1	A	4	B	16
B	1	B	4	C	16
D	1	C	4	F	32
C	1	D	8	D	33
E	1	E	8	I	33
F	1	G	8	E	37
G	1	I	8	G	37
I	1	F	9	H	42

These three levels of hierarchies depict the interrelation of the vertices of the various subnetworks. For instance, node H is first in the first and second hierarchies shown above, but it has the last position in the third hierarchy. This illustrates the different hierarchical 'roles' that a node can assume according to our approach.

In order to better explain our concept of *hierarchisation* in relation to our findings, let us imagine that the network of Figure 7.3 represents the structure of railway systems. In the first hierarchical level (see Figure 7.4a.) we identify the international railway network; the second hierarchical level (see Figure 7.4b.) represents the national freight railway network; and the third hierarchical level (see Figure 7.4c.) identifies the national passenger railway network. If, in the light of this example, we now examine the role of node F, we observe that the node belongs to the international railway network and has the highest interconnectivity among the nodes in the national freight network, but that it has medium-low interconnectivity among the nodes in the national passenger network. With this framework we may more precisely target policies for this specific node F, as for example, an increase in the interconnectivity of the node in the passenger national network level.

Finally, it is noteworthy that in principle, the previous approach may also be useful to analyse spatial dynamics by investigating the structural transformation in a network system (e.g., as a result of new nodes or an extension of current infrastructure). Such morphological changes in the hierarchy can then be analysed by comparing the evolution of hierarchy indices over time.

7.5   Conclusion

Networks are important organisational structures of complex phenomena. In this paper we have presented the concept of hierarchy as a system of 'Chinese boxes' first introduced by Simon in 1973. This approach differs from the more widespread definition of hierarchy, since it emphasises the interrelationships among the various parts of the network rather than defines a criterion that determines a hierarchy based upon dominance and subordination.

The technique that we have proposed focuses above all upon the interconnection among the subnetworks within the network. Such interconnectivity creates a lens through which we can observe the network by means of either a close-up or a global view according to the subnetworks which we examine. The approach that we have compared to our method considers the accessibility matrix as the discriminating factor among the nodes. The primary limitation of the latter approach is that the definition of hierarchy is developed through a single point of view, i.e. the accessibility value. Through the accessibility value, one focuses upon the dominant relationship among the nodes of the network, and therefore one can only generate a hierarchical classification based upon a pyramidal structure.

Our approach in contrast emphasises the nested characteristics of the networks. It may easily be extended to a dynamic analysis, where we can compare the development of the network through the addition and subtraction of subnetworks in, for instance, the analysis of the effects of a European network expansion upon national transport networks such as the high-speed train system. At present, two endeavours seem to be promising for further investigation into the operational definition of a nested hierarchy. First, there is the necessity to improve the analytical procedure of identifying the subnetworks within the network through the use of more sophisticated software programmes such as the GRADAP 2.0 software. Second, there is a need to test whether our definition of hierarchy is feasible in a comparative examination among different spatial network systems, such as between the railway system and the road system.

The preceding ideas on hierarchical networks are not only analytically interesting, but they also have an applied relevance in the framework of the far-reaching changes in European network configurations (e.g., the position of major metropolitan areas in the European space-economy). We have observed that the concept of hierarchy is a device to simplify and comprehend reality. For instance, in our case, we have examined the complexity of network systems. From this viewpoint, the hierarchical structure defined by the accessibility concept emerges as a device based upon a strong 'central places' approach. The 'central places' dimension has an impact on the definition of the accessibility hierarchies by creating a predominant position of the geographical element above both the organisation and coordination elements of the networks. This network interpretation, by definition, consigns peripheral regions to an inferior position.

European policies, beginning with the Maastricht Treaty, have advocated the *interoperability, integration* and *intermodality* of the European networks. In order to achieve these objectives, it is reasonable to examine networks as a multi-layered system and then to construct the *Chinese boxes* that represent the European networks. From this perspective, given the network layer that is examined, peripheral areas might assume the highest value in the defined nested hierarchies. Such information can be used to direct appropriate strategies toward the various nodes of the European network. For such an endeavour a comprehensive and systematic research effort is then necessary to map out structural transformations in the European network system.

References

Alba, R.D. and C. Kadushin (1976), "The Intersection of Social Circles. A New Measure of Social Proximity in Networks", *Sociological Methods & Research*, Vol. 5, No.1, 77-103.

Alba, R.D. and G. Moore (1978), "Elite Social Circles", *Sociological Methods & Research*, Vol.7, No.2, 167-189.

Abler, R., Adams J.S. and P. Gould (1972), *Spatial Organisation: the Geographer's View of the World*, Prentice/Hall International: London.

Barndorff-Nielsen, O.E., Jensen J.L. and W.S. Kendall (eds) (1994), *Networks and Chaos-Statistical and Probabilistic Aspects*, Chapman and Hall: London.

Berry, B.J.L. (1972), "Hierarchical Diffusion: the Basis of Developmental Filtering and Spread in a System of Growth Centers", in Hansen N.M (ed.), *Growth Centers in Regional Economics Development*, The Free Press: New York.

Boyce, R.R. (ed.) (1980), *Geography as Spatial Interaction*, University of Washington Press: Seattle.

Bunge, M. (1969), "The Metaphysics, Epistemology and Methodology of Levels", in Whyte L.L., Wilson A.G. and D. Wilson (eds), *Hierarchical Structures*, American Elsevier: New York.

Coffey, W.J. (1981), *Geography: Towards a General Spatial Systems Approach*, Methuen: New York.

Coffey, W.J. (ed.) (1988), *Geographical Systems and Systems of Geography*, The University of Western Ontario: Ontario.

Georgescu-Roegen, N. (1971), *The Entropy Law and the Economic Process*, Harvard University Press : Cambridge.

Grene, M. (1969), "Hierarchy: One Word, How Many Concepts?", in Whyte L.L., Wilson A.G. and D. Wilson (eds), *Hierarchical Structures*, American Elsevier: New York.

Grobstein, C. (1973), "Hierarchical Order and Neogenesis", in Pattee H.H.(ed.), *Hierarchy Theory: the Challenge of Complex Systems*, George Braziller: New York.

Hasan, M. (1978), *Social Network in Spatial Perspective*, discussion paper no.45, Dept. of Geography, Syracuse University.

Haggett, P. and R.J. Chorley (1969), *Network Analysis in Geography*, Edward Arnold: London.

Knoke, D. and J.H. Kuklinski (1982), *Network Analysis*, SAGE: Beverly Hills.

Koestler, A. (1967), *The Ghost in the Machine*, Macmillan Company: New York.

Meijer, O.G. (1988), *The Hierarchy Debate*, Free University Press: Amsterdam.

Muller, G. and R.P. Blanc (eds) (1986), *Networking in Open Systems*, Springer-Verlag: Berlin.

Pattee, W.H. (ed.) (1973), *Hierarchy Theory: the Challenge of Complex Systems*, George Braziller: New York.

Pearl, J. (1985), *On Evidential Reasoning in a Hierarchy of Hypotheses*, Technical Report University of California: Los Angeles.

Scott, J. (1991), *Social Network Analysis: a Handbook*, SAGE: London.

Simon, H.A. (1969), *The Sciences of the Artificial*, The M.I.T. Press: London.

Simon, H.A. (1973), "The Organisation of Complex Systems", in Pattee H.H. (ed.), *Hierarchy Theory: the Challenge of Complex Systems*, George Braziller: New York.

Taaffe, E.J. and H.L.Jr Gauthier, (1973), *Geography of Transportation*, Prentice-Hall: New York.

Thom, R. (1975), *Structural Stability and Morphogenesis*, The Benjamin Cummings Publishing Company: London.

Torenvliet, L. (1986), *Structural Concepts in Relativised Hierarchies*, University of Amsterdam: Amsterdam.

Veldman, W. (1981), *Investigations in Intuitionistic Hierarchy Theory*, Katholike Universiteit Nijmegen: Nijmegen.

Wasserman, S. and K. Faust (1994), *Social Network Analysis: Methods and Applications*, Cambridge University Press: New York.

Whyte, L.L, Wilson A.G. and D. Wilson (eds) (1969), *Hierarchical Structures*, American Elsevier: New York.

Woldenberg, M.J. and B.J.L. Berry (1967), "River and Central Places: Analogous Systems?", *Journal of Regional Science*, Vol.7, No.2, 128-139.

Woldenberg, M.J. (1985), *Models in Geomorphology*, Allen and Unwin: Boston.

PART B:
GOVERNANCE OF NETWORKS

8 Assessing Scenarios on European Transport Policies by Means of Multicriteria Analysis[1]

CHRISTIAN HEY, PETER NIJKAMP,
SYTZE A. RIENSTRA AND
DIETER ROTHENBERGER

8.1 The common transport policy of the European Union

The Maastricht Treaty states that the EU aims to 'promote a stable and non-inflationary growth which respects the environment'. As part of the required action, it calls for the integration of the principles of sustainable development into all EU policies. This includes the regulations governing the Structural Funds programme, which supports a large number of transport projects. As an elaboration of these objectives to the transport sector, the Common Transport Policy (CTP) of the EU has the following objectives (CEC, 1992):

- free movement of goods and persons;
- development of a coherent, integrated transport system using the best available technology;
- reducing disparities between regions, e.g. by infrastructure construction;
- sustainable patterns of development by respecting the environment;
- actions to promote safety;
- encouraging social cohesion;
- developing appropriate relations with third countries.

---

[1] The paper is based on the POSSUM (Policy Scenarios for sustainable mobility) project, which represents Strategic Research Task 13 in the 4th Framework Transport Programme of the European Union. Other members of the POSSUM group are: David Banister and Dominic Stead (UCL, London); Maria Giaoutzi and Zenia Dimitrakopoulou (NTUA, Athens); Jonas Akerman and Peter Steen (ESRG/FOA, Stockholm); Veli Himanen (VTT, Espoo); Wolclech Suchorzewski (WUT, Warsaw) and Viacheslav Arsenov (MTI, Moscow).

These objectives are, however, abstract in nature, while it is neither clear whether these objectives are complementary or conflicting. A scenario analysis is therefore extremely useful for analysing this problem. In order to focus the analysis and to find concrete targets for the CTP, the objectives concerned may be redefined in three issues (see also POSSUM, 1997): increasing the efficiency of transport systems, contributing to regional development and achieving environmental sustainability.

This paper will first set concrete targets for these three general objectives. Target setting cannot be a purely ivory tower task; it requires wide consensus. This paper tries to find a number of widely accepted statements and terms of reference from both scientific and official policy documents which might offer a basis for target definition. Next, scenarios are constructed by maximising these targets within two so-called external frameworks. Then we will analyse the extent to which the targets identified are fulfilled in the distinct scenarios, by means of a multicriteria analysis based on regime analysis. Finally, some strategic policy conclusions for future EU policies are formulated.

8.2   Targets for the environmental dimension

Setting targets is a very difficult and politically sensitive task. A general problem of target setting is that very general targets (like economic growth) may be achieved by different, sometimes even contradictory means (see Tinbergen, 1956). Therefore, target setting must be an open process; an objective threshold does not exist, but has to be defined in a social context. Transport can predominantly be regarded as a means - so one can assume very different transport policy strategies and transport policy targets, being derived from more general targets. We will focus here on both scientific and political terms of reference for target setting, and will discuss target setting for environmental, regional development and efficiency issues, respectively.

For environmental targets, the idea of environmental sustainability needs to be transformed into operational targets. There is a crucial difference to be made between strong and weak sustainability which results from different viewpoints with regard to ecological, economic and social aspects. In addition, more pragmatic targets may be chosen based on official policy targets. These issues will successively be discussed in Subsections 8.2.1-8.2.3.

8.2.1 Strong sustainability

The term 'sustainability' refers to policy choices that give priority to ecological objectives. This priority expresses the fact that any human activity is more or less contingent on some natural resource; therefore, beyond certain limits there is no justification for economic trade-off analysis concerning the use of natural resources. These limits are to be scientifically determined and constitute a political constraint for economic activities.

Strong sustainability can be derived from the characteristics of economic and technological processes with regard to thermodynamics and ecology. These processes can be described as irreversible, entropy-increasing and non-substitutional (with regard to natural and manufactured capital). Additionally, risk aversion is the underlying strategy of strong sustainability to deal with uncertainty about future environmental conditions. Strong sustainability is the basis for so-called management rules, such as:

- use of renewables has to be in line with their ability to regenerate;
- use of non-renewables has to be in line with the increase in productivity of renewables;
- there has to be a balance between the natural assimilation capacity and anthropogenic emissions and waste;
- there has to be a balance between time-scale of human impacts and natural processes.

Several more practical applications of the concept strong sustainability are defined in the literature.

8.2.1.1 Critical Loads/Levels Critical loads or levels can be defined as scientifically derived limits of environmental stress for receivers like ecosystems, parts of ecosystems, organisms and materials (SRU, 1994). This concept has also been adopted by The World Commission of the UN for Europe (UN-ECE) for different air pollution substances. The underlying assumption is, that there is no damage to be expected when the actual environmental stress levels are below Critical Levels or Loads.

8.2.1.2 Environmental Utilisation Space Another approach to strong sustainability is the concept of Environmental Utilisation Space, which can be seen as an approximation of the ecosystems' capacities to buffer stresses by human impacts (Opschoor and Wetering, 1992). Another definition is '... the space of the natural environment which can be utilised by humanity without damaging crucial characteristics'. This concept depends on the different conditions of ecosystems, e.g. carrying capacity. Besides, it is possible to enlarge the Environmental Utilisation Space through human activities like reforestation. Like in the concept of Critical Loads/Levels, priority is given to ecological limits and not to economic processes. Moreover, this approach stresses social aspects, since the distribution of resources is included. Using the assumption of equal rights for any human being to environmental safety, equally individual access to resources is postulated.

8.2.1.3 Maximum Scale The concept of Critical loads/Levels can be linked to Daly's (1992) concept of Maximum Scale. This approach does not consider a set of single environmental limits, but a physical measure for the size of the economic system in comparison with the natural system and its carrying capacity. The variables which determine this size (scale) are: population and standard of living (per capita consumption). Hardin (1992) describes the total human impact on the environment as population x per capita impact. The objective is to reduce the total human impact or the scale to a size compatible with the carrying capacity of nature.

8.2.1.4 Entropy Kümmel (1980) defines an indicator for the pressure put on the natural system by human activities. This indicator consists of social welfare losses, based on the relative increase of entropy caused by production and consumption and the entropy-reduction due to nature.

Advantages of the concept of strong sustainability are that the settings of ecological objectives are limits which should not be exceeded, resulting in a long term protection of proper conditions for human living. The decision about the use of ecological resources beyond these limits is withdrawn from individual and economic trade-offs. Another advantage is the scientific determination of these limits, which is not dependent on psychological factors and therefore less prone to mistakes.

However, one has to bear in mind that human knowledge about the complex issues of ecosystem dependence is far from perfect; therefore, there is no guarantee that the limits are set right. Another criticism is that the impact on economic and social systems is not considered. The limitation of economic use of resources can result in massive regional or sectoral disturbances.

Moreover, the concept of Environmental Utilisation Space is seen as imposing severe political interventions in the market system and a mechanism to distribute resources without considering regional differences. So, some critics see the danger of eroding the market system, limiting individual freedom and changing personal preferences due to the absolute priority of nature. This priority given to nature is expressed particularly within Daly's concept of maximum scale.

It can be concluded that the concepts discussed above are up to now not capable of providing clear targets for sustainable transport policies. Next, we will investigate whether 'weak sustainability' concepts can provide clear targets.

8.2.2 Weak sustainability

In contrast to strong sustainability the concept of weak sustainability puts much more emphasis on the impacts of environmental aims on the economic system. The concept is based on the assumption that natural capital can be substituted by manufactured capital, so that environmental losses can be compensated for by e.g. infrastructural gains. Weak sustainability copes with uncertainty in a rather risk-loving way, trying to maximise economic benefits by taking environmental risks. In the literature several approaches can be found.

8.2.2.1 The Corridor concept WBGU (1996) has developed a so-called Inverse-scenario for estimations of minimum global reduction efforts, using the example of the greenhouse effect. Starting from the effects of climate change on humans and nature, tolerable limits of future climate change are derived. With this information emission profiles can be calculated which ensure that the changes stay within the limits and that necessary reductions are easily identified. The starting point is the viewpoint of many economists that costs to adapt to climate change higher than 3-5 per cent of global GNP lead to heavy disturbances of economic and social systems. Calculations of the tolerable climate change are based on this figure.

The advantage of this approach is that exogenous climate data can be integrated within economic models and therefore be transformed into endogenous variables. The maximum tolerated climate change can be reached in many different ways, and society can choose which way to go (e.g., starting drastically or transforming gradually).

On the other hand, there are some problems inherent in this approach. To determine the limits one has to conduct economic-ecological impact assessments to analyse the economic impacts of environmental changes. The difficulties with these assessments are well known from the discussion about the monetarisation of damages to the environment. Especially with regard to the conventional method of discounting future values of goods, a wrong damage curve may be derived and used, resulting in the wrong tolerable climate change.

8.2.2.2 No Regrets Strategy No Regrets Strategy means that only measures are taken which have a positive economic effect and additional environmental

175

gains (Nijkamp et al., 1998; Rienstra, 1998). This strategy looks for reductions of environmental stress, which also induce cost savings which are as least as high as the costs of the measure (less water used, less energy consumed). The objective is to abolish all obstacles to the realisation of these measures and thereby to reduce the pressure on the environment without inducing costs for businesses or households. Therefore, political interventions should not impose new restrictions, but reduce transaction costs by abolishing lack of information and capital. Some studies found a potential for CO_2 emission reduction of about 10-20 per cent (Springman, 1991).

The advantage of this approach is the possible change of attitudes towards environmental protection, because it loses its character as a cost-driver. Furthermore, win-win solutions may be established, which leads to high acceptance. On the other hand, the realisation of this change is doubtful, because the individual maximisation of benefits still does not include environmental issues. Besides, the fact that the societal benefits from environmental improvements are ignored means that the social optimum is not reached.

8.2.2.3 The Solow Model As a measure for the sustainable use of capital Solow (1986) proposes the maximum consumption per head which can be sustained indefinitely. This implies that not natural capital but total capital must remain constant, and that natural capital can be substituted by man-made capital. As a result, intergenerational equity is established; investing in non-renewables to increase the productivity of other input factors - such as infrastructure, education, and modern machines - may compensate for the loss of natural resources. The advantage of this concept is the legitimisation of the use of non-renewables, which is to date unavoidable, but the assumption of complete substitution is highly disputed.

Although the weak sustainability concepts are somewhat more concrete than the strong sustainability concepts, it is again not possible to define clear targets based on these concepts. Therefore, we will turn now to a more pragmatic way of defining targets; viz. analysing which targets are found in official documents.

8.2.3 Taking official policy targets

The reasoning behind official policy targets is often much more fragmented and ad hoc, than the above described top-down approaches. The logic is political rather than rational in a scientific sense. This may be illustrated by a few examples:

- the SO_2 reduction targets of the EU from 1988 have been calculated on the basis of the 'BATNEEC-Concept' (Best available technology not exceeding excessive costs) (Héritier et al., 1994). This concept implies, that only technologies are assumed, which have reached a sufficient degree of market diffusion and do not cause excessive - politically acceptable - costs;
- the EU CO_2 stabilisation target from 1990 is based on the positive side-effects of industrial decline in Eastern Germany on the CO_2 balance of the EU. So most countries could afford CO_2 emission increases and only a few already committed countries were to achieve a slight decrease of CO_2 emissions (Haigh, 1996);
- the proposed 25 per cent reduction target of Germany is based on available evidence on climate change and on the technical potential to reduce CO_2 emissions (Beuermann and Jäger, 1996). The ambitious target was announced before elections to attract greening conservative voters.

The state of official environmental targets of the EU related to transport is presented in Table 8.1; for the sake of comparison, also the targets of the German Environmental Protection Agency are included.

Table 8.1
Environmental targets of the European Union and Germany

Issue	EU reduction targets	German EPA reduction targets
CO_2 emissions	Stabilisation (1990-2000)	25% (1990-2005)
NO_x emissions	30% (1990-2005)	80% (1990-2005)
Dioxine	90% (1985-2005)	--
Heavy metals	70% (by 1995)	70% (by 1995)
Noise	threshold: 65db; no additional noise beyond 55db	threshold: 50db (by 2030)
Nature protection	'Natura 2000' network; habitat and birds directives	no additional net surface covered by roads
Benzol	--	90% (1988-2010)
VOC	30% (1990-1900)	80% (1987-2005)

Source: EU: CEC, 1993a; Germany: Gorissen, 1995.
Note: In March 1997 the EU ministers of environment agreed upon a 15 per cent CO_2 reduction target for the year 2010 as an offer for the UN Earth Summit Conference.

One may argue that political goals, which have been formulated for 2005 or 2010 might become more widely accepted for the period until 2020, which is the time frame for our scenarios. Targets may now be chosen based on indicators for environmental sustainability which are based on several criteria

(POSSUM, 1997; Rienstra et al., 1997; Rienstra, 1998): first, the number of indicators should be as small as possible in order to keep the analysis manageable; second, the indicators should relate to all main environmental problems caused by transport. This analysis resulted in CO_2 and NO_x emissions as the most important indicators.

8.2.3.1 CO2 emissions When in addition to the above table also other sources are taken into consideration, it can be concluded that a 25-30 per cent overall CO_2 emission reduction target for the year 2020 is in the lower range of what is required to avoid major environmental damage (see e.g., WBGU, 1996). If one assumes an overall 30 per cent target and that different sectors have different cost-effective potentials, not every sector should have the same CO_2 reduction target. Stead (1997) suggests to take the predicted trends as a rough indicator for the cost-effective reduction potential. So it is assumed, that low growth sectors have a higher reduction potential than high growth sectors. According to the CEC (1996) overall CO_2 growth between 1992 and 2020 will be 15 per cent, when current trends continue. Compared to the trend, a 30 per cent target means a reduction of 39 per cent. Overall mobility growth is estimated to be 22 per cent. If one calculates the above reduction target for the year 2020, a 25 per cent reduction from 1995 levels is required.

8.2.3.2 NOx emissions The same type of analysis may be applied to NO_x emissions, which is the second hardest objective to achieve and also an important indicator for several environmental impacts. When 1995 is taken as a reference year, up to 2020 a reduction of 80 per cent is in line with the objectives stated in Table 8.1 and other sources.

It can be concluded that scientific concepts may provide insights into the necessary reduction of external factors, but that it is up to now too complex to set concrete targets based on these concepts. Therefore, targets are pragmatically chosen based on current policy documents. Next, we will turn to setting targets for the regional dimension.

8.3 Targets for the regional dimension

As mentioned in Section 1, social and economic cohesion is one of the fundamental objectives of the EU. However, a widely accepted and operational definition of cohesion does not exist. Cohesion is politically defined as the socially acceptable difference of economic and social welfare between regions or groups. The thresholds for acceptable differences differ from region to region and from context to context. This makes a target definition difficult to find.

Even the term 'convergence', which aims at the gradual reduction of differences in wealth, GDP or unemployment rates, gives little help. Most regions would prefer high growth rates (even at the price of relative decline) to convergence at the price of low growth. The following goals for regional planning can be distinguished (Schleicher-Tappeser et al., 1996):

- *functionally balanced regions*; this derives from the idea to create equal living conditions in each region. Due to the diversity of European regions this model could not be implemented - despite considerable financial support;
- *spatial functional division of labour*; this approach refers to specialisation and the reliance on comparative advantages, which culminated in concepts like 'tourist region', 'industrial region' or 'refuse disposal regions';
- *endogenous regional development*, stressing regional independence; endogenous development aims at allowing a region's inhabitants a 'satisfying' standard of living. Living conditions may vary according to specific natural and economic potentials, regional cultures and modes of institutional regulation.

Objective 1 regions - which receive more than 70 per cent of the Structural EU Funds - are defined to have less than 75 per cent of average per capita income of the EU (CEC, 1993b). On this basis a minimum target for regional development is a steady improvement of income and employment for these regions. Economic growth of objective 1 regions should therefore be higher than the EU average.

Furthermore, an objective for the cohesion within peripheral regions should be defined. Unemployment seems to be a rough but easily available indicator. In this sense decreasing unemployment (say with an unemployment rate less than 5 per cent) might be used as a target for the equity dimension between regions.

8.3.1   Regional development objectives and transport policies

What this means for transport policies depends on more specific goals of regional planning, the associated policy strategies and hence on the underlying theories of regional development and on the different economic structures. A uniform goal for a transport policy promoting regional development cannot be defined, since this depends on the specific situation and the choices within regions.

On this basis one can distinguish two different ideal type orientations: an export-led growth orientation requiring accessibility to the centres, and an inward-oriented orientation focusing on the quality of intraregional communication networks. Also analytically it is difficult to assess the regional development impact of new high-quality infrastructures to peripheral regions.

There is no linear correlation between regional development and the quality of transport links between the regions and other economic centres (Bruinsma et al., 1997; Vickerman, 1995). Due to different specific economic structures different regions have different transport needs. Some scientists even argue, that better transport links between strong and competitive centres and economically weak peripheries may increase polarisation instead of cohesion (see the literature survey by Hey et al., 1996).

Furthermore, specific targets have to be related to indicators. But as Vickerman (1995) argues, traditional accessibility indicators focusing on time or distance between a peripheral region and a set of economic centres do not match the complexity of the issue. Accessibility indicators have to consider, that peripheral regions are dependent on the network quality within transit regions, discontinuities exist and interchanges become important. Furthermore, not only infrastructure, but also frequencies are relevant for measuring accessibility. Finally, different sectors have different needs with respect to connectivity, speed, price or modal choice (Vickerman, 1996).

Finally, good access for a regional centre may mean more peripherality for any other location along a corridor. On this basis Vickerman (1996) suggests a complex and eclectical mix of different accessibility indicators, taking into account frequency, modal choices, economic structure, modal discontinuities etc. Although this would be an accurate choice, it is too complicated for assessing scenarios focusing on general trends. Therefore, a simplified approach is required. We will apply two approaches, a traditional and an innovative one.

8.3.2.1 The traditional approach This approach starts from the traditional idea of accessibility. A transport policy target is the improvement of 'access' to economic centres. This implies short travel times, user choices and low transport costs - normally between the regional centres and the most important international centres of economic activity. CEC (1994) applies a BFLR-index, which measures the potential population that can be reached within a given travel time by using the best available modes. This index identifies 194 centres from regions at the NUTS III scale and measures the resident population which can be reached within 3 hours. Actually there is a difference between regions with the lowest and the highest accessibility by a factor 4. Due to geographical differences this difference can never be equalised but only improved. A general target may therefore be to improve the accessibility of peripheral centres by 50-100 per cent by the year 2020. A Gini-coefficient of accessibility based upon the BFLR-Index might be a tool to measure the dynamics of more equitable access of peripheral regions.

8.3.3.2 The innovative approach This approach is more concerned with accessibility within regions. As several authors state (e.g., Vickerman, 1996) most traffic takes place within regions. Hence, the focus of this strategy is to improve accessibility within regions. On a European scale the objective of such a strategy is to give intraregional accessibility priority over interregional accessibility. This could be measured by a coefficient which compares intraregional (A_i) with interregional accessibility (A_e). A general target is to improve A_i/A_e by more than 25 per cent. This measure would accept the given natural differences of accessibility between regions, but nevertheless would seek for a relative improvement. For A_e the BFLR-index can be used, for A_i an analogous indicator may be constructed identifying the centres within a NUTS III region.

8.4 Targets for the efficiency dimension

Reference points for efficiency targets may be found in general welfare economic theories, other theoretical reflections or policy documents of the EU. General welfare economics has identified two different criteria for efficiency improvements: the strict Pareto criterion and the wider Kaldor-Hicks criterion. The Pareto criterion is met, when a change induces an increase of welfare levels without reducing the welfare of any other individual. Generally, it is assumed that this can be best achieved under market conditions. The Kaldor-Hicks criterion is met when total welfare increases for one group due to the change are higher than the total losses of others.

So a starting point for both efficiency definitions is maximising economic growth from a given set of resources. It is less evident what this may mean for the transport sector. In general, one could argue that transport policies should facilitate economic development. But this can be achieved by different sets of subtargets. Two approaches can now be identified for defining efficiency targets: taking transport as a resource or treating transport as a sector contributing to economic growth.

181

8.4.1   Transport as a source

A wide perspective treats transport itself as a resource and tries to maximise economic growth (Peake, 1994). So a transport efficient economy minimises its transport needs to maintain a certain growth path. Dematerialisation and the substitution of physical flows by non-physical flows (Pestel and Johnston, 1996) might be vital characteristics of a transport efficient economy. This certainly applies to freight transport. In the case of passenger transport however, mobility is not only a means (so as to find access to certain facilities), but also as final consumption (mainly leisure activities). This is a problem for the definition of transport as a resource for the economy.

Despite this reservation one may argue that, taking the link between energy use and economic development as a historical model (Peake, 1994), the decoupling of economic growth from mobility growth (both for passengers and freight) is a fundamental efficiency goal (for example, no mobility growth combined with 2.5 per cent real BNP growth). Assuming that economic growth will be 100 per cent over the next 20-30 years, decoupling would mean halving the transport intensity of the economy. As a target this would mean improving the transport efficiency of the economy by a factor 2.

8.4.2   Transport as contributor to economic growth

Yet, efficiency may also be characterised by the contribution of the transport sector to economic growth in a totally opposite sense. CEC (1993b) highlights the essential relationship between the functioning of the internal market, the competitiveness of the European economy and a fast, flexible and low cost transport system, which reduces natural spatial barriers as much as possible. The efficiency goal is not related to the overall economy, but rather to the transport sector itself, which is supposed to maximise its performance under a given set of public and private expenditures for transport services.

The traditional definition of efficiency relates to the transport sector itself (Van Gent and Nijkamp, 1991) and is essentially linked to the second definition. Transport is subordinated to the needs of the growing economy. Efficiency in this case means, to provide a transport service at the lowest possible costs. The definition of efficiency in a free and competitive transport market is no problem: marginal costs (including external costs) have to be equal to the marginal willingness to pay for transport users. Transport necessarily implies some degree of government intervention, especially in the case of infrastructure policies, safety regulations and social minimum standards to avoid dumping practices by operators. For governments efficiency implies the optimal use of public finance in terms of investment profitability and minimisation of public subsidies.

An efficiency goal for public investments into the transport sector might be, to realise at least the same rate of return for public investments, as for the average of the economy as a whole. A lower rate of return would indicate that more efficient uses of capital exist. A more ambitious efficiency target would be to set priorities for public investment priorities where the highest rates of return might be produced. Cost-Benefit Analysis offers a tool for the shadow-pricing of government investments (Hanley and Spash, 1993) - but this target is difficult to measure within general scenarios.

Another efficiency goal might be the minimisation of direct and indirect subsidies of the government and the general public (e.g., health insurance system; especially to railways, private damage and repair costs etc.). In short: an efficient transport system must fully cover its costs in order to be viable.

A third efficiency goal might be the rule of 'optimal government intervention': trying to find the equilibrium, where marginal benefits are equal to marginal costs. In short: the point of reference for efficiency is the real or hypothetical market equilibrium.

In general however, the gradual abolishment of public subsidies to the transport sector by the strengthening of market mechanisms and pricing external costs seems to be the best measurable concrete target.

It can be concluded that it is not easy to formulate widely accepted and operational targets for the three normative frames. Scientific approaches are often too abstract to define specific operational targets and most political objectives do not reach to the year 2020. Hence a certain degree of voluntarism is unavoidable in setting targets. This may be justified by a reiterative and participatory approach.

Here, we choose a minimum threshold approach for each of the targets. On the basis of a review of different political and scientific reference points, several targets have been identified for the distinct policy dimensions. Now, we will give scores to these targets for six scenarios, which will be constructed first. Next, these scenarios will be assessed by means of multicriteria analysis.

8.5   Description of the scenarios

The future of transport is largely influenced by institutional, economic and social-psychological developments (Nijkamp et al., 1998; Rienstra, 1998). Scenarios should therefore take into account these trends. On the other hand, treating all factors as internal ones may make the construction too complex and broad, so that lessons cannot be learned. Therefore, we will construct two - so-called external - frameworks 'Polarisation' and 'Cooperation', which describe these trends in rather contrasting ways. In this way, we can test in this scenario analysis for the impacts of these external trends (see Table 8.2). The reference year in the analysis is 2020.

Table 8.2
Contents of the Polarisation and Cooperation external frameworks

The Polarisation Framework	The Cooperation Framework
Institutional/economic developments • EU integration is stopped (e.g., no new member states, no EMU) • No European coordination of transport and environmental policies • Little cooperation in R & D • Low economic growth	*Institutional/economic developments* • EU integrates further (CEC-countries, EMU) • Strong coordination of transport and environmental policies • European coordination R & D • High economic growth
Social developments • Little support transport and environ-mental policy measures • Equity no important policy objective	*Social developments* • Much support for transport and environmental measures • Social cohesion/equity is an important issue

In Table 8.3 these scenarios are concisely presented by focusing on 'efficiency', 'regional development' and 'environment' issues, within both frameworks. Because we focus in the present paper on scenario assessments instead of descriptions, we will not further elaborate on the contents of the scenarios. For an extensive description of the scenarios and the methodology we refer to POSSUM (1997), Rienstra et al. (1997) and Rienstra (1998).

Table 8.3 Summary of the scenarios

Competitive nations Economic efficiency - Polarisation	Competitive Europe Economic efficiency – Cooperation
• Privatisation • Moderate pricing in all forms • Investments based on economic return • Growth mainly in European core zone • Public transport subsidy reduced • Public transport systems reduced • More energy efficient cars • Limited HST-network • Low mobility growth	• Large scale privatisation • Road and other pricing introduced very much • Investments based on maximum return • Stimulation for peripheral regions • Little new technologies • Some closure of public transport • Limited HST-development • Low mobility growth
Equitable Nations Regional development-Polarisation	Equitable Europe Regional development – Cooperation
• Some privatisation • No road pricing or fuel price increases • Little new transport infrastructure • Core zone declines, periphery high growth rates based on own strength • Public transport declines • Little technical development • Low mobility growth	• No privatisation • No pricing measures • High growth in periphery initiated by European funds • Telecommunications important • HST and airport investments • Little new technologies • Reduced public transport use • High mobility growth
Environmental Nations Environment – Polarisation	Environmental Europe Environment – Cooperation
• No privatisation • Limited road and other pricing • Core dominant and dense development • HST-network completed • Public transport expanded • Large scale investments in new fuels • Low mobility growth	• No privatisation • Much road and other pricing • Large scale investments in public transport • Car use restricted • Core zone dominant • New fuels introduced • Public transport dominant • Very low mobility growth

Next it is interesting to what extent the targets which are identified in Sections 8.2-8.4 are achieved. This is presented in Table 8.4, which is based on the analysis of Dreborg et al. (1997) and POSSUM (1997), as well as an internal POSSUM workshop and discussions via the Internet.

Table 8.4
Qualitative scores[1] for the targets in the distinct scenarios

	Comp. Nations	Eq. Nations	Env. Nations	Comp. Europe	Eq. Europe	Env. Europe
Environmental						
25% reduction CO_2	2	2	4	4	1	5
80% reduction NO_x	4	3	5	4	2	5
Regional development						
incr. Gini-coefficient	2	4	2	2	5	2
unempl. obj. 1 reg.	2	4	1	2	5	3
Efficiency						
decoupling	2	2	3	3	1	4
full cost coverage	5	2	1	5	1	2

Note: 1) The scores indicate: 1 = situation worsens very much; 2 = situation worsens; 3 = no clear change; 4 = situation improves; 5 = target achieved

Now we will assess by means of regime analysis to what extent the scenarios achieve the distinct targets and which scenario is most attractive.

8.6   Assessing scenarios by applying multicriteria analysis

8.6.1   Introduction to multicriteria and regime analysis

The various future policy options developed and presented in Section 5 are mainly qualitative in nature. There is no way to order one. In addition, each of these options does not have a single performance measure, but a multiplicity of performance indicators or characteristics. This is a typical case of a multicriteria decision problem, where one preferred choice possibility out of a distinct number of options has to be selected. The typical information needed for a multicriteria analysis is the availability of an impact matrix (i.e., the scores of all relevant policy criteria for all alternatives to be considered) and a relative importance attached to each of the criteria (preferably in the focus of policy weights).

There is a wide variety of multicriteria decision methods, ranging from simple frequency countings to more complicated mathematical exercises. We refer to Nijkamp et al. (1991) for a comprehensive overview. In the past years, various multicriteria methods have become very popular in policy analysis, especially when the impacts to be assessed were qualitative in nature. In our case study, we will use the so-called regime method. This method has been applied on various occasions and has proven its validity for many multicriteria choice problems. The method is essentially based on pairwise comparisons and aims to identify the maximum cardinal information possible from a set of qualitative data. It is also available as user-friendly software. The advantage of the regime method is twofold:

- it allows to deal with different categories of information precision, viz. ordinal cardinal and mixed ordinal-cardinal information for both the impact scores and the weights;
- it allows to derive unambiguous statements on the relative dominance of each alternative considered by offering as a result an aggregate performance score which may be interpreted as the probability that a given alternative may be the most preferred one.

For details we refer to Nijkamp et al. (1991). We will now offer the outcomes of some of our multicriteria decision experiments.

8.6.2   Results of the scenario assessment

In order to analyse which of the scenarios presented in Section 8.5 are more or less preferable, we will apply the above-mentioned regime analysis to the scores for the targets given in Table 8.4. We carried out two types of analysis successively: first, all targets are treated equally (i.e. equal weights), while in the second experiment with our multicriteria analysis, priority is given to one of the three classes of targets.

8.6.2.1   Treating all targets equally First, we applied a multicriteria analysis in which all targets 'unknown' and 'equal' priorities, respectively. There is clearly a difference between 'unknown' and 'equal weights'. 'Unknown' means that it is assumed that there is no information on any weight of any target, so that all qualitative rankings of weights are equally probable. 'Equal weights' means that the value of all weights is identical; the results of these analyses are presented in Table 8.5.

The rank order of the scenarios in terms of their political importance appears to be equal in both analyses. 'Environmental Europe' appears to be the most preferable scenario in which the mix of targets is optimised; also 'Competitive Europe' is an attractive scenario according to these results. Apparently, the Cooperation framework combined with environmental or efficiency priorities results in the best possible achievement of the targets found earlier. This is probably the case, because both scenarios place an emphasis on pricing measures (road pricing, fuel price increases), which have

Table 8.5
Results of the scenario assessments with unknown and equal priorities

Scenario	Priorities unknown	Scenario	Priorities equal
Environmental Europe	0.933	Environmental Europe	1.000
Competitive Europe	0.733	Competitive Europe	0.800
Equitable Nations	0.447	Environmental Nations	0.500
Environmental Nations	0.444	Equitable Nations	0.400
Competitive Nations	0.329	Competitive Nations	0.300
Equitable Europe	0.114	Equitable Europe	0.000

positive impacts on both environmental and efficiency objectives, while at the same time regional development issues are not neglected because of general cooperation trends (Rienstra et al., 1997).

Next, the Polarisation framework appears to result in less attractive scenarios: generally, the scores found by applying the regime analysis are low. A final striking result is that both scenarios aiming at regional development appear not to be very attractive when all targets are taken into account. This is especially the case within the Cooperation framework; here the Polarisation framework scores better than the Cooperation framework. This is likely the case, because regional development issues result in higher mobility levels and high investments in infrastructure, resulting in negative environmental impacts and an inefficient and unprofitable transport system.

8.6.2.2 Giving priority to one of the objectives The scenarios are constructed by means of maximising one of the three issues while suppressing the impacts on the other ones. Therefore, it is interesting to give different weights to the distinct targets in order to analyse to which extent the preference order of the scenarios differs. For example, in one analysis a high priority is given to both environmental targets, whereas the other targets receive a low priority; in this case one would expect higher scores for both environmental scenarios. The results of these analyses are presented in Table 8.6.

Table 8.6 Results of the scenario assessments with different priorities

Environment high	Sc	Regional dev. high	Sc	Efficiency high	Sc
Environm. Europe	1.000	Environm. Europe	0.901	Environm. Europe	0.899
Competitive Europe	0.800	Competitive Europe	0.800	Competitive Europe	0.800
Environm. Nations	0.500	Equitable Nations	0.699	Equitable Nations	0.701
Equitable Nations	0.500	Competitive Nations	0.299	Competitive Nations	0.301
Competitive Nations	0.200	Environm. Nations	0.202	Environm. Nations	0.199
Equitable Europe	0.000	Equitable Europe	0.099	Equitable Europe	0.101

Strikingly, the Environmental Europe and Competitive Europe are the most attractive scenarios in all cases, while Equitable Europe scores the lowest in all analyses. The Environmental Nations scenario becomes more attractive when environmental targets receive priority, but again it can be concluded that the Polarisation framework is not very favourable for the achievement of targets. The same holds for the regional development scenarios when these targets receive the highest priorities. Striking is also that there is hardly a difference between the scores when regional development or efficiency targets receive priority.

In conclusion, in all assessments the Cooperation framework is preferable to the Polarisation framework for efficiency and environmental issues; for regional development issues this is less clear. Environmental and Competitive Europe are the most favourable scenarios, while regional development scenarios are much less preferable, even if regional development issues receive the highest priority.

8.7   Conclusions for European transport policies

The EU has not set concrete measurable targets for the Common Transport Policy (CTP) up to now. For analysing policy packages and researching their impacts it is however necessary to set concretely and objectively defined policy targets. In general terms, the general CTP objectives may be redefined in efficiency, regional development and environmental issues. Setting objective targets in the environmental field based on scientific frameworks is very difficult, because of the lack of knowledge about important issues like the greenhouse effect; also moneterising external costs still causes numerous problems. In addition, it is an extremely politically sensitive issue. Nevertheless, scientific frameworks provide interesting insights and inputs for target setting. For defining measurable targets however, it is still necessary to depend on policy documents in the environmental field. Reducing CO_2 and NO_x emissions appear to be the best targets, which are indicators for the most important externalities caused by transport.

The fields of economic efficiency and regional development provide better opportunities for defining targets, but also here no concrete measurable targets are found, so that again a more pragmatic approach is required. Improved accessibility of regions and unemployment rates in objective 1 regions are taken as regional development targets. For efficiency, decoupling mobility growth from economic growth and a full cost coverage of the transport system are defined as the main targets.

When targets are set, it becomes possible to assess future developments and policy packages, e.g. by regime analysis as applied in this paper to CTP policy scenarios for the year 2020. Six scenarios are assessed, through which two external social and institutional frameworks - Cooperation and Polarisation - and three policy directions - optimising efficiency, regional development and environmental objectives - are investigated.

From the assessment, it appears that cooperation in society and among European countries may be preferable for the achievement of efficiency and environmental targets. This may especially be explained by the fact that price measures can relatively easily be introduced in the Cooperation framework, so that these targets may be achieved to a large extent. Strikingly, a European focus on regional development will have very negative impacts on both efficiency and environmental targets, mainly due to large unprofitable investments and a large mobility growth.

Polarisation in Europe and in society has more negative impacts, although general mobility levels may be lower in such an external framework. Policy measures can less easily be introduced because of societal resistance and free rider behaviour of individual countries, which may hamper the development of effective transport policies. These conclusions even hold when the regional development targets receive a high priority in the analysis compared to the other targets.

From this analysis, it can be concluded that European and societal cooperation and policies aiming at increasing efficiency and environmental objectives (especially by means of price measures) may result in an optimal achievement of transport policy targets.

References

Beuermann C. and J. Jäger (1996), "Climate Change Politics in Germany: How Long Will the Double Dividend Last?", in: O'Riordan T. and J. Jäger (eds), *Politics of Climate Change. A European Perspective*, 186-227, Routledge: London.

Bruinsma F.R., Rienstra S.A. and P. Rietveld (1997), "Economic Impacts of the Construction of a Transport Corridor; A Multi-Level and Multi-Approach Case Study for the Construction of the A1 Highway in the Netherlands", *Regional Studies*, Vol. 31-4, 391-402.

CEC (Commission of the European Communities) (1992), The Future Development of the Common Transport Policy: A Global Approach to the Construction of a Community Framework for Sustainable Mobility, Brussels.

CEC (1993a), Towards Sustainability. A European Community Programme of Policy and Action in Relation to the Environment and Sustainable Development (Fifth Environmental Action Programme), Brussels.

CEC (1993b), Wachstum, Wettbewerbsfähigkeit, Beschäftigung. Herausforderungen der Gegenwart und Wege ins 21. Jahrhundert, Brussels.

CEC (1994), Europa 2000+. Europäische Zusammenarbeit bei der Raumentwicklung, Brussels.

CEC (1996), Die Energie in Europa bis zum Jahre 2020. Ein Szenarien-Ansatz, DG XVII, Brussels.

Daly H.E. (1992), "Elements of Environmental Macroeconomics", in: Costanza R. (ed.), *Ecological Economics - The Science and Management of Sustainability*, 32-46, Columbia University Press: New York.

Dreborg K.H., Hedberg L., Steen P. and J. Akerman (1997), *Comparing Targets with Reference Images*, POSSUM-working paper 15/04-97/ESRG/2.1, Stockholm.

Gent H. van and P. Nijkamp (1991), "Devolution of Transport Policy in Europe", in Button K. and D. Pitfield (eds), *Transportation Deregulation; An International Movement*, Basingstoke: MacMillan Press, 25-35.

Gorissen N. (1995), *Massnahmenplan Umwelt und Verkehr. Konzept für ein Nachhaltig Umwelt-verträgliches Verkehrgeschehen in Deutschland*, paper presented at the Environment Conference ENVITEC, Düsseldorf 21-21 June, Dept. of Environment, Berlin.

Haigh N. (1996), "Climate Change Policies and Politics in the European Community", in O'Rior-dan T. and J. Jäger (eds), *Politics of Climate Change. A European Perspective*, Routledge: London, 155-185.

Hanley N. and C.L. Spash (1993), *Cost-Benefit Analysis and the Environment*, Aldershot: Gower.

Hardin G. (1992), "Paramount Positions in Ecological Economics", in: Costanza R. (ed.), *Ecological Economics - The Science and Management of Sustainability*, Columbia University Press: New York, 47-57.

Héritier A., et al. (1994), Die Veränderung von Staatlichkeit in Europa. Ein Regulativer Wettbewerb: Deutschland, Großbritannien, Frankreich, Opladen: Leske & Budrich.

Hey C., Pfeiffer T. and A. Topan (1996), *The Economic Impact of Motorways in the Peripheral Regions of the EU*, EURES-report no. 7, Freiburg.

Kümmel R. (1980), "Growth Dynamics of the Energy Dependent Economy", in Beckenbach F. (ed.), *Die Ökologische Herausforderung für die Ökonomische Theorie*, Marburg.

Nijkamp P., Rienstra S.A. and J.M. Vleugel (1998), *Transportation Planning and the Future*, John Wiley: Chichester.

Nijkamp P., Rietveld P. and H. Voogd (1991), *Multicriteria Evaluation in Physical Planning*, Amsterdam: North Holland.

191

9 Sustainability and the Transportation Sector
The use of a general equilibrium model to calculate sustainable prices
KNUT S ERIKSEN[1]

9.1   Introduction

Managing climate risks and optimising the use of depletable resources have become a more important part of our political everyday life. This is partly due to the fact that environmental and resource problems are felt by a growing number of people. It is also partly due to the recent results of research, which indicate that factors that are not perceived to be a problem in people's everyday lives, may, all the same, represent huge problems in the long run. A well-known example of this is emissions of CO_2 and its effects on climate in the long run.

The concept of sustainability plays a central part in the discussion of what should be the correct level of pollution and of consumption of resources. In this paper we will give a review of different ways of defining sustainable development. A method of obtaining a set of prices or «shadow prices» associated with a sustainable development will be demonstrated. This will be implemented by means of the general equilibrium model GODMOD.

The paper discusses the concept of sustainable development and the way some criteria for consumption of exhaustible recourses meet this definition. Our aim has been to find a criterion that may lead to operational rules of handling depletable resources. The Chichilnisky criterion seems to meet the theoretical and practical needs in a satisfactory way. We then describe how shadow prices associated with an optimal development may be defined.

Next we discuss how uncertainty concerning the environment affects the optimising behaviour of economic agents, including utilisation of scarce resources.

[1] Thanks to Harald Minken and Peter Christensen, TØI for comments on an earlier version.

In the last sequence we use a CGE model, GODMOD to calculate examples of shadow prices associated with certain sustainable paths. The repercussions for the transport sector and the rest of the economy are discussed.

9.2   The concept of sustainability

9.2.1   Definition

By the term "sustainable development" we usually understand a path with respect to environment and the use of resources that is feasible and acceptable in the long run. Disagreement usually arises when it is necessary to decide what development will hold in the long run. In the Brundtland report (WCED 1987) the concept of sustainability is defined as: *"...development that meets the needs of the present without compromising the ability of future generations to meet their own needs."*

This definition, too, is of course subject to discussion, as it is left open on what level the resources should be maintained in the future. Should all resources be kept on at least the same level as it is now, or should it be possible to trade some exhaustible resources for others? Is the existence of all species and natural resources a necessary condition, or should it be possible to exhaust some resources if they may be replaced by other and equally useful resources? We will not try to give a full discussion of these matters, as they are discussed extensively elsewhere, i. e. in the Brundtland report. We will just describe some theoretical criteria. These are however not sufficient to give an answer to the question of how sustainability should be reached in real life.

The concept of sustainability and the theoretical conditions of equity for the future generations have been discussed thoroughly by a number of authors. See among others Asheim (1991a) and (1991b) and Chichilnisky (1994). The handbooks Kneese and Sweeney (1993) and Goldin and Winters (1994) comprise several important contributions to the subject.

We will try to establish some practical rules of calculating the path of a sustainable development that has at least some theoretical basis.

9.2.2   Discounted utility

The classical way of treating the intertemporal comparison of income and costs is by discounting these streams to the present value. The discount rate used should reflect the society's valuation of future benefits compared to present ones. As we shall see, this method will not give a weight to the

194

distant future that it is compatible with the notion of sustainability. The following chapters will to a great extent be based on works by Geoffrey Heal, e. g. Heal (1995, 1996), Heal (1993) and Beltrati, Chichilnisky and Heal (1994). The models that will be presented here are subject to several limitations.

a) We are looking at one resource at a time.
b) There is no substitution between resources.
c) The resource is not renewable.
d) No technological progress and no investment.

Several of these limitations may be eased as discussed by Heal (1996). For clarity I will stick to the simple version of the model.

We will suppose that the utility of the consumer depends upon the size of the consumption as well as the remaining stock of the resource in question. As an example of this we may think of a forest, which may be enjoyed as a recreational facility as well as a source of wood material for consumption. This may be formulated as:

$$u_t = u(c_t, s_t) = u_1(c_t) + u_2(s_t) \qquad (9.2.1)$$

Here u_t is the level of utility which is a function of consumption, c_t and stock, s_t, all at time t. We will assume that the utility function is separable, which means that the utility of consumption is independent of the size of the stock and vice versa. This is done to simplify the analytical discussion. The results will be of a more general character, as separability is not essential to the conclusion (Heal 1996, Ch. 3.3). At least the utility function should be strictly concave.

The discount rate is i and is a measure of the value of consumption today compared to future consumption. Discounting the flow of income from this resource to present value then will give us a first formulation of the problem to be solved:

$$\text{max.} \int_0^\infty u(c_t, s_t) \cdot e^{-it} \text{ subject to the conditions} \qquad (9.2.2)$$

$$\dot{s}_t = ds_t/dt = -c_t \text{ and } s_t \geq 0 \qquad (9.2.3)$$

The first of these conditions says that the reduction of the level of the stock at every moment will be equal to the consumption of the stock. The problem may be solved by optimal control theory, as we form the Hamiltonian function with the parameter p_t:

195

$$H = u\,(c_t, s_t)\,e^{-it} - p_t \cdot e^{-it}\,c_t \tag{9.2.4}$$

The maximising of this subject to consumption and stock gives us:

$$u'_1\,(c_t) = p_t \tag{9.2.5}$$

$$\dot{p}_t - i\,p_t = -\,u'_2\,(s_t) \tag{9.2.6}$$

Here p_t may be interpreted as the shadow price of the resource along the optimal path. Thus pt is a function of time.

From (9.2.3) it is obvious that in a stationary solution the consumption will have to be zero. In a stationary situation we therefore have

$$i = u'_2\,(s^*)\,/\,u'_1(0) \tag{9.2.7}$$

This means that in a stationary situation the ratio between the marginal utility of the stock and the marginal utility of consumption at zero consumption will equal the discount rate. Here s* denotes the constant value of the remaining stock. This may also be interpreted another way. By rewriting (9.2.7) as $u'_1(0) = u'_2\,(s^*)\,/i$, we can see that the marginal utility of consumption must equal the present value of the stream of utility of a marginal increase in the stock.

The optimal path of this system may be described by the two equations

$$u_1'' \cdot \dot{c}_t - i\,u_1' = -\,u_2'$$

$$\dot{s}_t = -\,c_t$$

We assume that the utility function is strictly concave, so that $u'' < 0$. Here $\dot{s}_t$ will always be non-positive, and c_t will decrease as $i\,u_1' > u_2'$. Thus we will move towards a stationary solution if such a solution exists.

The size of the optimal stock will, as we see from (9.2.7), depend upon the ratio of the marginal utilities at zero consumption and the discount rate. Whether there will be a stationary solution is depending on the form of the utility functions. If the marginal utility goes to infinity as consumption goes to zero, then there is no solution to the problem of reaching stationary state. The marginal utility of zero consumption must also exceed zero. From this we see that in a stationary solution the only utility the consumer will derive, is what he gets from the stock of resources. Consumption will equal zero.

9.2.2.1 The Green Golden Rule

9.2.2.1 The Green Golden Rule If our aim is to maximise utility in the long run, that is for generations of the distant future, then the solution must be no consumption at all. This is easily seen from the following: Maximise u(0, s), where $s \leq s_0$. As long as marginal utility is positive, the solution must be $s = s_0$.

The general problem is

$$\text{max. } \lim_{t \to \infty} u(c_t, s_t) \qquad (9.2.8)$$

The solution to this problem is what Heal calls *"the green golden rule"*, which is the path that maximises the level of utility in the long run. This criterion at least carries some good qualities that may be related to the concept of sustainability. The utility level is not discounted to the present situation, but valued at its future level.

9.2.2.2 Depletion of resources

9.2.2.2 Depletion of resources We will now return to (9.2.1) and look at a special case, which in the theory seems to be the most common one. That is the case where we consider the size of the stock to have no existence value for the consumer. Then the utility function is reduced to

$$u = u\,(c_t) \qquad (9.2.9)$$

The maximising problem and the conditions are of the same kind as described earlier. The solution, however, is simple as (9.2.6) is reduced to

$$u'\,(c_t) = p_t \qquad (9.2.10)$$

$$\dot{p}_t - i\,p_t = 0, \qquad \text{or} \qquad p_t = p_0\,e^{it} \qquad (9.2.11)$$

This describes an optimal path of exhausting a resource over time, so that the marginal utility of consumption utility of consumption, which is equal to the shadow price, will have to grow at a rate that equals the discount rate. Therefore the present value will stay constant as long as consumption is positive. This is called *Hotelling's rule*. It can easily be shown that consumption drops over time following the below pattern

$$\dot{c}/c = -i\,/\eta \qquad (9.2.12)$$

197

Here $\eta = - c_t u''(c_t)/u'(c_t)$. This is the elasticity of the marginal utility of consumption and will always exceed zero. The utility function is often supposed to have a form, e. g. logarithmic, that makes this elasticity constant. Then consumption over time will drop by a rate that is proportional to the elasticity of the discount rate and to the inverse of the elasticity of the marginal utility of consumption.

Here it is not possible to apply the green golden rule. Positive utility can only be obtained as long as consumption exceeds zero. A sustainable path is not possible here, even if the discount rate is set to zero. A zero discount rate will of course give no solution to the problem.

9.2.3   The Chichilnisky criterion

It is frequently argued against discounted utility as a criterion that not enough weight is given to the utility of future generations. If the utility of consumption is positive then the resource will be exhausted given a utility function like (9.2.9), even with an extremely small discount rate. Setting the discount rate equal to zero will not help us, since in many cases the integral (9.2.2) then will be indefinite. On the other hand a utility function like (9.2.1) and the green golden rule will lead to no consumption at all. All of the resource is left to eternity.

We can clearly see that there is a conflict between what we may call *"the dictatorship of the present"* and *"the dictatorship of the future"*. That is to say that it is not trivial by discounting alone to find a good balance between the utility of the present generation and the utility of the future generations which fulfils the conditions of sustainability. Here we will look into some of the characteristics of one such criterion.

As a way of combining the needs of the present and of the future Chichilnisky (1993) has proposed the following criterion

$$\text{max. } \alpha \int_0^\infty u(c_t,s_t)e^{-it}dt + (1-\alpha) \lim_{t\to\infty} u(c_t,s_t) , \qquad (9.2.13)$$

where $0 < \alpha < 1$

It may be shown that the first part of the expression, that is the integral identical with (9.2.2), represents the dictatorship of the present, while the second part $\lim u(c_t, s_t)$ represents the dictatorship of the future. The weighted sum of them will be neither of the two and is the only way of avoiding either kind of dictatorship. This seems intuitively correct, but it can also be proved formally, as done by Chichilnisky.

The time dependency expression, e^{-it}, may be replaced by any other measure of time, $f(t)$, that fulfils certain criteria, for instance that utility that is close to the present is given stronger weight than utility that is not so close.

If $\alpha = 0$, we will have The Green Golden Rule, with preservation of the whole initial stock. Then if $\alpha = 1$, the whole initial resource will be consumed, unless the size of the stock itself has a value for the consumer. In that case part of the resource will be kept for the far future, as we have seen from the previous chapter.

It may also be shown that values of α between 0 and 1 will lead to the conservation of a certain part of the initial stock. The smaller α is, the bigger will the stock that is preserved "forever" be.

Figure 9.1 shows the time paths for the stock of the resource under different criteria.

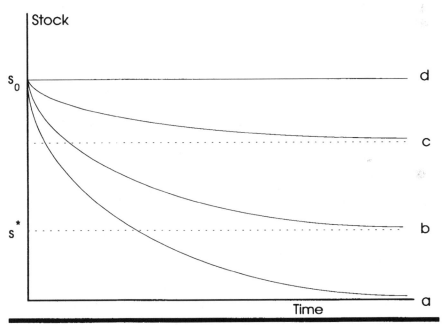

Figure 9.1
Alternative time paths for the stock of an exhaustible resource

All paths will start in s_0. The letters by the end of curves denotes the alternative optimality criteria for the use of the stock over time:

a) Hotelling's Rule for depletion of resources over time.
b) Utility from both stock and consumption.
c) The Chichilnisky criterion.
d) The Green Golden Rule.

9.2.4   Other cases

Several other criteria for ranking developing paths for the utilisation of a depletable resource have been introduced. A common feature is that they seem to have a high degree of logical precision, but it appears to be easy to find examples of situations where the criteria do not work and therefore are of no use in calculating the optimal path. One example that we have already dealt with is the case of zero discount rate. This will give the utility of all future points of time the same weight. In many cases this will be useful, but as seen, it will not help us to decide the optimal depletion path over time.

It is possible to analyse special cases of the models described above. Resources may be considered renewable, or the research effects of finding a replacement for the threatened resource may be included in the model. This will complicate the difference between the four criteria described above, but it will not change the principal difference between them. In the following we will therefore stick to the simple models we have described earlier in this chapter.

9.2.5   Shadow prices

The four criteria described above makes it possible to define shadow prices in different situations. The shadow price may be used for calculating the cost of using the resource. This is to provide a framework for cost-benefit analysis and project evaluation. In many cases the market prices will not give a correct impression of the "real" costs of the resource. This is treated in the theory of cost-benefit analysis. The shadow prices are supposed to measure the values that society place upon scarce resources.

It can easily be deferred from the conditions of optimum referred in sections 9.2.2 and 9.2.3 that for the shadow prices in the initial situation we will have

$$p_{0d} > p_{0c} > p_{0b} > p_{0a} \tag{9.2.14}$$

Here p_{0a} is the price of the resource when criterion **a** is applied and so on.

As we may see the stronger the restrictions put on the resource is, the smaller the consumption must be, and the higher the shadow price will be.

The value of a resource will equal the total discounted value of the services of the resource.

It is possible, at least in principle, to calculate the time path of the shadow price of a certain resource when the criterion of optimality has been chosen. The problem when it comes to implementing is to determine the sustainable level of consumption of a resource. By resource we will here also understand goods like fresh air and a nice climate. That is to say that polluting the atmosphere by sending large quantities of carbon dioxide or nitrogen oxides into it means the same as to deplete the resources good climate and fresh air. The use of fossil fuel will pollute the atmosphere with a variety of gases in addition to the fact that fossil fuel is in itself a scarce resource. The total outcome of this process decides the size of the shadow price. These resources usually will have positive market prices, but market prices are not reflecting the real value of the resources for the society valued by the long-term criteria depicted above. We can see this from (9.2.14), as p_{0a} is the market price with no future restrictions placed upon it. The more restrictions are placed upon the resource, the higher the price, and the more in favour of the future the path will be.

9.3   The effects of uncertainty

9.3.1   General

Uncertainty about the future will influence decisions concerning how to approach a sustainable development. Traditionally there have been many ways to treat uncertainty in cost-benefit analyses and other economic evaluations. Among these we will concentrate on one of the methods, which we may call «The value of waiting» or the option approach. This method is inspired by the theory of financial options and deals with the value of having the options of investing now or delaying the decision of whether or not to invest till later. Thus a project will have to compete not only with other projects, but also with itself, implemented at a later time. What you get from waiting may be more information about how income and cost flows from the project may develop over time. Thereby you may avoid possible losses. The main point is the irreversibility of the decision to invest (or huge costs of reversing it).

There has been an increasing amount of literature in this field in recent years. An important source is Dixit and Pindyck (1994). Here we just want to discuss how this theory may influence the way sustainability is addressed in transport projects.

Given the growth factor and the variance of the income of a project, this theory can be used to decide whether to invest now or to await further information. The function describing the value of the project, including the value of waiting may be derived from this by applying a Taylor series expansion (called Ito's Lemma). The investor will want to invest when the value of keeping the project on the hand no longer exceeds the expected net revenue of implementing the project. By linking this together we also may determine the parameters of the function.

From this process we get the new investment criterion, telling us to invest when the ratio between the net revenue of the project and the project costs exceeds a certain limit that is *larger* than unity. In traditional cost-benefit analysis this limit is unity.

9.3.2   Uncertainty and sustainability

Using the Chichilnisky criterion to decide how much of the initial stock that should be preserved, will lead to a higher shadow price for the resource compared to a situation where no part of the initial stock is preserved for the distant posterity. This means that uncertainty about the correct level of the future shadow price should be accounted for when calculating criteria for investment under uncertainty.

For our purpose it is important to notice that for transport investment decisions there is frequently more than one uncertainty factor interacting. Future traffic generated by the project and the shadow price of the environment resource may both be quite uncertain. Total uncertainty will then increase substantially since the traffic and the resource price are multiplied to give the environment cost.

Uncertainty about the environmental consequences makes it rational for the decision-maker to postpone investment decisions to possibly get more information. This would be the case both for major investment decisions to make environment improving investments or special regulations that will look expensive for the society in the short run. This may seem like a very defensive policy, but it is quite rational from the point of view of the decision-maker to postpone the investment in environment improvement, given that the uncertainty of the benefits of the project is large.

On the other hand keeping a security stock of a scarce resource will be rational for society until sufficiently close substitutes eventually are found.

Therefore it should be profitable not to postpone an environment decision to make sure the "insurance" does not come too late.

These two statements seem contradictory – as the first one may lead to a wait-and-see attitude – and the second statement should mean safety first. This may offer part of the explanation of why it is so difficult to make decisions concerning environment improvement. How these two theories may be integrated needs further investigation.

One further point can be made here. Uncertainty may not be the same for all decision makers. It may depend upon where in the hierarchy our decision-maker is. What matters is the relevant uncertainty, which may vary between different decision levels. The relevant uncertainty is the one that our project is contributing to the total uncertainty of the decision makers total activity. Therefore the covariance between "our" project and other projects should be considered, since it is the variance of the net benefit from the whole of our activity that matters.

It is thus important that decisions should be made on a sufficiently high level. It is also wise to try to reduce total risk by combining investment packages where the uncertainty of the member projects, at least partially, will neutralise each other.

9.4 The calculation of sustainable prices

9.4.1 Sustainability constraints

Returning now to the criteria for sustainability we ask whether it is possible on the basis of the theoretical conditions to determine a set of prices that will support a sustainable development. If we choose the Chichilnisky criterion as our criterion of sustainability, we first have to decide the size of α in the formula (9.2.13). This means that we have to decide what ratio of each resource that should be kept for the eternity (or really the very far future). Then the task is to find a set of prices that will realise this set of sustainability conditions.

We start from the Hotelling situation with depletion of the resources and assume a constant elasticity of the marginal utility of consumption. Then, as we let time go to infinity, we have from (9.2.2), (9.2.3) and (9.2.12)

$$c_0 = s_0 \cdot i / \eta \tag{9.4.1}$$

This means that the "correct" amount of consumption in the initial situation will be a fixed proportion of initial stock.

203

With an analogy from Hotelling to Chichilnisky, the same rules may be applied to the part of the initial stock, s_0^*, that may be consumed. The ratio of the consumable part to whole stock will be β, leaving $1-\beta$ to "eternity". We see that determining the size of α, is the same as determining β. We then have

$$s_0^* = \beta s_0 \tag{9.4.2}$$

Combining (9.4.1) and (9.4.2) we have

$$c_0^* = \beta c_0 \tag{9.4.3}$$

This means that the sustainable consumption may be calculated as the same ratio of the initial consumption as the consumable stock is to the whole stock of the resource.

To agree to how much of a resource should be set aside for the distant future does not seem to be an easy task. Formally determining this is the problem of maximising (9.2.13), determining optimal α. This is however not easy, as long as the consequences of depletion are not fully known. If the consequences of total exhaustion of a resource are very serious, then a quite large part should be shielded from being used up. If there is a hope that research may bring a substitute for the resource, then this part may be lower. In the end deciding the size of the part that is kept for posterity should be a political decision only advised by experts in the actual field.

When it comes to carbon dioxide the situation is a little more complicated. We may call the resource "depot for carbon dioxide". This means that to keep the concentration of CO_2 in the atmosphere under a certain level, emissions must be reduced by a certain percentage. According to some climate experts it may be wise to reduce the emissions as much as 50 per cent, or even more, in the long run.

As the changes in quantities are supposed to be big and there also may be a great deal of dependency between the price of one commodity and the quantity of others, we choose to use a general equilibrium model to calculate the prices that may give us the "correct" initial consumption of definite resources. In the next chapter we will present a model which we will use for some example calculations.

9.4.2 The GODMOD-model

At the Institute of Transport Economics one has developed a CGE model (Computable General Equilibrium) of the Norwegian economy. The model has been named GODMOD, not primarily by reference to its divinely conceived structure, but because particular emphasis has been put on the detailed MODelling of commodity (GOoDs) transport supply and demand. Technically, the model has been constructed by means of the MPS-GE programming format of Thomas Rutherford (1989). Trond Jensen at the Institute of Transport Economics has mainly been responsible for developing the model. The model has been described in Jensen (1993), Jensen (1997) and in Jensen, Eriksen, Katz and Larsen (1997).

In a general equilibrium model, explicit account is taken of the interrelationships between multiple sectors or markets, in the form of common resource constraints, technology, preferences and input-output relations. In principle, externally induced supply or demand shocks affect not only the market for the product in question, but all other markets as well, through budget, substitution, and input-output effects.

GODMOD is generally based on the assumption of competitive markets, as defined by Walras' law. This implies that in equilibrium, there can be no (positive) excess demand for any commodity, and all available resources are fully utilised, when carrying a positive price. Principally all factors are assumed to have full mobility, but it is possible to restrict mobility for some of them. All prices will be given as the value of the marginal product. Other forms of market organisation, such as monopoly, duopoly, or price or quantity constraints, can, however, also be implemented within the MPS-GE model format.

In GODMODs description of the Norwegian economy, there are 30 separate production sectors defined, including one sector for the production of public services. These sectors produce commodities, services, energy, passenger transport and commodity transport. There are 8 commodity transport sectors, 6 passenger transport sectors and 16 general sectors for commodity and service production. Each of the domestically produced commodities can be substituted for a similar foreign commodity. It is assumed that commodities produced domestically and abroad are not perfect substitutes.

Commodity transport as well as passenger transport are inputs of production, linked - physically and economically - to the use of other inputs. Thus, transport demand is derived from the use of input commodities in production. In addition passenger transport is a product which is also purchased by the private consumer. The substitution between different modes of transportation, which may be rather complex, leads to changes in the demand for different energy sources like hydroelectric power and fossil fuels.

All production and utility functions are specified as CES (constant elasticity of substitution) functions, of which the Cobb-Douglas and Leontief production function are special cases. These functions are mathematically

205

convenient and provide economically interpretable solutions over their entire domain. In practice, the CES assumption can be relaxed through the construction of hierarchically nested production or utility functions. Thus the parameters of the function, which may be interpreted as the elasticity of substitution, may differ for nearly all pairs of input factors to a production process.

Cost and utility functions are calibrated from the Norwegian national accounts for 1992 - the "benchmark" year, which is assumed to represent one point of equilibrium. All results will thus be given in 1992 base year prices.

The nested structure of the production sectors is determined in an estimation process where the parameters of the cost functions are estimated. Most parameters are estimated econometrically or calculated based on previous econometric studies. In a few cases the values used may be characterised as "guestimates".

GODMOD is a static model, which for each run calculates an equilibrium for the entire economy. All costs can be interpreted as one-year rental prices for the respective factors. In the model, all decisions are assumed to be made under perfect insight. The treatment of capital stocks and the assumptions made concerning the numerical values of elasticities are such that the equilibria computed by the model are most plausibly interpreted as medium term solutions, i.e. effects applicable at a three to five years' horizon.

9.5   Example calculations

The GODMOD model is, as mentioned, basically a static model, but it may be used to simulate a growth process, given the necessary exogenous input data for each year. Thus it may be used to calculate the price path associated with an optimal use of scarce resources. This path may be similar to the Hotelling-Chichilnisky price path depicted in section 9.2.5, provided that we are able to get the relevant input data for each year, among this the remaining stock of the limited variables in question. The uncertainty aspects are expressed in the model only via the shadow prices that may reflect uncertainty about the size of and the future demand for the remaining stock of the resource. The shadow price of the recourse may be interpreted as a tax-rate that reduces the utilisation of the resource to the desired level.

We use «climate» as an example resource, as it seems to be the opinion among researchers that the emission of carbon dioxide reduces this resource. To be more specific, the resource can be defined as depot for carbon dioxide. The exact link between the size of the depot left and the level of human made CO_2 -emissions is not defined here, as there is a natural turnover of CO_2 as well, but this not important as long as such a link *can* be established. As mentioned in chapter 4.1 some climate experts have advised that emissions should be reduced by as much as 40 or 50 per cent. The example may also be interpreted more directly as restrictions on the use of scarce fossil energy recourses.

Since we are not too certain about how well the model describes the way the economy would react to the big changes in consumption, we have decided to settle for a 20 per cent cut in CO_2-emissions as our main example, which will be described in detail. We will also calculate three other examples, namely CO_2-emission cuts of 10, 30 and 40 per cent.

We start with a reference solution where no extra measures are taken to reduce the CO_2-emissions. This solution is based on national account figures for the year 1992. The existing CO_2-taxation is not equally distributed between sectors, as sectors exposed to foreign competition are entitled to reduced rates. We calculate four scenarios as mentioned above. The CO_2-tax changes are meant to be revenue neutral. This means that the increased public revenue from the carbon tax is given back to the private sector by a neutral tax reduction. A weakness in this way of calculation is that the CO_2-tax is levied equally on all sectors according to how many tons of CO_2 that is emitted. This comes as an addition to the existing taxes based on CO_2-emission or energy use which are not «justly» distributed among sectors.

The emission constraints are easily incorporated within the model, which will calculate the necessary tax-rate to meet each constraint or shadow price of the resource at that specific level.

Table 9.1 Rate of tax needed to reduce emission of carbon dioxide

	Reference alternative	10% reduction	20% reduction	30% reduction	40% reduction
CO_2-emissions. Billion tonnes	34.4	30.95	27.52	24.07	20.64
Tax per tonne CO_2. NOK.	-	400	924	1653	2740

Table 9.1 shows that an increase in the CO_2-tax will make the production sectors try to reduce the use of heavily taxed production factors, and as the tax rate increases it is getting more difficult to reduce the use of CO_2-emitting factors further. We thus can see that the first ten per cent of reduction, costs 400 NOK per tonne. The next 10 per cent, cost us an extra 524 NOK. A further reduction of 10 per cent costs 729 NOK in addition to that, and the last step of reduction from thirty to forty per cent will cost 1087 NOK on top of the rest. This means that the curve of cost of the reduction becomes increasingly steeper as CO_2-emissions get lower. A CO_2-tax of 2740 NOK per tonne represents an additional tax of 8.70 NOK per kilogram gasoline. This is also shown in Figure 9.2.

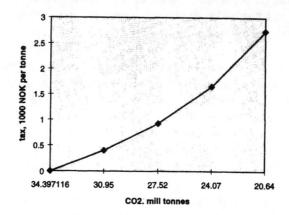

Figure 9.2 CO_2-tax and emission

Gross production drops by 0.9 per cent at a 10 per cent CO_2-tax, by 1.8 at a 20 per cent tax, by 3.0 at a 30 per cent and by 4.5 per cent by a 40 CO_2-tax.

The welfare index is a measure of private utility and includes consumption of goods and services. The index does not comprise the utility of a good climate. Even so, as Figure 9.3 indicates there is a small increase in the welfare index for a small tax increase. For further tax increase and reduction of emission, the index will start to fall. The reason for this is probably that several of the sectors producing consumer goods are not very heavily CO_2-taxed. So they get a relative benefit compared to the fossil fuel intensive (CO_2-producing) sectors as to the price of the input factors. As the tax increases further, the gross national production will decrease. Mathiesen (1996) also describes similar effects. The point is that the initial situation may be considered "not optimal". The long term utility of having the CO_2-level reduced is not included in this welfare index.

In the 20 per cent CO_2 tax alternative the production is reduced by nearly 40 per cent in the metal industry compared to the reference alternative, and by nearly 30 per cent in oil refining. Oil and gas production is reduced by 8 per cent. Total private consumption is not changed, but the use of private cars is reduced by 17 per cent.

Sectors gaining are public metro transport by 9 per cent and railway transport by 3.5 per cent. This is due to the price increase of fuel. Also other transport sectors like the taxi industry and some sectors producing consumer goods show a small increase. The change in production due to the tax for some selected sectors is shown in 9.2. We see that even a general CO_2-tax favours public transport that is not very fossil energy consuming. The reason that taxi industry is gaining and the bus industry is losing is the high substitutability between taxis and private cars.

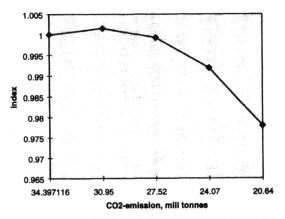

Figure 9.3 Welfare indicator and CO_2 emission

Table 9.2 Changes in gross production in communication-
and transport sectors due to a 20 per cent carbon tax

Sector:	Per cent change
Post & telecom	-2.91 %
Tram & metro	8.58 %
Taxi	2.52 %
Air transport	-0.79 %
Buss & coach transport	-0.15 %
Domestic shipping	-1.85 %
Railway	3.46 %
Hired truck transport, medium size	-0.93 %
Own truck transport, medium size	-1.94 %

In these examples all sectors get to pay the same additional CO_2-tax per tonne. In real life, at least in Norway, there seems to be a tendency to discriminate against domestic transport and the private car sector in the form of heavy tax rates. One might also consider the case where the whole CO_2-tax is levied on these sectors, letting the goods producing sectors go free for foreign competition reasons. It is not shown here, but it is obvious that the most efficient way to reduce CO_2-emissions is the way we have done it with an equal tax rate for every CO_2 producing sector. Excluding some sectors from the tax will reduce the efficiency of the total economy, given.

209

The prices calculated here are to be interpreted as the initial shadow prices. From here the prices will follow an increasing path as depicted earlier. The best thing is probably to recalculate the model for several future years given the new values of the exogenous variables for each of the example years. The example calculations by GODMOD show:

- Production loss is substantial with high CO_2-tax rates.
- The tax rate needs to be progressively increased to bring CO_2-emissions further down.
- Some industries, e.g. the metal industry may be protected from heavy CO_2-taxation.
- Non fossil fuel transport sectors will gain from the tax.

In the case of unilateral measures in the Norwegian economy, as may be the case here, the result may show us that tax measures of these proportions may lead to fatal consequences for certain industries.

The model has many weaknesses, and we are not certain about how well it describes the mechanisms of really big tax rate changes. The calculations indicate, however, that the effects of heavy CO_2-taxation not may be dramatic to society as a whole. But for parts of it the effects may be dramatic, indicating that the tax-rate should be somewhat gradually increased.

Conclusions

We have seen that among several criteria that are consistent with the definition of sustainability the Chichilnisky criterion is one that can easily be made operational. The criterion gives a theoretical reason for saving a fixed part of the known stock of a resource for "eternity" - or rather the far future. Keeping a safety stock is also consistent with the theory of the value of waiting, as it would be wise to assign a higher price than market price to the use of a limited resource if we are uncertain whether it will become really scarce in the future. This will give society the time and motivation to develop close substitutes to the imperilled resources. This theory does not, however, help in deciding the size of the safety-stock.

The CGE-model GODMOD seems to be a useful tool to calculate the initial level of the shadow prices of presumably scarce resources and thus indicating at what level the environment tax level should be to make society limit the use of specific resources to a certain level. The calculations should be interpreted bearing in mind that conclusions should not be drawn from changes in variables that are far outside their initial values. But all the same it seems that the shadow price will have to be increased progressively to obtain a linear decrease path in consumption of the resource.

The three parts of this paper are closely related, but they are still not quite integrated as parts of *one* theory of the optimal utilisation of limited resources under uncertainty. This integration seems to be an interesting but difficult task to be dealt with in the future.

References

Asheim, G.B. (1991a), Sustainable Management of Common Property Resources: Possible Institutional Structures and Incentive Mechanisms. LOS-senter Notat 91/40, Bergen.

Asheim, G.B. (1991b), "Unjust Intergenerational Allocations". *Journal of Economic Theory 54, 1991.*

Asheim, G.B. (1991c), *Defining sustainability when Resource Management does not have Deterministic Consequences.* Working Paper No. 77/1991.

Beltrati, A., G. Chichilnisky and G. Heal (1994), *Sustainable Growth and the Green Golden Rule,* in Goldin and Winters, 1994).

Chichilnisky, G. (1994), *What is sustainable development?* Technical Report No. 65. Stanford Institute for Theoretical Economics. Stanford, CA.

Chichilnisky, G. and G. Heal (1993), "Global Environmental Risks", *Journal of Ec. Perspectives. No. 4.*

Dasgupta, P. (1994*), Optimal Development and the Idea of Net National Product.* I Goldin and Winters.

Dixit, A. and R. Pindyck (1994): *Investment under Uncertainty,* Princeton University Press.

Goldin, I. and L.A. Winters (1994), *The Economics of Sustainable Development,* Cambridge University Press: Cambridge, U K.

Heal, G. (1993), *The Optimal Use of Exhaustible Resources.* In: Kneese and Sweeney.

Heal, G.(1995), *Lecture Notes on Sustainability.* Memo. No. 16. Department of Economics. University of Oslo. To be published as part of Heal (1996).

Heal, G. (1996), *Valuing the Future: Economic Theory and Sustainability.* To be published as book.

Howarth, R.B. (1995), *Sustainabilty under Uncertainty: A Deontological Approach.* Land Economics. November 1995.

Jensen, T. (1993), *En generell likevektsmodell for godstransportanalyser.* TØI-rapport 163. (English Summary). Transportøkonomisk institutt, Oslo.

Jensen, T. (1995), *GODMOD 2.0. Ny versjon av TØIs nasjonale modell for godstransport.* Arbeidsdok. TØ/713/94. Transport-økonomisk institutt, Oslo.

211

Jensen, T., K. Eriksen. A. Katz, B. Larsen (1997), *Transport og Makroøkonomi* – En samkjøring av MSG-6 og GODMOD-3, Statistisk Sentralbyrå, Oslo.

Jensen, T. (1997) *GODMOD-3 - En makroøkonomisk modell for transportanalyser.* Oslo, Transportøkonomisk institutt. TØI rapport, 345/1997. (English Summary).

Mathiesen, L. (1996), *Skog og skogproduksjon som virkemiddel for å binde klimagasser:* En CGE-analyse. Sosialøkonomen nr. 5. Mai 1996, Oslo.

Kneese, A. and J. Sweeney (1993), *Handbook of Natural Resources and Energy Economics,* Vol. III, Elsevier: Amsterdam.

Lund, D. (1993), Samfunnsøkonomisk vurdering av usikkerhet. *Norsk Økonomisk Tidsskrift 107, 1993.*

World Commission on Environment and Development (WCED) (1987), *Our Common Future,* Oxford University Press.

10 New Governance Principles for Sustainable Urban Transport

ROBERTO CAMAGNI, ROBERTA CAPELLO AND PETER NIJKAMP

10.1 The city: pro and contra[1]

Human settlements are a spatial mapping of socio-economic and cultural political ramifications of society. In the past century, we have witnessed the emergence of large cities as a result of economies of density and scale. These forms of human settlement suffer often from environmental hazards and health risks posed by air, water and surface pollution, substandard housing, poor sanitation and in general, lack of basic services. These negative urban factors are disproportionately distributed among urban inhabitants. Especially in Third World cities the poor tend to live in ecologically vulnerable areas and on marginal lands. Thus, large cities often show an unsustainable picture of economic efficiency, social equity and environmental decay. This tension will increase in the future, as the main part of the growth of world population will reside in urban areas, a trend which will likely be accelerated due to the liberalisation of the world economy and the transition towards a global network society in which urban nodes will play a key role. A critical question is then whether urban management and local political leadership will be sufficiently strong and effective so as to implement a proper proactive urban policy in a multi-faceted field fraught with conflicts: traffic, pollution, waste, energy, congestion, infrastructure, sanitation, or public services.

The above rather pessimistic view on the city is even aggravated, if one introduces the notion of the so-called "footprint of cities", by which is meant

---

[1] R. Camagni is at the Economics Department of the Politecnico of Milan, Piazza Leonardo da Vinci 32, 20133 Milan, R. Capello is at the Economics Department of the University of Molise and at the Economics Department of the Politecnico of Milan, Piazza Leonardo da Vinci 32, 20133 Milan, while P. Nijkamp is at the Regional Economics Department, Free University, De Boelelaan 1105, 1081 HV Amsterdam. Though the paper is the result of a common research work, R. Camagni wrote Sections 10.2, 10.3, 10.7.1-10.7.4, R. Capello wrote Sections 10.4, 10.6 and 10.7.5, while P. Nijkamp wrote Sections 10.1, 10.5, 10.8.

the total land use which would be necessary to supply a given city with sufficient food or timber, as well as the total area of growing vegetation which would be needed to absorb the CO_2 emission of that city. Such calculations lead usually to excessively high estimates of the indirect spatial requirements for the survival of cities. They contribute to a view on the modern city that is characterised by threat and decay, but fail to assess the direct and indirect spatial demands of alternative patterns of human settlements (e.g. deconcentrated ways of living). Moreover, many publications on modern city life seem to forget that the city has more opportunities to cope with negative factors than any other way of living (Capello and Nijkamp, 1998). Furthermore, it should be noted that the urban environment does not only concern pollution and waste, but also the cultural heritage and the built environment which offer massive positive factors to both citizens and visitors (cf. Coccossis and Nijkamp, 1995). Thus, a reflection on the urban environment comprises many aspects of urban life. We may refer here to Lynch, 1981, who asserted: "So that settlement is a good which enhances the continuity of culture and the survival of its people, increases a sense of connection in time and space, and permits or spurs individual growth: development, within continuity, via openness and connection" (p.117).

The critical role of a city in an industrialised society appears to turn increasingly into a centripetal role in a modern network society; cities are becoming "local networks in networks of cities". In their setting we focus on the central role of transport and communications systems which offer many economic opportunities and social advantages (i.e., social benefits), but also many threats in terms of environmental decay, traffic insecurity and congestion. This requires a careful tuning of various types of policies to transport policy, guided by the idea that free readership has to be penalised and - following sound economic principles - social costs of transport have to be charged to the sources of negative factors.

The quality of the urban habitat will at the same time decisively be determined by its accessibility by means of both physical and non-physical network infrastructure. This means that transportation and communication are in principle vehicles for urban sustainability, provided all social costs (and benefits) involved are charged to all users in such a way that a socially acceptable and equitable market result emerges. The recent popularity of market-based policy principles for sustainable urban development (e.g., tradable area licensing schemes, or tradable car emission permits as experimented at present in e.g., Mexico City) illustrated that creative policies are necessary in order to ensure that cities are - and remain - the "home of man".

The paper deals with the role of transport and telecommunications networks on urban environment, underlining the well-known negative factors caused by transport in urban areas, as well as the positive effects that may generate from the exploitation of telecommunications technologies. However, the paper takes also a more unusual perspective, by providing elements and suggestions for claiming that transport has positive effects on urban development and that transport restraint policies are not always the right and more efficient strategies to put in place for a sustainable city. The paper is organised as follows. In Section 10.2 the role of cities in the modern economy is emphasised, both in terms of cities as nodes and as places. Section 10.3 deals with the new emerging urban paradigm, a new model of growth typical of urban areas, that of city networks. Section 10.4 takes into consideration the role of transport and communications in the modern economy, underlining the negative and positive effects that these technologies generate on urban growth, for both underdeveloped and developed cities. Sections 10.5 and 10.6 deal with the role of transport and telecommunications infrastructure on Urban Sustainability, while Section 10.7 provides a taxonomy of all policies which may be used in the field of transport to keep social costs under control. Some final remarks conclude the paper.

10.2   The modern city as a node in the new network society

Cities are increasingly playing a central role in our modern society, due to their threefold nature of "gateways" in the internationalisation of their regional setting, of "nodes" in international information and communication networks, and of "places" bearing an economic and demographic weight, a specificity and a "vocation".

10.2.1   Cities as gateways to internationalisation, multinationalisation and globalisation

As a result of the presence of dynamic agglomeration economies, cities have always been recognised as the loci of modernisation and technological innovation and as the engines of economic growth and social transformation. In this respect, they have always developed or attracted the most advanced, economically rewarding and politically crucial functions (Braudel, 1979; Nijkamp, 1986). Traditionally, all this developed for a long time into multiple forms of territorial control and economic hierarchisation, but has also given rise to opposite processes of diffusion of know-how and economic activities, in a never ending cyclical process of concentration and diffusion.

More recently, in presence of an acceleration in the process of international integration due to political, economic and institutional backgrounds, cities are

215

taking up a novel crucial role: the role of gateways in the internationalisation process of their surrounding regions.

We may distinguish three different processes within the general international integration of the different economies (Gordon, 1994):

- internationalisation, which refers to international trade and increasing market integration;
- multinationalisation, which refers to integration in the production sphere, through foreign investment and the selective location decisions of multinational corporations;
- globalisation, which refers to integration in know-how and innovative activities, through transnational cooperation agreements and strategic alliances.

When these processes refer to specific regions, their territorial connection takes place through those guideposts or gateways we call cities. On the one hand, external firms interested in the control of new regional markets, in off-shore branch-plant location or in potential technological joint-ventures establish their guideposts in the economic heart of the different regions; on the other hand, regional activities dispersed throughout the territory find in the big city the competences, the tools and the channels for their international projection. It is not incidental, for example, that the economic upswing determined in Europe by the launching of the Single Market Project in 1985 coincided with the relaunching of almost all big cities in the countries of the European Union (Camagni, 1991).

10.2.2   Cities as nodes in the city-network

The capability of the city of connecting economic activities throughout the world derives from its nature of a node in international communication and information networks. In all times, efficient links (relative to the existing technological level) connected cities with one another; today, airplanes, high-speed trains, fibre-optics cables annihilate physical distances and simplify the geography of centres by the dichotomy "to be or not to be in the network".

Against this statement, one could argue that some networks are nowadays extremely diffused on the relevant territory (like the telephone network), and that other communication technologies, using the ether as a medium, overcome not just space but also physical networks and nodes, reaching whatever place the receiver is located. In this picture, nodality seems to lose importance.

The counter-argument may be straightforward: it is certainly true that each economic unit might act and might be considered as a node in the information network, but what really matters is the coexistence of different networks in a single node, or, using an increasingly popular terminology in transportation research, their interconnection. In consequence, if nodality still matters for some kinds of networks (like transportation networks), nodality still matters for the interconnection among them.

While in the past the rank of a city was determined by the number of functions that concentrated in that city, nowadays its rank is more and more determined by the number of networks it allows to interconnect: financial networks, technological networks, headquarters networks, cultural and leisure networks, high-speed trains networks and so on.

As a consequence of these evolutions, cities (as nodes) link up with other cities and nodes in ways that cannot be analysed and understood with the traditional tools of urban geography. The traditional models of city-systems considered only one class of city-networks: hierarchical networks, where each city interacted only with smaller urban units situated inside its regional hinterland. These types of relationships remain important, but are complemented by other more important relationships, that give rise to three kinds of city networks (Camagni, 1993):

- complementary networks, linking cities performing different roles within the spatial division of labour (e.g.: the cities of the Randstad Holland, relatively specialised in different functions);
- synergy networks, linking cities performing similar roles and allowing the integration of the local markets (e.g., the international financial centres acting on a unique virtual worldwide market; art cities linked within tourist itineraries);
- innovation networks, linking cities cooperating on common projects (e.g., airports, railways, etc.).

In all these cases, two complementary elements are necessary at the same time: efficient physical networks and a specific function played by the city within the network. The existence of efficient physical networks is a condition *sine qua non* for the development of high order functions and the internationalisation of the city; the existence of an actual role of a strategy to build it up is a condition for the effectiveness of the investments in the networks.

217

10.2.3   Cities as places

This last element brings us to the consideration of the third nature of cities: cities as places characterised by a physical dimension, an identity, an image. The use of the network metaphor in fact does not exhaust the multiform facets that characterise the city, and may even be misleading: the city cannot be interpreted as (and its image reduced to) an airport, a railway station or an electronic switch addressing telephone calls to the right direction. Cities bear a geographic, demographic, physical and economic dimension that nourish and determine its internal functioning and its role.

The functions performed are always biased towards tertiary and non-material tasks, planning and control, contact and interaction; one in the modern city, towards internationalisation. In order to host and attract these functions the city has to supply efficient external accessibility through long distance networks and linkages, but also an efficiently managed internal territory allowing a good quality of life and an easy utilisation of space for internal movement and residential activities.

10.2.4   Nodes and places: an increasingly difficult integration

As we have seen above, the territorial and the network natures of the city are widely complementary, but may become conflicting with each other. On the one hand, the quality and quantity of the urban functions demand, and highly benefit from the supply of, external infrastructures; in turn, infrastructure provision needs an actual and effective demand in order to be profitable. But on the other hand, highly efficient long-distance networks have to end up into specific sites within the city; they have to interconnect with each other; therefore they enter in a direct contact with the physical aspects of the city, with its traffic and congestion, with its costs. Users mainly branched on the air or fast train networks can stand less and less the inefficiency and the slow rhythm of the central city, even though they need a wide CBD, a diversified local economy, an equilibrated blend of economic and leisure assets. The market, and in particular the urban land market, provides an initial answer to this possible conflict. The city selectively loses the activities and the functions that make a less efficient use of its assets (which are in general those activities which are less willing to pay its costs), through their suburbanisation or disappearance. But at the same time a wide part of the adjustment process happens at the expense of the urban quality of life, the urban efficiency, and in the long run its sustainability.

An effective policy response is needed, especially in terms of proper urban form, internal transport infrastructure and effective interconnections among the different transport means inside the city. Many recent studies about international cities point out in fact that not only the internationalisation of internal urban functions is needed, but also an efficient interconnection between the airport and the CBD, the high-speed trains station and the major highways (Bonneville, 1991; Bonnafous, 1993).

10.3 The new emerging urban paradigm: The multicentric network city

As we have seen, one of the possible answers to the problem of urban diseconomies of scale and to the increasing contradiction between the abstract node function of the city and its heavy physical realm consists in rethinking in an integrated way the general city form. The international debate on this issue is intense (see for example Breheny, 1992; Owens, 1992) and many international institutions have contributed to it (OECD, 1990 and 1995; CEC, 1990) launching a plea in favour of "compact" city forms. Arguments for and against this suggestion have multiplied recently, as, on the one hand, the compact, monocentric, big city has shown in the past a low "sustainability", due to excessive density of functions, congestion costs and slow pace of internal renewal, while, on the other hand, also the low-density, spread city, with its heavy dependence on private transport means and its high land consumption, has added new problems to the traditional ones.

Nevertheless, one general conclusion has come out in a sufficiently clear way. A possible land-use pattern that can avoid the limits of the two extreme patterns might be found in the multicentric network-city. This pattern in fact maintains the "urban effect" linked to the agglomeration of different functions in compact centres, avoiding at the same time the diseconomies coming from excessive size of the single centre through the multiplication of the centres. The necessary conditions for the effectiveness of this new (or better revisited) "paradigm" may be described as follows (Camagni and Gibelli, 1994):

a) the single centres have to bear a diversification of functions, possibly linked with each other "en filière" (intersectoral linkages, residence/leisure/production linkages, etc.), in order to contain inside the centre the widest possible share of trips. In such cases, mono-functional centres should be avoided, as they maximise trip generation with respect to other centres;

b) the centres should be linked with each other through a network of effective transport links, organised both in a radial and an orbital way with respect to the major city-centre;

c) each centre should keep or develop its specific image and character, in order to work as a magnet (with respect to both trips and locations) and not as a repeller (emphasising spread trends).

Northern European countries such as Holland and Denmark have for a long time oriented their land-use planning towards integrated systems of medium-sized, compact centres, and this pattern is increasingly seen as a policy benchmark and an effective solution in many big cities around the world (OECD, 1995).

In policy terms, the new paradigm implies first of all, a deep integration between transportation and land use planning, and secondly, an anticipatory policy intervention with respect to actual development processes. It may also be implemented at different spatial scales:

- at the regional scale, distributing high order functions (e.g., in the public administration and government activities) among different centres;
- at the metropolitan scale, maintaining the urban fringe as a continuous and compact area and concentrating development in newly developed centres, spatially separated and linked to one another;
- at the urban scale, trying to re-concentrate and push some polarisation effects in the already urbanised, middle-density urban peripheries, through the selection of what French planners call some "lieux magiques", bearing a symbolic meaning for local population, and recreating around them an "urban atmosphere".

A major question involved in designing a new paradigm for the city concerns the transportation and communications function. This has a direct impact on urban sustainability, and will be discussed in the next sections.

10.4   The role of transport and communication in the modern economy

During the eighties much attention was devoted to the structural changes taking place in modern economies. During those years, the rapid rise of the service sector - not only for domestic but also for international activities - mirrors the fact that the western world is increasingly marked by a wide variety of communication and interaction patterns ranging from a local up to a global scale. This tendency is reinforced by the rapid and deep technological changes taking place in the transport and communications sector, which have been regarded as the driving forces pushing modern society into the so-called "Information Economy"; this term refers to an economy where a large share of all economic activities is associated with the production, distribution and consumption of information.

The pioneering study of Machlup (1962), followed by Porat (1977), was the first one to stress the significance of a "knowledge-based" economy in those years when Bell (1973) was signalling the emergence of a "services-dominated economy in post-industrial society". From these early works, a series of theoretical and empirical analyses have followed, strengthening the development of an economy governed by different rules and dependent upon different strategic resources. Jonscher (1983) described the emergence of the "Information Economy" by classifying economic activities into two classes, viz. "production tasks", i.e. tasks associated with the manufacturing and delivery of products and services, and "information tasks", i.e. tasks associated with the coordination and manipulation of production activities. The major source of added value appeared to shift from production tasks to information tasks.

All these studies witness the emergence of an information economy, characterised by a growth and intensification of activities (both investment and employment) associated with the collection, manipulation, storage and transfer of information. *Knowledge-based* and *information-based* activities were becoming important strategic resources upon which the competitiveness of firms and comparative advantages of regions would increasingly depend (Bar et al., 1989; Capello et al., 1990; Gillespie et al., 1989; Gillespie and Williams, 1988). Thus, a modern economy tends to go through a period of transformation, marked by the move from "*capital-intensive*" production systems to "*information-intensive*" production systems (Willinger and Zuscovitch, 1988), where information and knowledge are inextricably linked strategic resources for economic development. The emergence of the "Information Economy" is seen to be highly dependent upon the widespread diffusion and adoption of new communications technologies, originating from the interaction of computers and telecommunications, which give rise to new ways of storing, manipulating, organising and transmitting information.

It is evident that a delay in the adoption and exploitation of modern transport and communication technologies will imply a loss of opportunities and hence cause significant costs. This is true for developed countries and developed cities, which define their competitive edge on the basis of the speed of adoption of these new technologies. This is even more true for developing countries, and developing cities; for them new transport and communications technologies represent a new threat which their economic systems have to face in the near future. The lack of adequate transport and telecommunications infrastructure may imply that local economic systems (i.e. regions and cities) may become isolated from development processes and from integration processes characterising modern economies.

By the same token, a great attention was given in the same years to transport infrastructures and communications services as tools for urban economic development and competitiveness. There are strong commonalities between the two sectors which can better explain why they are always analysed together, also in the case of urban sustainability studies:

- accessibility to an urban area depends on the existence (and efficiency) of transport and communications systems (Banister and Button, 1993; Banister et al, 1995);
- in the last two decades, a radical technological revolution has taken place in both sectors, allowing a revolutionary upgrading of all technologies. In the words of Freeman (1987), radical innovations have taken place in the two sectors, which are now followed by numerous incremental innovations, opening the way to a new techno-economic paradigm;
- both transport and communications systems impact on the spatial organisation of economic and social activities, and can thus have a very important role on sustainability. The extremely high potentialities of these two sectors to reshape the spatial organisation of industrial and social activities represent an important opportunity for creating more sustainable urban forms, at least in the long run (Capello and Gillespie, 1993);
- in the light of what has just been said, transport and communications are the physical carriers of the new "city-network" paradigm which seems to emerge in modern economies. As was shown before, this paradigm implies the development of non-hierarchical relationships among specialised centres, providing external factors from complementarity/vertical integration or from cooperation among centres.

However, transport technologies do not offer only advantages. As they imply mobility, energy consumption, noise, and, when overexploited, congestion costs, they have huge negative environmental impacts, especially in the case of cities. Mobility of commodities and people plays a conflicting role in the development of any economy (Nijkamp, 1994a): on the one hand it enhances the productivity of the capital stock and the welfare of the population, but on the other it causes high costs of affecting the urban quality of life and the structure of the urban environment and by eroding the stock of natural resources.

The negative feedback of transport activities are not irrelevant in modern societies, and risk to become even greater if efficient intervention policies in favour of environmental protection are not put in place. The list of costs is a long one: air and water pollution, noise and vibration, road casualties, are just some of the examples. If we look at some data, the picture is quite dramatic.

According to Swedish studies, urban air pollution causes between 300 to 2000 new cases of cancer annually. Traffic accounts for 70 per cent of the emissions of carcinogenic substances that may affect the genes of people living in urban areas. In Switzerland, concentration of NO_x regularly exceeds the standards for cities laid down in the 1985 Order for the Protection of air. The costs of local air pollution, although rather difficult to calculate, have been estimated at about 0.3 per cent of GDP in OECD countries; for the European Union, a figure of 0.3 per cent to 0.4 per cent of GDP, with 90 per cent of the costs attributed to road transport, is quoted in the EU Green Paper (OECD, 1995). All these data witness the severity of the problem, which becomes even greater if one thinks that transport infrastructures are vital for economic development and daily life. At a first glance, it seems a paradox without a solution.

A way out to this impasse may be found at a higher level of abstraction of the problem, with the introduction of two different concepts: *accessibility, defined as the potential interaction among sites based on ease of contact/flows* (i.e. travel time, capacity of links) and *mobility, defined as the actual interaction based on the ease of contacts/flows and costs.*

Accessibility represents the real value of transport infrastructure, as it embodies all the advantages of spatial interaction: exchange of goods, information, know-how and experience. Mobility, in turn, is the way by which the advantages of accessibility are realised, but it creates social costs and, through congestion of the network, impinges on accessibility itself. A possible solution for the preceding paradox is to conceive policies that reduce mobility without limiting accessibility, acting on mobility costs (e.g. by internalising its social costs) rather than on circulation restrictions. If similar policies are successfully implemented, one can reach the positive effects:

- reduce mobility costs and congestion costs;
- anticipate the effects of congestion on mobility without jeopardising accessibility;
- increase public financial resources, that can be mobilised for improving public transport infrastructure.

An interesting aspect to draw attention to is the relationship between accessibility, economic development and sustainability. The logic characterising the relationship is different in cities located in developing and developed countries. For what concerns *developed countries*, the virtual circle is depicted in Figure 10.1. The mechanism is put in place by exogenous factors; policies supplying transport infrastructure and services have an immediate positive impact on urban accessibility. After this first pushing effect, a double cycle is activated:

- *a virtuous cycle*, as improved *accessibility* means improved *sustainability* of urban development via reduced congestion and better air quality. The improved *sustainability has a positive effect on development*. Urban quality becomes a strategic local factor, and thus a discriminating feature in the competitiveness of urban systems. The city becomes an ideal location for managerial and residential activities, and for high quality social interaction. The case of the Swiss cities is an example in this respect, where natural quality, economic efficiency and pleasant social life are mixed together and guarantee an increase in economic welfare;
- *a vicious cycle*, as *development generates more mobility* and *more mobility has a negative impact on accessibility*. The elasticity of mobility to income has been estimated around 1.2 in OECD countries (OECD, 1995). Moreover, it has been proved that the increase in income has a positive effect on car ownership, which is increasing in all European countries. Even in USA, where 58 per cent of households own two or more cars and 20 per cent have three or more, there is little sign of saturation, as one would expect (OECD, 1995); and the upward trend of car ownerships is expected to continue in all countries. The rising trend is even more problematic, if data on travel choice mode are analysed. Car represents the mode by which more than 30 to 50 per cent of urban trips are made in European cities, and the one which generates the highest external costs. On the other hand, the increase in congestion generated by more mobility has an economic cost, in terms of loss of economic activities within the city and of loss of efficiency of the economic system as a whole. OECD data report that using the definition of "additional time spent travelling compared with free-flowing travel", congestion is estimated to cost the equivalent of about 2 per cent of GDP (Quinet, 1994, as quoted in OECD, 1995).

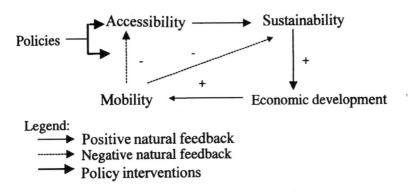

Legend:
⟶ Positive natural feedback
┈┈▶ Negative natural feedback
⟶ Policy interventions

Figure 10.1 Positive and negative feedback of transport activities in developed cities

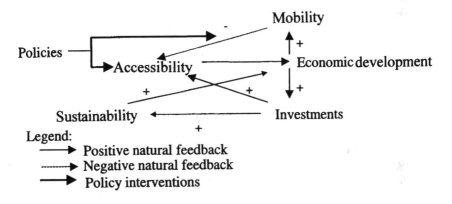

Legend:
⟶ Positive natural feedback
┈┈▶ Negative natural feedback
⟶ Policy interventions

Figure 10.2 Positive and negative feedback of transport activities in developing cities

It is on the negative feedback of the "circle" that appropriate transport policies play a crucial role. Appropriate policies should be able to move along a difficult "razor edge" path, increasing accessibility of cities (the real value of transport) and at the same time keeping the negative social costs of transport activities under control.

As far as cities in *developing countries* are concerned, the virtuous circle does not look the same as before (Figure 10.2). Also in this case, the mechanism is activated with supply driven policies which develop transport infrastructures in cities. The first impact on accessibility is the same as in the case of developing countries, but then:

- *more accessibility generates more development*, as new activities are attracted or generated (transport infrastructure is a direct precondition for development); *more development has two kinds of effects: from one side it acts on sustainability* through more investments in the quality of social services sewerage systems and sanitary infrastructures, at present very low in developing cities (Lea and Courtney, 1986). All this has a positive impact on the quality of life in urban areas, and thus on sustainability. *From the other side, economic and social development has a positive effect on mobility* of people and commodities, as in the previous case. Studies on the effects of per capita income growth in developing countries have underlined the fast rise by the consumption of non-durable goods such as cars and electric appliances, usually second-hand, high energy-consuming ones. What is even more worrying is the fact that forecasts on the number of car ownerships in developing countries estimate a substantial increase by the year 2025 (see Button, 1992);
- as is the case for developed cities, in the long run more *mobility generates more congestion and thus less accessibility*. Most of developing cities are in fact already affected by congestion on urban roads, which is the result of an increase in car trips and a very poor quality of transport infrastructures (roads and public transport services). Bangkok is a clear example of a highly congested city, with severe traffic problems: overall, Bangkok's public transport carries only 33 per cent of the total annual passenger kilometres in the city, compared to an average of 64 per cent in Singapore, Tokyo and Hong Kong. At the same time, Bangkok has 51 per cent of daily trips by private transport, and is recognised to be the most severely congested city in the world (Poboon and Kenworthy, 1995).

An important message stems from these considerations; there is a need that appropriate policies are formulated in the transport field, which lead to a cut in costs caused by mobility and to the protection of the real value of transport, i.e. accessibility. The main problem is that such a strategy has thus far never been implemented, as we will show in the next section.

10.5   The role of transport infrastructure on urban sustainability

The relationship between transport systems design and use on the one hand and urban sustainability on the other hand is an intricate one, as both positive and negative factors can be observed. In addition, this complex relationship varies throughout the history of cities. Ancient cities already regarded infrastructure as a necessary condition for industrial, commercial and residential activities. It is plausible to state that accessibility is almost an

226

indicator for urban economic performance. Clearly, the costs of accessibility -reflected in the costs of infrastructure and in the costs of transportation - may be significant (see Button, 1992; Desai, 1990; Dimitriou, 1990; ESCAP, 1990). In most countries, for instance, the energy share of the transportation sector exceeds 25 per cent of total energy use. Also the amount of public resources in infrastructure construction, environmental decay and traffic insecurity is significant. Although there is a wide spectrum of various transport modes (cars, trains, buses, undergrounds, trams, bicycles, airplanes, ferries etc.), it turns out that - despite urban poverty - in almost all cities private surface transport is becoming the dominant mode (see Button and Ngoe, 1991). Although this is conceivable in light of the obvious advantages of the latter mode, it also means that the most polluting mode has become the most popular. This social trap can only be remedied if all social costs are properly charged to all transport users. If this is not done, urban accessibility - which is a critical success factor for economic success - is under serious threat. Thus ways would have to be found that ensure urban sustainability through market based policies.

It is also worth noting that there is a close connection between transport needs and land use (see Wegener, 1995). If there is no strict physical planning which addresses also explicitly the transportation needs of new residential, industrial or commercial areas, urban sustainability is not likely to emerge. Thus a strict coordination between urban transport policy and urban land use policy is badly needed, a strategy in which also public transportation would have to play a critical role. Distortion of the urban transport market via subsidies, unfeasible regulatory measures or unpriced factors will no doubt aggregate environmental quality conditions in the city. It seems a wiser policy to adhere to economic principles which would pave the road to sustainable urban development (see also OECD, 1994).

It goes without saying that the dynamics of urban transport technologies runs parallel to that of the urban morphology. Various types of cities have emerged and each arche-type results in specific urban energy use patterns, environmental quality conditions, safety and congestion patterns, and land use patterns (see also Banister and Banister, 1995; Breheny, 1992; Newman and Kenworthy, 1989; Rickaby, 1991 and Warren, 1993). An interesting overview of indicative effects of various types of urban morphology - from the viewpoint of transportation - can be found in Verroen and Hilbers (1994). They distinguish four types of development patterns of a city, viz. the compact city, new towns, edge cities and uncontrolled development.

The implications of diverse patterns of urban transport and urban morphology for urban sustainability are not entirely clear at the outset, as each city is facing site-specific physical conditions and behaviour-specific responses of citizens, which makes it difficult to make unambiguous statements on the consequences of transport and land use in the city for the urban sustainability. However, in light of the dynamic evolution of both phenomena it seems plausible to suggest that in new urban land use development the notion of urban sustainability - in terms of economic efficiency, social equity and environmental quality - is taken as an explicit starting point for urban policy (cf. Hay and Trinder, 1991). Market-based policy measures may then be developed to make sure that future mobility patterns contribute to a reinforcement of urban sustainability. This message is particularly important for Third World cities, which are threatened by a "mobility avalanche". Without a mobility policy driven by market principles, Third World cities will not turn into islands of local opportunities, but rather into pollution havens. Traffic restraint policies, road pricing and land use policies need to be developed in a proper combination to pave the road to urban sustainability. Needless to say that this requires a strong urban management based on business-oriented guidelines, coupled with environmental-friendly land use planning.

A few examples may help to clarify the above notions. In a recent paper, Goddard (1995) has proposed for Mexico City demand side management policies for making urban areas sustainable by managing vehicle use as part of a cost-effective programme for controlling vehicle emissions and congestion. The allocation system for achieving this result is based on a tradable permit system for vehicles which combines the objectives of efficiency, equity and environmental quality, at the expense, however, of very high transaction costs for users. In another study, area licensing schemes are proposed in order to reach an environmentally-benign transportation system (see Ramjerdi, 1992a). This approach is based on the maximisation of user benefits, taking into consideration time preferences of users and marginal utilities of incomes of users. The analysis was applied for new transport policy schemes in Stockholm. The same author (Ramjerdi, 1992b) has also extensively studied the road pricing (essentially a cordon toll system) developed in the city of Oslo.

It may be concluded that there is not a single uniform market solution for transport policy in a sustainable city. There are various options and - depending on site-specific considerations - a choice has to be made. Recent experiences provide testimony of the fact that the use of economic principles in urban transport policy is necessary for ensuring accessibility and thus urban sustainability.

A convincing support for the above mentioned need for a client-oriented and market-instigated transport policy and infrastructure provision is found in the World Development Report 1994 published by the World Bank (1994a) which was entirely devoted to "infrastructure for development". According to this study, infrastructure can generate significant benefits in economic growth, poverty alleviation, and environmental sustainability, provided it delivers services that respond to effective demand and does so efficiently. Thus infrastructure policy has to be instrumental in fulfilling market needs Therefore, infrastructure policy must be seen as a service industry, driven by commercial management, competition and stakeholder involvement. As a consequence, the following guidelines are formulated by the World Bank (1994a):

• manage infrastructure like a business, not a bureaucracy.
• introduce competition - directly if feasible, indirectly if not.
• give users and other stakeholders and strong voice and real responsibility.

Clearly, there should be much more scope for private-public partnerships in the provision and financing of infrastructure. One thing is clear: governments will have a definite - though changed - role in infrastructure, especially in setting up efficient policy and regulatory frameworks safeguarding the interests of economically deprived people and the interest of the environment and in developing initiatives that induce private involvement in the provision of infrastructure services.

If we accept the idea that a positive relationship can exist between transport development and sustainability, given appropriate policies to overcome social costs, urban policies which limit transport development do not seem the most appropriate. At least two aspects act against these kinds of policies:

• the *high costs implied by limiting the emerging strong social behaviours*. In fact, many structural phenomena cause the role of transport to rise rather than to decline. Examples of such phenomena are: at a micro level, increased female labour force participation, increase in leisure time and income, and at a macro level, the rise of a global economy (Nijkamp, 1994b). Policies oriented towards the reduction of transport activities would hamper these structural socio-economic trends but in the long run it will not prevent them from taking place, exacerbating congestion and environmental damages;
• the *high economic costs involved in such policies*. The risk is that in the short term an increase in pure environmental values is achieved, but at the expense of economic competitiveness and growth. In the long run, the weak economic position would lead cities to invest less in environmental quality.

10.6 The role of telecommunications technologies on urban sustainability

New information and communications technologies represent a great opportunity for both developed and developing cities, since they can act as countervailing powers to environmental decay caused by transport activities. In principle, these technologies may play a double role in leading cities in terms of sustainability:

- they act on *accessibility*, without generating the negative environmental feedback caused by transport systems. In this way, they act on development without the negative effects of mobility;
- they act as *policy tools to solve some negative aspects of transport activities*, through an increase of their efficiency. Examples of these potentialities are multimodal transport systems aiming at optimising the performance of the transport systems as a whole, telematics aiming at optimising drivers' behaviour through the provision of real time information, fleet control serving to reduce transport cost.

In the last two decades there has been a wide spectrum of technological upgrading in telecommunications systems, particularly computer networks and data systems, fax machines and electronic mail, whose effect has been to increase accessibility, by shrinking time and distance. All these technological opportunities have dramatically widened the choice of location for many workers, allowing them to work whenever these tools are available, including the home; this means a high potential reduction of mobility for journey to work trips within cities. In the United States, for example, the share of people working at home, for at least part of the time, is estimated to be as high as 30 per cent of the labour force. An estimated two million of these people are full-time employees, who would otherwise commute daily to an office or on other work place. Estimates for telecommuters in the United States are between 7.5 and 15 million by 2002 (OECD, 1995).

Telecommuting can be an effective component of travel demand management and can contribute to reducing traffic congestion, air pollution, road casualties and energy consumption. In developing countries the application of telecommuting would only be possible for high qualified jobs and high level trained employees, which represent a very low percentage of daily commuters. The impact on travel demand is then likely to be lower than in developed cities. Other advanced telecommunications technologies, like teleshopping, home-banking, videoconferencing are expected to have an impact on transport mobility, but even in developed countries the rate of adoption is still very low and the foreseeable effect will be limited.

A more promising area in which telematic applications will ultimately represent an effective policy tool for reducing road congestion is the implementation of information technology on road transport and public services (see for an extensive discussion Nijkamp et al, 1996). Traffic management will benefit from integrated systems incorporating real-time, adaptive computer programs that will optimise traffic-signal timings and give bus priorities, making use of information from accidents to congestion detector systems. It has been estimated that traffic management measures, which remove much of the "stop-go" from urban driving, coupled with congestion pricing, could reduce NO_x emissions from trucks by up to 70 per cent, apart from any savings in fuel consumption (OECD, 1995).

Telematics applications have also an important role to play in public transport operation.

Despite all positive aspects related to telecommunications technologies described above, it would be too simplistic to affirm that these technologies represent the perfect solution to the problem of negative external costs associated with transport activities. Many barriers and limits exist which may hamper their widespread adoption and exploitation:

- limits to the adoption;
- limits on the expected positive effects.

The limits to the adoption stem from the often "taken for granted" idea that telecommunications and transport technologies are perfect substitutes, and thus that telecommuting, teleshopping, videoconferencing will soon achieve a high penetration level.

Some theoretical considerations may be offered here. Both transport and communication systems enter a production function, and present a certain degree of substitution, given the fact that both reply to the accessibility needs of firms. But this degree is very low, as substitution between the two technologies is an *imperfect one*, since it depends on (Camagni and Capello, 1991; Capello and Williams, 1992; Capello, 1994a and 1994b):

a) habits of individuals and economic actors;
b) organisational factors at industrial and urban level;
c) learning processes related to the use and exploitation of these new technologies, especially in the case of telecommunications technologies.

As a consequence, a change in the relative prices of the two inputs (e.g. an increase in the transport costs due to congestion) does not drive directly towards substitution, as is suggested by the traditional neo-classical equilibrium model. Other external conditions must be present, either

231

exogenous to the economic system (like the Gulf war in 1991 responsible for the rise of the videoconference service and the drop of air transport demand), or endogenous to the economic systems. In this latter case we refer to policies encouraging telecommunications demand, not in terms of financial support to adoption, but especially in terms of specific measures to overcome the three above-mentioned critical aspects explaining imperfect substitution. These telecommunications related policies become, in a more general framework, urban sustainability policies aiming at increasing the degree of substitution between transport and telecommunications systems.

The expectations related to the positive side effects of the use of telematics applications in reducing the negative impacts of transport on the environment are usually very high; it is instead worth mentioning that, even if positive effects are envisaged as a consequence of the introduction of transport-substituting activities like telecommuting and teleshopping, in the long run these advantages may be eroded if newly-generated traffic is not restrained. In fact, telecommuting will certainly bring about changes in travel patterns. Whether the total travel will decrease or not is not clear at this stage, but there will be considerable redistribution of travel in time and space. Telecommuting might stimulate urban sprawl and have other adverse effects on land use and public transport use, if suitable counter measures are not taken (OECD, 1995).

The above limits and barriers to an efficient telecommunications policy for urban environmental quality stem mainly from the *demand side*. It is worth mentioning that also at *the supply side* there are aspects which are strongly related to the potential effects generated by these policies. There are two main areas which deserve particular attention when telecommunications policies are implemented:

- the *"appropriateness"* of these technologies, which guarantees the best exploitation of the technological potentialities, and;
- the *"vintage of the technology"*, which in the long run has an impact on both the efficiency of the technology itself and on environmental quality.

10.7 Transport policies for sustainable urban development strategies

10.7.1 Foreseeable trends and the need for appropriate sustainability policies

Before addressing the issue of the appropriate policy strategies for sustainable urban development focusing on transport and communications, a brief scenario of the foreseeable trends in urban transport demand looks necessary.

Extrapolating recent trends, international institutions like the OECD forecast a doubling of urban private traffic for both cars and goods vehicles in the next 30 to 40 years (OECD, 1995). We can subscribe to this forecast as far as demand elements are concerned; but in the face of increasing bottlenecks and contradictions arising on the mobility supply side, aggregate growth will probably slow down or find other territorial patterns of expansion (growth of new centres, flow of activities in developing countries, substitutions among transport modes and between transport and communications modes).

Moreover, these forecasts do not take into account the countervailing effects of transportation and land-use policies implemented by local and national government, preoccupied by the evident non-sustainability of the aggregate scenario and willing to anticipate the disruptive effects of spontaneous trends (on local well-being and global sustainability) and feedback (potential crisis of existing cities and spread of activities on the entire regional territory with disastrous long-term effects). Demand forecasts have nevertheless the advantage of clearly showing the contradictions of spontaneous trends, if the present situation in which social costs of urban mobility are not but partially internalised by private activities is going to continue.

The forecasts of a rapidly increasing urban travel demand derives from the evidence of an aggregate elasticity with respect to income higher than one, and of the continuing success of an urban environment to provide the information and contact assets that are requested by modern economies and to reduce the uncertainty embedded in a more and more turbulent and innovative economic environment (Camagni, 1996).

In developed countries, cities will not probably grow in terms of population and jobs, but in terms of income controlled and produced and in terms of physical space utilised. The decentralisation of population will continue, albeit at slower rates than in the past, as a consequence of increasing land prices in the centre and of increasing congestion. Edge-city shopping malls and leisure centres, decentralised headquarters and science-parks will flourish, especially in those countries where they have remained a rare phenomena up to now.

The average tri-lengths will increase, as a consequence of the widening of the "bassins de vie" of the households, and of the widening of the urban labour market to which individuals address themselves as long as income levels, professionality and personal specialisation increase. The increase in women participation rates and consequently two-income families reduce the possibility of optimisation of the household location with respect to journey-to-work length.

Even if technological improvements were to reduce the toxic emissions of cars, the problems of noise and CO_2 emissions will remain, and will remain also the problem of increasing use of urban land for roads and increasing use of roads for private parking.

Trends in energy use, toxic emissions, congestion and traffic domination in cities will probably be exacerbated. This will especially show up in new industrial and developing countries where a wider space for rural-to-urban migration exists and the urban hierarchy is widely biased in favour of primate cities. The attractiveness of cities as pleasant places to live and efficient places to work will be jeopardised.

The forecasted trends are preoccupying also from the point of view of global sustainability. Transport is not the major source of CO_2 emissions but the fastest growing one: the case for a precautionary intervention strategy to limit private mobility in cities is evident.

10.7.2 The main policy goals

Given the preceding worrisome scenarios referring to urban travel demand, the main general goals of a transport policy for sustainable urban development may be summarised as follows:

a) maintaining for cities their character of efficient forms of organisation of human societies, a character that they have always maintained in history and that is more and more threatened by the contradictions issued from increased size, sub-optimal city form, growing urban travel demand, increased use of the private car. In fact, their role as nodes of interaction, engines of economic growth, triggers of modernisation and change, instruments of social well-being and cultural upgrading might be jeopardised by the increase of the above-mentioned environmental diseconomies;

b) avoiding diseconomies of large scale through appropriate urban forms, stimulated and realised through an appropriate blending of anticipatory intervention, land-use regulations and effective orientation of market forces;

234

c) avoiding traffic domination in the urban landscape without reducing accessibility of the different parts of the city, including the more congested ones like the city-centre;
d) encouraging a more environmentally sensitive use of the vehicles stocks, in terms of a more selective use, better maintenance, better energy-efficiency;
e) increasing the efficiency and attractiveness of public transport;
f) stimulating the communication substitution for people, paper and goods mobility.

10.7.3   Policy principles and policy styles

The complexity of the system we present to control the multiplicity of the goals of an urban sustainability policy, the lack of really successful policy experiences to which to refer, are all elements that suggest that the resource to a single and simple policy principle would not be possible or sufficient: an eclectic approach would prove more effective. But even in an eclectic approach some principles emerge as the most relevant and appropriate. The first principle under this respect should be the resource to market forces whenever it is possible.

In fact, when the behaviour of a host of individuals is under scrutiny, the market proves to be a much more efficient, flexible and equitable instrument of resources allocation than governmental regulations. On the other hand these latter have often proved costly, easy to contour, inflexible, open to negative side effects and incapable of dealing with the complexity of urban phenomena.

Or course, the market we are speaking about is often a corrected market, integrated by a system of environmental taxes in order to take into account all the costs implied by individual behaviour and to deliver more correct signals (as in the case of the resource to a "polluter pays" principle, addressed to the internalisation of social costs and negative factors), or created voluntarily in order to allow an easier adaptation of the private system to the environmental benchmarks which look necessary (this is notably the case of the transferable emission rights).

A relevant part of the excessive mobility demand we are facing in cities stems from a traditional policy of cheap transport cost that for decades was implicitly or explicitly implemented, in the persuasion that mobility is a value per se, eligible for government support, and transport a powerful development factor. Transport-intensive mobility patterns and organisational methods (like for example just-in-time organisation) were consequently implemented in a condition where (private) transport inputs were not paid their full investment costs, operational costs and social negative externalities. Today it is time to restore a sounder equilibrium in this respect, allowing the market to adjust to more reasonable prices for this production or consumption input. And this can be achieved through fuel taxes, carbon taxes or road pricing (or congestion pricing). But a purely market principle should be complemented by other forms of intervention in a number of theoretically relevant cases:

a) first of all, when the market requires long run reference frameworks, as in the case of land-use regulations on new urban expansions. With the external situation, this is another case of market failure, in presence of important benefits allowed by inter-individual coordination and cooperation;

b) secondly, when the market, even corrected for external factors, does not allow the required protection of environmental conditions, like in the case of abnormally high pollution loads and emergency traffic conditions. It is generally agreed that in these cases the market mechanism would be accompanied by some forms of regulatory control over maximum pollution loads (Pezzey, 1988);

c) thirdly, when the resort to a market mechanism does not allow (or even jeopardises) the possibility of reaching a second goal in sustainable urban policies, namely that of environmental equity. A huge transport tax could easily prove to be a regressive fiscal device, as low income classes spend a much wider share of their income on transportation. Regulatory devices and traffic restrictions, applying to everybody, do not have this side effect and should accompany the former intervention strategy at least partially;

d) fourthly, when the mechanism of market correction or the creation of tradable permits encounters huge transaction or control costs. It is the case, for example, of emission permits on car use in the city, as proposed by Haynes Goddard for Mexico City (1995; see also Nijkamp and Ursem, 1998), an instrument which looks sound from an abstract point of view, but that is going to rise multiple organisational problems in the implementation phase:

- direct transaction costs for the user: the commodity traded is not in fact and homogeneous one, as the circulation permit has to refer to specific weeks and has in principle to be traded continuously;
- easy possibility of illegal permits emission, unless a costly control procedure is built (the *bona fide* holder is not going to be prosecuted);
- the increase in intensity of car use that is going to be determined in the allowed days.

236

The most relevant point is of course the first, which refers to the necessity of giving the market the necessary long-term guidelines. It is widely accepted in fact that the market allows the most efficient adjustment to these guidelines, but cannot supply them. These guidelines should refer to:

- general environmental targets: types of gasoline allowed, maximum emissions of exhaust gases per car (control of the efficiency of mufflers, etc.)
- general expansion axes of the city and land-use guidelines; projected territorial pattern of the transport network architecture.

But a bridging mechanism should be conceived in order to integrate better the two principles and avoid negative reactions on the side of private activities. The regulations introduced should be in principle:

- addressed to clearly stated and easily perceivable collective goals;
- accepted by the public and the goals widely shared, through new forms of public debate and consensus building;
- effective with respect to both short-term emergencies and long-term issues;
- based on sound long-term analyses and plans;
- delivered and marketed in a reliable way, in order to convey effective signals to the private decision making;
- shared from the beginning by the relevant interest groups whose behaviour the success of the public initiative widely depends on;
- politically acceptable, which means that they have to appear equitable, non penalising with respect to special categories of citizens, fiscally neutral (a new relevant tax should in principle be counterbalanced by the release of a previous one).

The policy style that all this implies is close to the one proposed by the new paradigm that is increasingly adopted in local policy management, namely "strategic planning" (Bryson and Einsweiler, 1988; Gibelli, 1993 and 1995). Policies in fact should refer to the building of a shared vision of the community future, merging traditional methods of long term land-use planning with socio-economic analyses of the viability (or sustainability) of the development trajectories envisaged and with strong involvement in consensus building, grass-roots participation, private/public partnership.

In developed countries, the same role of information dissemination, interest building in policy issues and involvement of local communities might be performed by NGOs, collaborating with local authorities and international organisations. In fact, they are already active in collecting the needs and concerns of local people and reflecting their perspectives in local project design and implementation (World Bank, 1994b).

A last element which is relevant in the discussion about market vs. regulation policy styles, regards the problem of guaranteeing an equal treatment of equal land property owners in case that planning regulations become increasingly selective in terms of development permits. In fact, once a territorial development axis is chosen for a "compact" urbanisation and surrounding areas are due to open to green spaces, a problem of equity is involved. In this case, the institute of transferable development rights guaranteeing the same potential building rights to all land parcels, but forcing the actual utilisation to particular sites through rights exchange - which is usually employed in case of inner city rehabilitation - could be used in the case of new urbanisation, as it guarantees a fair treatment of property rights and lowers the case for illegal practices.[2]

10.7.4 Towards anticipatory and precautionary short-term and long-term policies

Territorial phenomena are subject to huge irreversibility given the long-term persistence of social overhead capital and buildings, the cumulative effects linking transport infrastructures and location decisions, the forced outcomes in terms of transport use of the different land-use patterns and city-forms (Camagni, 1998). The same irreversible shape the development trajectories of technologies (and transport technologies in our case), due to rapid learning effects that reinforce the profitability of early-developed technologies.

In this framework, the necessary short-term policies have to be complemented, developed together and even anticipated by far-looking, long-term policies, addressed to avoiding the previously mentioned irreversibility.

Short-term policies are by definition policies that assume the present state of technologies, private and social capital stock and land-use patterns, and are primarily addressed to the stimulation of more environmentally friendly use of the production functions through the substitution of high energy and natural resources-intensive inputs and the stimulation of the use of mass transit facilities. On the other hand, long-term policies pursue the same goals through the orientation of technological change and the shaping of more sustainable urban forms (Camagni et al, 1996).

---

[2] This institutional tool is increasingly utilised in the U.S. for greenfield urbanisation; for its full operationality it requires high financial and planning skills by the local government and has to be used on areas of similar potential economic value (see Camagni, 1994; Jabobs, 1994).

The latter policies have a crucial role in a sustainable urban development strategy, as the bulk of negative factors from transport demand and use inescapably derive from such structural elements as transport technologies, the architecture of transport infrastructure, the urban form and from their cumulative evolution.

Therefore, long-term policies should not be relegated to the package of those things whose implementation "would be so good but will never happen". They are the most important elements of a successful strategy of sustainable development.

Hopefully, many short-term measures are likely to have potentially beneficial effects on the long-term trends (e.g. a tax on fuel consumption not only reduces car use but is likely to stimulate the orientation of both car demand and car technology towards more energy efficient products). But this is not true in all cases, in particular as far as land-use regulations are concerned, given the large degrees of freedom that a market response to land-use restrictions maintains; moreover, the favourable long-term result is only possible, but not guaranteed.

10.7.5 Towards an integrated approach

The pure environmental issue to an urban sustainable development is in a way far too limiting to solve urban problems for at least two reasons: a) the city is a more complex reality, where three (economic/ environmental / social) subsystems interact and give rise to advantages and disadvantages on the quality of life in cities; b) urban sustainable development is a process of co-evolution of these positive interactive effects and cross-factors which are generated by the three fields.

A wide variety of policies and measures is available to governments at all levels to tackle the problems of transport and urban sustainability. However, in light of the approach used in this paper, it would be a contradiction in itself to suggest separated urban sustainable intervention policies in different fields, without taking into consideration the positive cross-factors, feedback and co-evolution of the three different elements constituting the city.

For this reason, and in the light of the perspective followed in the all paper, the best way to approach environmental problems and all related negative externalities associated to transport and high mobility in urban areas, is to suggest *an integrated approach of policy interventions*, which should act exactly on the positive interaction effects and positive cross-factors that the different fields which characterise an urban setting generate; at the same time, countervailing policies should be put in place to dominate the negative aspects and the social costs associated with these interaction effects.

The major advantage of an integrated approach is that a careful combination of carefully-selected policies *reinforce* each other. Some policies blend naturally with others: for example the combination of restraint measures of private transport modes in city centres and improved public transport policy increase the effectiveness of the transit improvements. Moreover, integrated policies not only reinforce each other, but may have the great advantage of avoiding, or in some cases limiting, the adverse side-effects of the policy. In the example given above, the restraint of private cars in city centres without an increase in public transport efficiency would have major adverse effects on the mobility of people, and thus would make the impact on car drivers less unpleasant.

Two issues come at this stage: if an integrated approach to intervention policies is envisaged as the most appropriate way of tackling urban transport policies, which are the phases of the intervention policies and the fields where integration is mostly favourable.

For what concerns the first issue, the integration of policies should take place at different stages of the decision making process. In particular:

- the design of the policy, in terms of intermediate and final objectives has to be developed by policy makers acting in these fields involved;
- the building of political consensus around the proposed policy;
- the decision concerning the timing of action.

Instead, the implementation stage has to be left to each responsible body in each field for two main reasons: a) it may very well be that tools and strategies need different times to be implemented, and the integration of the two could only postpone the implementation of short-term interventions, although integrated policy actions should run parallel; b) specific know-how and experiences are required in different fields, and thus each contributor acts with its own specialisation.

As far as the second aspect is concerned, there are four fields of action in which integrated policies have for sure a positive impact and generate cumulative positive cross-factors (see Table 10.1):

Table 10.1
Short and long-term policies in different integrated fields of action

Policies / Fields of action	Short term	Long term
Integrated transport and land-use policies	Restraints on central city Request for private parking availability in newly-built residential lots	Strategic land-use/transport planning Compact city and urban containment Multicentric city Mixed land-uses Designated growth areas and new towns Guiding the location of travel generating land-uses
Integrated transport and environment policies	Restraints on private traffic in particular areas Restrictions on heavy goods vehicles movements in the city New logistics of goods distribution in the city Enforcement of better performing catalytic converters and their frequent renewal	Investments in public transport service, infrastructure, management and image
Integrated transport and communications policies	Urban traffic management through telematic systems Improve control systems for public transport Telematic systems for bus/ tramways priority Drivers' information a telematic networks	Incentives for telecommuting/ teleshopping infrastructures Incentives for telecommuting/ teleshopping use
Integrated transport and local public policies	Fuel taxes Congestion pricing, road pricing Selective tariffs of parking with decreasing distance Enforces use of less polluting fuels Incentives to a faster renewal of car fleet	Incentives to design energy efficient engines Incentives to research on electric vehicles Incentives to reduce peak-hours travels

241

a) the first field is *transport and land-use planning*. This field of interaction has already been widely studied (see among others Banister et al, 1994; Breheny, 1992; Owens ,1992; Rickaby, 1991), and its relationship quite easy to foresee. Territorial dimensions, such as density, dimension, urban form, functional territorial organisation are all critical variables for environmental quality, especially in terms of energy consumption. The OECD has put much attention on the role that land-use planning may have on car use, and its use limit, through two main mechanisms: a) reducing the need to travel, ensuring reasonable proximity between places of residence, employment and other facilities; b) increasing the scope for non-motorised travel, such as cycling and walking, or by public transport modes (OECD, 1995);

b) the second field where integrated policies may be put in place with extremely positive results is between *transport and environmental policies*. The intervention policies in the field of transport, which may have positive effects on environmental policies cover a wide spectrum. All technological improvements in car emissions (i.e. catalytic converters), efficiency of fuel consumption and fuel-substituting technologies (e.g. electric cars), have a major impact on air pollution in cities. In this field, the improvement of public transport services remains one of the leading intervention policies, not only in terms of infrastructure development, but also in terms of quality, reliability and attractiveness of the service, as we will see in one of the next sections;

c) the third field regards the integration of policies concerning *transport and telecommunications*. As we mentioned already in Section 5, in this area there is ample space for giving incentives for the use and exploitation of transport-substituting technologies, with the intention of avoiding simplistic approaches which emphasise mainly the technological capabilities and overlook other organisational, managerial and cultural aspects crucial for adoption processes of telecommunications technologies and thus for the substitution effect to take place;

d) the last field of integrated intervention policies is between *transport and public finance*. Here, a large variety of economic levers exist, which may act on transport, both in terms of traffic management and of social costs involved, although some measures are more efficient than others. For example, it has extensively been recognised that the elasticity of fuel demand to prices is extremely inelastic and thus a tax on fuel in developed countries has unfortunately a very limited impact on the demand for car trips. OECD has estimated that an increase of 5 per cent above the rate of inflation every year, thus doubling the amount of duty paid after 14 years and trebling after 21 years is still less than the rate of increase which

242

would be required to reduce CO_2 levels to the that recommended by the Intergovernmental Panel on Climate Change (OECD, 1995).

10.8 Concluding remarks

Policies aiming at urban sustainability have to find a balance between economic efficiency, social equity and environmental equity. In particular the interfaces between these three major policy orientations have to be given due attention, as these shape the conditions for an equilibrated solution in a multi-faceted force field. In a long-term perspective one has to emphasise also the dynamics of interactive forces, as cumulative processes and irreversibilities are the rules in this field.

Transport and communications in the urban area are not necessarily a burden or threat, but rather they are vital for sustained economic development. It ought to be emphasised that cities in both the developed and the developing world will not favour urban sustainability by discouraging urban mobility through artificial, inflexible and generalised regulations. Mobility is a necessary consequence of the need for accessibility, which in turn offers the necessary conditions for vital cities as islands of opportunities. Thus, the often assumed conflict between urban transport and the environment has to be looked at also from the viewpoint of dynamic positive externalities.

Clearly, the negative factors of transport have to be coped with by devising proper policy measures, e.g., environmentally-benign transport technologies, traffic regulations and user charge principles. Priority should be given to urban land use policies, as such physical planning instruments are able to influence urban transport patterns in a structural way. This requires in both developing and developed cities a strong and professional urban management. Such a business orientation towards urban policy - in light of significant differences among cities - clearly does not give a simple uniform remedy, but rather a policy guidance based on the viewpoint that cities are the driving forces for the national economy (in both the developed and the developing world). In a way similar to corporate firms, cities are (and have to be) networked with the rest of the world to be competitive and they should be aware of the need for globalisation at the local level.

Clearly, there is not a uniform pattern or position of cities: they differ in institutional, historical, cultural and economic respects. Furthermore, it is noteworthy that in developing countries there is generally a close dynamic interaction between urban and rural areas and it should be avoided that the expansion of the former were driven by the crisis of the latter rather than by their own development potential.

From an environmental viewpoint it would be noted that - despite similarities in various technologies - the vintage of these technologies is different (causing a higher ecological stress on developing countries). In this respect, there is still a long way to go for cities in developing countries, as the degree of introduction and acceptance of (tele)communication systems is still rather low. This may be detrimental for cities with a low penetration rate of network technologies, as such cities run the risk of being exploited by more technologically advanced cities in their own country. Therefore, policies should aim at a rapid introduction of and access to modern communication technologies in all cities. This seems to be a plausible strategy for enhancing the quality of urban life, to improve the urban habitat and to favour urban sustainability.

The urban economy creates scale advantages through synergy and proximity of all human activities, connected through networks inside and between cities. Sustainable urban development implies a maximisation of synergy within strict social and environmental constraints (see CEC, 1990). The social fabric of the city is vulnerable and therefore it is a formidable challenge for urban governments to develop a management style which introduces economic principles for city governance, while enhancing the quality of the environment and the human habitat under conditions of increasing social opportunities, defending historical heritage and promoting urban culture. In all these aspects, the design and maintenance of physical and immaterial infrastructure networks is a necessary condition. Networks open many opportunities for a varied and dense city life, for security and protection, for flexibility and participation.

The design of urban networks which manifest themselves in manifold configurations is a major task for city governments. Networks offer enabling opportunities, although it has to be emphasised that the use of networks incurs private and social costs which have to be borne by the user or actor. Active network policy is of strategic importance for a proper urban governance. This does not only require physical and non-material transport and communication policy but also science networks, organisational networks, neighbourhood networks etc.

In view of environmental factors, particular emphasis has to be laid upon coping with the social costs of transport. Apart from developing market-orientated strategies for controlling mobility (e.g., tradable mobility rights, road pricing), also land use policy is a prerequisite for urban sustainability. There is certainly scope for more rationality and business orientation in urban planning.

Focal points of policy attention at the interface of transport and urban development are:

- strict land use planning (including prevention of illegal land use);
- provision of satisfactory housing for a sustainable habitat (including prevention of squatter movement);
- access to collective transport (including user change for external factors caused by private transport);
- development of environmental infrastructure (water sewage systems, waste treatment plants, renewable energy systems etc.);
- stimulation of a competitive urban economic environment (including sufficient accessibility via modern infrastructure).

Different tasks for governments may be distinguished in this context, depending on the level of competence. Examples are:

- *national* governments: in charge of national environmental and health standards, main infrastructure provision and social amenities, using both regulatory and economic incentives, with a particular view on reinforcing local government competence and management
- *urban* governments: in charge of active involvement in local sustainability by providing the necessary overhead capital and stimulating new initiatives, using *inter alia* market-orientated strategies and strict enforcement of sustainability regulations (e.g. environmental impact analysis).

As far as the problem of financing new public infrastructure provision is concerned, two elements may help to provide the necessary resources:

- the revenues from environmental taxes, fuel taxes, road and parking pricing levied at the urban level should be short-circuited to investment in local infrastructure;
- if investment in public transport and communication infrastructure helps urban sustainability, and sustainability implies long-term development, and development drives demand for urban locations and use of urban infrastructure, it follows that the initial investment cost can be easily matched by a combination of betterment levies on rising real estate and urban land rents and privately managed project-financing schemes addressed to the building and operation of the infrastructure.

In order for this virtuous circle to be closed, many conditions are necessary, belonging mainly to the cultural, political and public administration spheres: intense environmental concern, efficiency of the planning officials, trust between public and private partners, and local community participation and consent.

References

Banister, D., and C. Banister (1995), Energy Consumption in Transport in Great Britain, *Transportation Research A*, Vol. 29A, 21-32.

Banister, D. and K. Button (eds) (1993), *Transport, the Environment and Sustainable Development*, E & FN Spon: London.

Banister, D., R. Capello and P. Nijkamp (eds) (1995), *European Transport and Communications Networks in Europe: Policy Evolution and Change*, Belhaven Press: London.

Banister, D., S. Watson and C. Wood (1994), *The Relationship between Energy Use in Transport and Urban Form*, Working Paper n. 10, Planning and Development Research Centre, The Bartlett, University College: London.

Bar, F., M. Borrus M. and B. Coriat (1989), "Information Networks and Competitive Advantages: the Issues for Government Policy and Corporate Strategy", OECD-BRIE Telecommunications User Project, Paris.

Bell, D. (1973), *The Coming of Post-industrial Society*, Basic Books: New York.

Bonnafous, A. (1993), *Les Systèmes de Transport, Facteurs de Développement des Métropoles?*, paper presented at the Seminar on "Métropoles et Aménagement du Territoire", Université de Paris Dauphine, May.

Bonneville, M. et al. (1991), *Villes Européennes et Internationalisation*, Lyon, PPSH Rhône Alpes.

Braudel, F. (1979), *Civilisation Materielle, Economie et Capitalisme*, Vol. 1, "Les Structures du Quotidien", Armand Colin: Paris.

Breheny, M.J. (ed.) (1992), *Sustainable Development and Urban Form*, Pion: London.

Bryson, J. and R. Einsweiler (1988), *Strategic Planning*, Planners Press: New York.

Button, K. (1992), "Transport Regulation and the Environment in Low Income Countries", *Utilities Policy*, July, 248-257.

Button, K., and N. Ngoe (1991), "Vehicle Ownership and Use Forecasting in Low Income Countries", Transport and Road Research Laboratory, Dept. of Transport, Crowthorne: Berkshire.

Camagni, R. (1991), "Metropolitan Areas and the Effects of 1992", in M. Quévit, *Regional Development Trajectories and the Attainment of the European Internal Market*, GREMI - RIDER, Louvain-la Neuve.

246

Camagni, R. (1993), "From City-hierarchy to City-network: Reflections about an Emerging Paradigm", in: T.R. Lakshmanan and P. Nijkamp (eds) (1993), *Structure and Change in The Space Economy*, Springer Verlag.

Camagni, R. (1994), "Processi di Utilizzazione e Difesa dei Suoli nelle Fasce Periurbane: dal Conflitto alla Cooperazione fra Città e Campagna", in: Boscacci and Camagni (eds), *Fra Città e Campagna: Periurbanizzazione e Politiche Territoriali*, IP Mulino: Bologna.

Camagni, R. (1995), "Global Network and Local Milieu: towards a Theory of Economic Space", in: S. Conti, E. Malecki and P. Oinas (eds), *The Industrial Enterprise and its Environment: Spatial Perspectives*, Avebury: Aldershot, 195-216.

Camagni, R. (1998), "Sustainable Urban Development: Definition and Reasons for a Research Programme", in: Capello, R. and P. Nijkamp (eds), *Sustainable Cities*, special issue of the International Journal of Environment and Pollution, Vol. 10, No. 1, 6-27.

Camagni, R. and Capello R. (1991), "Le Caratteristiche delle Nuove Tecnologie di Comunicazione e loro Interazione con la Domanda", in: Camagni, R. (1991) (ed.) *Computer Networks: Mercati e Prospettive delle Tecnologie di Comunicazione*, Etas Libri: Milan.

Camagni, R. and Gibelli M.C. (1994), "Réseaux de Villes et Politiques Urbaines", *FLUX*, No. 16, April.

Camagni, R., R. Capello and P. Nijkamp (1996), "Sustainabile City Policy: Economic, Environmental, Technological", in: Van der Meulen G. e Erkelens P. (eds), *Urban Habitat: the Environment of Tomorrow*, Technische Universiteit: Eindhoven, 35-57.

Capello, R. (1994a), "Towards New Industrial and Spatial Systems: the Role of New Technologies", *Papers in Regional Science*, Vol. 73, No. 2, 189-208.

Capello, R. (1994b), *Spatial Economic Analysis of Telecommunications Network Externalities*, Avebury: Aldershot.

Capello, R. and A. Gillespie (1993), "Transport, Communication and Spatial Organisation: Future Trends and Conceptual Frameworks", in P. Nijkamp (ed.), *Europe on the Move*, Avebury: Aldershot, 43-66.

Capello, R. and P. Nijkamp (eds) (1998), special issue of the International Journal of Environment and Pollution, Vol. 10, No. 1.

Capello, R., J. Taylor and H. Williams (1990), "Computer Networks and Competitive Advantage in Building Society", *International Journal of Information Management*, Vol. 10, 54-66.

Capello, R. and H. Williams (1992), "Computer Network Trajectories and Organisational Dynamics: a Cross-national Review", in Antonelli, C. (ed.), *The Economics of Information Networks*, North Holland, Amsterdam, 347-362.

CEC (Commission of the European Communities) (1990), *Green Paper on the Urban Environment*, Brussels.

Coccossis, H. and P. Nijkamp (eds) (1995), *Planning for a Cultural Heritage*, Avebury: Aldershot, UK.

Dimitriou, H. (ed.) (1990), *Transport Planning for Third World Countries*, Routledge: London.

ESCAP (1990), Report on Identification of Major Problems on Urban Transport in the ESCAP Region, Bangkok.

Freeman, C. (1987), *Technology Policy and Economic Performance*, Frances Pinter: London.

Froger, G. (1993), "Les Modèles Théoriques de Développement Soutenable: une Synthèse des Approches Methodologiques", Cahier du C3E n. 93-19.

Gillespie, A. and H. Williams (1988), "Telecommunications and the Reconstruction of Regional Comparative Advantage", *Environment and Planning A*, Vol. 2, 1311-1321.

Gillespie, A., J. Goddard, F. Robinson, I. Smith and A. Thwaites (1984), *The Effects of New Technology on the Less-Favoured Regions of the Community*, Studies Collection, Regional Policy Series, EEC, No. 23.

Goddard, H. (1995), "Sustainability, Tradeble Permits and the World's Largest Cities", paper presented at the International VSB Conference on "Traffic and the Global Environment", held in Amsterdam, 9-10 February.

Gordon, R. (1994), "Internationalisation, Multinationalisation, Globalisation: Contradictory World Economies and New Spatial Division of Labour", *Working Paper Series*, Centre for the Study of Global Transformation, University of California: Santa Cruz, n. 94-10.

Hall, P. (1994), "Squaring the Circle: Can We Resolve the Clarkian Paradox?", *Environment & Planning B*, Vol. 21, 579-594.

Hay, A., and E. Trinder (1991), Concepts of Equity, Fairness and Justice Expressed by Local Transport Policy makers, *Environment & Planning C*, Vol. 9, 453-465.

Jacobs, R. (1994), "Transferable Development Rights in the U.S. Experience", in: F. Boscacci and R. Camagni (eds).

Jonscher, C. (1983), "Information Resources and Economic Productivity", *Information Economics and Policy*, 13-35, Vol. 1.

Lea, J.P. and J.M. Courtney (eds) (1985), *Cities in Conflict: Studies in the Planning and Management of Asian Cities*, The World Bank: Washington D.C.

Lynch, K. (1981), *A Theory of Good City Form*, MIT Press: Cambridge, Mass.

Machlup, F. (1962), *The Production and Distribution of Knowledge in the United States*, Princeton University Press: New York.

Nijkamp, P. (ed.) (1986), *Technological Change, Employment and Spatial Dynamics*, Springer Verlag: Berlin.

Nijkamp, P. (1994a), "Roads Towards Environmentally Sustainable Transport", *Transportation Research*, Vol. 28 A, No. 4, 261-271.

Nijkamp, P. (1994b), "Improving Urban Environmental Quality: Socio-economic Possibilities and Limits", in Pernia E.M. (ed.), *Urban Poverty in Asia*, Oxford University Press: Oxford, 241-292.

Nijkamp, P. and T. Ursem (1998), "Market Solutions for Sustainable Cities", in: Capello, R. and P. Nijkamp (eds), in: *Sustainable Cities*, special issue of the International Journal of Environment and Pollution, Vol. 10, No. 1, 46-65.

Nijkamp, P., D. Banister and G. Pepping (1996), *Telematics and Transport Behaviour*, Springer Verlag: Berlin.

OECD (1990), *L'Environnement Urbain: quelles Politiques pour les Années 1990?*, Paris.

OECD (1994), *Managing the Environment: the Role of Economic Instruments*, Paris.

OECD (1995), *Urban Travel and Sustainable Development*, ECMT, Paris.

Owens, S. (1992), "Energy, Environmental Sustainability and Land-use Planning", in: Breheny M. (1992).

Pezzey, J. (1988), "Market Mechanism of Pollution Control: Polluter Pays, Economic and Practical Aspects" in: Turner R.K., *Sustainable Environmental Management*, Belhaven Press: London.

Poboon, C. and J. Kenworthy (1995), "Bangkok: Towards a Sustainable Traffic Solution", paper presented at the International Habitat Conference, held in Delft, 15-17 February.

Porat, M. (1977), The Information Economy: Definition and Measurement, Special publications 77.22 (1), Office of Telecommunications, US Department of Commerce, Washington D.C.

Ramjerdi, F. (1992a), "Cost-Benefit Analysis and Distributional Consequences of an Area Licensing Scheme for Stockholm", *Transport Policies* (Proceedings 6th World Conference on Transport Research), Lyon, 2043-2054.

Ramjerdi, F. (1992b), "Road Pricing in Urban Areas, the Case of Oslo", *Transport Policies* (Proceedings 6th World Conference on Transport Research), Lyon, 2055-2065.

Rickaby, P.A. (1991), "Energy and Urban Development in an Archetypical English Town", *Environment and Planning B*, Vol. 18, No. 2, 153-176.

Verroen, E.J., and H.D. Hilbers (1994), Op Zoek naar Mobiliteitsvriendelijke Vormen van Verstedelijking, *Implementatie van Beleid* (Colloquium Vervoersplanologisch Speurwerk 1994) (J.M. Jager, ed.), CVS: Delft, 1269-1286.

Warren, W.D. (1993), "A Transportation View of the Morphology of Cities", *Transportation Quarterly*, Vol. 47, No. 3, 367-377.

Wegener, M. (1995), "Reduction of CO_2 Emissions of Transport by Reorganisation of Urban Activities, Transport", in Hayashi Y. and J.R. Roy (eds), *Transport, Land Use and the Environment*, Kluwer: Dordrecht, (forthcoming).

Whitelegg, J. (1988), *Transport for a Sustainable Future*, John Wiley & Sons: New York.

Willinger, C. and E. Zuscovitch (1988), "Towards the Economics of iInformation-Intensive Production Systems: the Case of Advanced Materials", in: Dosi, G., C. Freeman, R. Nelson, G. Silverberg and L. Soete (eds), *Technical Change and Economic Theory*, Pinter Publisher: London, 239-255.

World Bank (1994a), *World Development Report 1994*, Washington, D.C.

World Bank (1994b), *Making Development Sustainable*, The World Bank, Washington D.C.

11 Regionalism, Planning and Strategic Investment in the Transportation Sector

ROBERT E. PAASWELL

11.1 Introduction

At a time in the United States when scarce resources should dictate long-term strategic thinking and planning resulting in judicious infrastructure investments, just the opposite is taking place. A case in point is the New York City Urbanized Area. Desperately trying to gain relief from congestion, improve accessibility and lower transportation costs, local governments, nonetheless, defeat regional infrastructure investments and the mitigating impact on future economic growth and competitiveness such investments might have. This paper will examine two current (1996) major regional[i] strategic initiatives, "Access to the Region's Core" (ARC), a joint project of three regional agencies and the Regional Plan Associations (RPA) third regional plan "Region at Risk". Both start with the assumption that the long-term regional economic health is reflected in the health of the core. One, ARC, takes a core perspective, and uses transportation infrastructure as critical to improving the core. The second, RPA, addresses needs of the entire region, but also sees core infrastructure as critical to the region's health. The paper will discuss the context into which these plans are introduced, their objectives and proposals and discuss their likelihood of success. The objective of the paper is to illustrate the difficulties traditional planning has in facilitating rational investment decisions. It further focuses on the heart of investment decisions - the location and impact of those investments, and the willingness or desire to strengthen urban cores or to live with and adopt to dispersion. These incredibly complex issues are being decided in political meetings and not in the planning literature. They are decided around personal and community values, issues of personal freedom and, of course, issues of race. Discussions of these latter issues are beyond the scope of this paper. In trying to understand the current rationality of U.S. planning, the author, together with many planners believes that strong urban centers are crucial for economic and social growth. That is the genesis of the plans discussed in this paper.

251

11.2 Background

The New York City Metropolitan Region covers a land area of more than 12,700 square kilometers, and includes a population of 18 million people and a resident labor force of 9 million people. But, as table 11.1 shows, this region is composed from areas of three states, New York, New Jersey and Connecticut. This creates fractions in governance making both planning for and implementation of strategic regional infrastructure investments quite difficult. At the heart of the 12,700 sq. km. region is the Manhattan CBD, or the Core. The Core will refer to the Area of the Borough of Manhattan south of 59th Street. The "Extended Core" will refer to this area plus Western Queens and portions of nearby Northern New Jersey (See Figure 11.1).

Table 11.1 Tri State New York metropolitan region demographics

STATE	POPULATION	RESIDENT LABOR FORCE	HOUSING UNITS
NEW YORK	11,820,017	5,459,800	4,645,536
NEW JERSEY	5,008,800	2,613,400	1,965,023
CONNECTICUT	1,693,232	891,765	695,268
REGION	18,602,049	8,964,965	7,305,827

The largest metropolitan area in the United States, the region relies upon a high performing transportation network for its viability. The Intermodal Surface Transportation Efficiency Act (ISTEA) of 1991[ii] has required the region to address three major issues: congestion, air quality and financial constraints. The basic premises underlying these issues are:

- through relief of motor vehicle road congestion, personal costs of travel will decrease, increasing accessibility,
- improvements in air quality, through more efficient management of traffic will decrease regional health costs, and
- any new investments can occur only after full project capital costs have been identified, assuring project commitment and reliable programming.

ISTEA mandates that these issues be resolved regionally, using planning as the underlying tool for project implementation. The ability to adopt the intent of ISTEA on a regional basis has been hindered by one basic reality - the region is made up of hundreds of local governments that have a say in the

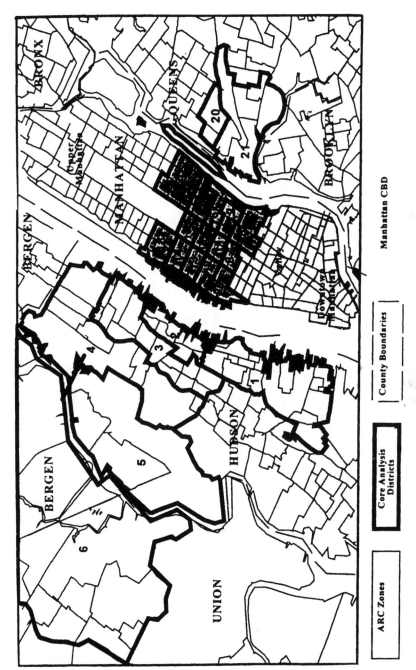

Figure 11.1 The extended core

local planning and implementation of transportation infrastructure and projects. The actual projects that have emanated from ISTEA in the New York region have varied greatly among the states. While New Jersey has been moving rapidly with new rail transit initiatives, New York State has been reducing support for transit in New York City, and moving ahead with a highway improvement program. In a highly political climate, competition for economic advantage - often, short term, becomes the local driving force for any major transportation innovation. This competition goes right to the state borders, diffusing the impact that regional planning and investment might have.

The competition among regional bodies (the city of New York, Northern New Jersey, the role of the Port Authority) has been over the allocation of scarce funds to address the needs of highly local projects. This is exacerbated by highly short term views on solving infrastructure problems. In fact, ISTEA, a piece of legislation full of promise, actually demands gaining full efficiency from existing investments before thinking of new capital projects. While, at first blush, this seems to be the obvious approach, the strategic plans emanating from the New York region reinforce this idea, which, in turn, reinforces local approaches to addressing regional problems. That is one major failure of ISTEA.[iii]

Another failure of ISTEA has been the way in which planning authority has been designated. Planning is the responsibility of the Metropolitan Planning Organization (MPO), designated by the governor of each state for each metropolitan area within that state. In the New York area there are separate MPOs for New York, New Jersey and Connecticut, with no overall mandate to coordinate or cooperate. In fact there are incentives for each state to aggressively push their own program to their own advantage.

11.3   Jobs, the economy and infrastructure

As important as transportation is to a regional economy, it is never the primary item on a decision maker's agenda. The most fundamental issue now driving political decision making in the region is the creation and sustaining of jobs. Jobs are incomes and income multipliers, and jobs imply regional growth. Driving the local equations are two major factors:

- in the last decade, the core area, Manhattan, lost more jobs -200,000 - than any other part of the region, and
- rapid suburbanization has created job relocation outside the core, with all the economic implications of regional shifts in income.

254

Each such political area competes for these jobs, and tries to make advantageous critical investments that will build on this changing economic momentum. Lost in the actual decision making is the broad picture of what makes the region so successful: agglomeration of industries and activities, innovation in financial dealings, capital creation, and interactions with the electronic media, factors identified[iv] by a number of prominent economists, planners and regional leaders.

11.4   Investments

To improve the climate for job creation and retention, regional organizations make use of many programs - tax incentives, building of new facilities, training programs - hoping these programs will reduce costs to businesses. One of the most critical components, in the New York Region of business decisions is transportation. Transportation has impact on labor force availability, reliability and cost of moving goods, and the reliability and safety of moving people. While congestion is the most apparent symptom of increasing transportation costs, system reliability is, for New York, another critical issue. New York's infrastructure, especially its many bridges and 100 year old transit system, need maintenance and rehabilitation expenditures three times the amount being spent annually. The slowness of repair is seen in bridge and tunnel lane closings and large numbers of slow zones in transit. To address these maintenance issues actual annual expenditures must concentrate on system preservation, or keeping the system in a state of good repair, rather than looking more broadly to improving regional links. With such high demand for maintaining the current system in a state of good repair funds for new capacity initiatives are difficult to identify. While the region has changed its distribution of activities in the last decades, local governments address only local problems, losing sight of the potential impact of more broad regional investment.

11.5   Planning and dynamics of suburbanization

The region is now faced with two sets of competing forces that will influence the identification of regional infrastructure investments influencing regional objectives to meet job growth, competitiveness and regional equity:

1. The first force is the local infrastructure investment needs, identified through the ISTEA planning process, and directed to local improvements focused on capacity needs and congestion relief. These improvements are based on historic

models of population and economic growth and activity. The greatest amount of regional money goes to the five boroughs of New York. Furthermore, the greatest amount of funds are for transit, throughout the region. However, these transit funds are primarily for vehicle replacement and for projects to bring the system into a state of "good repair". The funds actually utilized throughout the region for capacity, i.e., expansion of facilities is only 5.1 per cent. Northern New Jersey is somewhat more aggressive with capital expansion. Seventeen per cent of highway funds and 35 per cent of transit funds are going into system expansion. It should be noted that much of the new transit expansion is to improve connections into New York City. However, the significant amount of highway spending is to improve capacity in rapidly growing employment and commercial centers, many of which are perceived to compete with core (Manhattan) activities.

2. The second force is the need for major regional infrastructure capital investment based upon New York's role in national and international markets and its identity as a world city. Regional planners have identified a broad range of projects that cross political boundaries, involve multiple public agencies and demand great sources of funds. The studies and plans that are the basis for the identification of these projects are the focus of this paper.

The realities of investment of the past two decades draw significant attention away from the core, while they underscore the impacts of dispersion and the inter regionoal development rivalries.

The most important reality is the dynamics of suburbanization. For example, from 1985 -1990, new housing was added in the suburbs of the greater New York Region (NY, NJ, Conn.) at a rate four times that of the ten largest cities (the RPA Centers) in the region. During this same period of growth, 1980 to 1990, of the nearly 1,000,000 net jobs added in the region, only one third were added in NYC, which contains about one quarter of the region's jobs. Not surprisingly, over this same period, household vehicle ownership increased significantly, VMT increased at a rate greater than population while transit ridership in general stayed constant or declined.

The decision to invest in specific types of infrastructure has had significant impact on mode choice and the resultant land uses followed by demonstrable impact on intra regional economic equity. A simple examination of the difference between highway and transit investments will illustrate this point. Transit investments are made to sustain personal mobility and accessibility, and most often focus on the work trip. Highway investments serve both goods and people, and all trip purposes. Quite simply, a dollar spent on highways serves more markets than a dollar spent on transit. Transportation investment in New Jersey in the last two decades can be used to illustrate this point:

- first, transit investment in rail on the Northeast (Rail) Corridor was sustained and significant. New Jersey Transit rail and PATH provide high levels of service within the corridor, but focus on New York City and Newark.
- second, Interstate Construction continued, e.g. I-287, a suburban Interstate highway,
- third, employment growth in the region occurred primarily outside the five boroughs of NYC and Newark, and primarily along highway corridors,[v] and
- goods movement, to serve these newly dispersed activity and residential centers were most effective by truck, increasing the demand for truck services and reducing the suitability and availability of rail.

As noted earlier, over the last decade, housing expanded in the suburbs four times as fast as in the largest cities, and jobs in the suburbs grew at rates three times that of the largest cities. Simultaneously, as our region became more suburban and auto/truck oriented, significant decisions on rail rationalization, new truck, break-bulk and warehouse facilities were made that reinforced increased need for and utilization of highway networks. Conrail concentrated its freight activity in New Jersey, and substantially reduces freight rail access to New York City. Major warehousing has relocated from New York City and its immediate environs to more central counties in New Jersey, and upstate New York. The intra regional equity issues that result from these investments can then be identified:

- movement of jobs to the suburbs favored employees who had access to these jobs with cars. While much has been written of the jobs- residence imbalance, the most significant parts of that imbalance occur in the lowest income areas of the largest urban areas, primarily NYC and Newark. These groups have low car ownership, and are dependent upon rides and transit to reach not only jobs, but other activities that are not within their neighborhoods.
- A relocation of activities, from central shopping streets to malls, in response to auto oriented shopping creates jobs displacements and patterns of inaccessibility for those without cars. On a grander scale, a relocation of major markets (e.g., to the New Jersey Meadowlands a mega sports, office, commercial residential complex) creates real winners and losers intra regionally, even though the net regional gain might be positive. Such relocations occur because of shifting markets, and the increased accessibility, by and to these markets. When it is less costly to have all goods moved by truck, access to major highway corridors becomes a prime location determinant.

257

- An increased reliance on goods movement by truck and reduced capability of rail movement into New York City has increased the costs of moving goods in and about New York and has decreased the desirability of New York as a business location for truck dependent enterprises. As truck movements increase on a yearly basis, and compete for street space with growing numbers of autos, costs of moving and delivering goods will continue to increase congestion. RPA estimates there are 85,000 truck movements in and out of the NYC CBD every day.[vi]

In 1990, it was apparent that the Central Cities were losing both jobs and access to those jobs to the suburbs. Furthermore, in a truck dominated goods movement environment, businesses were better served by locating in suburban Areas. The winners were New Jersey suburban locations adjacent to good Interstate or tollway facilities, and upstate New York Counties.

Regional planners have consistently addressed these growing inequities. While recognizing that loss of core vitality can be economically devastating to the region these planners have been doing what political leaders have not - developing regional strategic plans. Two major studies have been undertaken which address regional issues and regional investment solutions. These are:

I. *Access to the Region's Core (ARC).* This study concentrates on capital improvements, primarily rail based, that will improve access to the lower half of Manhattan, identified as the single most concentrated employment center in the region and the heart of those activities that give New York its international identity and uniqueness - finance, media and entertainment, publishing and high fashion. The study is supported by a unique arrangement of three regional agencies, New York Metropolitan Transportation Authority (MTA), the operator of New York City Transit and the New York based commuter rail lines, New Jersey Transit (NJT), operator of commuter rail and bus throughout New Jersey, but, in particular, into Manhattan, and The Port Authority of New York and New Jersey (PA), operator of regional bus terminals, trans Hudson River bridges and the PATH system, a subway system from nearby northern New Jersey into Manhattan.

II. *A Region at Risk, The Third Regional Plan for the New York -New Jersey - Connecticut Metropolitan Area.* This study, in the tradition of grand plans of the mid decades of this Century, examines not only transportation, but land uses, open spaces, and human resources. It was developed by the Regional Plan Association, an independent (i.e., non government) planning body.

11.6   Plan objectives

In an introduction to a document accompanying the NYMTC long range plan,[vii] it was emphatically stated that, "Simply put, regional issues and challenges require regional solutions". The dynamics of economic development and activity in the region in the last two decades have created a set of planning problems that seem insurmountable. These problems can be restated as:

- *sustained dynamics of suburbanization.* While 25 per cent of regional suburban workers work in the Core, obviously, 75 per cent do not. In the New York suburbs, resident workers in those areas increased by 15 per cent from 1980-1990. In fact suburban workers generate more than 1,000,000 inter suburban work trips every day. Living and working in the suburbs, these workers and the households they represent also demand to shop, get medical treatment and be entertained in the suburbs, generating more secondary employment. Strong as the core is and unique as it is, this is a dynamic that can't be denied and creates strong local political forces demanding local expenditures to address local problems.
- *reinforcing suburban developments.* Strong localized expenditures, e.g., upgrade of Newark Airport, the Meadowlands office and sports complex, tax free shopping zones, sustained Port of Newark investments, are examples of infrastructure and fiscal investments designed to give New Jersey a competitive edge within the region. Movement of activity from one location to another in the region is seen as a gain for one area and a loss for another rather than sustaining the net regional economic product.
- *fiscal austerity and local problems demand local solutions.* The pervading political philosophy is that there is little public money available and what is available can best be allocated at the most local level. This philosophy mitigates against both thinking big (remember Olmstead, "Make No Small Plans"), and thinking regionally.

Both of the above plans are attempts to gain regional support to reverse the impacts of the three problems stated above. They both use the same structure; first, to state the impacts of our current course of actions in recent programs of infrastructure investment, second to quantify the economic consequences of continued disinvestment or new investment, particularly by showing the importance of the core and uniqueness of the region, and finally by proposing courses of action.

259

11.6.1 ARC

The ARC plan is coordinated by three agencies, as noted above, that operate rail systems and terminals terminating in the core. The agencies are not integrated. There are no common fare or scheduling policies, there are no transfer arrangements nor seamless trip making, and all do their planning independently. A trip from New Jersey to Long Island might involve all three agencies, with the passenger making ticket and transfer arrangements on their own. This is the operating environment into which ARC comes. What makes ARC limited in scope is that (1) it defines the core as the most critical target for planning and then bases all the design on the certainty of that location, and (2) it brings to the solution only the vision and experience of rail operators. While neither of these limits are *a priori* wrong or even misleading, it does not allow the test of the dynamics of suburbanization (see Figures 11.2 and 11.3 for population and employment dynamics) and the realities of the changing nature of work and the household. It does however base the planning logic on a set of fundamental measures.[viii]

- the earnings of workers in the core are twice those of U.S. employees, and they are especially high in financial services, a segment unique to the core,
- as a result of both incomes and services, the core generates taxes for a number of surrounding communities, who become dependent upon core employment for their residents,
- it is, as noted earlier, an international Center for arts, entertainment and the media, high fashion and avant garde fashion and trend setting, and tourism. It is a place where people want to be.

ARC sets out with specific goals, and targets their solution to improvements in the core. The goals are: (1) To maintain and enhance the economic viability and productivity of the New York/New Jersey region, (2) to improve the quality of life in the region and (3) to invest and use resources productively, efficiently and effectively. The objectives to achieve these are then essentially accessibility based objectives, keyed to reduced transportation costs through transportation improvements. The most important objectives incorporate rail transit improvements through new linkages and multi modal terminal improvements, all involving the extended core (see Figure 11.4).

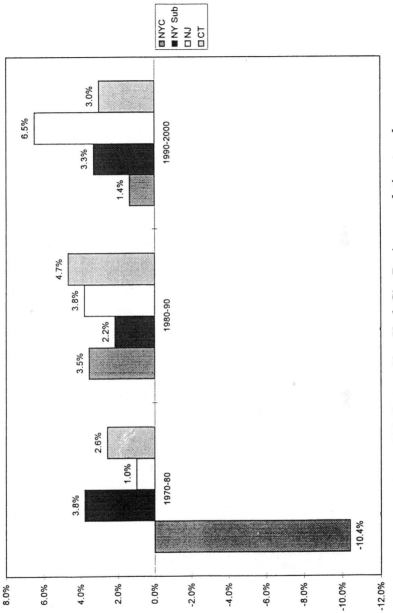

Figure 11.2 Greater New York City Region population trends
Percent changes 1970 – 2000

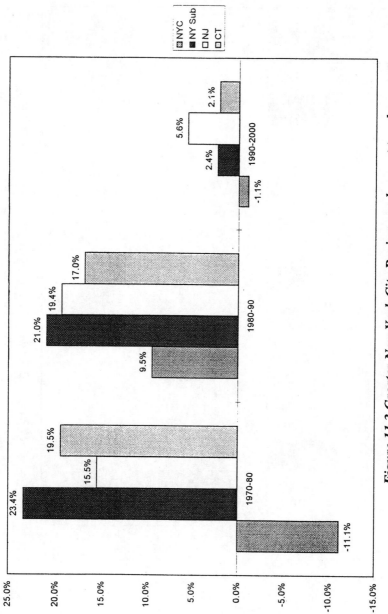

Figure 11.3 Greater New York City Region employment trends
Percent changes 1970 – 2000

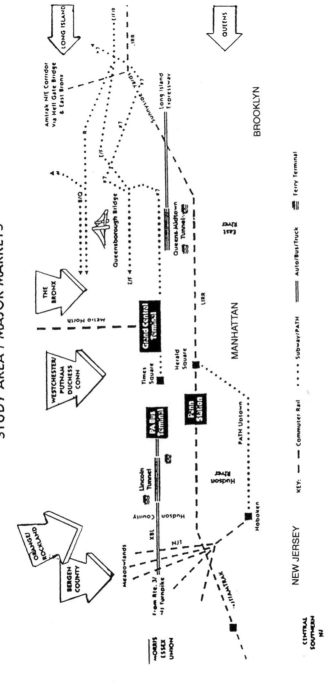

Figure 11.4 Access to the region's core
Study area/major markets

Some of these objectives are:

- link all significant regional activity centers to the extended core with efficient public transit
- provide improved means of goods movement across the extended core and accessibility of services to extended core areas.

The core is at a critical point in its history where the forces of dispersion are draining some of the economic segments, while pressures to sustain the "uniqueness of place" are attempting to sustain businesses, and to grow new businesses. The ARC proposal would have immediate impact in that it would reduce the cost of commuting. That is it would have the accessibility impact of shrinking the size of the region. A worker, suddenly lives five to ten minutes closer to work, or conversely, employment opportunities for workers from the outer Boroughs would increase.[ix] Secondly, it would reinforce the concept of Central Place or uniqueness, critical for the industry segments, identified here. In addition, such current agglomerations of particular industry types has led to new start up industries in the core, the most important example being entertainment related computer software. Based upon advances in computer technology and communications, and using media related entertainment as a source of support, hundreds of new start up businesses have come together in a small area of the Core (Soho), relying on the availability of start up financing, appropriate legal instruments, support services and, most critical, a unique and well trained labor force. The purpose of ARC is to facilitate those interactions and that development.

ARC brought together a number of plans currently being examined by the separate agencies as well as suggesting new initiatives. A very large set of alternative plans has been reduced to a current six alternatives using an elaborate set of evaluation criteria. These criteria include support for regional and economic development, quality of service, fiscal impact, cost effectiveness, dependability, equity, environmental protection and adding to freight movement capacity.

The six alternatives that resulted include: a no-build, or continue with on book plans; a number of commuter rail improvements and new links; new light rail lines; new subway links; combinations of these and transportation management strategies. They include better use of the existing major core termini, Grand Central and Pennsylvania Stations, additional links between New Jersey and the core, additional access to Long Island, including access to the East Side of the core by tracks into Grand Central and new light rail loops in Manhattan. Each of these are sets of specific projects, i.e., activate and complete a tunnel giving more access to a terminal, build a new rail link on 2nd avenue in Manhattan, build a new Hudson River tunnel. Each of these requires coordination of more than one agency as well as substantial funding from more than one source. Each alternative, a set of high cost projects, addresses the evaluation criteria, or the overall project goals. Each then would require substantial inter agency agreements, not only now for design and funding, but later, to insure smooth operations. No single organization in the region now can address any of the alternatives.

11.6.2 RPA

The third regional plan, carried out by a private planning organization representing the tri state area (see Figure 11.5), recognizes the importance of the core. But, reflecting a constituency different from those represented in ARC, attempts to balance the economic growth of all areas of the region, maximizing the opportunity for the region to sustain world leadership.

The RPA plan addresses and works with the population and economic dynamics of the last decades. It noted that "at the beginning of the 1980s the suburban ring accounted for 13 per cent of the regions total inventory [of office construction]. By the 1990s it was 35 per cent".

The plan then assumes that the dynamics of dispersion will continue, but is counterproductive to economic growth and towards achieving long-term regional objectives. The plan concludes that it must develop regional strategies that can reverse the consequences of suburbanization, without reversing the process of dispersion itself.

The RPA plan identifies five campaigns essential to addressing issues concerning the economy, equity and the environment in the next decades. These campaigns are: (1) greensward - addressing open spaces, (2) [regional] centers - sustaining down towns in the core and in other important cities and towns, (3) mobility - transportation needs, (4) workforce - addressing needs of the underemployed, a major equity issue and (5) governance - the ability of local institutions to address needed change and come to consensus on investment.

The Plan takes important note of well defined forces that serve as the overwhelming context in which planning decisions will be made. One, sustained dispersion has been mentioned above. Two others, which may be representational of issues of growing concern in European Cities are (1) personal equity, "the huge challenge we face is that the region is becoming more inequitable as it becomes more disperse"[x] and (2) institutional ability to manage regional change. The 1990s finds the region with marked physical separation of the higher and lower income population. A growing proportion of lower income households in the region resulted from the employment shifts of the 1980s and the out migration of labor. Coupled with a regional,

265

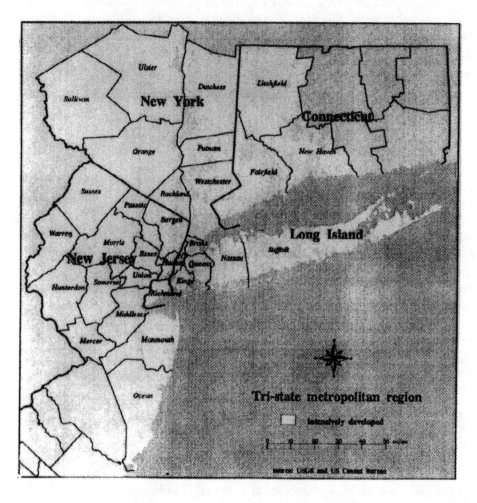

Figure 11.5 Tri-state metropolitan region

national and international redistribution of high paying manufacturing jobs (the largest segment to lose jobs in the region) is the growing impact of productivity - fewer people can produce more goods and services. In addition to problems of underemployment is the jobs - housing imbalance, the fact that poor communities are isolated. This problem, well documented in the US literature and beginning to be recognized in some European Cities, is exacerbated in the New York Region where housing prices (affordability) is about the highest in the country.

In addressing ways of meeting the needs of equity, environment and the economy through the five campaigns, alternative investment changes must begin to solve these issues. For example, to address the issue of equity and jobs - housing imbalance, a traditional transportation plan would look primarily at reverse commuting and improved accessibility. The RPA plan examines changes necessary through all five campaigns as integral, i.e., necessary and sufficient, to address this issue.

To focus on infrastructure investment, two of the five campaigns will be studied. These are the Centers campaign and the Mobility Campaign. The Centers campaign restates the importance of the Core (i.e., the Manhattan CBD) as the prime focus. Decline in this core will stimulate decline in the region. But it notes there are eleven other regional "down towns". Somewhat lost or out of focus due to the dispersing impacts of suburbanization, these eleven centers should be rebuilt and strengthened to offset the continued costs of dispersion. Simply, it recommends that job growth not taking place in the core be directed to these centers. These centers should contain new or revitalized institutions (arts, education, etc.) And as in other concentrations should be transit and pedestrian friendly.

The mobility campaign provides one of the plan's greatest challenges as it calls for implementation and investment of billions of dollars. The mobility campaign begins by noting that the principal components of improved mobility include greater access to transit throughout the region, relief of highway congestion and a reconfigured freight system. The region's transportation systems are disjointed, they have many operators and these operators are usually identified by geography. This has limited making obvious regional connections that reflect the geographic dynamics of household and employment location. The rail system, especially the New York City subway, is old and needs substantial repair and upgrading. Because of the simultaneous strength of the core, suburbanization, and the high use of trucks to move goods, congestion remains a most critical problem. Finally, the cost of moving goods and the impact on business and competitive regional costs are high, functions, again, of a disjointed freight movement system. The mobility campaign recommends four areas to concentrate on in order to achieve their transportation objectives. These are,

(1) transit upgrades, (2) new rail routes and a Regional Express - Rx -, (3) relieve congestion through new capacity and market based demand management, and (4) examine congestion pricing.

The heart of the mobility campaign is the Rx (see Figure 11.6). Identifying a number of ongoing regional transportation planning initiatives, including ARC, Rx proposes a limited number of critical linkages among existing rail services that would have significant impact on regional centers and core accessibility. The twenty five new miles of Rx is designed to address employment access through overall regional changes in accessibility. These changes will occur through creation of an integrated regional network, fewer and more seamless transfers and lower costs of travel. It is anticipated such changes will also stimulate new employment centers to locate near appropriate transit stations. And, of course, the plan would stimulate new transit riders at the expense of the Single Occupant Vehicle. The mobility transportation objectives have concentrated on relief of congestion and discontinuities at the heart of the regional system network, with an [unexpressed] assumption that improving accessibility will address the overarching issues of economics, environment and equity.

11.7 Plan impacts

Having lived through three decades of increasing regulation addressing the environment, both plans respond to more sustainable environments. First, ISTEA demands that this occur.[xi] ISTEA mandates that all new capital investments fully meet the requirements of the Clean Air Acts of 1970 and 1990. That is, any new investments must move air quality towards national standards. Energy, through use of gasoline (petrol) is addressed through clean air; ISTEA encourages alternative transportation plans to move towards High Occupancy Vehicles and reinforces those choices with funded programs. The most difficult impact to address remains land use. While concepts such as transit oriented design, and "neo classical" town plans are part of the emerging planners jargon, one fact remains paramount. In the U.S., all development is local and communities often go with the money - the developers. The plans discussed above urge changes to that principle, The RPA plan in particular suggests legislative and institutional changes. The reality is that the plan projects will come much before any institutional change.

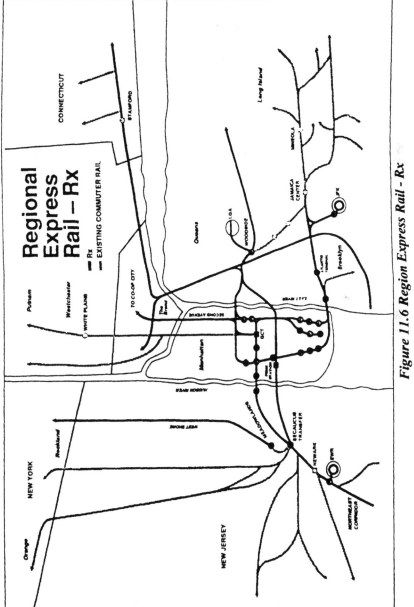

Figure 11.6 Region Express Rail - Rx

11.8 Realities and process

As noted in a previous section, ISTEA requires an annual Transportation Improvement Program (TIP), whose list of projects reflects the region's approach to addressing long-term needs. The New York City TIP, $79 billion, concentrates on state of good repair projects. The Northern New Jersey TIP designates more than two thirds of its $6 billion budget to state of good repair and management. That is the current reality, and reflects the current momentum of investment.

Both the ARC and RPA plans have some overlapping objectives. Among the most important are the sustained prominence and future development of the region's economy. The economic strength is seen as emanating from the core. This then generates a set of plan objectives that concentrate first on greatly improved accessibility to the core. Both note that these improvements would have positive impact on labor force commuting, reduce business costs and stimulate the unique set of forces that are reflected by the diversity of people, institutions, activities and jobs that make up the core.

Meeting a broad set of important regional goals would presume that the next steps, choice of alternatives or programming of necessary projects would commence.

11.9 Next steps

ARC is currently a brilliant project without a single client. Although it has been reviewed by a broad array of regional planners and community officials, it must go through a complex procedure to begin implementation. While a plan that is a product of three strong regional transportation operators, it will, when completed, become one of four Major Investment studies (MIS) of the MTA. MTA will then (1997) discuss whether to include the ARC recommendation in its overall Long Range Plan. If so, the project elements become eligible for funding by the regional MPO under the annual transportation Improvement Program. This is not simple. First, as a multi agency program, the MTA must have a strategy for funding and operation that includes the other two operating agencies. This strategy is part of the final tasks of ARC and has not been addressed yet. Second, the MTA Board must be convinced that these regionally oriented programs have greater priority than the traditional MTA capital plans - some of which are program sub elements of ARC.

RPA is also a plan without a client. It obviously contains almost every element in its transportation program considered in ARC. In addition it provides transportation programs that meet broader regional objectives. But

270

transportation is only one of five elements to meet the broad goals of economics, equity and the environment captured in RPA. The RPA plan recognizes the difficulties in posing regional solutions to local governments and suggests approaches to address the prime issue - institutional change. At the heart of the recommendations is a suggestion to mobilize what is now known as the third sector - not for profit and community organizations - whose agendas go beyond political boundaries. But RPA notes institutions must change and recommends a new regional transportation authority that incorporates existing operators, using the old Greater London Council, Portland or Toronto Metros as examples, and the creation of a metropolitan service commission to address land acquisition and land use regulatory issues. RPA suggests an infrastructure bank, based upon tri state compacts and funded from user fees and gasoline taxes. These are all grounded in current examples, but would be great departures from the current approach to planning and implementation. However, RPA has convened a type of regional forum, where the plan elements become the ad -hoc investments to discuss. This has stimulated agencies to renew planning for some core related projects - consistent with RPA objectives.

11.10 Conclusions

The forces of dispersion and congestion, fed by increasing motor vehicle use[xii] have created a two fold problem for the New York Metropolitan Region. The first concerns the viability of the core - how well can it sustain the forces of decentralization. The second concerns the growing problems of congestion and inefficient land uses. The results of both are growing inequities - both to the region and to segments of the population.

Two plans address these issues and they both come to a basic conclusion: that the presently existing institutional support must change. Local governments and agencies, designed to manage transportation systems in the 1960s are not valid for the Year 2000. The RPA plan takes a more aggressive posture in recommending new forms of regional governance and funding - modeled on existing examples.

Untested and unmeasured in both plans are the true dynamics of the core. As noted, the undefinable (i.e., quantifiable) characteristic of being "the place to be" might overcome the forces of dispersion, or might even be supported by inter regional activity shifts that remove an old industry and replace it with a newer one. That is the subject of the next research paper.

11.11 Acknowledgments

The author would like to thank Jeffrey Zupan of the Regional Planning Association, David Phraner and Iris Berman of the Port Authority of New York and New Jersey, and Martin Hofler of North Jersey Transportation Planning Authority for their help in gathering data for this paper. Special thanks to Yuko Nakanishi, Assistant Director for Research for UTRC for research and data gathering and interpretation necessary for the paper. The author also thanks the paper reviewers for their perceptive and helpful comments. The contents and ideas remain the responsibility of the author.

Endnotes

i. The region that the Greater New York Metropolitan Area is chosen is that it contains a wide range of problems familiar not only to the U.S. audience, but also to the European audience.

ii. 1991 is selected as the year of implementation of ISTEA - a major piece of transportation legislation in the US. This has been discussed in two previous papers by the author, presented at the Nectar conferences in London (1994) and Espinho (1995). Issues leading to adoption of ISTEA had of course been in existence for many years previous.

iii. As noted in "Urban Transport Policies: United States Lessons", presented at the Conference on European Transport and Communication Networks, Espinho, Portugal, April 1995, the actual spending in the New York region will be against highway and bridge maintenance and repair, and transit vehicle replacement. Any new initiatives are left to an uncertain future.

iv. See, "Proceedings of the Regional Policy Roundtables", Port Authority of New York and New Jersey, 1994.

v. In fact Wolpert and Danielson (Transportation and the Distribution of Metropolitan Economic Growth, Princeton U. 1992), found that employment growth in New Jersey during the period 1970 -1987 was not correlated with train connectivity but was with highway densities (la - mi/ sq mi).

vi. J. Zupan et al. *Goods Movement in the New York Region.* RPA, March 1992.

vii. NYMTC, *We are a region*, Feb., 1996.

viii. See "Future of the Extended Core, *op.cit.*

ix. See, for example, J. Berechman and R. Paaswell, "The Implications of Travel for Transportation Investment", J of Transportation, 24, PP51-77, 1997.

x. The RPA Plan notes two factors which influence the nature of work - one is the huge immigration of population and the role these immigrants play in New York's dynamic work force. The second is the fact that things get worse for those at the bottom end of the income ladder. The lowest 20 per cent of the families lost 14 per cent of their share of the regional income in the last decade.

xi. The author discussed the details of ISTEA and the land use requirements in , "ISTEA: Infrastructure Investment and Land Use", in: *Transport and Urban Development*, D. Banister (ed.), Chapman and Hall. 1995.

xii. See discussion of rapid growth of VMT and household motor vehicle ownership in: Paaswell, R., "Urban Transport Policies: United States Lessons", *op.cit.*

12 Success and Failure Factors for Multimodal Transport Policy in Europe

KOSTAS BITHAS AND PETER NIJKAMP

12.1 Introduction

The development of a (more) efficient and effective trans-European transport network (TEN) is of great importance. Such a network is included among those activities emanating from the European Commission's White Paper on Growth, Competitiveness and Employment endorsed by the Heads of States and Governments in 1993. The overall vision regarding the development of these networks is coloured by the concept of multi-modality. This has particular relevance for the freight sector in Europe. Freight transport constitutes a considerable share of the total transport activities. Furthermore, freight transport is of tremendous importance for the creation of an effective and efficient single European market. This is also witnessed by the fact that international freight transport has risen with more than 10 per cent annually in the past years.

The present study aims to examine the conditions for developing an efficient and effective multi-modal freight transport system which may also offer a solution to the current environmental and transportation problems in Europe. Our study initially deals with the concept of multi-modal transport in the framework of combined road-rail transport. Then an operational framework for the evaluation of the current state and performance of this network is discussed. Finally, a survey questionnaire is used for identifying the main barriers that limit the development of an effective and efficient multi-modal (rail-road) freight transport network in Europe. The survey addresses the views of transport experts from all European countries. The paper closes with a number of strategic remarks on European transport policy.

12.2 The new scene of the transport sector

Transportation is an activity of decisive importance from both social and economic perspectives. Passenger transport is strongly related to socio-cultural exchange and development, while commodity shipment is strongly oriented towards economic development in Europe. Transportation of goods and passengers forms a cornerstone activity in the way towards a single European market (Button and Banister, 1990). Especially, as the European territory expands by the integration of new countries and as a greater variety and magnitude of raw materials and products are expected to move within this territory, freight transport is going to be either a decisive promoter or a strong barrier to an efficient common market. The direct user's transport costs as well as the relevant hidden costs (bottlenecks, congestion, etc.) determine, to a considerable extent, the costs of production and of distribution processes and hence the competitiveness of the European market. In addition, these factors codetermine the economic effectiveness of the regional economies within Europe and hence future European development. Furthermore, freight transportation is going to influence the question whether national firms will become European firms by realizing the concept of the 'extended firm', exploring the comparative advantages of each member country (Nijkamp *et al.*, 1993).

In the far past, freight transport was based on railways due to the relative advantages of this particular mode of transport - compared to road transport. Indeed, since the last part of the century the rail infrastructure has been considerably extended and for many years has proved more reliable than the road system. We also note that at that stage rail infrastructure served other social purposes, e.g. national defence. At the same time, the transport demand turned out to be well met by the railway system. Indeed, the main goods to be transported were raw materials of low value or heavy final products. As the western economies moved towards a service and post-industrial economy, transport demand changed drastically. Light products of high value, just-in-time-products, decreasing stock size, etc. appeared to require a different type of transport. Besides, road transport had in the mean time acquired an extensive infrastructure which permitted it to be flexible, speedy, reliable and cheap. Road transport therefore has increased its share in freight transport in recent years (European Conference of Ministers of Transport, 1992).

Nowadays, freight characteristics are changing towards valuable and sophisticated products, express delivery, and door-to-door delivery. The transportation sector is no longer a single economic activity-agency. It provides a chain of value added activities that are performed by different actors who utilize the existing infrastructure and offer a reliable service which the user is willing to pay for. It is worth mentioning here that the infrastructure expansion and the restructuring (both in infrastructure and in operation) of transport supply create a new demand in the sector, as we can observe from recent relevant trends.

Simultaneously, the technical development in the transport sector may be characterized as an important driving force in recent years. New infrastructure opportunities which offer attractive transport properties are introduced, for example, magnetic levitation, high speed trains, vacuum tunnels, etc. In transport operation, the use of informatics new cost-saving measures and increasing speed and reliability: for example, telematics, new signalling methods, and energy saving measures. However, although these developments seem promising, they have not yet been introduced widely and their results depend largely on the current transport policy (EC, Road Freight Transport in the Single European Market, 1994).

On the other hand, transport is strongly related to severe problems in our present society. The most important factor is environmental decay. Indeed, transport contributes to a considerable degree to both air pollution at a local level and global warming at a global level. In addition, the increase in total energy consumption depletes the necessary but limited resources of our world. At the same time, serious amenity disturbances are envisaged including noise, ecosystems separation, land requirements, sight-amenity problems, etc. It seems that the severity of this calls for direct and immediate action. In this context, several European countries are designing a number of regulatory and economic counter-measures (Austria, Germany, France, etc.). These measures tend to impose barriers to freight transportation that may affect its economic functioning. In addition, the inevitable problem of road congestion on important European corridors obstructs an efficient transportation operation. All these issues call for a concrete and coherent European transport policy [3]. Otherwise, the emerging inefficiency will lead to cost increases which will hamper the efficient functioning of the single market, and moreover the external problems will be intensified. Indeed, the design of a European freight transport policy is imperative. In this context, a new institutional framework for increasing efficiency emerges, where deregulation and privatisation are increasingly promoted for rail transport. This mode should pass from bureaucratic management to a market oriented operation. In addition, a single national orientation of each rail operator is discouraged. In this course, the separation of the railway infrastructure from its own operation is pursued, which is a necessary condition for a free entry market (contestable market). As far as road transport is concerned, this policy may promote the internalisation of the negative external costs via the application of the 'user pays' principle, for example.

In the present study, the intriguing issue in this respect is to define the necessary and sufficient conditions for a satisfactory freight transport network in Europe. A network is defined here as a cohesive set of infrastructure links (edges) connecting concentrations of people or economic activity centres (so-called nodes), with a view to the utilisation of these infrastructure links by transport actors. As noted above, the present study is mainly concerned with the rail-road multi-modal freight transport network (Nijkamp and Blaas, 1994).

A network of this kind has three main characteristics. Firstly, the interoperability which refers mainly to operational and technical uniformity and allows actors and operators to use a network for different simultaneous or sequential purposes. Secondly, the inter-connectivity which in particular is concerned with horizontal coordination and access to the network from different geographical areas. The third aspect is the inter-modality which addresses the issue of a combined use of different transport modes in the chain of freight transport (Nijkamp and Blaas, 1994; Nijkamp *et al.*, 1993).

The present study aims first to evaluate the current state of the rail-road freight network in Europe and then to outline the properties of a satisfactory network. Finally it defines the relevant necessary and sufficient conditions. In this perspective, the study adopts a European view on infrastructure networks as seen by relevant decision-makers who have to design a policy for improving the present system. The network will be assessed on three main dimensions: environmental, economic and services (customers' satisfaction). Instead of a maximisation process in one dimension, a trade-off will be adopted, since competitive elements between these issues are involved.

The main background issues that are taken into account in our study are the following:

The severe environmental problems caused by current road-rail freight transport should be systematically considered and taken into account when the characteristics of a satisfactory system are examined.

The crucial technical, managerial and institutional barriers should be identified and their relative importance assessed. Preferably they should be removed so that the .evolution of the system can promote a more environmentally sustainable behaviour.

The service delivered by the network should be sufficient, according to current European market conditions and the relevant desired evolution. The institutional framework of rail operations would have to be reoriented towards a business activity which produces the services the consumer desires.

It appears at first glance that rail and road transport are by definition competitors and will maintain this relationship in the future. But a tentative evaluation of the network may reveal possibilities for synergy that create mutual benefits and increase the overall efficiency of the system. The potential for such a synergy will be outlined in the study. The relevant barriers will be examined on institutional, managerial and technical grounds.

In order to study the rail-road freight transport network some important aspects of each mode should be examined; these aspects may be considered as 'rational principles' that underlie the function of each mode and therefore, they should be taken into account by relevant policy-makers (Nijkamp and Blaas, 1994). These aspects are:

- *performance*
- value added
- distribution of benefits

- *synergy with other models*
- cohesion
- scale
- morphology

- *buyer's market*
- customer driven
- motives
- internalisation

- *tariffication*
- transport as commercial market
- clean pricing policy
- economic instruments
- market for transport (e.g. permits)

- *capacity limits*
- technomax
- enviromax
- sociomax
- perimax
- terminomax

- *multi-actor's market*
- price/quality ratio
- typology of actors

- *information for policy design*
- data collection
- data processing
- data monitoring
- modelling
- scenario design
- policy experiments

The above issues call for further empirical work and are elaborated in Section 3.

12.3   Approach adopted

In our paper, an operational methodology for the evaluation of road-rail freight transport operation will be established. This methodology is aimed at the following targets:

- cross-national, international and intra-national evaluation of the characteristics and performance of   each mode and the system as a whole.
- The performance and the characteristics of the network will be viewed from various main angles: environmental, economic and service/network appropriateness (interoperability, inter-connectivity, inter-modality).

In this context, the evaluation framework boils down to a number of indicators which serve these concepts. The indicators fulfil certain prerequisites:

- relative ease of data collection
- relative ease in application
- comprehensibility by policy-makers and the public
- sensitivity to controllability

The above described evaluation framework will be applied for assessing the efficiency and the state of each mode separately and of the network as a whole. This will be pursued at two levels. In the first instance, the technical elements and their operational aspects will be evaluated. Thereafter, the operational-managerial characteristics will be considered.

In effect, the crucial relative advantages and disadvantages of each mode will be identified and the relevant trends will be assessed. This approach leads to the determination of the characteristics (environmental, economic, service/network) of a good/satisfactorily operating freight transport network. Such desired trends will be defined for each mode and for the entire system. The aim of a good network directly addresses the issue of the desired relation between the two modes; should they collaborate or compete, and to what extent?

The information that will be used at this stage of the study originates from existing European statistics as well as from a questionnaire addressed to a broadly composed panel of transport experts in Europe.

In this step the study will outline, identify and assess the decisive barriers that prevent a well-functioning operation of the freight road-rail network. These factors will be outlined at two levels: at the supply and at the demand side. The issue of achieving a satisfactory freight transport network will be examined. To design the necessary policy, the crucial success factors have to be carefully studied and their relative importance systematically assessed. For the identification of both current barriers and success factors the so-called pentagon model will be used. This model divides the relevant barriers into five main categories: financial, organisational, hardware, software and ecological barriers (Nijkamp and Blaas, 1994; OECD, 1992).

An evaluation framework for European transport systems should consider all physical, economic and institutional perspectives of the system. An ideal evaluation would be to define a reference point or benchmark by means of which the system might be characterized as good. This might also be done separately for the main aspects of the system. However, such an absolute evaluation is hardly achieved in open, partial and small systems.

By necessity, therefore, an evaluation framework based on the relative assessment of the system is often adopted. For the freight transport sector, we cannot define reference-point levels at which the system can be said to be environmentally sustainable, economically efficient and socially appropriate. All we can do is to assess the relative environmental, economic and social performance of the system. Relative evaluation means to compare the system's performance with the respective performance of another system of a similar type or with its performance in the past or future (i.e. a benchmark approach).

The performance of the freight transport (rail-road) system can be evaluated by using efficiency indicators. Indeed, the system receives material and energy input, as well as labour and capital services from outside. This results in useful output (transport service) and some material and energy waste (pollution). The efficiency of the system is defined by the way it utilizes its input in order to create the useful output, and also by the rate of reducing the waste production. At this point, we can distinguish two classes of efficiency: environmental and economic efficiency. Environmental efficiency involves the relative environmental friendliness of the sector. It examines both the exploitation of natural resources and environmental degradation.

Resource exploitation is related to energy and material input. The relevant efficiency must therefore take into consideration the relationship between the input and the useful results of the sector. Environmental degradation refers to the waste pollution produced during the system's operation. Thus, the relevant efficiency is assessed on the basis of the relationship between useful results and useless waste. It goes without saying that environmental efficiency is measured by quotients whose numerator is expressed in physical terms and the denominator in output (service) units which can be either monetary units (value of transport) or physical units (ton-km). Economic efficiency can be assessed via the productivity of all inputs that have an economic cost.

The identification and assessment of the relative importance of the barriers in a transport system are faced with considerable difficulties, since the relevant literature and statistics are limited - in particular when the analysis concerns all European community countries, each one presenting individual characteristics and specific problems. Therefore, in the present study a survey approach will be used. It aims at identifying the crucial barriers at national and international (European) levels.

12.4 Identification the conditions of an effective multi-modal freight transport network: a survey approach

The question is now whether multi-modal transport reaches a sufficient or desired level in Europe; and if not, which are the main barriers that prohibit such a development? Clearly, the direct assessment of the state of multi-modal transport as well as the identification of the relevant obstacles face incommensurable problems, since both relevant studies and empirical statistics are scarce. In order to cope with this, a survey study has been designed in the framework of the present research. Its basis is a comprehensive questionnaire distributed among European experts which deals with two issues in its respective parts. Part 1 asks for an assessment of the gap between the current inter-modal transport and the corresponding desired level. Since a critical factor for an effective multi-modal network is the existence of inter-modal terminals, Part 1 assesses also their present availability in relation to the respective desired level. All assessments take place at both national and international (European) levels.

Part 2 deals with the main barriers preventing the development of effective multi-modal transport. These barriers are classified in the five groups: financial, organisational, software, psychological and hardware (a pentagon model). All groups contain several distinct items, each one depicted by a separate question.

The questionnaire was addressed to freight transport experts in all Western and Central European Community countries plus Switzerland. No additional information was provided to the experts. The opinion of each expert was asked separately for the respective national and (European) international level. A five-point ordinal scale was used to assess the answers. It represents respectively the following possible answers: no barrier, intermediate barrier, strong barrier, extremely strong barrier. Each expert was asked to give his opinion first about the gap between the existing level of inter-modal transport and the relevant desired level, as well as about the gap between the current inter-modal terminals and the desired ones.

Each expert indicated a personal opinion about the relevant barriers by choosing, for each barrier considered, a point in the ordinal scale. A presentation of the questions and the results are presented in Annex 12.1.

The total response to the questionnaire was 60 (response rate 75%). Clearly, this sample is insufficient to apply standard statistical methods. Therefore, a recently developed non-parametric statistical method for data analysis was used. This is a rough-set analysis developed by Pawlak (1991) and Slowinski (1993). We will first give a concise introduction to rough-set theory (see also (Pawlak, 1991; Pawlak, 1982; Slowinski, 1993; Matarazzo, 1996).

A rough-set is a set for which it is uncertain in advance which objects belong precisely to that set, although it is in principle possible to identify all objects which may belong to the set at hand. Rough-set theory takes for granted the existence of a finite set of objects for which some information is known in terms of factual (qualitative or numerical) knowledge on a class of attributes (features, characteristics). These attributes may also act as equivalence relationships for these objects, so that an observer can classify objects into distinct equivalence classes. Objects in the same equivalence class are - on the basis of these features - indiscernible. In case of multiple attributes, each attribute is associated with a different equivalence relationship. The intersection of multiple equivalence relationships is called the indiscernibility relationship with respect to the attributes involved. This intersection generates a family of equivalence classes that is a more precise classification of the objects than that based on a single equivalence relationship. The family of equivalence classes which is generated by the intersection of all equivalence relationships is called the family of elementary sets. The classification of objects as given by the elementary sets is the most precise classification possible, on the basis of the available information.

The indiscernibility relationship and the equivalence classes generated by this relationship make up the basic concepts and building blocks of rough-set theory. A set is now termed 'rough' if it is impossible to build it up from one or more elementary sets. In other words, a set is rough if it is not equal to a union of elementary sets.

Now we may introduce the concept of a reduct. A reduct is a subset of the set of all attributes with the following characteristic: adding another attribute to a reduct does not lead to a more accurate classification of objects, while elimination of an attribute from a reduct does lead to a less accurate classification of objects.

Finally, the core of a set is the class of all indispensable equivalence relationships. An attribute is indispensable if the classification of the objects becomes less precise when that attribute is not taken into account (given the fact that all attributes have been considered until then). The core may be an empty set and is, in general, not a reduct. An indispensable element occurs in all reducts. The core is essentially the intersection of all reducts.

Based on the previous concepts, rough-set theory is now able to specify various decision rules of an 'if then' nature. For specifying decision rules, it is useful to represent our prior knowledge on reality by means of an information table. An information table is a matrix (objects row-wise, attributes column-wise) that contains the values of the attributes of all objects. In an information table, the attributes may be partitioned into condition (background) and decision (response) attributes. A decision rule is then an implication relationship between the description of the condition attributes and that of a decision attribute. Such a rule may be exact or approximate. A rule is exact, if the combination of the values of the condition attributes in that rule implies only one single combination of the values of the decision attributes, while an approximate rule only states that more than one combination of values of the decision attributes correspond to the same values of the condition attributes. Decision rules may thus be expressed as conditional statements ('if then').

In this way one may analyse in greater depth the information contained in the original table and to enrich it, specifying additional decision rules directly by means of suitable interviews or discussions with experts. In other words, it is possible to acquire information also directly in the form of decision rules supplied by experts, thereby enriching the original information contained in the decision table.

The relevance of rough-set analysis for the present study refers to the ability of the rough-set method to identify crucial variables, among a great number of variables, which explain the classification of some objects to certain classes. The classification variables and the classes could be considered as the explanatory variables and the dependent variables respectively. The crucial variables are reported by the core when it is identifiable. However, when the core cannot be estimated, the relevant reducts give an approximation of the decisive variables for the classification. Note the relevance between classes and decision rules as well as between classification variables and attributes.

We will now present the results of the rough-set method on the survey questionnaire of our study. Although rough-set analysis may be used for identifying decision rules and performing multi-attribute sorting, we will rely in particular on the concepts of a reduct and the core of attributes which are used in our analysis. Every expert questionnaire is considered as an object in the rough-set method. There are four independent variables (decision variables):

- the gap of current inter-modal transport with respect to the desired level at the national level
- the gap of current inter-modal transport with respect to the desired level at European level
- the gap of current inter-modal terminals with respect to the desired level at national level
- the gap of current inter-modal terminals with respect to the desired level at European level.

Therefore, the analysis will be subdivided into four cases, each one considering one dependent variable in relation to the relevant independent and explanatory variables.

As explanatory variables (attributes), we consider all the remaining questions to be entities of the questionnaire. For a detailed presentation we refer to Annex 12.1, where the whole structure of the questionnaire is illustrated. The explanatory variables are classified into five, pentagon groups: financial, organisational, software, psychological and hardware.

In all cases, three meta-variables are added to the analysis in order to test their importance for the development of effective multi-modal transport. These meta-variables are: population, surface of the country considered, and the geographical position of the country (central or peripheral in the European territory).

In each case, rough-set analysis examines which are the subsets of explanatory variables/barriers that lead to the same accurate classification with all variables considered. In this way, reducts of barriers are estimated; each reduct presents a set of important explanatory variables (barriers). Next, the core of all reducts, if it exists, consists of all important barriers.

The analysis initially identifies the reducts within each one of the five groups of barriers (financial, organisational, software, psychological, hardware). This process indicates the most important barriers in each group. Next, the sum of the most important variables is considered, and thereupon the reducts are estimated. These reducts and the respective core, if they exist, may be interpreted as important barriers.

12.5   Results of the analysis

12.5.1   The gap between existing and desired inter-modal transport at the national level

The independent variable is the gap between existing inter-modal transport at national level in relation to the relevant desired level; in rough-set theory terms this is the classification/decision variable. Each expert's opinion is classified into one of the five groups (non-existing gap, very small, small, high, extremely high) according to the answer to the dependent variable. In order to identify the relative importance of each barrier variable for the classification of the answers (which in fact means to identify the relative importance of each barrier for the gap between existing inter-modal transport at national level to the relevant desired level) we apply rough-set analysis. First, we examine the relative importance of each group of barriers (financial, organisational, psychological, software, hardware, meta-variables) as a whole

285

and then we examine the relative importance of the barriers within each group.

The group of *financial* barriers has a relatively high importance for the classification, since the barrier variables of this group alone suffice to give an accurate classification of high quality - they form a reduct in rough-set analysis. In reality this means that the financial barriers are a critical obstacle for the development of an effective inter-modal freight transport at national level. Within this group the relative importance of the 'user cost in inter-modal transport' and the 'user cost at inter-modal terminals' is very high, although they do not form a reduct in rough-set analysis. The 'investment cost of inter-modal infrastructure' and the 'investment cost of rail infrastructure' follow with a relatively lower importance which nevertheless remains considerable. It is noteworthy that in rough-set analysis there is no core of attributes/barriers within the financial group.

The group of *organisational* barriers is also of great importance since the organisational barriers alone lead to an accurate classification of high quality for the objects: they form a reduct in rough-set analysis. As far as the relative importance within this group is concerned, we may conclude that the 'institutional barriers which prevent inter-modal transport between different countries' and the 'bureaucratic organisation and management in rail mode' are the most important barriers. The 'lack of express delivery in inter-modal transport' and the 'lack of just-in-time delivery in inter-modal transport' are of secondary importance. We note that there is no core of attributes/barriers within the organisational barriers group.

Next, both the groups of *software* and *psychological* barriers, when considered individually, appear to be of little importance, and therefore their explanatory power for the classification of objects is low. If these groups are considered together, then their importance increases; however, it still remains far lower than that of the financial and organisational groups; they do not form a reduct in rough-set theory.

The group of *hardware* barriers is of great importance, since this group alone leads to an accurate classification of the objects: the barriers of this group form a reduct in rough-set theory. It turns out that among the variables of this group the most decisive barrier is the 'lack of inter-modal terminals'. The 'lack of rail infrastructure' then follows, while the remaining barriers have almost the same (lower) importance.

Finally, the group of the *meta-variables* appears to have the lowest importance among all groups.

At this point of our analysis, we are able to select the most important barrier variables of each group and to check their importance at a more general level. It appears that the *financial* and *hardware* barriers are the most important ones. Specifically, the 'lack of interoperability of railways at

European level' alone, the group of 'investment costs for inter-modal infrastructure' together with 'investment cost for rail infrastructure' and the group of the 'user cost at inter-modal terminals' together with the 'user cost in inter-modal transport' appear to be the most decisive ones. It is noteworthy that there is no core of attributes neither for the whole set of attributes considered nor for the set of the most important ones.

Another general conclusion, which may be drawn from the analysis up to this stage, is that the barriers prohibiting the development of an efficient inter-modal freight transport at national level differ considerably from country to country. It seems that the decisive mixture of variables is different in each country. For instance, in one case we find that the financial barriers together with software barriers prevail, while in another case a combination of hardware together with organisational barriers is the main obstacle.

Nevertheless, the analysis so far indicates that the importance of hardware and financial barriers are the most common and severe obstacles for the development of an effective and efficient inter-modal freight transport at national level.

12.5.2 The gap between existing inter-modal and desired transport at European level

In this second step of our analysis, the independent variable is the gap between the existing inter-modal transport in relation to the desired level, at international (European) level. In rough-set theory, this variable stands for the classification/decision variable. The issue here is to identify the relative importance of the independent variables/barriers for the classification. This, in turn, means to identify the contribution of each barrier in the gap. Following the same mode of analysis as in the previous section, the importance of each group of barriers is examined separately.

The group of *financial* barriers leads to a classification of high quality and therefore it is of relatively great importance: the barriers of this group form a reduct in rough-set theory. The most important barrier variables are the 'investment cost for rail infrastructure', the 'investment cost for inter-modal infrastructure' and the 'user cost in rail mode' which also form the core of the attribute-barriers according to rough-set analysis (Slowinski 1993).

Next, the group of *organisational* barriers alone cannot establish an accurate classification and hence is of secondary importance: these barriers do not form a reduct. Nevertheless, among the barriers of this group, the barriers 'lack of express delivery in inter-modal transport', 'lack of just in time delivery in inter-modal transport' and 'delays at inter-modal terminals' appear to emerge with the relatively highest importance.

The group of *software* and the group of physiological barriers also appear to be of relatively low interest. Even when both groups are examined together, they do not lead to an accurate classification of the objects, and therefore their explanatory power is low.

The *hardware* group clearly has high explanatory power and the barriers of this group obviously form a reduct. The barrier 'lack of interoperability of railways at the European level' appears to be the most interesting. The subgroup consisting of the barriers 'lack of specific rail vehicles suitable for inter-modal transport' together with 'lack of specific track vehicles suitable for inter-modal transport' has considerable explanatory power, while the barrier 'lack of rail infrastructure' comes third in the ranking of importance.

At this point we are able to select the most important variables from all groups and to examine the relative importance between them. It appears that the barrier 'lack of interoperability of railways at the European level' is the most decisive one, while the barriers 'investment cost for inter-modal infrastructure' and 'investment cost for rail infrastructure' follow next. The barriers 'lack of specific rail vehicles suitable for inter-modal transport', 'lack of specific track vehicles suitable for inter-modal transport' and 'lack of rail infrastructure' are also of great importance.

Consequently, it appears that the most powerful explanatory barrier variables belong to the groups of hardware and financial barriers. This result is more evident at international (European) level than at national level. Moreover, in contrast to the national level, it seems that the prohibitive obstacles for the development of a European inter-modal freight transport network are perceived to be rather common at European level.

12.5.3 The gap between the existing and desired inter-modal terminals at the national level

It is an almost common perception among European scientists and experts that the role of the inter-modal terminals is decisive for the development of an effective multi-modal freight transport system. In this context, the dependent variable, in this part, is the gap between the existing inter-modal terminals in relation to the desired level, at national level. We have to explain the existence of this gap by the relative power of the relevant barriers as explanatory variables. We apply the same type of analysis as in the previous two subsections.

It should be mentioned immediately that no group of barrier variables alone leads to an accurate classification. Therefore, the identification of the most decisive barrier should take place at a general level where all variables are considered simultaneously. By applying rough-set analysis, it appears that the most important barriers are related to *financial* and *hardware* issues.

Specifically, the 'lack of suitable rail infrastructure' and the relevant investment costs composed of 'investment cost for rail infrastructure' and the 'investment cost for inter-modal terminals' emerge as the most serious prohibitive barriers.

In contrast to an intuitive expectation, our analysis shows that the *meta-variables* (population, surface, location of the country) show up as irrelevant factors. Here again, the mixture of the decisive barriers differs significantly between countries (our rough-set analysis results in weak accuracy of classification when a subset of barriers is examined).

12.5.4 The gap between existing and desired inter-modal terminals at the European level

Here, the dependent variable is the gap between existing inter-modal terminals in relation to the desired level, at European level. The problem of explaining this variable on the basis of the relevant barriers functioning as the explanatory variables in our analysis, is dealt with in the same way as in the previous part of the analysis.

The *financial* and *hardware* barriers, considered together, account for the lack in the development of inter-modal terminals at European level. Specifically, the 'lack of rail infrastructure' and the 'lack of interoperability of railways at European level emerge as the barriers with the most decisive power. Similarly, the *financial* barriers 'investment cost for rail infrastructure' and 'investment cost for inter-modal infrastructure' are strong. We also note that the above mentioned four variables offer a classification of the same accuracy as the classification resulting from all variables and form a reduct in terms of rough-set theory. Besides, the *organisational* issues 'institutional barriers which prevent inter-modal transport between different countries' and 'bureaucratic organisation and management of railways' provide significant explanations for classification and therefore constitute important barriers.

In this framework, we may conclude that at international level the analysis concerning the lack of inter-modal terminals, leads to more rigid results than is the case in the same analysis at the national level, since the experts consider that common barriers exist at European level. In this respect, rough-set analysis leads to a better approximation of the relevant classification compared to the analysis at national level.

Table 12.1 Survey of the results

	Crucial Barriers	Medium Barriers	Low Barriers
Gap between existing and «desired» inter-modal transport. *National* level	financial hardware	organisational	software psychological meta-variables
Gap between existing and "desired" inter-modal transport. *European* level	financial hardware		organisational software psychological
Gap between existing and "desired" inter-modal terminals. *National* level	financial hardware		software psychological organisational meta-variables
Gap between existing and "desired" inter-modal terminals. *European* level	financial hardware	organisational	software psychological

12.6   Application of factor and regression analysis

We will now confront the results of the rough-set analysis with those from conventional statistical techniques. This section presents the results of the application of certain standard statistical methods on the survey questionnaire. Evidently, the magnitude of the sample is not sufficient for applying exclusively standard statistical methods. However, we may use them as a kind of additional experimentation on the robustness of the results of rough-set analysis. We will use the standard factor analysis, principal components analysis, and regression analysis (Sneath and Sokal, 1973; Wittink, 1988).

Specifically, by using the standard factor analysis, and principal components analysis in each group of the explanatory variables (financial, organisational, software, psychological, hardware) we identify a smaller number of 'combined' explanatory variables which appears to have a statistically significant explanatory power. As a result we eliminate the number of the relevant explanatory variables within each of the five groups.

Then, by applying standard regression analysis on all the combined explanatory variables, we outline their relative explanatory power and hence the relative explanatory power of the five groups of the explanatory variables.

Note that the relevant statistical estimations are not presented. This is because of the fact that the statistical analysis is not a comprehensive approach but rather an additional experimentation which lies in the margins of statistical methods. So, the relevant results are of indicative nature.

12.6.1 The gap between existing and desired inter-modal transport at national level

For each group of the financial, organisational, software, psychological and hardware variables, factor analysis determines two 'combined variables' factors. Subsequently we apply regression analysis for the eight 'combined' variables. The linear regression model indicates that the *financial* barriers, and especially those ones related to the infrastructure costs, have the highest explanatory power. These variables may exclusively explain the variation of the dependent variable.

12.6.2 The gap between existing inter-modal and desired transport at European level

The factor analysis identifies two 'combined variables', factors for each of the financial, organisational, software, psychological and hardware variables. Using these eight 'combined' variables, we apply regression analysis. It indicates that the *financial* and *hardware* barriers are the most decisive ones, while organisational barriers play also a significant role which is, however, statistically less important than the former ones.

12.6.3 The gap between the existing and desired inter-modal terminals at national level

The factor analysis determines three 'combined variables' factors for all groups of the explanatory variables examined together. Then, regression analysis proposes that the *organisational* and *financial* barriers are statistically the most powerful ones.

12.6.4 The gap between existing and desired inter-modal terminals at European level

The factor analysis composes three 'combined' variables out of all the explanatory variables. However, regression analysis cannot lead to robust

291

results. It would seem that the magnitude of the sample plays a decisive prohibitive role here.

In general, the results of the standard statistical methods are rather similar to those of rough-set analysis. Especially, for the first two dependent variables, the decisive explanatory variables determined by both methodologies, are the same. For three dependent variables, the standard statistical methods indicate a marginally different outcome; while for the fourth dependent variable the standard statistical methods cannot be applied. The limitations imposed by the magnitude of the sample appear to be very important for the standard statistical analysis. On the other hand, its use as a reference point for the robustness of rough-set analysis may be considered as an acceptable endeavour, at least on an experimentation level.

12.7   Concluding remarks

The development of a well functioning multi-modal transport framework emerges as a promising solution for some of the current transport problems as well as for relevant external factors. However, it appears that the existing state of multi-modal networks lags far behind desired levels, especially in the case of road-rail cooperation. The survey conducted in the framework of the present study, shows clearly that transport experts in Europe attach much value to the development of an efficient and effective multi modal network, which will also be beneficial to the transport sector and society in general.

However, this evolution is burdened by serious obstacles. Prohibitive financial, technical, organisational and other problems exist. Especially, the cooperation between European countries for the development of a fully inter-operable railways system is rather weak at present - and railways play a vital role in the development of an effective network. Other technical problems related to the existence of specific rolling material, also emerge as decisive barriers and should be taken into account. Furthermore, financial issues related to the creation of sufficient rail infrastructure and inter-modal terminals turn out to be a rather prohibitive obstacle in almost all European Countries and relevant institutions.

On the other hand, the importance of the proper inter-modal terminals is considered fundamental by most European experts. They indicate that there is a great lack of inter-modal terminals to facilitate an effective rail-road network. Alas, the development of proper terminals is burdened by serious financial and inter-European cooperation obstacles.

In this context, the recommendations stemming from our study concern the development of a policy for removing financial and hardware technical barriers, since multi-modal freight transport emerges as a promising evolution in economic, social and environmental terms. Such a policy may have a European (international) perspective, which takes into account, however, the particular national characteristics of each country. In this framework, the adoption of common technical standards for railway operations and the introduction of new financial schemes, are prerequisites.

This evolution may require certain legislation and social adjustments related to the market structure, the management and the ownership conditions in the transport sector.

References

Button, K. and D. Banister (eds) (1990), *Transport in a Free Market Economy*, MacMillan: London.

European Conference of Ministers of Transport (1992), *Statistical Trends in Transport 1965-1988*, ECMT, Paris.

Group Transport 2000 Plus (1991), *Transport in a Fast Changing Europe, DG VII*, European Community, Brussels.

EC (July 1994), *Road Freight Transport in the Single European Market*, Report of the Committee of Inquiry, Brussels.

Matarazzo, B. (1996), "Basic Principles of Rough Set Analysis", in: P. Nijkamp, J.C.M.J. van den Bergh and G. Pepping (eds), *Meta-Analysis of Environmental Strategies and Policies at a Meso Level*, Report European Commission: Brussels.

Mitra, A., Jenkins, G.D. and Gupta, N. (1992), "A Meta-analytic Review of the Relationship between Absence and Turnover", *Journal of Applied Psychology*, 879-889.

Nijkamp, P. and E. Blaas (1994), *Impact Assessment and Evaluation in Transportation Planning*, Kluwer: Boston/Dordrecht.

Nijkamp, P., J. Vleugel, R. Maggi and I. Masser (1993), *Missing Transport Networks in Europe*, Avebury:Aldershot.

OECD (1992), *Advanced Logistics and Road Freight Transport*, Paris.

Pawlak, Z. (1982), "Rough Sets", *International Journal of Information and Computer Sciences*, Vol. 11, No. 5, 341-356.

Pawlak, Z. (1991), *Rough Sets, Theoretical Aspects of Reasoning about Data*, Kluwer: Dordrecht.

Slowinski, R. (ed.) (1993), *Intelligent Decision Support. Handbook of Applications and Advances of Rough Sets Theory*, Kluwer: Dordrecht.

Sneath, P. and R. Sokal (1973), *Numerical Taxonomy*, Freeman: San Francisco.

Wittink, D. (1988), *The Application of Regression Analysis*, Allyn and Bacon: Massachusetts.

Annex 12.1 Tables of data and results

Table 12.A1 Frequencies of the dependent variables

	Current inter-modal transport compared to the desired level. *National*	Current inter-modal transport compared to the desired level. *European*	Current inter-modal terminals. *National*	Current inter-modal terminals. *European*
non-existing	0%	0	2.3	0
very small	4.7	0	4.7	2.3
small	23.3	25.6	34.9	27.9
high	65.1	51.2	39.5	48.8
extremely high	7	23.3	18.6	20.9

Table 12.A2
The questionnaire and the relevant answers (in percentages)

	no (barrier)		light		intermediate		strong		extremely strong	
FINANCIAL BARRIERS										
inter-modal infrastructure investment cost	2.3 %		18.6	27.9	39.5	37.9	25.6	23.3	14	11.6
rail infrastructure investment cost	2.3		20.9	20.9	30.2	32.6	30.2	32.6	16.3	16.3
user cost at inter-modal terminals	4.8	4.8	19	23.8	52.4	52.4	19	14.3	4.8	2.4
user cost in inter-modal transport	4.8	4.8	21.4	19	52.4	57	19	16.7	2.4	2.4
user cost in rail transport	7.1	2.4	28.6	42.9	38.1	31	26.2	23.8	0	

Table 12.A2 continued

ORGANISATIONAL									
lack of express delivery in inter-modal transport	9.5	*9.3*	26.2	*18.6*	26.2	*44.2*	28.6	*20.9*	9.5	*7*
lack of just in time delivery in inter-modal transport	2.3	*4.7*	23.3	*16.3*	27.9	*30.2*	30.2	*39.5*	16.3	*9.3*
delays at inter-modal terminals	2.4		31.7	*26.8*	22	*36.6*	34.1	*26.8*	9.8	*9.8*
institutional barriers that prevent inter-modal transport between different countries	7.5	*9.5*	20	*9.5*	32.5	*38.1*	25	*23.8*	15	*19*
bureaucratic organisation of rail mode	2.4	*2.4*	16.7	*7.1*	19	*33.3*	35.7	*21.4*	26.2	*35.7*
SOFTWARE									
insufficient informatics system in rail mode	2.4		29.3	*29.3*	36.6	*31.7*	14.6	*26.8*	17.1	*12.2*
insufficient informatics system used by freight transport operators	2.4		26.8	*26.8*	39	*41.5*	22	*29.3*	9.8	*2.4*
PSYCHOLOGICAL									
unjustified prejudice against rail mode	15	*15.4*	25	*17.9*	35	*41*	15	*15.4*	10	*10.3*
justified prejudice against rail mode	2.4	*4.9*	17.1	*12.2*	39	*46.3*	22	*24.4*	19.5	*12.2*

295

Table 12.A2 continued

HARDWARE										
lack of inter-modal terminals	7		23.3	20.9	25.6	44.2	32.6	27.9	11.6	7
lack of rail infrastructure	14	11.9	20.9	28.6	34.9	23.8	20.9	31	9.3	4.8
lack of specific rail vehicles suitable for inter-modal infrastructure	7.3	4.9	48.8	41.5	24.4	34.1	9.8	14.6	9.8	4.9
lack of specific truck vehicles suitable for inter-modal transport	17.1	17.1	41.5	34.1	19.5	31.7	19.5	17.1	2.4	0
lack of interoperability of railways at the European level	5.4	2.3	16.2	7	24.3	27.9	37.8	37.2	16.2	25.6

13 Options for Transport Telematics

MATTIAS HÖJER

13.1 Introduction[1]

The conflict between collective good and individual utility maximisation is a classical problem of "tragedy of the commons" (Hardin 1968). In the following, a study using a scenario method that can be used to limit such conflicts by increasing the knowledge of available options among policy makers and citizens is presented. The consequences on the collective good can thereby be incorporated in the public debate and taken into account in policy formation.

The study focused on how transport telematics in cities could be implemented in order to facilitate a sustainable development. Sustainable development was used as a high level policy goal (Gudmundsson and Höjer 1996; Höjer 1996). As such it supports the holistic, problem-oriented view that is seldom seen in the transport telematics literature. The scope involved the design of systems aimed at reaching such a goal. It was formulated as a question: "What systems should be designed to get the best out of the new technology?"

The main issues here have been to suggest how functions can combine into systems, to visualise barriers to feasibility, to discuss the impact from different technologies and to investigate potential markets for different systems. A benefit of the scenario technique is that the functions' dependence on their environment is emphasised.

This is expected to highlight the opportunities and risks that transport telematics entail. The study can then lay the basis for a policy formulation on future implementation strategies. The scenario descriptions can also be used as a basis for public debate on how to use information technology in the future transport system.

Below follows a description of the study's methodology including four complete scenario descriptions. The empirical results, i.e. the experts' reactions to the scenario descriptions are summarised at the end of this chapter. The quantitative

---

[1] This chapter is drawn upon the results of a research project performed at the Royal Institute of Technology between April 1995 and April 1997. The complete results are published in Höjer 1997. Funds for the study have been provided by the Swedish Telecommunications and Transport Research Board (KFB).

analysis of the results are not presented here, due to restrictions of space. However, a more comprehensive presentation of these can be found in Höjer 1997.

13.2 Visualising policy options with scenarios

A combination of backcasting and Delphi surveys was used in the survey. Backcasting aims at presenting images of the future, visions that can be used in contemporary policy formation. The idea is to highlight interesting (possible, but not necessarily probable) shifts in society's development by organising the images around such shifts. A backcasting study can be useful when directional studies and forecasts indicate that targets will not be met, i.e. when non-marginal changes are needed. In such cases, visions of the future that fulfil targets can be generated. The images are not supposed to spring out of forecasts. Instead, they should visualise a state when the target is met. One point with backcasting is to see beyond the trends. Therefore, the time perspective is often long – 20 years and more. Figure 13.1 illustrates the applicability of backcasting. When the visions have been described the task is to outline paths between current situation and the visions (Dreborg 1996).

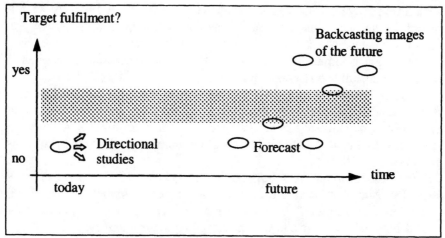

Figure 13.1 Applicability of backcasting
Backcasting is motivated when forecasts and directional studies indicate that targets will not be met. Figure developed from Steen and Åkerman 1994.

In Delphi surveys, a number of experts are asked repeated questions about their views of the future in a number of respects. The classical field for the method has been technological forecasting. In early Delphi surveys (e.g. Gordon and Helmer 1964) the experts were asked quantifiable questions such as "Within how many years will something specific happen?" or "How many units of something will there be in 20 years?" During the more than thirty years that have passed since the Delphi method was developed, the method has taken different directions. Van Dijk 1990, summarises the Delphi method as "... a set of familiar questioning techniques with the common features of some kind of interactive communication and intermediate feedback of results." Masser and Foley 1987 see three basic components of the Delphi method: "...the creation of a panel of experts that can be consulted, the use of a series of questionnaires for consultation purposes, and the provision that is made for the feedback of findings to respondents..."

In the current study a structured scenario technique and an expert panel were used. The scenario technique made it possible to present IT-functions in their environment. This aimed at dismantling advantages and shortcomings with the separate parts of a system. The point of using experts was to take advantage of the knowledge and ideas that already exist around the world. Hopefully, experts can deliver thoughtful ideas and share their experiences.

One starting point when developing the current method, the marriage between backcasting and Delphi, was the criticism that has been formulated against the Delphi technique by e.g. Sackman 1974 and Asplund 1979. The critique focused on conventional Delphi studies, where the aim is to produce a reliable forecast. In this study the purpose was to lay the basis for a policy formation. Some of the most criticised parts of the Delphi-technique are the use of experts and the consensus forming methods. In the current study the experts have not been used as oracles, i.e. they have not been asked to predict the future. Instead they have been asked to share their own thoughts on how a couple of alternative transport telematics systems could be used. Moreover, a consensus statement from the experts has not been sought for explicitly.

The contribution from backcasting to the development of the method in this study has been related to the scenario writing. No attempts have been made to forecast the most probable development or dissemination path of a certain technology. Instead, the problem-oriented perspective has been allowed to dominate. The idea has been to formulate scenarios that have a potential for adjusting the transport system towards sustainable development. This is an example of a problem where current trends and forecasts indicate that the target will not be met (see Figure 13.1), according to e.g. Steen et al. (1997). The second part of a backcasting study, the outline of a path leading towards the scenarios, has not been carried out here.

In order to create interesting scenario descriptions or images of the future, a solid basis of knowledge about the performance of the state of the art technology is a prerequisite. But this basis can be hard to build since the expertise might not be united on where state of the art is. Moreover, the expertise to a specific scenario description might come from several different disciplines.

In this study, the Delphi method was used to overcome these problems in scenario design. First, scenarios were developed within the research project and then repeatedly exposed to organised external critique, in a Delphi-like manner. This made it possible to improve the scenario descriptions by grinding off parts that received too much critique and adding parts that were suggested by the expert panel. Thus, the feedback to respondents that both van Dijk 1990 and Masser and Foley 1987 mention had the shape of adjustments to the scenario descriptions. The repetition also made it possible to check the stability of the experts' responses. The interactions between improvement of scenario descriptions and exposure of them for criticism could in principle keep on for several rounds. In the present case two rounds have been performed – the initial round plus one improvement round.

13.3   The survey

Initially, components to the scenarios were found in the literature. The literature from the Swedish RTI-program, such as the TOSCA-project (e.g. Lind 1992; Lukasic 1994) was of central importance. Ideas from the Nordic Road Association 1992 and from the Danish RUF-system (Miljøstyrelsen 1992), were added. Provisional scenario descriptions and questionnaires were generated and discussed in a reference group connected to the study. After these discussions, a testing round with 10 experts was carried out. The comments from these ten experts led to some final adjustments of the scenario descriptions and questionnaire.

The first round of the survey was sent out in April 1995 and the second in January 1996. The survey consisted of a cover letter, strictly structured scenario descriptions and a questionnaire.

13.3.1   The scenario descriptions

The scenarios were formulated as descriptions of the function and use of technical systems, i.e. a kind of technical scenario. They were placed in the context of passenger transport in industrialised cities, and focused on the use of IT in transport. They did not include e.g. teleworking. The year of the scenarios was deliberately unspecified. In this study there was no need to argue about exact years of introduction for different scenarios. It was looked upon as more interesting to try to compare scenarios of different technical complexity within the same framework.

All scenarios followed the same structure. They began with a few lines on the basic ideas with the scenario and continued with a description of the functioning of some crucial features. This was followed by examples of how trips could be carried out and explanations of some more specific details in the scenario. They all ended with a list of the most important functions contained in the scenario.

All scenarios had some items in common. Physical similarities were the presence of smart cards and pocket terminals. Three functions that were taken advantage of in all scenarios were traffic centres (for traffic control and/or traffic information), route guidance systems and road user charges. However, the items were not used the same way in all scenarios. Four scenarios were developed. One of them was based on the private car (Dynamic Route Choice), one was based on public transport (Extended Public Transport) and two were combinations of private and public transport (Car Pooling and Dual Mode). See also box 1, 2, 3 and 4 below.

The scenarios did not exclude each other technically, but they took different paths towards fulfilling the basic transport mission. In actual fact, all four scenarios could be implemented side-by-side. This would of course be very costly indeed. And the systems and sub-systems would both complement and substitute each other. So the benefit might turn out to be limited.

It was obvious that some parts of the scenario descriptions in round one were poorly formulated, thus leading to different interpretations of how the scenarios were expected to work. To avoid such misunderstandings in the second round, some small changes of formulations were made to the descriptions.

The evaluation of the first round responses showed that Car Pooling received heavy criticism. Therefore, this scenario was not included in round two. Instead, a much looser form of car pooling was incorporated in Dynamic Route Choice. The other two scenarios went through only minor changes.

Car Pooling was designed to show how information technology could raise the vehicle load factor, i.e. number of passengers per car. This was going to be achieved with a system for automatic matching of travellers who wanted a ride with drivers who could pick up passengers. The scenario also included a system for payment of the ride via automatic transfers from the passenger's account to the driver's account and road user fees. Some of the basic ideas for this scenario came from a vision described by Hans Bendtsen (Nordic Road Association 1992). See also box 13.1.

Dynamic Route Choice was designed to optimise the performance of the urban transport system with the help of dynamic road user fees. The fees were to include estimated internal as well as external costs of traffic. The fees in co-operation with an efficient traffic control centre would direct traffic the best way, i.e. the drivers could chose between driving the cheapest and the fastest route between two points. Many central functions for this scenario are described in Lind 1996. See also box 13.2.

Extended Public Transport was aimed at raising the attraction of public transport by improving information and extending the public transport information service to include taxis and rental cars. A number of bicycle features were also included. A

301

related scenario is described in a British report from the Cabinet Office 1995. See also box 13.3.

In Dual Mode, the challenge was to combine the potential for efficient energy use in rail transport and the advantages of electric vehicles with the flexibility of the private car. It differed from the others in that it was more futuristic, e.g. by the requirement of a new infrastructure of monorails and dual mode vehicles. The scenario is a version of a Danish system that is under development (Jensen 1996). See also box 13.4.

Box 13.1 The full scenario description of Car Pooling, round 1

Car pooling implies that all cars can be used as taxis. The system is founded on the idea that a person who wants a lift orders a trip through a traffic control centre and that a driver who is prepared to pick up passengers announces a planned trip to the same centre.

The main task for the traffic control centre is to co-ordinate passengers' orders with drivers' announcements. A route guidance system, that can help drivers find the best way, is connected to the traffic control centre. The traffic control centre delivers information about current traffic situation, as well as traffic forecasts, to the route guidance system.

The cars in the system are connected to the traffic control centre so that they can get information about where passengers are waiting. They are equipped with card readers that are connected to a bank. All money transfers from passengers to drivers are handled this way. Transfers due to a road user fee are made from the drivers' accounts to an account administered by the traffic control centre. The cars cannot be started unless a qualified smart card is in the card reader and the code belonging to the card has been entered.

The driver has three alternatives in this system:

1. She can get into the car, put the card in the card reader, tell the traffic control centre where she is, where she is going and that she is prepared to pick up passengers. Then the traffic control centre can allot a passenger to the driver at any time during the drive. The message from the traffic control centre consists of address and a description of the waiting passenger. The route guidance system automatically adjusts the instructions in accordance with the new destination. The driver is obliged to accept all passengers that the traffic control centre suggests, and to follow the route choices made by the guidance system. The road user fee is lower if she announces her trip some time in advance. Such an announcement can be made from the same terminals that are used by passengers to order trips. The passenger pays for the trip to the driver by putting his card in the car's card reader before the trip begins.

2. The driver can get into the car, put the card in the card reader, tell the traffic control centre where she is, where she is going and that she is not interested in picking up passengers. The road user fee then automatically goes up and the driver is informed about this. An exception to the fee rise is made when there are already passengers in the car.

3. The driver can get into the car, put her card in the card reader and drive away. This gives a high road user fee which she is automatically informed about.

The high fee for driving freely is motivated by the traffic control centre's few possibilities of planning traffic for vehicles that run without a known destination. Drivers who do not follow the directions from the route guidance system in the examples above will pay the same high road user fee.

The passenger can order his trip from a terminal at home, from terminals at major meeting places and from a pocket terminal that is connected to the traffic control centre by a modem and a mobile telephone. The passenger orders a trip by telling where he is, where he is going and when he wants to start the trip. He can specify his wishes further (more than one passenger, direct trip to destination, luggage, child safety seats). In such cases the waiting time can be longer and the fee will be higher. The message from the traffic control centre consists of the driver's name, the colour, model and registration number of the vehicle and the expected time when the car will arrive. If no lift can be offered within reasonable time from the ordering moment, a taxi is offered to a price corresponding to the car pooling price. In such cases other passengers might be left or picked up on the way to the destination.

The passenger fee consists of a fixed fee plus a certain share of the driver's road user fee. Three different price levels for drivers have been mentioned above. The fee for passengers vary with the number of passengers and their trip specifications. All fees vary with time of day, day of week and place.

All cars have special sensors that register the number of passengers. This way the computer in the card reader can control that the correct fee is used.

Safety is handled through special procedures. Drivers in the system are obliged to have special driving licences, that demand more of the drivers than ordinary licences do. The licences can be suspended or taken away altogether in cases of traffic offences and crimes. Passengers can also be expelled from the system if they commit violent crimes, harass drivers or misuse the system in other ways. Women can demand to go with, or pick up, other women only. There are also alarm buttons at all seats in the car. Everybody who wants to use the system will be identified automatically with the personal smart card in combination with a code.

This is included in the system:
- a traffic control centre that co-ordinates passengers' orders with drivers' announcements
- a route guidance system
- a system that calculates the price for the passengers' trips
- an in-vehicle computer that calculates the road user fee and controls that the fee is paid
- cars equipped with card readers and equipment for communication
- smart cards that can be used for identification, money transfers and as locks to the starters
- pocket terminals, terminals in homes and at meeting points
- sensors that control the number of passengers in the cars
- alarm buttons at all seats in the car.

303

Box 13.2
The full scenario description of Dynamic Route Choice, round 2

Dynamic route choice implies that road traffic is directed with the help of a route choice model. A route guidance system and a system for vehicle intersection control are available for all drivers that follow the suggestions from the model. Road user fees are charged to cover the damages caused by traffic. The fee varies with time of departure, place and vehicle, but it is normally fixed once a driver has accepted an offered price for a drive between an origin and a destination. A system for fee calculation and fee-collection and a system for parking place reservation are also included in the scenario.

Damages from traffic on global and regional ecosystems are paid for via a fuel tax. Local disturbances caused by traffic, e.g. air pollution, congestion, noise, safety risks and perceived threats (road users' as well as pedestrians') are covered by road user fees. This implies roughly that it is more expensive to drive old, big cars, to drive in city centres or housing areas and to drive in peak hours. On the countryside no fees apply – only the fuel tax is paid. The exact levels of the tax and the charges are in practice compromises between the estimated costs for traffic damages and what is politically feasible.

A traffic control centre collects information about ongoing and planned trips. The centre also gets continuous information about air quality, state of the roads, road repairs and accidents affecting the traffic. Based on this information and on past and present traffic situations, the centre makes short-term (minutes) traffic forecasts.

The information about present situation, the forecasts and the politically decided charges for traffic are used as bases for regular recalculations of fees on the road links. From this a route choice model can calculate the cheapest and the quickest route between two places for a specific vehicle. All fees except the congestion fee are vehicle-specific so that energy-efficient, low-noise, small, light vehicles with low emissions pay lower fees. The payment is made through a rechargeable card that is placed in a card reader in the car.

Vehicle intersection control is implemented. This means that vehicles and traffic signals communicate so that the signals are adjusted to approaching vehicles and the in-vehicle computer calculates a suitable speed and recommends it to the driver.

A certain amount of the parking places are reserved for drivers using the route guidance system. These places have sensors connected to the traffic control centre that register if they are available. The parking places can be booked while driving. After a reservation the guidance system takes the car to the reserved place. The parking fee is paid with the rechargeable card. If a vehicle is parked on a place that is already reserved the traffic control centre sends an urgent request to move it immediately. If this is not done it will get a parking fine and the car that had reserved the place is given another alternative.

All information is given to the driver on a display in the car. The driver can also get the information from a pocket terminal before he gets into the car, and so he has the opportunity to adjust his departure time to the present traffic situation.

The driver places his card in the card-reader and announces his origin, destination and vehicle characteristics to the traffic control centre via the in-vehicle computer before the trip begins. The centre returns information about total cost and expected time use for the cheapest and the fastest routes. If the driver accepts one of these two routes, the price is fixed and the route guidance system will guide him to the destination. If he decides to go somewhere else other than the original destination, he can contact the traffic control centre. The centre recalculates the cost and the route guidance system adjusts its information.

If the driver does not want to state origin/destination, or if he does not follow the instructions from the route guidance system above, he will neither be able to use the route guidance system, nor the vehicle intersection control. If he has placed a rechargeable card in the card reader a fee will be charged at the beginning of each link. The in-vehicle computer gets a signal from roadside transmitters telling the link fees. The charges are the same as the ones used by the route choice model, and thus they vary with traffic situation, air pollution, vehicle type etc. The opportunity to fix the cost before driving is not available, since the traffic control centre has no information about where the driver is going. Visitors can buy rechargeable cards before entering the urban region.

If the driver does not want to use/does not have a card, the number plate of the car will be photographed each time it enters a pre-defined zone. By the end of the month all entries are summed and multiplied with a fixed charge. A bill is then sent to the owner of the car. This leads to higher charges than when a rechargeable card is used.

The motivation for car pooling rises when the costs for each trip are displayed. And it is easy to share costs, since several cards can be entered at the same time in the in-vehicle card readers. The road user fees are always divided equally between the cards in the card reader. Moreover, pools with neighbours and colleagues are supported by the introduction of a "car pooling software" in local computer networks of any size (e.g. at huge places of work, among a couple of thousand households). Anyone who is connected to such a network can either announce that he wants a ride or that he is prepared to pick up passengers. The matching procedure is supported by the software.

This is included in the system:
- a route guidance system
- vehicle intersection control
- a traffic control centre that collects and processes information and administers parking
- sensors for air quality and for information about the state of the roads
- a traffic forecast model and a model for calculation of the cheapest and the fastest path
- rechargeable cards
- vehicles equipped with card readers, computers and displays
- sensors at parking places
- pocket terminals for information from the traffic control centre
- local computer networks that facilitate co-ordination of passengers with drivers

Box 13.3
The full scenario description of Extended Public Transport, round 2

Extended public transport implies both that public transport gets advantages in relation to private car traffic, and that the public transport system is integrated with rental car, taxi and bicycle systems.

The nucleus of the system is a traffic information centre. The centre has information about all public transport time tables and all delays in relation to these. A telephone register with names and addresses and a road register are also connected to the centre.

Moreover, the information centre knows if there are any available parking lots at park-and-ride facilities and it calculates an approximate "peak index". The peak index indicates how full the major public transport vehicles are at a given moment. It is based on reports from a number of key vehicles. All this information can be retrieved through the pocket terminals.

The traffic information centre is connected to a taxi system. If you want a taxi to wait at the destination of your public transport trip, this can be arranged via the traffic information centre. The centre forwards the order to a taxi company together with the expected arrival time. Delays in the public transport system are automatically reported to the taxi system. Taxi trips can also be ordered from inter-city trains.

The traffic information centre is also connected to rental car-companies. Rental cars are available at all major stations. Cars can be booked via the information centre. The client gets a code and registration number of the car to confirm the booking. The car will then be waiting at the station. A personal smart card and a code, but no key, is needed to start the car. The payment is taken care of through a card reader. Rental cars can also be ordered from inter-city trains.

All communication between the traffic information centre and the traveller is taken care of through pocket terminals, terminals at public places and terminals at home.

Traffic signals are adjusted to give priority for buses and separate bus lanes are built, so that public buses get higher average speeds and better punctuality, achieving priority from other vehicles.

Payments are handled with a smart card that is put in a card reader placed at the stations. The cards can be refilled at cash dispensers by means of transfers from the card holder's account, or with cash deposited at the dispensers.

The public transport fares are higher at peak hours than at off-peak hours. The fares are co-ordinated with a system for road user charges, so that at all hours it is more expensive to go by car than by public transport. The differences in price between car driving and public transport are highest at peak hours.

Bicycling is encouraged by building covered bicycle tracks along the most popular routes and separated crossings through the city centre. The commuter trains are equipped with places for bicycles that can be booked in advance via the terminals mentioned above. A route guidance system for bicycles helps the cyclist find the best way to a destination. The information from the route guidance system is received by the pocket terminal that can be fastened at the handlebars. At major meeting points, such as stations, there are bicycles for loan. To borrow a bicycle a personal smart card that identifies the user must be inserted in a card reader. This unlocks a bicycle and a deposit is taken from the user's account. The deposit is paid back when the bicycle is returned. The system is financed by sponsors having their names on the bicycles.

The traveller begins the trip by sending departure time, origin and destination (or a name of the company or person she wants to visit) to the traffic information centre. The traffic information centre responds with information about alternative route choices with public transport and bicycle (optional) between the two addresses. If only a name has been given as destination, the traffic information centre looks up the address in the telephone register before sending the above information. The information about the public transport contains transport mode, departure and arrival times, changes, peak index and price. The information about the bicycle alternative consists of the length of the trip, wind-force and wind direction. When the traveller has chosen one of the alternatives she confirms the choice. If delays that affect the confirmed trip appear somewhere in the system, the traffic information centre will announce this promptly, and suggest alternative choices.

This is included in the system:
- a traffic information centre that has information about public transport and that is connected to taxi- and rental car-companies
- a register of roads, addresses and bicycle tracks
- locks to rental cars that can only be opened with a smart card and code
- terminals at public places, homes and in pocket-size
- public transport regularisation
- rechargeable cards
- card readers at stations
- cash dispensers where the cards can be recharged
- separate spaces for bicycles on trains
- a booking system for bicycles on commuter trains
- a route guidance system for bicycles
- borrow-a-bicycle facilities

Box 13.4 The full scenario description of Dual Mode, round 2

Dual-mode vehicle system implies a new physical infrastructure. The system consists of light vehicles with electric propulsion that run automatically on light monorails with low friction. The vehicles can also leave the rail and run on ordinary roads with manual driving. The rails can be built on ground, in tunnels or be raised above ground.

The vehicles are constructed so that front and end fit each other. On rails where speeds are high (70-200 km/h), trains of vehicles can be formed to minimise air resistance. Normal braking is regenerative, but emergency braking is taken care of with disc brakes that squeeze the rail. This is efficient and stable since the brakes are placed close to the vehicles' centre of gravity. The vehicles can be privately owned, hired for longer periods from traffic operators or for public use. The public vehicles are cleaned daily at special stations.

All trips on the rail network are announced to a traffic control centre that directs the traffic. Driving on the network is automatic. The route choice on the network is consequently decided by the traffic control centre. Another task for the centre is to automatically connect and disconnect trains of vehicles on the network. The centre is also administering the user fees. The fees are designed to avoid congestion on the network. Vehicles can be denied entrance to the rail network if the maximum capacity is reached.

In city the network is very dense with many stations. The system works as a Personal Rapid Transit-system, i.e. the traveller is offered automatically guided trips from one station directly to another. Empty vehicles are distributed in the system to be available within reasonable time from ordering.

The vehicles use electric propulsion and batteries when running on roads. A hybrid unit with a diesel engine, a generator and a fuel tank can be placed under the vehicle to make longer trips possible. This way the vehicles can be used like conventional cars, at the cost of not being able to run on the rails. Hybrid units can be hired at all major exits from the rail network. The batteries are charged when the vehicle runs on rails, when the hybrid unit is used and when the vehicle is connected to a socket.

Switching from rail to road (road to rail) is done in a semiautomatic way. The vehicle slows down to 30 km/h and the driver takes over (handles over) the control gradually.

When the vehicle runs on rail the user fees vary with the amount of traffic. When running on the road a fixed fee is charged per kilometre. It is much cheaper to run on rail than on the road, and it is cheaper to go with a public vehicle than with one that is privately owned or hired for a longer time. This is because public vehicles have a higher utilisation rate, since they can be used by anyone. Conventional cars pay zone-based fees each time they enter a new zone in the urban area.

The payment is handled via a smart card. The card, together with a code, makes it possible to hire public vehicles that are parked in the streets and at stations for shorter or longer periods. The driver must prove her identity to mitigate the risk for vandalising and theft. Misuse of the system can lead to expulsion. The smart card holds information about the owner's driving license to stop drivers without a licence from leaving the network with a public vehicle.

A trip can be made in mainly two ways in this system (apart from driving on roads like today with either a conventional vehicle or with one of the dual-mode vehicles):

1. The driver can take her vehicle (privately owned or hired), drive to the nearest rail, continue automatically to her destination, leave the rail and park the vehicle.
2. The driver can order a trip with a public vehicle by stating destination and desired time of departure to the traffic control centre. There are terminals in homes, at meeting points

and stations and for pocket use, from which the order can be sent. The trip can be specified with e.g. desires of room for extra luggage and child safety seats.

When it is hard to find parking places for the privately owned vehicle, it can be left on the rail network at a low cost. The empty vehicle will then circulate in the system, or be parked at a station with excess capacity, without anyone else being able to use it. When the owner needs the vehicle again she uses a terminal to send for it from wherever she is.

This is included in the system:
- vehicles with electric propulsion that can run on either rail or road
- hybrid units with a diesel engine, a generator and a fuel tank
- a traffic control centre that directs traffic on the rail network and administers charges
- a monorail network with entrances and exits to the road system and with stations
- smart cards that give access to public vehicles and handle identification (when a vehicle is hired) and payment
- terminals for ordering public vehicles or sending for parked private and hired vehicles

13.3.2 The questionnaires

The purpose of the questionnaires was to structure the responses from the experts. The responses to the questions would give an idea of what the experts regard as pitfalls and advantages of the scenarios. In the first questionnaire the experts were asked to assess feasibility (technical and acceptance), impact (market penetration and effects) and economy (changes in land values and investment costs) of the four scenarios. The second questionnaire was changed so that the questions on feasibility were adjusted to the new scenario descriptions. The question on long-term effects was sharpened and questions on the need for subsidies as well as probability and desirability were added. The questions on market penetration were not repeated in round two. Extensive space were given to comments in plain text in both questionnaires.

13.3.3 The experts

The expert panel was selected from members of the Regional Science Association International, from networks where the project's researchers were involved and from networks with individuals from organisations of environmental groups and the car industry. In figure 13.2, the experts' personal and professional profiles are illustrated. The profiles include all the 97 experts who took part in the survey. Roughly 25 per cent of them came from Sweden. Less than 10 per cent came from countries outside Europe. Most worked at universities and nearly 90 per cent were men.

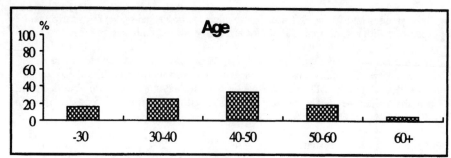

Figure 13.2a

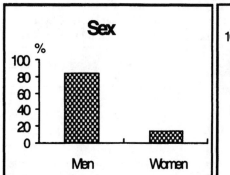

Figure 13.2b

Figure 13.2c

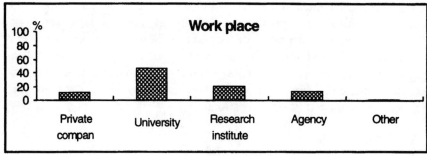

Figure 13.2c

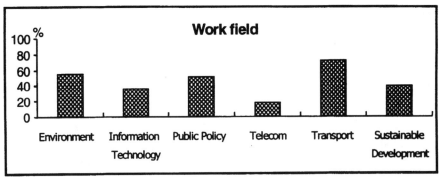

Figure 13.2e

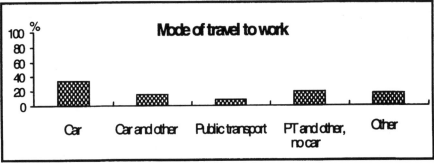

Figure 13.2a-f Socio-cultural profile of the experts (age, sex, country, work field and mode of travel).

The first questionnaire was responded to by 86 out of 310 experts (28 per cent). The second questionnaire was responded to by 54 out of the 86 who responded to the first questionnaire (63 per cent) and 11 out of 20 who only received the second questionnaire.

What happened to the 72 per cent who did not respond to the first questionnaire? Obviously, it cannot be known for sure. We are left with the material that was sent back. The point was not to get a representative selection of experts. Rather, the idea was to gather a sufficient number of questionnaires to have a basis for the evaluation of the scenarios. The views expressed there were to be collected, organised and analysed in order to develop a scenario technique and to build a basis for policy discussion on what we want from information technology in urban transport systems. For these purposes the number of filled in questionnaires were sufficient.

An analysis of systematic biases in the characteristics of the experts who responded in comparison to the set of experts who were selected, reveals that the response rate was slightly higher for women (38 per cent of 29 questionnaires were returned) than for men (27 per cent of 281) and that the response rates decreased with distance (Sweden: 35 per cent of 68; Other Nordic countries: 34 per cent of 38; Netherlands: 26 per cent of 46; Rest of Europe: 24 per cent of 112 and rest of the world: 21 per cent of 46).

13.4   Results and discussion

The Backcasting Delphi method turned out to work well. This can be concluded from the many positive remarks made by the respondents, by the stability of responses to comparable questions between the two rounds and by the improved evaluation of the scenario descriptions (data on this can be found in Höjer 1997). The experts also seem to have spent quite some time considering the questions, as can be concluded from the number of comments (an average of 8 comments/expert in the first questionnaire and 5 comments/expert in the shorter second questionnaire).

It could be interesting to use the Backcasting Delphi method, i.e. scenario development with the help of a panel, as a part of the implementation of telematics systems in a region. If the panel is made up by citizens, it can work as a way of engaging the public in town planning, and to collect ideas from those who are directly affected by the changes, before final decisions are made.

Table 13.1 Summary of evaluation of the four scenarios

	Car Pooling	*Dynamic Route Choice*	*Extended Public Transport*	*Dual Mode*
Feasibility, main barriers	*Acceptance barrier*	*Complexity barrier*	*No barriers found*	*Technical barriers*
Market penetration	*Smaller cities*	*Same as today's car market*	*Same as today's public transport market*	*Same as today's car market*
Effect	*Reduced CO2-emissions, not shorter travel times*	*Shorter travel times, some other positive effects*	*Many positive effects, longer travel times and decreased comfort*	*Improved safety, some other positive effects*
Economy	*Low cost*	*Best finances*	*Low cost*	*Very costly*

The experts rejected the feasibility of Car Pooling mainly due to peoples' expected reluctance to go with strangers. Probably, systems with less compulsory elements would be more feasible. Given the high expectation in the possibility to reduce CO_2-emissions, it could be interesting to develop e.g. some of the already existing systems for ride-sharing that use the Internet further (see also Table 13.1).

The experts thought that Dynamic Route Choice could shorten travel times and that it also could have some other positive effects. The finances of this scenario was expected to be better than for the other scenarios. However, there was a fear that the overall technical complexity of the scenario could become a problem (see also Table 13.1).

Extended public transport was the scenario that received the best evaluations. The experts found no serious technical or acceptance barriers and the evaluation of its impact on long-term effects was by far the best (see also Table 13.1).

Dual Mode involves a number of severe technical uncertainties, but it seemed to be the only scenario with the power of changing existing travel patterns. It can be worth following the technical development of dual-mode systems in future, since a technical breakthrough here can lead to a number of positive changes in transport. However, for the moment the experts find this scenario costly and technically too advanced (see also table 13.1).

One common fear from the experts had to do with privacy intrusion. Since the scenarios include a traffic centre with the task of assembling information and organising traffic, the inherent opportunities for control are high. At the same time, this handling of masses of information may hold a potential for substantial efficiency improvements for urban traffic. Obviously, there is a conflict between risks of violation of privacy on one side, and potential efficiency improvements with gains for all users on the other. A similar conflict exists with mobile phones. It is technically possible to keep track of all mobile phone users as long as the phone is on. This conflict between privacy and collective good is a political question (see also Höjer 1996).

In future studies, it can be interesting to develop scenarios that depend less on centralised information – scenarios that concentrate in offering opportunities, without the degree of enforcement that has been included here. Such systems will probably get a higher feasibility evaluation. However, it might be difficult to develop the systems in a way that leads to high gains in terms of e.g. CO_2-reductions.

The future development of transport telematics may change the conditions for peoples' mobility. The current study contributes to the illumination of the potentials and risks with transport telematics, so that future research and decisions can be made with those in mind. There are obvious inherent conflicts between private and public interests, in the centralised way of implementing transport telematics that has been assessed here. A higher degree of centralisation (and risk for privacy intrusion) may be more compatible with lower environmental degradation (which is a public interest). Therefore, the implementation and future development of transport telematics is very much a political question. As such it should be addressed more thoroughly by social scientists.

In summary, the experts in this study regard highly the potential of transport telematics. Many of them see substantial improvements on a number of long-term environmental and other effects. It is also clear that the strongest improvements are expected to come from a systematic introduction of transport telematics for public transport. A related conclusion has been reached in a study from the British Cabinet Office 1995, where a scenario based on information to the traveller is highlighted as one out of three "transport foresight projects".

The implementation can be financed with the use of dynamic road user fees, along the lines for road pricing that was described in Dynamic Route Choice. Such fees limit the necessity for subsidies in two ways: directly by the revenue from the road user fees, and indirectly through the higher prices on transport, which makes it feasible to raise user prices for public transport as well. The fees will lead to lower subsidies to road transport, thus levelling out the differences between private and public transport. Finally, it should be possible to integrate some of the ideas from Dual Mode, mainly the transport-on-demand, with Extended Public Transport, in order to relax the time constraints during the parts of the day when demand is low.

The current study lays the foundation for the systematic implementation of improved public transport with telematics. A conclusion is that future development and design of transport telematics should focus much more on public transport applications, than has been suggested by e.g. the Swedish Delegation for Transport Telematics 1996. This implies a shift in current development programs.

References

Asplund, J. (1979), *Teorier om Framtiden* (Theories about the Future, in Swedish), Liber: Falköping.

Cabinet Office (1995), *Technology Foresight 5: Progress Through Partnership – Transport*, HMSO: London.

van Dijk, J. A. G. M. (1990), "Delphi questionnaires versus individual and group Delphi – a comparison case", *Technological Forecasting and Social Change*, Vol. 37, pp. 293-304.

Dreborg, K. (1996), "Essence of Backcasting", *Futures*, Vol. 28, No. 9, pp. 813-28.

Gordon, T. J. and O. Helmer (1964), *Report on a long-range forecasting study*, P-2982, The RAND Corporation: Santa Monica.

Gudmundsson, H. and M. Höjer (1996), "Sustainable development principles and their implications for transport", *Ecological Economics*, Vol. 19, No. 3, pp. 269-82.

Hardin, G. (1968), "The Tragedy of the Commons", *Science*, Vol. 162, pp. 1243-48.

Höjer, M. (1996), "Urban transport, information technology and sustainable development", *World Transport Policy and Practice*, Vol. 2, No. 1-2, pp. 46-51.

Höjer, M. (1997), *Telematics in Urban transport – a Delphi survey using scenarios*, Report TRITA-IP FR 97-23, Department of Infrastructure and Planning, Royal Institute of Technology: Stockholm.

Jensen, P. (1996), *The RUF-system*, RUF International: Copenhagen.

Lind, G. (1992), *Test-site oriented scenario assessment (TOSCA)*, TFB-report 1992:26, The Swedish Transport Research Board: Stockholm.

Lind, G. (1996), *Test-site oriented scenario assessment – possible effects of transport telematics in the Göteborg region*, KFB-report 1996:13, The Swedish Transport and Communications Research Board: Stockholm.

Lukasic, V. (1994), *Technical RTI systems – a study of equipment and costs*, TOSCA II project, Deliverable 22, Transek: Solna.

Masser, I. and P. Foley (1987), "Delphi revisited: Expert opinion in urban analysis", *Urban Studies*, Vol. 24, pp. 217-25.

Miljøstyrelsen (1992), *RUF-systemet* ("The RUF system", in Danish), Work report No. 48 from Miljøstyrelsen, The Ministry of Environment: Copenhagen.

Nordic Road Association (1992), *Ett miljöanpassat transportsystem – tre framtidsbilder* ("An environmentally sound transport system - three images of the future", in Swedish with English summary), The environment committee, Report 12:1992, The Swedish National Road Administration: Borlänge.

315

Sackman, H. (1974), *Delphi Assessment: Expert Opinion, Forecasting, and Group Process*, R-1283-PR, The RAND Corporation: Santa Monica.

Steen, P. and J. Åkerman (1994), *Syntes av studier över omställning av energi- och transportsystemen i Sverige* ("Synthesis of studies on the adaptation of the Swedish energy and transport systems", in Swedish), in: *Report from the committee on climate*, Official report, SOU 1994:138, The ministry of environment: Stockholm.

Steen, P., Dreborg, K-H., Henriksson, G., Hunhammar, S., Höjer, M., Rignér, J. and Åkerman, J. (1997), *Färder i framtiden - transporter i ett bärkraftigt samhälle* ("Travel in future - transport in a sustainable society", in Swedish), KFB-report 1997:7, Swedish Transport and Communications Research Board: Stockholm.

Swedish Delegation for Transport Telematics (1996), *Transportinformatik för Sverige* ("Transport informatics for Sweden", in Swedish with an English summary), Official report, SOU 1996:186, The Ministry of Transport and Communications: Stockholm.

14 Behaviour of Western European Scheduled Airlines During the Market Liberalisation Process

MILAN JANIC

14.1 Introduction

The world's aviation industry has been exposed to significant changes during the past two decades. These changes have had their origins in both the aviation industry and external institutional bodies, which have created the appropriate legislation regulating the rules and procedures for the industry's operations. It is likely that the most important institutional change that has ever occurred was the deregulation of the U.S. airline industry in 1978. A few years after deregulation, significant welfare effects and benefits for the airlines, their users and society as a whole had been gained. This generated the pressures for creating more liberal aviation markets in the other areas including Canada, Australia, and of course, Europe (Bailey et al., 1985; Button, 1989 a, b; Morisson and Winston, 1986).

To match growing liberalisation trends, the EU (European Union) launched 'Three Liberalisation Packages' during the past decade. They were aimed to gradually liberalise the aviation market of Member States (Stasinopoulos, 1992, 1993; Vincent and Stasinopoulos, 1990). Confronted with new institutional and operating conditions at 'home', the particular EU airlines were under pressure to change their business practice and policy and adapt themselves to new market conditions.

The objective of this paper is to investigate the airline behaviour under conditions of gradual liberalisation of the EU's aviation market. For that purpose it has been necessary to create a suitable methodology for monitoring the structural changes that might happen over time in the structure of industry, the aviation market and at particular airlines. Only a section of the airline industry represented by the scheduled airlines operating in the network of international routes connecting particular Member States has been under focus.

Besides this introductory Section, the paper consists of five Sections. Section 14.2 describes the main characteristics of 'Three Liberalisation Packages'. Section 14.3 briefly describes the structure of the Western European airline industry and some aspects of the airline behaviour such as its 'growth' upon entering the various kinds of mergers and alliances, and competition/cooperation in the EU air route network. Section 4 discusses the models that have empirically quantified the specific aspects of the EU airline behaviour during the first phase of the market liberalisation (1989/1993). These are the model of economies of scale, the model of airline growth and financial performances and the model of airline relationships on the EU (European Union) air route network. Section 5 describes some of the other aspects of airline behaviour and the factors influencing them. The last section contains the conclusions.

14.2   Aviation legislation in the European Union

The general institutional basis for aviation industry operations all over the world is covered by the Chicago Convention (1944). It has determined basic traffic rights which have guaranteed five different 'freedoms' to scheduled and non-scheduled (charter) airlines. These freedoms have comprised the airline rights to fly over a country without stopping, land and/or take-off due to technical reasons (e.g. to take fuel, change crew, etc.), carry passengers and freight from the country of origin to another foreign country, carry passengers and freight from a foreign country to their home country, carry passengers and freight from a foreign country to a third country, and vice versa (ICAO, 1988; OECD, 1988).

The first two 'freedoms' not involving commercial rights have always been included in the multilateral agreements. The other three 'freedoms' were granted in bilateral agreements which had been contracted between particular countries. They were based on the Bermuda Agreement reached between the US and the United Kingdom in 1946. According to ICAO (1988), the main purpose of a typical bilateral agreement has been to protect the general national and specific interest of domestic airlines which has inherently created a solid regulatory structure. However, such a structure has shown to be useful and justified only to a certain level of development of aviation industry (for instance, in the U.S. until 1978, in Europe until 1987, etc.) (Button, 1989 a,b; Stasinopoulos, 1992, 1993; Vincent and Stasinopoulos, 1990).

In 1978, the US domestic aviation market was deregulated by a single Act. Over night, the US airlines found themselves in the position to continue their business in a completely new, free operational environment. They were allowed to fly everywhere they wanted to and they set up the airfares freely. In addition, the airlines were no longer allowed any sort of governmental subsidies for non-profitable services (Bailey et. al., 1985). In the EU, alleviating of rigidities and inflexibility of the aviation services between particular Member States was realised as a gradual process in three phases: Each phase was determined by implementation of one of the 'Liberalisation Packages'. The process was completed in 1997 (Stasinopoulos, 1993).

The main features of the particular Packages have been the following:

1. The First Package was approved on 7 December 1987. It consisted of the following market liberalisation measures:

- The *capacity shares* on the particular route(s) were permitted up to a certain threshold.
- The *'third'*, *'fourth'* and the *'fifth freedom'* services up to 30 per cent of the offered capacity were permitted between the *Category 1 airports* and *regional airports* located in the different Member States,
- The *airfares* still remained under control. Discount fare and deep discount fare could be set up to 65-90 per cent and 45-60 per cent of the reference, and *the average economy class* fare, respectively.

2. The Second Package was approved in June 1990. It launched additional 'freedoms' which can be summarised as follows:

- The *capacity share*, *access to the markets* and *setting-up the airfares* were liberalised.
- The use of *the airline capacity for the 'fifth freedom'* traffic rose from 30 to 50 per cent. The airport derogation in the position of the fourth freedom services and loosening capacity sharing contracts were removed.
- Air cargo was allowed to operate the *'third'*, *'fourth'* and *'fifth freedom'* operations.
- The airlines originating from the Member States were granted the right *to cabbage* in all Member States.
- The airfares were allowed to be 'deep' discounted *without* governmental (double) approval. *Lower discount* limit was reduced to 30 per cent of the reference fare. The limit of *deep discount* fare was set up to 30-75 per cent of the reference fare. *Discount fares* were allowed to vary between 80 and 94 per cent of the normal economy (reference) fares. The appropriate mechanisms for controlling and sanctioning predatory pricing were contained in the Package, too.

3. The Third Package was approved in June 1991. It went into effect on 1 January 1993. The Package provided the following:

- *Protection* of the airlines *against discrimination* with respect to their nationality in *the cases of getting the licences* in different Member States;
- *Complete elimination of the capacity sharing* for the airlines flying between the Member States. Also, an airline from one *Member State* was allowed to fly between *any two places (cities)* in *the other Member States.* Until April 1997, the airlines were permitted to board a maximum of 50 per cent of seats during the stops in the another Member State including the *'seventh freedom'* right too, e.g., the transport of passengers and freight between any two Member States being other than the country of the airline origin.
- Airfares could be set up freely with barriers to predatory pricing.

These Three Packages have institutionally opened the national aviation markets of the fifteen Member States. Their airlines have been allowed to freely enter and leave from the particular markets and compete with the flight frequency and fare. Nevertheless, some external problems are still unresolved. The most important problem has seemed to be related to the regulation of access of the EU airlines to the markets of the third (non-EU) countries, and vice versa. For example, the modifications of the Packages applicable to some non-EU countries such as Norway and Switzerland, and the aviation market of the USA, Eastern and Central Europe and Asia, have become particularly interesting for EU airlines. Also, provision of the concessions of the traffic rights to the third countries may impact the functioning of the internal EU aviation market. The actions that have been undertaken by third countries may bring benefits to some and discriminate against other EU airlines, etc. (Nijkamp, 1996; Stasinopoulos, 1993).

14.3   Structure of the EU airline industry

An analysis of the structure and behaviour of Western European airlines has been carried out to illustrate their most important characteristics.

14.3.1   Structure of the industry

Broadly, Western European airlines can be classified into *scheduled airlines* and *charter airlines* (CAA, 1993; Doganis, 1992). *Scheduled airlines* can be further divided into flag-scheduled and sub-class non-flag scheduled airlines (CAA, 1993).

Flag-scheduled airlines always have been considered as the most important airlines in their countries. Typically, they have been mostly governmentally owned and controlled. They have also enjoyed a high level of government protection consisting of subsidies for non-profitable services and covering the losses. Very often, they have served, apart from their own, other general and specific political and social-economic interests of their major owners.

Non-flag airlines appeared on the markets later. Because they are privately owned, they have never enjoyed such a high level of protection as their 'older' and usually much bigger 'brothers', the flags.

Western European *flag and non-flag airlines* have been of various sizes, scale and scope of operations. About 100 flag and non-flag airlines have performed scheduled services in the EU (European Union) Member States (Airline Business, 1994/1995; CAA, 1993).

The size of the airlines may be expressed in distinct ways. First, it can be expressed in terms of size and structure of their fleets. The size and structure of the airline fleet, in turn, can be expressed by the number of aircraft of different capacity and number of personnel, which both reflect the size of the airline's available static resources.

Secondly, the size of an airline can be measured by the volume of its annual output expressed in millions of the Revenue Passenger (or Tonne) Kilometres (RPK). This measure has reflected efficiency of utilisation of the available airline 'static' resources (fleet, personnel) in an absolute sense. Some characteristics of the size of particular West European scheduled airlines in 1993 are presented in Table 14.1 and 14.2, respectively.

In Table 14.1, the *flag airlines* have been *ranked* according to *the volume of their annual output*. As can be seen, there are clear boundaries between their outputs allowing one to make another ranking and sub-classification. For example, *the flags* can be divided into three sub-groups. The first one is represented by British Airways, Lufthansa and Air France.

The annual output of these airlines was greater than RPK 40,000 million. KLM, Alitalia, Iberia, SAS, and Swissair formed another group, which produced between RPK 15,000 and 40,000 million. The last sub-group consists of the airlines with annual output of RPK 10,000 million. These were: Finnair, Olympic, TAP-Air Portugal, Sabena, Air Lingus, Icelandair, and Luxair.

A similar sub-classification of the *non-flag scheduled airlines* can be carried out. Table 14.2 shows that the first sub-class consists of the airlines that produce over RPK 5000 million per year (Britannia, Air 2000, Monarch, Virgin Atlantic, Air Inter and Martinair). Another sub-group contains 10 airlines of which produced between RPK 1000 and 5000 million. The last sub-group consists of 16 airlines, which each carried out less than RPK 1000 million.

By comparing the outputs presented in Table 14.1 and 14.2, it can be seen that some non-flag airlines have operated larger fleets and produced a greater volume of output than certain smaller flag airlines. For example, the non-flags from the first sub-class in Table 14.2 may be compared with some flags from the third sub-class in Table 14.1, etc.

Table 14.1
Some characteristics of the western European flag airlines (1993)

Airline	Output (Million of RPK)	No. of Employees	No. of Aircraft	Load Factor (%)
British Airways	79306	48960	244	71,0
Lufthansa	51367	42841	206	68,0
Air France	43642	39965	140	67,6
KLM	37455	26163	94	71,2
Alitalia	28368	20363	161	65,5
Iberia	23268	26000	142	66,6
SAS	18170	20000	153	63,4
Finnair	8275	7714	56	58,0
Olympic	7971	9600	40	61,0
TAP-Air Portugal	7869	10700	41	70,0
Sabena	6485	9500	51	55,5
Air Lingus	4362	12500	31	68,0
Icelandair	2049	1280	11	66,0
Luxair	606	1000	9	60,0
Swissair	17227	19100	62	61,5

Sources: Airline Business, 1995; Air Transport World, 1995; ICAO, 1986/1994.

According to the type of operations and origins and destinations of their routes (flights), the scheduled airlines may be divided into the group performing both domestic and international traffic, and the group operating either only domestic or only international services. The majority of Western European scheduled airlines have usually performed both kinds of operations. Subject to the length of routes, these airlines have performed short flights (those carried out in their own countries and between some close regions (airports) in different Member States), medium flights (those performed mainly between the places (airports) in different Member States), and long haul flights (those connecting EU with the other continents) (CAA, 1993; 1994).

Table 14.2 Some characteristics of western european non-flag scheduled airlines (1993)

Airline/Country	Output (Millions of RPK)	No. of Employees	No. of Aircrafts
Britannia (UK)	18092	3300	43
Air 2000 (UK)	10400	1259	19
Monarch (UK)	9500	2000	25
Air Inter (France)	9491	11142	58
Virgin Atlantic (UK)	9001	3013	10
Martinair (Netherlands)	7424	2025	15
AeroLloyd (Germany)	4700	830	10
Transavia (Netherlands)	3933	1003	16
British Midland (UK)	3365	3720	28
Air Europe (UK)	3088	300	6
Aviaco (Spain)	2383	1696	41
Meridiana (Italy)	2200	1150	17
Maerskair (UK)	1343	120	27
Eurobelgian (Belgium)	1154	100	6
Viva Air (Spain)	1116	457	8
Air UK (UK)	1109	1800	34
AirBelgium (Belgium)	757	55	2
GB Airways (UK)	529	160	4
Eurowings (Germany)	517	950	26
British World (UK)	431	400	19
Binter Canarias (Spain)	318	230	11
Manx (UK)	211	601	15
Brymon (UK)	153	170	13
Air Littoral (France)	152	727	12
Karair (Finland)	139	250	7
City Flyer Express (UK)	136	196	7
Finnaviation (Finland)	74	180	6
Air Dolomiti (Italy)	58	50	3
Binter Mediteraneo(Spain)	57	120	5
Business Air (UK)	44	140	8
Gillair (UK)	31	160	12
Avianova (Italy)	26	150	11

Sources: Airline Business,1995; Air Transport World, 1995; ICAO, 1986/1994.

Charter airlines represent another broad class of the airlines operating in the the European aviation industry expressed in annual RPK (CAA, 1993; Pelkmans, 1991). As is the case with the scheduled airlines, the charters can also be ranked and classified subject to different criteria considering, among the other characteristics, also their specific connections and type of vertical integration with other schedule airlines, travel agents and tour operators (CAA, 1993; Janic, 1996). particular Member States. They are distinguished from the scheduled airlines according to the pattern of operations, segments and type of demand they have primarily served, as well as internal organisational structure. Very often, such specific structures and operating conditions have allowed them to operate as the 'low-cost' carriers. Opposite to the scheduled airlines serving mostly the business trips, the charters have specialised to serve predominantly the leisure (holiday) journeys. Thus they have realised more than half of the total output.

14.3.2   Airline growth, mergers and alliances, and competition

Growth of the airlines means continuous increase in their output that can be measured by the annual revenues, costs and volume of the passenger and freight kilometres. This growth can be achieved by use of the internal resources, acquisitions, and/or various merging and alliances.

Table 14.3 shows an example of the airline average growth rates for the period 1986-1994. Generally, these rates have been higher among smaller airlines than larger ones. Also, among particularly larger airlines they have seemed constrained: namely, at higher volumes of output they have diminished (Janic, 1996).

There are two explanations for the main causes behind the continuous growth of airlines. Firstly, the airlines have been growing in order to satisfy increasing demand and to enjoy the advantages of economies of scale. These airlines have expected to produce a larger volume of output at lower unit cost (Antoniou, 1991; Youseff and Hansen, 1994). Secondly, any expansion of the airline output is bound to bring positive marginal revenues. That means that each additional service (product) is going to be appropriately sold (Train, 1991; Weisman, 1990).

Mergers and alliances have been recognised as another typical form of behaviour of Western European airlines. They have been particularly enhanced during the first phase of the market liberalisation (1987/1991) and afterwards. Three types of airline mergers can be identified. These are: corporate mergers, airline alliances of 'marketing agreement' types, and strong airline alliances involving holding of stakes or equities by mergers in the partners (Tretheway, 1990).

Table 14.3 Some characteristics of the airline growth (1986-1994)

The western european airlines	Average annual rate of growth (%)	Scale of output (Million of RTK*)
Air France	9,9	5100 - 10 000
Austrian Airlines	17,7	150 - 530
Alitalia	9,7	1900 - 4200
British Airways	10,4	5700 - 12 500
KLM	9,8	3400 - 7400
Lufthansa	11,4	5500 - 13 000
SAS	4,5	1500 - 2000
Swissair	6,5	1900 - 3300
British Midland	10,7	60 - 300
Lauda Air	23,7	95 - 325

* Revenue Tonne Kilometres

Sources: Airline Business, 1995; Air Transport World, 1995; ICAO, 1986/1994; Janic, 1996.

Corporate merger is a form of joining the airlines from different countries into the common corporation. The airlines participating in the merger had first been bought and then merged. SAS in Europe 'originating' from three Scandinavian countries, and Air Afrique, established by 12 countries in West Africa, have been considered as the typical examples of corporate merging.

Simple airline alliance involves marketing agreement(s) between particular airlines originating from the same and/or different countries. The prime aim for these airlines has been to exchange traffic more easily. Among European flag airlines, 'marketing agreements' have usually included arrangements such as: joint venture and pooling agreements on the particular routes, sharing capacities and services of the airport terminals and air staff, co-ordination of timetables and ground handling operations, block space agreements, code sharing on particular routes, sharing the same CRS (Computer Reservation System). Also other forms of co-operation are involved, such as ticket reservations and sales, developing information systems, FFP (Frequent Flyer Programmes), maintenance of aircraft, training of staff, etc.(Airline Business, 1995; Janic, 1996). Marketing agreements have been shown to be an effective cooperative tool for obtaining benefits for both airlines and passengers. However, their inherent, crucial disadvantage proves to be the difficulty to cancel at any given time.

Strong airline alliances involving holding of stakes in partner companies through the merger(s) have been practised by the EU airlines as a convenient 'tool' for sustaining institutional stability of the relationships. Generally, by buying a part and/or majority of the partner(s), the merger(s) established either partly or full control. In this case, all activities carried out in the 'marketing alliances' have been included (Tretheway, 1990; Janic, 1996).

The number and types of merges and alliances which were in effect among EU scheduled airlines in 1995 are shown in Table 14.4 It can be seen that the number of alliances of type 'marketing agreement' has been greater than those contracted by holding of stakes (or equity) in the partner(s) with the majority of the airlines. Also, larger airlines, through mergers, have contracted a greater number of alliances of both types than the smaller ones. Evidently, the airlines originating from the European 'peripheral' regions (countries) have contracted more alliances than it could be expected considering their size (Alitalia, Austrian Airlines, British Midland, SAS and TAP-Air Portugal). Air France has contracted most alliances by holding of stakes with domestic smaller non-flag airlines - other European regional airlines and the airlines from France's former colonies. The airlines, Air France, Iberia, Lufthansa, British Midland, SAS and Swissair have entered approximately the same number of alliances of a 'marketing agreement' type with partners from Europe and from the other continents. Unlike Alitalia, Austrian Airlines and KLM have contracted many more of these alliances with European rather than non-European partners.

Several factors have driven the most famous (leading) EU flags to enter the 'strong alliances' by buying up stakes (or equity) from their partners. First, they have aimed to enlarge their catchment area by establishing 'links' with the airline(s) originating from a high demand generating areas and with those assumed to be capable of feeding their continental and intercontinental flights. In addition, they have aimed to alleviate and/or even completely prevent competition at domestic markets that might come from existing smaller non-flag airlines and new entrants (i.e. in many cases 'buying of stakes' has meant taking control over domestic and foreign non-flag and charter airlines). Secondly, they have intended to provide more efficient access to strategically positioned airports being the hub(s) of their partner(s). This has enabled them to benefit from the partners' slots at congested airports and enter the markets of the other flag airlines in EU (i.e. buying of stakes in smaller airlines abroad has allowed the mergers to start indirect competition with the flags on their domestic markets). Finally, the mergers have intended to establish closer relationships and stronger control over the other flags in Europe, and to improve access to markets on the other continents (e.g. to get 'the rights beyond the market entry gates') (CAA, 1993, 1994; IFAPA, 1988; Janic, 1996; Kim Han and Signal, 1993; Tretheway, 1990; Youssef and Hansen, 1994).

Table 14.4 The mergers and alliances of the european airlines (1995)

Airline	Number of mergers and alliances by type*					
	A_0	A_{01}	A_{02}	A_1	A_{11}	A_{12}
Air France	16	9	7	13	4	9
Alitalia	6	1	5	1	1	0
British Airways	5	2	3	3	2	1
Cyprus Airways	5	2	3	0	0	0
Iberia	23	11	12	4	1	3
KLM	10	7	3	3	1	2
Lufthansa	22	10	12	4	4	0
Luxair	0	0	0	1	1	0
Sabena	1	1	0	1	0	1
SAS	7	3	4	2	2	0
Swissair	5	2	3	4	2	2
Austrian Airlines	15	12	3	3	2	1
British Midland	9	4	5	2	1	1
TAP Air Portugal	5	2	3	0	0	0

* A_{0i}-The mergers and alliances without holding of stakes or equity in the partner; A_{1i}- The mergers and alliances with holding of stakes or equity in the partner (i = 0, total number; i = 1, number with European partners; i = 2, number with non-European partners).
Sources: Airline Business, 1995; Janic, 1996.

Competition between EU scheduled airlines with charter airlines and other transport modes has been recognised as another aspect of their behaviour. Both institutional and marketing conditions for developing the competition in the EU aviation market have been significantly different than those in US. Firstly, as opposed to the instant liberalisation of the US market by single Act, the EU aviation market has been liberalised as a process. Second, in comparison to the US market, the EU aviation market has been mostly international (cross-border) and highly fragmented among the flags, non-flags and charters. For example, our sample has consisted of 15 flag, 33 non-flag and 26 charter airlines (Janic, 1996). Thirdly, the networks of the flags have already existed as large strong 'star-shaped' configurations. The routes of typically large flag airlines containing a significant proportion of profitable long-haul (intercontinental) flights have originated and sunk at single hub airports. Last, but not least, some monopoly rights are still in effect on the particular routes (Pelkmans, 1991).

Evidently, the flag airlines have not been completely prepared to accept neither frequency nor price competition. A few 'strong' reasons have supported these assertions. These are: inappropriate cost structure and ownership; high percent of government shares supporting cost-inefficient behaviour; limited freedom to manage much better both the costs and the ownership structure due to high influence of various trade unions; limited size and inherent weakness of domestic markets; permanent expectation for attracting governmental (or EU) subsidies; and prevailing recessive conditions at 'home' and all over the world in the time of the implementation of the Liberalisation Packages. The modest price competition has been launched by some smaller non-flag airlines, mostly on specific dense routes. They have employed smaller lower cost aircraft permitting much easier intensive competition by flight frequencies and airfares. The flags have answered such challenges by reducing their fares on particular routes for specific classes of users.

Competition between scheduled and charter airlines in the EU aviation market has been modest due to the constraints in the industry and markets themselves. Namely, many charters have been completely or partly under ownership and control of the flag airlines. They have predominantly served holiday routes that have been spatially separated from the main business routes served by scheduled airlines. Many of the charters have been vertically integrated with large tour operators who have considerably influenced their business policy and pattern of operations (CAA, 1993; Janic, 1996).

Permanent scarcity of capacity of the aviation infrastructure has appeared to be another factor influencing development of competition in the EU aviation market. Particularly, the most famous European airports are already congested. At these airports the domestic large flags have dominated by keeping more than 50 per cent of the available slots dedicated thanks to 'grandfather's' rights. Since capacity of these airports is going to increase only slightly in the near future, its scarcity will likely continue to be a barrier for developing the competition (CAA, 1993; Janic, 1996). It will be particularly difficult for smaller airlines to enter these particular markets. Hence, they will be forced to enter the various forms of merging and alliances with the incumbents. Thus, they will be able to share the incumbents' slots at saturated airports and airspace (Airline Business, 1995; CAA, 1993; Janic, 1996).

14.4　Models of airline behaviour

Behaviour of Western European scheduled airlines has been examined using three models. These are: a model of economies of scale, a model of airline growth and financial performances and a model of airline relationships on the network of international EU air routes (Janic, 1996). Regression analysis has been applied over relevant data.

14.4.1　Model of economies of scale

Economies of scale have emerged as on of the main instigators behind the growth of airline industries. Two models have been estimated by use of least-square regression techniques applied over cross sectional data to confirm or refute this hypothesis with the Western European airline industry. In the first model the average unit cost per airline output (dependent variable) has been regressed with an annual volume of its output (independent (explanatory) variable). For 32 flag and non-flag airlines operating within the Western European airline industry, the model has taken the following form (Airline Business, 1994/1996; ICAO, 1986/1994; Janic, 1996):

$$AC(X) = 475,235\ X^{-0.401}$$

$$R^2 = 0,523,\ N = 32 \tag{1a}$$

where

$A(X)$	is average airline cost per RPK (Revenue Passenger Kilometre)
X	is annual volume of airline output (million of RPK)

Evidently the airlines that produced larger outputs had lower unit costs. This allowed them to be either more profitable (regulated prices) or more competitive (free prices) than their smaller competitors. Such an advantage may be one of the main forces behind their grow.

Another model represents the relationship between the average cost per flight (dependent variable), and route length and aircraft seat capacity (independent, explanatory variables). It confirms the hypothesis that economies of scale, on an average route operated by Western European airlines, do exist. The model has been applied to the sample of 21 scheduled airlines. Its form is as follows (ICAO, 1986/1994; Janic, 1996):

$$C(n, d) = 7,934 \ n^{0,603} \ d^{0,656}$$
$$\quad\quad\quad (3,266) \quad (4,339) \quad (4,773)$$

$$R^2_{adj} = 0,896; \ F = 77,477; \ DW = 1,692; \ N = 21 \tag{1b}$$

where

$C(n, d)$	is the average cost per flight,
n	is aircraft seating capacity,
d	is route length.

In the above regression equation, the statistics t, F, R^2_{adj}, and DW *(Durbin-Watson)* indicate that the equation itself and its coefficients are significant at the level of 5 per cent and 1 per cent. The coefficients, being less than one, indicate that the cost per flight has risen at a decreasing rate with flying distance and aircraft seat capacity. This means that the average unit cost obtained by division of the total cost either with route length, aircraft capacity, or both have diminished under the same conditions (Weisman, 1990). This might be one of the strong reasons for Western European scheduled airlines to further consolidate and 'enrich' their air route networks by inclusion of new long (intercontinental) routes allowing engagement of large long-range aircraft. This might also justify engagement of larger aircraft on some short and medium high density routes (Janic, 1996).

14.4.2 Model of airline growth and financial performances

The model of airline growth and financial performances is based on the estimation of its revenue/output and cost/output function. For the particular airlines such estimation has been carried out by using empirical data for the period 1986/1994 (ICAO, 1986/1994). The *total annual output* of an airline expressed by the total available tonne kilometres has been taken as independent (explanatory) variable. The *total airline annual revenues* and/or *total annual costs* (in $US) have been adopted as dependent variable. The sample was small. It consisted only of 9 pairs of observations. Therefore, the outcome should be interpreted very cautiously despite the existence of high correlation between the variables in the regression equations. Both revenue/output and cost/output function have been estimated for Air France, British Airways and Lufthansa (Janic, 1996). The results are presented in Table 14.5. As can be seen, three types of regression equations have been obtained. These are: 'linear', 'log-linear' and 'semi- logarithmic'. They all indicate that both the total revenues and costs have increased with growth of the airline annual output. This means that the airlines have spent and earned more money by expanding the volume (scale and scope) of their operations.

By dividing the total *revenues/costs* by the volume of output, the average revenue/cost per unit of output can be obtained. This average depends on the form of the basic revenue/cost function. In the linear case of Air France the revenue/cost has increased at a decreasing rate towards the marginal value. In the semi-log case (British Airways) the average revenue/cost has decreased with increase in the output. In the case of Lufthansa (log-linear case) the exponent of both R and C functions has been positive indicating that their averages have increased at a decreasing rate with an increase in the output (Janic, 1996).

Analytically, *marginal revenue/cost* can be obtained as the first derivative of the total revenues/costs-output function, i.e., MR = $\partial R/\partial X$ and MC = $\partial C/\partial X$. At the linear function (Air France) both marginal revenue and marginal cost have been constant and not dependent on output. At semi-logarithmic function (British Airways) the marginal revenue and marginal cost have been constantly diminishing and dependent on output. At log-linear relationship (Lufthansa) the marginal revenues and costs have been either increasing or decreasing with output (Janic, 1996).

Table 14.5 Examples of Airline Revenues/Costs-Output Functions

Airline	Function	Volume of output (X) (10^6tkm)
1. Air France	R = - 3324,836 + 0,841 (X), $R^2 = 0,950$ C = - 4190,631 + 0,915 (X), $R^2 = 0,956$	8000 - 15000
2. British Airways	R = -54220,113 + 7717,342 ln (X), $R^2 = 0,938$ C = -59230,656 + 7023,447 ln (X), $R^2 = 0,938$	8000 - 19000
3. Lufthansa	R = 0,0046 $(X)^{1,568}$, $R^2 = 0,979$ C = 0,0029 $(X)^{1,578}$, $R^2 = 0,979$	8500 - 19000

R, C - Total Annual Revenues/Costs (Million of $US); X - Total Annual Output;
N = 9 Observations.
Sources: Airline Business, 1995; ICAO, 1986/1994; Janic, 1996.

The concept of the marginal revenues may be applied to explain one of the main reasons for the airline growth. Namely, the marginal revenue has always been positive independently of the form of the revenues/output function. It indicates that every expansion of airline operations has always produced positive marginal revenues (Train, 1991). In the above examples each new unit of output has been sold at constant (Air France), decreasing (British Airways), and increasing marginal rate (Lufthansa) (Janic, 1996).

The concept of average and marginal costs may be applied to detect any possible economies of scale at the particular airlines. For that purpose the following measure has been applied (Weisman, 1990): $l(X) = AC(X)/MC(X)$, where $AC(X)$ and $MC(X)$ are the average and marginal cost per unit of output, respectively, and X is annual volume of the airline output. If $l(X) > 1$, there are economies of scale; if $l(X) = 1$ there is constant return to scale; and if $l(X) < 1$, there is diseconomies of scale at given volume of output. In the example shown in Table 14.5, the following functions of $l(X)$ have been obtained: Air France: $l(X) = -4579$, $925/X+1$(it indicates diseconomies of scale that have been improving with an increase in the volume of output; British Airways: $l(X) = -8,433+\ln(X)$ (this indicates economies of scale that have been improving with increasing of the volume of output); Lufthansa: $l(X) = 0,634$ (this shows decreasing return to scale with increase in the volume of output). These outcomes should be considered with caution primarily due to highly limited sample applied for estimation of the cost/output functions and inherent simplicity of these functions.

14.4.3 Model of relationships on the EU air route network

The relationships between Western European scheduled airlines represented by co-operation and competitions have been modelled on the EU network of international air routes (Janic, 1996). Its simplified scheme is shown in Figure 14.1. The network consists of the following cities (places) assumed to be its nodes: Amsterdam (The Netherlands), Berlin (Germany), Brussels (Belgium), Copenhagen (Denmark), Dublin (Ireland), Dusseldorf (Germany), Geneva (Switzerland), Frankfurt (Germany), London (Great Britain), Madrid (Spain), Milan (Italy), Oslo (Norway), Paris (France), Rome (Italy), Zurich (Switzerland), and Vienna (Austria). As the most populated, economically developed and politically important in the EU, these places and wider urban agglomerations surrounding them have generated and attracted the most of the EU scheduled air traffic consisting mostly of business passengers (Button, 1995; CAA, 1993).

The relationships between Western European airlines on this network have been analysed by investigating their market shares and market concentration, quality of services and pricing policy. The data for three periods have been used to estimate the impacts of particular 'Liberalisation Packages' on the airline relationships. These are data for 1989 (two years after the implementation of the First Package), data for 1991 (one year after approving the Second Package, the year that the Third Package was published, and the year of the Gulf War and deepening recession in Europe and rest of the world), and data for 1993 (the year of common start of all Three Liberalisation Packages, and the last year for which there were data available) (ICAO, 1991/1995).

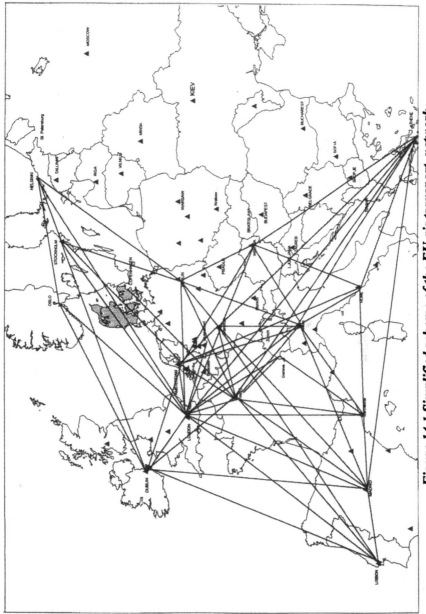

Figure 14.1 Simplified scheme of the EU air transport network

14.4.3.1 Airline market share and market concentration Market share can be expressed by proportion of the total demand (i.e., the number of passengers) that is served by an airline operating on the market (route, and/or network) in question together with the other airlines. Market share is expected to be mostly dependent on the proportion of capacity supplied by the airline in question. This capacity is always expressed by the number of seats and/or flights. Useful indicators to measure the 'strength' of competition in any aviation market can be HHI[1] (Hirchman-Herfindahl Index of market concentration) and the number of airlines operating there (Bailey et. al., 1985; Leahy, 1994; Janic, 1996).The analysis of airline market share and market concentration has been carried out using appropriate data for 131 route of the EU network. The results expressed by the statistical estimates (the means and standard deviations) relating to the airline market share MS, capacity share (SS-seat share and FS-flight share), index of market concentration and average number of airlines operating on an average route of the network, are given in Table 14.6. It shows that, on average, an airline has been able to keep around 30 per cent of the market share by sharing around 30 per cent of total capacity (either flights or seats) offered on the market.

This illustrates that there has been close relationship between the market and capacity indicators. Appropriate statistical tests have been carried out to investigate a relative stability of the airline market and capacity indicators over time. The test of null hypothesis H_o (H_0: MS (SS; FS)$_{1989}$ = MS (SS; FS)$_{1991}$ = MS (SS; FS)$_{1993}$) and alternative hypothesis H_1 (H_1: MS (SS; FS)$_{1989}$ $\neq$ MS (SS; FS)$_{1991}$ $\neq$ MS (SS; FS)$_{1993}$) has confirmed the null hypothesis. Namely, under the conditions of liberalisation the market in which the airlines have taken care of their current market position on particular routes (markets) by adjusting either overall number of flights, number of seats, or both. This implies that, apart

---

[1] In this case *HHI* has been computed as the sum of squares of market shares of particular airlines flying on the routes (markets) of the network (Bailey et. al., 1985), i.e. $HHI_k = \sum_{i=1}^{N_k} MS_{ki}$ *for k = 1,2, ... , N* , where MS_{ki} is the market share of the airline (*i*) operating on the route (*k*), N_k is the number of airlines operating on the route (*k*), N is the number of routes in the network. *HHI* can take any value from 0 to 1 (or from 0 to 10 000, when it is expressed in percentages). When it approaches zero the market is considered to be less concentrated indicating the existence of stronger competition between the airlines. If *HHI* moves towards its upper limit (1 or 10 000), there is a higher market concentration indicating 'weaker' airline competition.

from various bi-lateral agreements, mergers and alliances, some other collusive agreements might be negotiated in order to support their position on the market. Due to the reasons described above the new smaller airlines entering the particular markets (routes) have not meanwhile been able to considerably influence and change such solid relationships. Also it can be seen that both the average HHI and average number of airlines flying on a route K have been relatively stable during observed period (Braverman, 1978). Their coefficients of variation (S.D./Mean) have varied around 30 per cent, thus pointing out that there has been a relatively high, but stable variability of the traffic (market) concentration across the EU network.

Table 14.6 The statisticale etimates of the airline market attributes on a route of the EU network

		Period			
Attribute	**1989**		**1991**		**1993**
	Mean **S.D.**		**Mean** **S.D.**		**Mean** **S.D.**
MS (%)	32,32 25,36		30,23 24,62		32,07 26,74
SS (%)	32,20 24,23		30,32 23,94		32,12 25,89
FS (%)	32,30 23,76		30,35 23,23		32,01 25,34
HHI	0,52 0,26		0,50 0,14		0,54 0,19
K	2,61 0,79		2,55 1,06		2.35 0,97

MS - Airline Market Share (%); SS, FS - Airline Seat and Flight Share, respectively
HHI-Hirchman-Herfindahl Index; K- Number of Airlines Operating on a Route;
S.D.-Standard Deviation.

14.4.3.2 Quality of services on the route Quality of services on an average route of the EU network offered by an airline has been expressed by the following attributes: passenger schedule delay (e.g., defer time) defined as the difference between the time of passenger's desire to travel and the time of the first available departure; and average trip (non-stop flying) time[2] (Bowen et al., 1991; Headly and Bowen, 1992; Yeng, 1987).

Estimates of the particular attributes of this quality are given in Table 14.7. As can be seen, schedule delay has been shortened by about 50 per cent during the observed period, 1989/1993. This has been carried out by an increase in the number of flights on the particular routes of the network. The number of flights has been increased due to a few reasons such as satisfying demand, slight competition by flight frequency and increase in the flight frequencies on those routes where different airline mergers and alliances have taken place. Reduction of the schedule delay seems to be the most observable

---

[2] The passenger schedule delay is computed by formula $SD = (1/2)T/F(T)$, where T is the period of time in which the flights $F(T)$ have been scheduled.

benefit gained for the passengers during observed period. But there has not been any evidence indicating that the changes of supply causing reduction of the scheduled delays have been directly caused by gradual liberalisation of the EU aviation market. Average travel time has varied slightly since the airlines have 'slowed down' their aircraft during the observed period in order to increase fuel efficiency of their flights (i.e., to save fuel). This has been one of the measures for retaining the operating costs under control. Average load factor has varied due to simultaneous increase in the flight frequency and variations of air travel demand. Namely, during the observed period (1989/1993), overall development of air travel demand has been particularly impacted by Gulf War (in 1991) and deepening recession in Europe. The average aircraft size (seat capacity) has increased indicating the intention of the airlines to improve in-cabin comfort on the one side and to exploit economies of scale on the particular high density routes on the other (Janic, 1996).

Table14. 7
The Statistical Estimates of the Airline Quality of Services on a Route

Attribute	1989		Period 1991		1993	
	Mean	S.D.	Mean	S.D.	Mean	S.D.
Schedule delay(hr)	2,910	1,502	2,096	0,658	1,578	0,272
Non-stop flying time (hr)	1,472	0,990	1,517	1.039	1,437	0,984
Average load factor (%)	61,20	9,88	59,03	7,53	60,99	8,61
Average aircraft size (seats):	140,80	14,81	141,60	13,92	145,41	15,53

hr - hours; S.D. - Standard Deviation; N = 70 observations.

14.4.3.3 Airline pricing policy on a route The elements of the airline pricing policy have been analysed for the 'reduced' EU air route network consisting of 38 routes connecting the UK (United Kingdom) and the rest of the EU. Two fare classes have been considered: non-restricted and restricted business fares (OAG, 1995). To investigate the main factors influencing these airfares, the appropriate causal relationship has been estimated by least-square regression technique where the airfare was assumed to be a dependent variable. The independent (explanatory) variables have been adopted to be: the number of airlines operating on a route to explain the strength of the competition on a route, the length of a route (i.e., travel distance) to directly measure physical resistance to air travel and indirectly the flight cost on a route, and the aircraft type to emphasise the impact of aircraft type on the flight cost and airfare. The relationships obtained by experimentation with the model are presented in Table 14.8.

As can be seen, both classes of airfares have been (significantly) dependent on only two factors, length of route (travel distance) and aircraft size. The number of airlines operating on the route has not significantly influenced the airfares. This indicates that there may be two separate phenomena. First, the airlines set the prices primarily to cover their costs depending on the travel distance and aircraft capacity. Second, there has not been any price competition. The absence of price competition has been caused by a number of reasons. Namely, two types of scheduled airlines have operated on these routes: flags and smaller-non flags. Most of the smaller non-flags have been partly or fully controlled by their larger partners. Therefore, it is fair to assume that besides negotiating the prices by various bi-lateral and multilateral agreements, some collusive agreements have seemed to be contracted between the flags themselves, and the flags and their partners to alleviate and even completely 'prevent' 'price competition'.

Table 14.8 Dependence of the airfares on the number of airlines, route lengths and aircraft types

Class of airfare	Relationships
Non-restricted business:	$F_n = 96{,}941 + 2{,}717\,K + 0{,}170\,L + 37{,}970\,D_c$
	$\quad\quad\quad\ (2{,}264)\quad (0{,}329)\quad (9{,}444)\quad (2{,}930)$
	$R^2_{adj} = 0{,}779;\ F = 42{,}896;\ DW = 1{,}403;\ N = 38$
Restricted business:	$F_r = 14{,}367 - 2{,}044\,K + 0{,}133\,L + 90{,}187\,D_c$
	$\quad\quad\quad\ (0{,}155)\quad (0{,}119)\quad (9{,}023)\quad (3{,}604)$
	$R^2_{adj} = 0{,}431;\ F = 7{,}935;\ DW = 2{,}228;\ N = 38$

F_n, F_r - *Non-restricted and Restricted Business Airfare, respectively ($US);*
• -
Number of Airlines Operating on a Route (3 <=K <= 5); L -Route Length (km);
D_c *-Dummy Variable ($D_c = 0$, if the Aircraft Smaller than 100 Seats Is Used;*
$D_c = 1$, *if the Aircraft Greater than 100 Seats Is Used).*

14.5 The other aspects of the airline behaviour

Behaviour of the EU airlines has also some other aspects. These are: relationships with the 'fifth freedom' airlines and relationships with the other transport modes operating in the same market. The presence of the 'fifth freedom' airlines in the EU air route network (aviation market) has been important. Specifically, the 'fifth freedom' operations of the US airlines have been under focus since they could be seen as strong competition for the EU airlines once the concept of 'open skies' between USA and EU comes into effect. The US airlines have enjoyed the 'fifth freedom' rights in the Western Europe for a very long time. During the period 1989/1993 their policy significantly changed. Firstly, the average capacity of their aircraft was approximately halved (from 311 to 169 seats) causing an increase in average load factor from 37 per cent to 46 per cent. The load factor has increased despite there having been high variations (diminishing) in demand due to the general economic recession and the Gulf War in 1991. Change of the aircraft capacity has caused a significant change of their market and capacity shares on the particular routes of the EU air network. 'Opening up' the 'skies' between USA and EU will presumably contribute to growing presence of the airlines from both basins on both continents. Under more liberal conditions the presence of the EU airlines on the US domestic aviation market will increase thus contributing to further development of competition on both sides of the Atlantic (CAA, 1993; 1994; Janic, 1996).

Another important factor affecting future market positions of the airlines in question is their relationship with other transport modes operating within the EU common market. Apart from road transport, the most recent studies have shown that HSR has appeared to be competitive to air transport on short to medium hauls, up to 600/800 kilometres. Also, growing interests to locate rail stations at some large airports and thus include them into the HSR network, and vice versa, have been evidenced. This would instigate and support future development of two basic kinds of relationships between two modes: co-operation through providing complementary services, and competition (CEC, 1995; Janic, 1993).

In addition, some other aspects of the airline behaviour might be seen as a matter of future research. These are: access and use of the CRS (Computer Reservation System(s), modernisation and expansion of the FFP (Frequent Flyer Programme(s)), and predatory behaviour (CAA,1993; Dodgson et al., 1990; Janic, 1996; Kiriazidis, 1994; Nako, 1992; OECD, 1988; Williams, 1993).

14.6   Conclusions

This paper has analysed the main aspects of behaviour of Western European scheduled airlines during the first phase of gradual liberalisation (deregulation) of the aviation market in the EU (European Union). The approach has been based on the empirical estimates obtained by use of regression analysis and appropriate statistical techniques. Such an approach could be useful for analysts, planners, policy makers, and in particular airlines, as they intend to register the changes (and their causes) that may take place the airline industry (sector) over time.

The following aspects of airline behaviour have been investigated: internal growth; merging and alliances; co-operation and/or competition in the common EU aviation market; and relationships with the other transport modes operating in the same area (Member States). The results have indicated the following:

- Western European scheduled airlines have grown by constantly increasing their output. The effect of economies of scale has been observed at the airline industry. A similar effect has been uncovered at some airlines, however in this case it should be considered with caution due to a highly limited analysis.
- Merging and alliances have become common practice among many Western Europeans scheduled airlines. They have enabled them to cross the national borders more easily and provide reliable feeding of the return flights, start indirect competition with other airlines on their domestic markets, and alleviate potential direct competition on the same markets (routes).
- The average airline market and capacity share on an average route of the EU air network have been relatively stable during the observed period (1989/1993). This means that the airlines have carefully balanced their position on the market. The index of market concentration, HHI has also been stable. The average number of airlines on the particular routes of the EU network has not significantly changed. The capacity of aircraft increased slightly during the observed period.
- Overall quality of service has significantly improved during the observed period. This has been represented by increasing the flight frequencies and reducing the average schedule delay (defer time). This has seemed to be the most transparent benefit for passengers during the first phase of the market liberalisation process.
- The airfares have been much more dependent on the passenger, route and aircraft characteristics than on market conditions.

Finally, the results suggest that the implementation of 'Three Liberalisation Packages' has produced two kinds of changes during the first part of the liberalisation period. Firstly, the most significant and observable changes that have occurred in the airline global behaviour are related to various forms of integration. Secondly, a relatively minor change has occurred in the structure of the EU air route network itself and relationships between the airlines operating there.

Very likely, more observable and deeper changes were disrupted by the nature of the liberalisation process (gradual liberalisation), recessive social-economic conditions in Europe and weak economic conditions among many Western European scheduled airlines, which all prevailed during the observed period.

References

Airline Business, Various Issues, 1994/95/96.

Air Transport World, Various Issues, 1994/95.

Antoniou, A. (1991), "Economies of Scale in the Airline Industry: The Evidence Revisited", *Logistics and Transport Review*; Vol. 27, No. 2, 159-184.

Bailey , E. E., Graham D. R., Kaplan D. P. (1985), *Deregulating the Airlines*, The MIT Press: Cambridge, Massachusetts, London, England.

Bowen, D. B., Headly D.E., Luedtke J.R. (1991), *Airline Quality Rating*, NIAR Report 91-11, National Institute for Aviation Research, The Wichita State University, Wichita, Kansas, 67208-1595, USA.

Braverman, D. J. (1978), *Fundamentals of Business Statistics*, Int Ed., Academic Press: New York, USA.

Button, K. (1989 a, b), "The Deregulation of US Interstate Aviation: An Assessment of Causes and Consequences (Part 1 and 2)", *Transport Reviews*, Vol. 9, No. 2, 99-118, and Vol. 9, No. 3, 189-215.

Button, K. (1996), *Liberalising European Aviation: Is There An Empty Core Problem?*, Centre for Research in European Economics and Finance, Department of Economics, Loughborough University of Technology, Loughborough, UK.

CAA (1993), *Airline Competition in a Single European Market*; Civil Aviation Authority, CAP 623, London, UK.

CAA (1994), *Airline Competition on European Long-Haul Routes*, Civil Aviation Authority, CAP 639, London, UK.

CEC (1995), *Interactions Between High Speed Rail and Air Passenger Transport*, COST 318, Draft Interim Report, European Commission, IVT-ETH, Zurich, Switzerland.

Dodgson, S.J., Katsoulacos, Y., Pryke, S. W. R. (1990), *Predatory Behaviour in Aviation*, Commission of the European Communities, A Report to the Competition Directorate of the European Commission, Brussels, Belgium.

Doganis, R. (1992), *Flying off Course: The Economics of the International Aviation*, George Allen and Unwin Publishers, UK.

EUROSTAT (1995), *Yearbook '95 - A statistical Eye on Europe 1983-93*, Office for Official Publications of the European Communities, (Population), Luxembourg.

Headly, E. D., Bowen, D.B. (1992), *Airline Quality Issues 1992*, Proceedings of the International Forum on Airline Quality, NIAR (National Institute for Aviation Research), The Wichita State University, Wichita, Kansas, 67208-1595, USA.

ICAO (1988), *Digest of Bilateral Air Transport Agreements*, Doc. 9511, International Civil Aviation Organisation, Montreal, Canada.

ICAO (1986/1994), *Fleet, Personnel: Commercial Air Carriers*, International Civil.

Aviation Organisation; Digest of *Statistics*; Serial FP; Montreal, Canada.

ICAO (1991/1995), *Traffic by Flight Stage-1989/1991/1993*, International Civil.

Aviation Organisation, *Digest of Statistics*, Serial TF, Montreal, Canada.

IFAPA (1988), *European Airline Mergers: Implications for Passengers and Policy Options*, International Foundation for Airline Passenger Associations, Switzerland.

Janic, M. (1993), "A Model of Competition Between High Speed Rail and Air Transport", *Transportation Planning and Technology*, Vol. 17, 1-23.

Janic, M. (1996), *Airlines' Behaviour Under Changing Conditions*, Final Report on Research Fellowship, CN: 940304 F, The Phare ACE Programme, European Commission, CREEF, Department of Economics, Loughborough University of Technology, Loughborough, UK.

Kim Han, E., Signal, V. (1993), "Mergers and Market Power: Evidence from the Airline Industry", *The American Economic Review*, Vol. 83, No. 3, 549-569.

Kiriazidis, T. (1994), *European Transport: Problems and Policies* (Air Transport), Avebury: Aldershot, UK.

Leahy, S.A. (1994), "Concentration in the US Airline Industry", *International Journal of Transport Economics*, Vol. 21, No. 2, 209-215.

Morrison, S., Vinston, C. (1986), *The Economics of Airline Deregulation*, The Brookings Institution, Washington, DC, USA.

Nako, M. S. (1992), "Frequent Flyer Programmes and Business Travellers: An Empirical Investigation", *Logistics and Transport Review*, Vol. 28, No. 4, 393-414.

Nijkamp, P. (1996), "Liberalisation of Air Transport in Europe: The Survival of the Fittest?", *Swiss Journal of Economics and Statistics*, Vol. 132, No. 3, 257-278.

OAG (1995), *First and Business Class Travel*, Red Travel Group, (Special Ed.): UK.

Nijkamp, P. (1996), "Liberalisation of Air Transport in Europe: The Survival of the Fittest?", *Swiss Journal of Economics and Statistics*, Vol. 132, No. 3, 257-278.

OAG (1995), *First and Business Class Travel*, Red Travel Group, (Special Ed.): UK.

OECD (1988), *Deregulation and Airline Competition*, OECD, Cedex 16, Paris, France.

Pelkmans, J. (1991), "The Internal EC Market for Air Transport: Issues After 1992", in D. Banister and K.J. Button, Mc Millan (eds.), *Transport in a Free Market Economy*, Academic and Professional. Ltd., UK.

Stasinopoulos, D. (1992), "The Second Aviation Package of the European Community", *Journal of Transport Economic and Policy*, Vol. 26, 83-87.

Stasinopoulos, D. (1993), "The Third Phase of Liberalisation in Community Aviation and the Need for Supplementary Measures", *Journal of Transport Economics and Policy*, Vol. 27, 323-328.

Train, E. K. (1991), *Optimal Regulation: The Economics of Natural Monopoly*, The MIT Press: Cambridge, Massachusetts, London, UK.

Tretheway, W. M. (1990), "Globalization of the Airline Industry and Implications for Canada", *Logistics and Transport Review*, Vol. 26, No.4, 357-367.

UN (1994), *Statistical Yearbook*, United Nations, Department for Economic and Social Information and Policy Analysis, (Population), New York, USA.

Vincent, D., Stasinopoulos, D. (1990), "The Aviation Policy of the European Community", *Journal of Transport Economics and Policy*, Vol. 24, 95-100.

Weisman, E. (1990), *Trade in Services and Imperfect Competition: Application to International Aviation*, International Studies in Service and Economy, Cluwer Academic Publisher: London, UK.

Williams, G. (1993), *The Airline Industry and the Impact of Deregulation*, Ashgate, Ashgate Publishing Limited: UK.

Yeng, I. C. (1987), *Routing Strategies for an Idealised Airline Network*, PhD Thesis, University of California, Berkeley, USA.

Youssef, W., Hansen, M. (1994), "Consequences of Strategic Alliances Between International Airlines", *Transportation Research-A*, Vol. 28A, No. 5, 415-431.

15 Modelling Fees for Freight Transport Services in Eastern European Countries
WOLFGANG KOLLER

15.1 Introduction

Since the beginning of economic and political restructuring in Eastern Europe foreign trade between Western and Eastern European countries has been growing considerably. Together with this increase freight transport in both directions has gained in importance. The road transport sector has particularly profited from this development. Above all, imports to countries of Eastern Europe rely on this transport mode.

These trends, which can easily be extrapolated into the future, form the background to the main questions addressed in this chapter. How do the countries in question (Czech Republic, Slovakia, Hungary, Slovenia, Croatia, Poland, Romania and Bulgaria) compare in their performance of coping with the new transport needs? For the road transport sector, as well as quality and delivery time of transport services, an important performance measure is the price level of services. Differences of price level among countries of Eastern Europe and differences between Western and Eastern Europe indicate that there are differences in the regulation of the markets, competition, production functions or input prices.

This chapter presents an attempt to model these differences by hedonic price analysis. The empirical data stem from one of the largest Austrian shipping companies and cover a subsector of the transport sector, groupage transport. Groupage transport consists of collecting several smaller shipments which have a common destination and containerising them. Groupage transport between Vienna (Austria) and Eastern European destinations/origins is a very dynamic field, with more and more shipping companies opening regular services for Eastern European destinations. The following briefly characterises this segment:

- The average weight of shipments for the countries considered in this study varies from 500 to 1200 kilograms. Many of the shipments are under the average weight, some of them weighing only a few kilograms. Very few shipments reach weights above three tons.

- The trucks used in this market segment usually have a capacity of 15 tons. For less frequented or newly opened connections smaller trucks are also common.
- Larger shipping companies, like the one this study is based on, have one or more depots in each Eastern European country and have the shipments redistributed from there to the final destination by their local partners.
- Competition is strong since the predominance of smaller shipments allows for the market entrance of very small Eastern European carriers, that can offer lower prices, often due to illegal practices and missing insurance certificates.
- Regulatory measures in Eastern European countries change often and unexpectedly, uncertainties in many fields directly or indirectly affect the groupage transport sector. Among the most important restrictions is the shortage of foreign truck permits.

Groupage transport with origins in Vienna may serve as a representative example of examining the differences in price level of road transport services. Transport with reverse direction is not considered in this study.

In the following section of this chapter the question of applying hedonic price analysis to fees for transport services will first be discussed. The author owes the idea of applying this concept to fees for transport services to Maggi and Müller (1996). The idea to use it to calculate hedonic price indexes for Eastern European countries came as a natural extension. Another section of the chapter will be devoted to the methods used to preprocess the data. An innovative aspect is that a method is used to generate artificial data that show, with respect to the independent variables, distance and weight, more or less the same distribution as real world data. For the simulated transport services fees are calculated given the information gained by the shipping company. Then, empirical results are presented and discussed. In another section the calculated price indexes are discussed in the context of some influencing factors. Finally, some concluding remarks and an outlook will be given.

15.2   Hedonic price indexes

Hedonic price analysis has been developed to measure the effect of quality on price. One of the main contributors to the development of this method is Griliches (1961). Berndt (1991) gives an overview of the history and some econometric aspects of this method. From the beginning of hedonic price analysis the main motivation of empirical research has been to calculate price indexes which also allow for quality changes. The first study to pursue this is Court (1939). The idea behind it is to define a product as a bundle of quality characteristics, represented

344

by a vector $z = (z_1,..., z_n)$. The market price p of the product is seen as a function of the characteristics.

$$p = p(z_1,...,z_n) \qquad (1)$$

The market price guides both consumers and producers in their choice of quality packages. Marginal prices of quality characteristics z_n are defined as partial derivatives of function (1). It can be shown that in the market equilibrium marginal offer prices equal marginal market prices (Rosen, 1974). For the construction of a hedonic price index a hedonic regression equation has to be established that also includes dummy variables,

$$\ln p_i = \alpha + \alpha_1 D_{1,i} + ... + \alpha_m D_{m,i} + \beta_1 \ln z_{1,i} + ... + \beta_n \ln z_{n,i} \qquad (2)$$

where the α's and β's are unknown parameters to be estimated and the D_m's are variables that take on the value of 1 if the product i is from the year m and zero otherwise. One underlying assumption of the concept of hedonic price index is that the elasticities of quality characteristics, the β's, do not change over time. From equation (2) hedonic price indexes can be obtained easily as

$$PI_m = e^{\alpha_m} \qquad (3)$$

In the present study the concept of the hedonic price index is applied to fees for transport services. Distance ($DIST$) and weight ($WEIGHT$) of the offered transport service are taken as quality characteristics. Instead of years, the price index is calculated for countries. Thus, with the inclusion of an error term which is assumed to be normally distributed, the functional form of the models to be estimated looks like

$$\ln p_i = \alpha + \alpha_1 D_{1,i} + ... + \alpha_m D_{m,i} + \beta_1 \ln DIST_i + \beta_2 \ln WEIGHT_i + \varepsilon_i \qquad (4)$$

The double logarithmic form was not only chosen for the possibility to immediately obtain price indexes according to (3), but also for goodness of fit criteria.

15.3   Data

For the generation of the data set an Austrian shipping company placed its internal freight-tariff-basis for 11 European countries and some additional information (number of shipments, number of truckloads, average weight of shipment) at the disposal of the author. One of the main purposes is to propose a method to generate a data set by means of computer simulation, so that the distribution of the independent variables is approximately the same as in reality. The alternative would have been to select levels for each of these variables - a procedure which would have to be done arbitrarily. Therefore some information about the distribution of real-world transports was incorporated into the study in the following way.

- *The country's share in the data*: 10,000 data points have been generated, with each data point standing for one hypothetical transport service from Vienna to a selected European destination. Within this data set the destination countries are represented in varying degree. The share was determined by the foreign trade volume between Austria and the respective country. Thus in this study an Austrian point of view is adopted, by attaching more importance to countries with more foreign trade with Austria. Three Western European countries, France, Italy and Switzerland, have been chosen to represent Western Europe as the destination of groupage transports originating in Vienna. They account for about 60 per cent of the data points and therefore constitute the main influence at the estimation of the two coefficients for distance and weight.
- *Distance of the transport services*: These are measured in road kilometres. The distance of a transport can be split into two parts, the distance from Vienna to the hub in the destination country and the distance from there to the final destination (redistribution). The first part does not vary within country specific data, since it is assumed that all shipments destined for a foreign country pass through the same hub (even for Eastern European countries this assumption does not hold, nevertheless the data quality is not affected). The redistribution of the part-loads to the final consignee is carried out by partner companies of the Austrian company. The statistical distribution of the distance for that part of the overall transport depends on the economic geography of the country. In order to take into account country specific peculiarities two parameters have been introduced:
  1. a measure for the *relative economic importance* of the conurbation where the hub is situated; transport with destination within the borders of that conurbation are ascribed a distance of 1 km; in case of higher relative economic importance of the conurbation a higher percentage of the transports has a distance of 1 km.

2. a measure of the centrality of the economy; for more centralised economies longer distances are less probable (figure 15.1 gives an example of the resulting distribution.

- *Weight of the part-loads*: After inspection of real-world contracts for transport services it was concluded that the distribution of this variable can best be approximated by a truncated lognormal distribution. The real-world average weight for each country was used as the mean of the lognormal distribution. The variance of the lognormal distribution was assumed to be the same over all countries and chosen so that the simulated data covered all weight classes in a realistic way. Figure 15.2 displays an example of the resulting distribution.

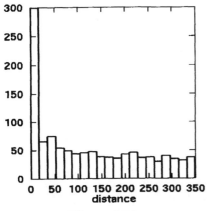

Figure 15.1
The distribution of local transport distances: the example of Hungary

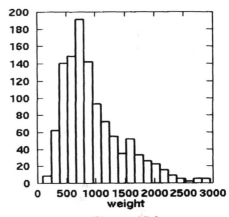

Figure 15.2
The distribution of part-load weights: the example of Hungary

The fees have been calculated according to the freight-tariff-basis of the shipping company. The calculation system used by the company consists, for most countries, of a grid of weight and distance categories which results in a non-steady price function. Corresponding to splitting up distances in two parts, prices can be divided into first the price for the transport from Vienna to the depot in the foreign country and second the price for redistribution to the consignee. This procedure is not without problems though, since prices for redistribution in reality do not exist independently of the overall transport. In subsequent estimations these data are nevertheless examined. Summarising the quality of the generated price data several causes of the error component in estimated models can be listed:

347

- The real-world freight-tariff-scheme is a non-steady function with, in some cases, considerable leaps. This applies particularly to the low-weight segment: a shipment of 3 kilograms costs the same as one of 95 kilograms.
- Due to practical reasons, for some countries seemingly illogical freight-tariff-schemes are valid and more distant destinations are sometimes cheaper than nearer ones. One example is Italy where transport to cities along the Ligurian coast is cheaper than transport along the Adriatic coast, making the calculation of distance-price pairs somewhat difficult.
- When pooling data for different countries, price data which follow different regimes and have a different accuracy are thrown together. The resulting error of the data is shown in figure 15.3. This residual plot stems from a model estimated on all 10,000 data points (see model d in the next section). Due to the use of dummy variables for Eastern European countries in this model the residuals for these countries have a mean of zero.

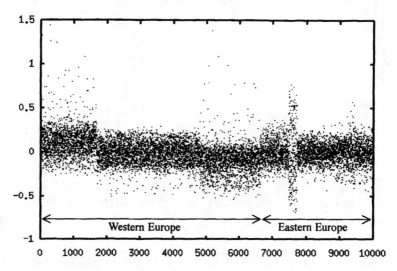

Figure 15.3 Residual plot for model d

15.4   Estimations

The aim of the following estimations is to allow different degrees of generalisation. As outlined in the previous section, the dependent variable used for these estimations, i.e. the price of the transport service, can principally be modelled as a completely deterministic function of the characteristics weight, distance and destination country. This function, the freight-tariff-basis as it was set by the shipping company, is very complicated. This is symbolised on the right side of figure 15.4. Whereas

348

many tables with many rows and columns are needed to predict prices for transport services, the estimated hedonic price function allows much more general but less precise price predictions. figure 15.4 attempts to visualise this in a schematic way.

On the data obtained by the procedures described in the previous section several models of the type of (4) were estimated, splitting up the data set in different ways and using different combinations of dummy variables. Table 15.1 gives an overview of these models.

Table 15.1 Overview of the selected models

	Vienna - hub	Vienna - dest.	Hub - dest.
All data points, 1 dummy variable for Eastern Europe	a)	b)	c)
All data points, 8 dummy variables for Eastern European countries	-	d)	e)
Only data for Eastern Europe, 7 dummy variables for the countries	-	-	f)
Data for each country separately	-	-	g)

As indicated in table 15.1, in the case of examining only the prices of transports from Vienna to the hub (column 1) the use of country specific dummies has not been considered. This is due to the fact that the variable *DIST* can only take on 11 different values and does not vary at all within each country. Thus the use of dummies and of the variable *DIST* can in the extreme case compensate each other completely (multicollinearity). The same applies, to a lesser extent, to the data set consisting of whole distances (column 2). Here it seemed only reasonable to include dummies when also using Western European data for estimation.

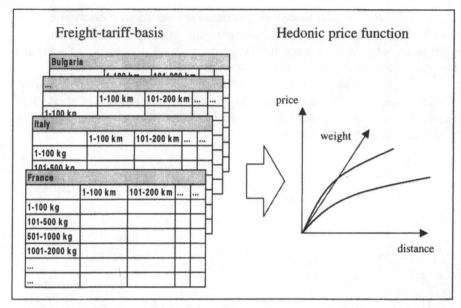

Figure 15.4 Hedonic price functions and the aim of generalisation

Table 15.2 reproduces the results of the models a, b and c. In the first of these models only that part of the transport is considered that is normally carried out by the Austrian shipping company itself. Therefore the results reflect to a high degree the price structure of the Western European freight transport sector. This is at least true for the used technology and manpower. But it should not be forgotten, that in the most cases only a minor part of the transport directed to an Eastern European destination is taking place within Austrian borders. Comparing the results of the first two estimations, it turns out that in both cases similar coefficients for the variables ln (*DIST*) and ln (*WEIGHT*) are obtained. Transport originating in Vienna and involving Eastern Europe is significantly more expensive than transport directed to Western Europe. This price disadvantage amounts to about 40 per cent in the first case and 20 per cent in the second. When applying the model only to transport from hub to final destination (model c) Eastern European transport is approximately 23 per cent cheaper than Western European comparable transports. Furthermore by comparing the coefficients for ln (*DIST*) and ln (*WEIGHT*) the conclusion can be drawn that distance has substantially less influence on price in the redistribution transports, than in the overall transports.

Table 15.2 Results of estimations for model a, b and c

Model a: Transports from Vienna to hub		
Number of Data Points: 10000		
Dependent Variable: ln(PRICE)		
R²: 0.844		
variable	coefficient	t-value
CONST	-0.291	-6.175
ln(DIST)	0.637	99.327
ln(WEIGHT)	0.534	211.534
Eastern Europe	0.415	45.897
Model b: Transports from Vienna to final destination		
Number of Data Points: 10000		
Dependent Variable: ln(PRICE)		
R²: 0.906		
variable	coefficient	t-value
CONST	0.182	4.716
ln(DIST)	0.585	114.239
ln(WEIGHT)	0.576	289.889
Eastern Europe	0.219	35.376
Model c: Transports from hub to final destination		
Number of Data Points: 10000		
Dependent Variable: ln(PRICE)		
R²: 0.875		
variable	coefficient	t-value
CONST	2.160	114.810
ln(DIST)	0.167	112.248
ln(WEIGHT)	0.635	236.294
Eastern Europe	-0.231	-41.674

Table 15.3 summarises the results of the estimations for models d, e and f. In these models, dummy variables for Eastern European countries have been included. From the coefficients of the dummy variables of these models price indexes were calculated by formula (3). The results are discussed in the next section (table 15.6).

The coefficients for ln ($DIST$) and ln ($WEIGHT$) obtained in the estimations of model d, e and f are very similar to the ones obtained in the models a, b and c. This is important especially for model d, because it means that the introduction of additional dummy variables did not lead to multicollinearity. All the coefficients for the dummy variables are highly significant. It is interesting to see if the coefficients are also significantly different from each other. Table 15.4 lists the t-values of this test procedure for all possible combinations of country specific coefficients.

Table 15.3 Results of estimations for model d, e and f

variable [1]	Model d		Model e		Model f	
OD-combin.	Vienna – final dest.		Hub – final dest.		Hub – final dest.	
Used data	all		all		only Eastern Europe	
N. of data p.	10000		10000		3380	
Dep. variable	ln(PRICE)		ln(PRICE)		ln(PRICE)	
R²	0.929		0.909		0.896	
variable [1]	coefficient	t-value	coefficient	t-value	coefficient	t-value
CONST	-0.064	-1.5	2.036	121.9	1.635	40.2
ln(DIST)	0.614	106.2	0.167	129.5	0.174	79.8
ln(WEIGHT)	0.582	323.9	0.654	273.7	0.634	114.2
CZR	0.134	15.9	-0.502	-61.1	------	------
SLK	0.358	24.5	-0.347	-24.2	0.141	9.5
HUN	0.299	35.4	-0.189	-25.7	0.317	34.4
SLN	0.073	7.6	-0.265	-23.7	0.217	16.5
CRO	0.733	57.3	0.494	29.9	0.968	55.9
POL	0.344	36.5	-0.111	-9.0	0.387	31.5
ROM	0.049	3.2	0.146	7.2	0.644	34.0
BUL	-0.152	-7.6	-0.340	-12.7	0.152	6.3

[1] CZR: Czech Republik, SLK: Slovakia, HUN: Hungary, SLN: Slovenia, CRO: Croatia, POL: Poland, BUL: Bulgaria, ROM: Romania.

Table 15.4 Testing for identity of coefficients (model d): t-values

Country	CZR	SLK	HUN	SLN	CRO	POL	ROM
SLK	11,2						
HUN	11,0	2,9					
SLN	4,1	14,1	14,9				
CRO	36,0	17,6	25,8	38,2			
POL	15,1	0,7	3,2	18,9	23,6		
ROM	4,8	14,7	14,3	1,3	34,1	16,2	
BUL	13,2	20,9	20,9	10,2	37,2	22,2	7,9

Table 15.5 presents the results of estimations of model g. Hedonic price functions have been estimated on the data of each country separately, without any dummy variables. The estimates are very similar. Only Poland and Bulgaria apparently have different elasticities for distance and weight of the shipment. These two particularities could in part be explained by specific problems of splitting up transport from Vienna to the final consignee into first international transport and second local redistribution. Incidentally, the portion of these two countries is not big enough to distort the results of models a - f.

Table 15.5

Results of estimations on country-specific data (model g)

Country/Area [1]	EEC	CZR	SLK	HUN	SLN	CRO	POL	ROM	BUL
Number of data	3380	850	250	1120	430	190	350	120	70
p.	.752	.894	.939	.847	.904	.911	.701	.889	.937
R^2	2.45	1.45	1.40	1.53	2.31	2.65	4.37	2.51	-0.09
CONST	0.17	0.16	0.11	0.18	0.19	0.16	0.22	0.11	0.37
ln(DIST)	55.4	45.1	20.5	56.0	23.3	17.4	26.2	15.0	17.9
t-value	0.55	0.66	0.73	0.69	0.53	0.63	0.25	0.63	0.76
ln(WEIGHT)	82.8	72.4	59.7	54.7	57.0	40.6	10.9	24.5	22.8
t-value									

[1] EEC: Eastern European countries together.

Discussion of price indexes

From the models d, e and f estimated in the previous section, country specific price indexes can be obtained. They are displayed in table 15.6, together with a selection of factors which form the context for their explanation. These price indexes measure the price levels for international transport (PI-international) and local transports (PI-local). The Czech Republic is used as the base country. In the case of PI-international Romania, Bulgaria and Slovenia have lower prices than the Czech Republic. In Slovakia, Hungary and Poland transport services are 15-25 per cent more expensive than in the Czech Republic. Croatia is an extreme case with an 82 per cent price difference.

It is clear that influences on these price indexes are very difficult to measure. Nevertheless, investigations and interviews with experts led to the conclusion that the main factors causing price differences for international transport services are the following:

- Regulatory measures: It seems to be very difficult to measure the extent of regulation as a complete concept. However, one important indicator of regulation is the number of foreign truck permits. These figures result from bilateral negotiations. In the last few years foreign truck permits have meant a severe bottleneck for international freight transports, leading to very uneven market partition between those carriers who temporarily dispose of a sufficient number of permits and those who do not. In table 15.6 these numbers are given for Austrian trucks. In order to get useful indicators for the shortness of permits it is necessary to relate the number of permits to freight transport volume and to consider that not only permits for the destination country are necessary but also for transit countries.

Table 15.6

Country specific price indexes and relevant influencing factors

	CZR	SLK	HUN	SLN	CRO	POL	ROM	BUL
PI-international(model d)	100.0	125.1	117.9	94.1	182.0	123.4	91.9	75.1
PI-local (model e [1])	100.0	116.8	136.8	126.7	270.7	147.8	191.2	117.6
PI-local (model f [1])	100.0	115.1	137.3	124.2	263.3	147.3	190.4	116.4
GDP p. Cap. [2]	4420	3247	4300	8908	3426	3002	1566	1513
Austria's exports [3]	1191	394	1759	752	352	554	195	126
Austria's imports [3]	1035	270	1171	373	149	378	97	39
Wage [4]	307.87	241.93	309.47	945.32	347.61	290.50	106.06	108.93
Foreign truck permits [5]	20500	38400	33000	24600	19000	8500	4000	15000
Road Infrastructure [6]	0.70	0.50	0.32	N.A.	N.A.	0.74	0.31	0.33

[1] Since model e and model f differ only in the data used for estimation and very similar estimates for the coefficients DIST and WEIGHT are obtained, the two price indexes have the same interpretation.

[2] Defined as GDP per Capita in USD at exchange rates, expected values for 1995; Source: Urban et al.(1996)

[3] Defined as Austria's exports/imports in millions USD 1994; Source: WIIW (1995)

[4] Defined as average gross monthly wage in USD, at exchange rates, expected values for 1995; Source: author's calculations; Urban et al. (1996)

[5] Defined as the sum of all types of single permits for Austrian trucks (loco, transit, third country) and permanent permits multiplied by 50 (i.e. they are assumed to be equivalent to 50 single permits), values for 1995; Source: author's calculations, BMfÖWV (personal communication)

[6] Defined as Road Network per area in km/km², 1989; Source: ECMT (1995)

- Trade parity: Austria's exports to Eastern European countries generally exceed imports from these countries, as is illustrated in table 15.6. Particularly in the segment of road affinitive goods there is a strong imparity between imports and exports and less-than-truckload transport cannot be avoided. This leads not only to a price difference between comparable transport services of reverse direction but also to higher price levels in general.
- Learning curves: Since the system change in Eastern Europe and the resulting reorientation in trade relationships is taking place in many Eastern European countries, the actors in the East European transport sector and their behaviour have changed considerably. Therefore it could be stated that a completely new learning curve came into effect with the start of the reforms: regulators on both sides have to gain a new understanding of their role, partner firms have to be found, bottlenecks have to be identified and optimal hub and spoke structures have to be worked out. Presenting indicators that describe the advances on this new learning curve is again very difficult. For future research the following indicators may form a first approach:

  1. for international transport services the learning process goes hand in hand with the increase of the trade volume between the involved countries in Western Europe and Eastern Europe. For the case study presented in this chapter this would mean the trade volume between Austria and the selected Eastern European countries (see the respective rows of table 15.6).
  2. for transport services in general per capita GDP as a general indicator of economic development could provide some information about the progress of the learning process.
- Road Infrastructure: There are different opinions about the impact of the quality of road infrastructure on transport prices. Although it can be expected that higher quality of road infrastructure makes transport cheaper, the extent of this impact has to be verified. The data quality on this issue is very unsatisfactory. The only comparable data available to the author constitute the length of road networks (a rather questionable indicator of infrastructure quality) and date from 1989 (see table 15.6).

Others: Several other indicators were identified as determinants of price levels. The most relevant among these are wage and real estate prices.

For the analysis of price differences of local transport, a different listing of possible causes would have to be presented, with other kinds of indicators reflecting the cost structure and aspects of regulation. A more detailed discussion of this issue would go beyond the purpose of this case study.

15.6   Conclusions and outlook

In this chapter hedonic price indexes have been calculated for transport services from one origin in Western Europe (Vienna) to destinations in several Eastern and Western European countries. Although there are studies, that have estimated hedonic price functions for transport services, they have focussed on calculating price elasticities and not on comparing price levels by means of hedonic price indexes.

Another innovative idea of the present study was to use artificially generated data. The generation of simulated data on the basis of the freight-tariff-basis of one of the largest Austrian shipping companies allowed the estimation of models with huge data sets. Nevertheless, the good statistical results (high R^2 and t-values) should not seduce one to overlook some principal problems of the underlying data. In particular, the summation of the international and the local redistribution part of the overall transport (or the separation of the overall transport into its two components) has to be undertaken carefully.

The results of the estimations indicate that there are considerable price differences in transport services between Eastern European and Western European countries. Additionally, different patterns can be observed if the price indexes are first calculated for international transport services and second for local transport services. It can be concluded that in the freight transport sector most of the Eastern European countries can increase their efficiency by providing a stable framework of regulatory measures, by investing in infrastructure and by fostering competition. Above all, it can be stated that efficiency will increase as an automatic consequence of the learning process that has begun with the transformation process in Eastern Europe.

References

Berndt, E. R. (1991), *The Practice of Econometrics: Classic and Contemporary*, Addison Wesley: Reading, Mass.

Court, A. (1939), "Hedonic Price Indexes with Automotive Examples", in: *The Dynamics of Automobile Demand*, New York: The General Motors Corporation, 99-117.

European Conference of Ministers of Transports (ECMT) (1995), *Transport Infrastructure in Central and Eastern European Countries. Selection Criteria and Funding*, ECMT:Paris.

Griliches, Z. (1961), "Hedonic Price Indexes for Automobiles: An Econometric Analysis of Quality Change", in *The Price Statistics of the Federal Government*, General Series No. 73, Columbia University Press for the National Bureau of Economic Research: New York, 137-196. Reprinted in Griliches Z. (ed) (1971), *Price Indexes and Quality Change: Studies in New Methods of Measurement*, Harvard University Press: Cambridge, Mas., 55-87.

Maggi, R. and K. Müller (1996), *Price offer services on a regulated network. A study on the European freight transport sector*, paper presented at the 41st International Atlantic Economic Conference, March 13-18, 1996 Paris.

Rosen, S. M. (1974), "Hedonic Prices and Implicit Markets: Product Differentiation in Pure Competition", *Journal of Political Economy*, 82, 1, 34-55.

Urban, W., L. Podkaminer (1996), "Kräftiges Wachstum in Ost-Mitteleuropa, weiterhin Rezession" in der GUS, *WIFO-Monatsberichte*, 5/96, 355-372.

Wiener Institut für Internationale Wirtschaftsvergleiche (WIIW) (1995), *Countries in Transition 1995*, WIIW: Wien.

357

List of Contributors

David Banister
University College London
The Bartlett, Wates House
22 Gordon Street
London WC1H 0QB
England

Michel Beuthe
FacultésUniversitaires Catholiques de
Mons
Chaussée de Binche 151
B-7000 Mons
Belgium

Kostas Bithas
Pantios School of Political Science
29, Aristotelous Street
Kallithea
Athens
Greece

Simona Bolis
Faculty of Economics
University of Lugano
Centrocivico
Via Ospedale 13
Lugano
Switzerland

Roberto Camagni
Politecnico of Milan
Dept. of Economics
Piazza Leonardo da Vinci, 32
20133 Milan
Italy

Roberta Capello
Politecnico of Milan
Dept. of Economics
Piazza Leonardo da Vinci, 32
20133 Milan
Italy

Laurent Demilie
Facultés Universitaires Catholiques
de Mons
Chaussée de Binche 151
B-7000 Mons
Belgium

Knut S Eriksen
Institute of Tranport Economics
P.O. Box 6110
Etterstad
0602 Oslo
Norway

Christian Hey
DG XI
European Commission
Rue de la Loi, 200
Brussels
Belgium

Mattias Höjer
FMS
Royal Institute of Technology
Box 2142
10314 Stockholm
Sweden

Milan Janic
ALFA
International Forwarding Agency
Gregorciceva
1000 Ljubljana
Slovenia

Bart Jourquin
Facultés Universitaires Catholiques
de Mons
Chaussée de Binche 151
B-7000 Mons
Belgium

Bo Terje Kalsaas
Dept. of Town and Regional Planning
University Administration
Alfred Getzvei 3
N-7034 Trondheim
Norway

Wolfgang Koller
Dept. of Economic and Social
Geography
Wirtschaftsuniversität Wien
Augasse 2-6
1090 Wien
Austria

Rico Maggi
Faculty of Economics
University of Lugano
Centrocivico
Via Ospedale 13
Lugano
Switzerland

Francesca Medda
Free University
Faculty of Economics
De Boelelaan 1105
1081 HV Amsterdam
The Netherlands

Peter Nijkamp
Free University
Faculty of Economics
De Boelelaan 1105
1081 HV Amsterdam
The Netherlands

Robert E. Paaswell
Institute for Transportation
City College New York
NY 10031, New York
USA

Aura Reggiani
Università di Bologna
Dipartimento di Scienze
Economiche
Piazza Scaravilli, 2
Bologna 40126
Italy

Sytze A. Rienstra
NEI
Postbus 4175
3006 AD Rotterdam
The Netherlands

Piet Rietveld
Free University
Dept. of Economics
De Boelelaan 1105
1081 HV Amsterdam
The Netherlands

Dieter Rothenberger
Institute for Regional Studies
(EURES)
Freiburg
Germany

Roger Vickerman
CERTE
Cornwallis Building
The University
Canterbury, Kent CT2 7NF
England